REMEMBERING THE ROMAN REPUBLIC

Culture, Politics, and History under the Principate

The Roman Principate was defined by its embrace of a central paradox – the ruling order strenuously advertised continuity with the past, even as the emperor's monarchical power represented a fundamental breach with the traditions of the "free" Republic it had replaced. Drawing on the evidence of coins, public monuments, and literary texts ranging from Tacitus and Pliny the Younger to Frontinus and Silius Italicus, this study traces a series of six crucial moments in which the memory of the Republic intruded upon Roman public discourse in the period from the fall of Nero to the height of Trajan's power. During these years, remembering the Republic was anything but a remote and antiquarian undertaking. It was instead a vital cultural process, through which emperors and their subjects attempted to navigate many of the fault lines that ran through Roman Imperial culture.

Andrew B. Gallia is Associate Professor of History at the University of Minnesota. His articles have appeared in *Classical Quarterly, Transactions of the American Philological Association*, and *The Journal of Roman Studies*.

D1354928

REMEMBERING THE ROMAN REPUBLIC

CULTURE, POLITICS, AND HISTORY UNDER THE PRINCIPATE

Andrew B. Gallia

University of Minnesota

CAMBRIDGE
UNIVERSITY PRESS

CAMBRIDGE
UNIVERSITY PRESS

32 Avenue of the Americas, New York NY 10013-2473, USA

Cambridge University Press is part of the University of Cambridge.

It furthers the University's mission by disseminating knowledge in the pursuit of education, learning and research at the highest international levels of excellence.

www.cambridge.org
Information on this title: www.cambridge.org/9781107429420

First published 2012
First paperback edition 2014

A catalogue record for this publication is available from the British Library

Library of Congress Cataloguing in Publication data

Gallia, Andrew B., 1974–
Remembering the Roman republic : culture, politics and history under the Principate /
Andrew B. Gallia.
    p.   cm.
Includes bibliographical references and index.
ISBN 978-1-107-01260-8 (hardback)
1. Rome – History – Flavians, 69–96.   2. Rome – History – Antonines, 96–192.
3. Republicanism – Rome.   4. Political culture – Rome.   I. Title.
DG286.G35   2011
937′.07–dc23   2011025077

ISBN 978-1-107-01260-8 Hardback
ISBN 978-1-107-42942-0 Paperback

For Carrie

CONTENTS

LIST OF FIGURES AND MAPS

ix

ACKNOWLEDGMENTS

This book began life as a doctoral dissertation at the University of Pennsylvania, under the supervision of Brent Shaw. I shall be eternally indebted to his clarion advice and unstinting encouragement. The other members of the dissertation committee, Ann Kuttner and Shane Butler, helped me shape the project in their distinctive ways. I want to thank these three and the entire faculty of Classical Studies and the Graduate Group in Ancient History at Penn for the vibrant intellectual community in which I was nurtured during my years in Philadelphia. For the long process of revising and expanding the dissertation into its current form, I have been very lucky to find myself in Minneapolis, where my colleagues in History and Classical and Near Eastern Studies at the University of Minnesota have provided the most stimulating and supportive environment in which anyone could hope to work. Financial support for some of the revisions was provided by generous grants from the McKnight Foundation and the University of Minnesota College of Liberal Arts.

Along the way, my thinking about this material has been enriched through discussions with Valentina Arena, Elaine Fantham, Harriet Flower, Eric Kondratieff, Michael Koortbojian, William Metcalf, Carlos Noreña, and Amanda Wilcox. When my family found itself in San Francisco for a year, progress might have ground to a halt had not Carlos also helped me gain access to UC Berkeley and its excellent libraries. Elena Stolyarik and Daria Lanzuolo provided help with the illustrations. I would also like to thank the readers for the Press for their comments and sage advice on an earlier version of the manuscript.

By far the greatest debt I owe is to my family. My parents' unconditional love and support gave me the confidence to pursue a path in life that has not always been easy. My children, Eddie and Rosie, are a constant source of joy. Their arrivals rejuvenated me as I have worked to bring this project to completion. Last but not least, my wife Carrie has put up with, and gotten me through, much in the last eleven years. Only she can appreciate how much I owe to her intellect, her sense of humor, and her limitless strength.

ABBREVIATIONS

Ancient authors are cited using the abbreviations listed at the front of S. Hornblower and A. Spawforth (eds.) (2003) *The Oxford Classical Dictionary*, 3rd ed. revised, Oxford, with occasional modifications. Editions used for problematic texts and collections of fragments are noted in the bibliography. The titles of periodicals are abbreviated as in *L'Annee Philologique* or, for works not listed there, the *American Journal of Archaeology*. Abbreviations for other modern works are as follows.

ANRW	H. Temporini and W. Haase (eds.) (1972–) *Aufstieg und Niedergang der römischen Welt: Geschichte und Kultur Roms im Spiegel der neueren Forschung*. Berlin.
BMCRE	H. Mattingly and R. A. G. Carson (1923–1962) *Coins of the Roman Empire in the British Museum*, 6 vols. London.
CAH X²	A. K. Bowman, E. Champlin, and A. Lintott (eds.) (1996) *Cambridge Ancient History. Vol. X. The Augustan Empire 43 B.C.–A.D. 69*. 2nd ed. Cambridge.
CAH XI²	A. K. Bowman, P. Garnsey, and D. Rathbone (eds.) (2000) *Cambridge Ancient History. Volume XI. The High Empire, A.D. 70–192*. 2nd ed. Cambridge.
CIL	(1863–) *Corpus inscriptionum Latinarum*. Berlin.
FOS	M.-T. Raepsaet-Charlier (1987) *Prosopographie des femmes de l'ordre sénatorial: Ier–IIe siècles*, 2 vols. Lovanni.
FS	J. Rüpke (2005) *Fasti Sacerdotum: Die Mitglieder der Priesterschaften und das sakrale Funktionspersonal römischer, griechischer, orientalischer und jüdisch-christlicher Kulte in der Stadt Rom von 300 v.Chr. bis 499 n.Chr.*, 3 vols. Stuttgart.
ILLRP	A. Degrassi (ed.) (1965) *Inscriptiones Latinae liberae rei publicae*. Vol. I. 2nd ed. Florence; *Imagines*. Berlin.

ILS	H. Dessau (ed.) (1892–1916) *Inscriptiones latinae selectae*, 3 vols. Berlin.
Inscr. It.	A. Degrassi (ed.) (1931–) *Inscriptiones Italiae*. Rome.
LIMC	Ackermann, H. C., and Gisler, J.-R. (eds.) (1981–1997) *Lexicon iconographicum mythologiae classicae*. Zurich.
LTUR	E. M. Steinby (ed.) (1993–2000) *Lexicon topographicum urbis Romae*, 6 vols. Rome.
MRR	T. R. S. Broughton (1951–1985) *The Magistrates of the Roman Republic*, 3 vols. New York.
MW	M. McCrum and A. G. Woodhead (eds.) (1961) *Select Documents of the Principates of the Flavian Emperors, Including the Years of Revolution, AD 68–96*. Cambridge.
PIR	E. Klebs and H. Dessau (eds.) (1897–8) *Prosopographia imperii Romani saeculi I. II. III*. Berlin.
PIR²	E. Groag et al. (eds.) (1933–) *Prosopographia imperii Romani saeculi I. II. III*. 2nd ed. Berlin.
RAC	T. Klauser et al. (eds.) (1950–) *Reallexikon für Antike und Christentum*. Stuttgart.
RDGE	R. K. Sherk (1969) *Roman Documents from the Greek East*. Baltimore.
RE	A. Pauly et al. (eds.) (1893–) *Real-Encyclopädie der classischen Alterumswissenschaft*. Stuttgart.
RIC	H. Mattingly et al. (1923–51) *The Roman Imperial Coinage*, 9 vols. London.
RIC I²	C. H. V. Sutherland and R. A. G. Carson (1984) *The Roman Imperial Coinage*. Vol. 1. Revised ed. London.
RIC II²	I. A. Carradice and T. V. Buttrey (2007) *The Roman Imperial Coinage*. Vol. II.1. 2nd rev. ed. London.
RPC	A. Burnett et al. (eds.) (1992–) *Roman Provincial Coinage*. London and Paris.
RRC	M. H. Crawford (1974) *Roman Republican Coinage*. 2 vols. London.
RS	M. H. Crawford (ed.) (1996) *Roman Statutes*. 2 vols. London.
Sm.	E. M. Smallwood (1966) *Documents Illustrating the Principates of Nerva, Trajan and Hadrian*. Cambridge.

INTRODUCTION

Remember the days of old, consider the years of many generations: ask thy
father and he will shew thee; thy elders, and they will tell thee.

Deuteronomy 32:7

"But how can you stop people remembering things?" cried Winston, again
momentarily forgetting the dial. "It is involuntary. It is outside oneself. How
can you control memory? You have not controlled mine!"

Nineteen Eighty-Four

As a cognitive process whose biological foundations in the structures and
chemistry of the brain neuroscientists have only recently begun to describe,
memory has long called on the lens of metaphor for its analysis.[1] One of
the most persistent of these metaphors is that presented by Plato in the
Theatetus, where Socrates compares the human mind to a lump of wax:

δῶρον τοίνυν αὐτὸ φῶμεν εἶναι τῆς τῶν Μουσῶν μητρὸς Μνημοσύνης, καὶ
εἰς τοῦτο ὅτι ἂν βουληθῶμεν μνημονεῦσαι ὧν ἂν ἴδωμεν ἢ ἀκούσωμεν ἢ
αὐτοὶ ἐννοήσωμεν, ὑπέχοντας αὐτὸ ταῖς αἰσθήσεσι καὶ ἐννοίαις, ἀποτυποῦσθαι,
ὥσπερ δακτυλίων σημεῖα ἐνσημαινομένους· καὶ ὃ μὲν ἂν ἐκμαγῇ, μνημονεύειν
τε καὶ ἐπίστασθαι ἕως ἂν ἐνῇ τὸ εἴδωλον αὐτοῦ· ὃ δ' ἂν ἐξαλειφθῇ ἢ μὴ οἷόν τε
γένηται ἐκμαγῆναι, ἐπιλελῆσθαί τε καὶ μὴ ἐπίστασθαι.

Let us say, then, that this [wax] is the gift of Mnemosyne (Memory), the
mother of the Muses, and that whenever we wish to remember anything
we see or hear or think of ourselves, we hold it under our perceptions and
thoughts and imprint them upon it, just as we make marks with seal rings,
and whatever is imprinted we remember and know as long as its image lasts,

[1] Kandel (2006), Rose (1992: 61–99), Assmann (1999: 149–78). Watkins (1990) offers a critique
of the quest for the biological "engram" as insufficient for understanding the complexity of
memory.

but whatever is rubbed out or cannot be imprinted we forget and do not know. (Pl. *Tht.* 191d-e)

Like all metaphors, Plato's framework for conceptualizing memory as a series of impressions in wax has both advantages and limitations. Most importantly, reference to an inscribed image accounts for the persistence that memory gives to fleeting thoughts and experiences. Additionally, the malleability of wax as the medium of these representations provides an explanation for the problem of forgetting and the selective nature of memory, because it allows for some items to be erased while others might not be recorded in the first place.

Plato's account is less successful, however, at explaining why certain sensory stimuli tend to prompt the recall of particular memories. Nor does it do anything to elucidate the process by which erroneous or false memories are produced. As these examples demonstrate, the critical shortcoming of any transcript model of memory (one that centers on inscriptions in wax, the arrangement of magnetized particles in a hard drive, or even the structure of neurons in the brain) lies in its failure to take into consideration the extent to which remembering depends not only on the storage of information, but on its recall as well.[2] As anyone who has had to relearn a once-familiar subject can attest, memories do not simply wait in an archive until they are needed. If not repeatedly reactivated by frequent recollection, they begin to fade almost as soon as they are formed.[3]

The importance of this distinction between memory as the storage of a series of static representations and remembering as an ongoing process of recall can be seen in Sallust's discussion of the peculiarly Roman practice of displaying wax masks of ancestors (*imagines maiorum*) in the main rooms of noble households:[4]

nam saepe ego audivi Q. Maxumum, P. Scipionem, <alios>praeterea civitatis nostrae praeclaros viros solitos ita dicere, quom maiorum imagines intuerentur, vehementissume sibi animum ad virtutem adcendi. scilicet non ceram illam neque figuram tantam vim in sese habere, sed memoria rerum gestarum eam flammam egregiis viris in pectore crescere neque prius sedari quam virtus eorum famam atque gloriam adaequaverit

[2] Fentress and Wickham (1992: 25), Assmann (1988: 13), Assmann (1999: 185). See also Schacter (2001: 88–160), Proust (1982: 50). For discussion of Plato's theory in relation to ancient practice of artificial memory, see Small (1997).

[3] Changeux and Ricoeur (2000: 138–9). This principle was first demonstrated in the pioneering study of Ebbinghaus (1913).

[4] See Flower (1996: 32–59, 195–202).

I have often heard that Quintus [Fabius] Maximus, Publius Scipio, and other illustrious men of our state used to say that when they looked upon their ancestors' portrait masks, these violently inflamed their spirits with a love for virtue. Certainly it was not that *the wax figure itself* had such power over them, but that the *memory of their deeds* fans a flame in the hearts of prominent men that does not subside until their own virtue has attained equal reputation and glory. (Sall. *Iug.* 4.5)

A fixed representation is insufficient on its own to produce the powerful response that these famous Romans experienced when they looked at the *imagines* of their ancestors. In Sallust's formulation, the memory that achieves this outcome is distinct from the visual signs that set it in motion.

In contrast to Plato, Sallust does not offer an explanation of the inner psychological mechanisms that produce particular memories. Notably, the physical traces to which he refers are real objects that exist in space, where anyone can see them and be prompted to remember. Moving from the internal record of Plato's wax seals to the wax *imagines* in the *atria* of noble households forces us to consider the broader framework within which memory functions. The memories that Sallust describes are not confined to the discrete and idiosyncratic mental processes of the individual; they are situated instead within their broader social and cultural context. Memory operates as it does for a Fabius or a Scipio because of a specific commemorative practice (the display of *imagines*) that helped to determine their position, and that of their families, within Roman society at large.[5]

Sallust's shift of emphasis from the psychological to the social points to the importance of what the French sociologist Maurice Halbwachs termed "collective memory."[6] Like Sallust, Halbwachs recognized that the ways in which memory functions for the individual are shaped by external social realities. Halbwachs' formulation is useful, but this approach to memory also comes with caveats. First, although it is evident that social realities play an important role in determining how information about the past is organized and transmitted within cultures, it can be misleading to speak of a cognitive process such as memory as if it belongs to a group rather than to individuals.[7] When we refer to "collective" – or better, "social" – "memory," it is important to bear in mind that we are speaking figuratively, redeploying the metaphors used to understand the memory of the individual to frame a discussion around a particular set of discursive

[5] Cf. Plb. 6.54.2–3. Flower (1996), Walter (2004: 84–130), Wallace-Hadrill (2008: 218–25).

[6] Halbwachs (1925, esp. 273–96), (1950: 51–87).

[7] Connerton (1989: 38), Margalit (2002: 48–69), also Gedi and Elam (1996). Other critiques: Confino (1997), Klein (2000).

practices common to the members of a group, which can only influence, but not establish, the distinct recollections of that membership.[8]

Halbwachs' concept of "collective memory" has also been criticized because of his tendency to position memory as a way of understanding the past that is fundamentally incompatible with the critical epistemology of history.[9] Postmodern critiques of historical positivism have done much to erode the theoretical coherence of this distinction, but that is not really what concerns us here. Insofar as it can be distinguished from later "scientific" traditions, ancient historiography clearly had a part to play in the operation of social memory – certainly Sallust did not regard his role as a historian as disconnected from the processes of memory he attributes to the Fabii and Scipiones.[10] From this perspective, the real problem with Halbwachs' formulation is not how he defines historiography, but rather how the distinction he draws between history and memory is embedded within a broader discourse about modernity, wherein scientific rationalism is felt to produce a break with earlier, more "authentic" traditions, here identified with "memory."[11] Pierre Nora draws on this line of thinking when he laments the corrosive impact that historical consciousness has had on traditional forms of social memory and suggests that modern societies have created artificial "sites of memory" to counteract the sense of alienation from the past that history creates.[12] Although the ideas of rupture and loss will be important to the discussion that follows, this nostalgia for a more cohesive sense of memory in an era defined by revolutionary change is, by definition, historically specific and not easily transferable to other cultures or time periods. To be sure, the Romans also worried about the implications of a breakdown in the social institutions of memory, but they did so on their own terms. Imposing a modernist distinction between "authentic" and "inauthentic" forms of memory can only hinder our investigation.

To account for the fact that socially conditioned memories often extend beyond the immediate personal experience of the individual to include ideas derived from a more distant, historical past, the Egyptologist Jan Assmann has introduced the concept of "cultural memory," which he

---

[8] On the preferability of the term "social memory," Fentress and Wickham (1992: 7).

[9] Assmann (1988: 11), Hutton (1988: 316–17), cf. Halbwachs (1950: 35–79).

[10] Castelli (2004: 26–8). See also White (1978), Wiseman (1979: 41–53).

[11] Le Goff (1992: 21–50), Kemp (1991: 149–78), cf. Koselleck (2004: 26–42), (2002: 154–69), also Connerton (1989: 13–14), Fentress and Wickham (1992: 144). Frow (1997: 218–24) provides an important critique.

[12] Nora (1989: 12): "These *lieux de mémoire* are fundamentally remains, the ultimate embodiments of a memorial consciousness that has barely survived in a historical age that calls out for memory because it has abandoned it." Cf. Yerushalmi (1982: 81–103), Le Goff (1992: 93–9).

distinguishes from the more informal kinds of "communicative memory" that provided the principal focus of Halbwachs' analysis.[13] Insofar as memory can be said to be situated in culture, its traces are there to be found in a wide variety of media. These include ritual, oral traditions, literature, the plastic arts, and the physical organization of space, to name the most prominent aspects of culture through which a person's recollections of the past may be formed.[14] The nature of cultural memory in a given context will depend on how these various channels of communication operate within a particular society. Like the neurobiologist who maps the cognitive processes associated with different kinds of memory onto the regions of the brain in which they occur, the historian of social memory pursues a project that is fundamentally descriptive. By examining the cultural frameworks within which memories are produced as well as the concepts, narratives, and semantic structures that give memory its shape, it is possible to gain a better understanding of how a given society understood its past.[15]

It is impossible to describe how memory operates without also considering its purpose, however. Of the many functions and consequences of remembering, one that stands out as critical for memory's social implications is its role in establishing a basis for the continuity of personal identity.[16] Without memory, it is impossible to claim credit (or bear responsibility) for one's past behavior, much less that of one's ancestors. Who we are, in an epistemological sense, depends on our memory. Applied to the cultural plane, this rule produces a reciprocal relationship, wherein memory is not only conditioned by the individual's participation in social life, but is also fundamental to the constitution of the very social groups in which he or she takes part. The Roman aristocrats in Sallust's example were expected to inherit their identities as members of noble families (and to display the characteristics that went with these identities) because they embraced the memory that attached to the wax *imagines* of their ancestors. In practice, of course, the contents of these social identities are rarely fixed in stone – but, then, neither is memory. The cultural channels of remembering thus offer an opportunity for a kind of communal autobiography,

---

[13] Assmann (1988: 10–14), (1992: 48–56), Assmann (1999: 13). Cf. Fentress and Wickham (1992: 44–84).

[14] Burke (1989: 100–2), Assmann (1999: 20–2).

[15] See esp. Olick and Robbins (1998). The "historical sociology of mnemonic practices" they propose differs in important regards from the broadly diachronic "mnemohistory" of Assmann (1997a: 6–22). For the importance of semantic structures to the operation of memory, see Fentress and Wickham (1992: 28–44), Bartlett (1932, esp. 247–80). On narrative, Fentress and Wickham (1992: 47–76), Schudson (1995: 355–8).

[16] Changeux and Ricoeur (2000: 138–9), Assmann (2006: 87–93).

through which individuals can assert their connection to a particular group or class, while the members of those groups work together to define some sense of what it means to belong to that collective.[17] As the sense of identity that attaches to a social group begins to change over time, we can be confident that the character of the social memory at work within that group will change as well.

Once we begin to speak of memory as operating in the social realm, we must inevitably consider its political dynamics.[18] This aspect of remembering is given special prominence in the history of the Roman Principate, which provides the context for the memories that are the focus of the present study. It should come as no surprise that the Roman emperors actively promoted memories that served their own interests and repressed forms of commemoration that they regarded as a threat to their power. The latter imperative can been seen in the restrictions that were occasionally imposed on the commemoration of individuals, especially the display of the wax *imagines* that Sallust regarded as an essential element in the social operation of elite Roman memory. Early in the reign of Tiberius, the senate imposed sanctions on the display of the *imago* of Cn. Calpurnius Piso as partial punishment for his crimes against the Imperial house. This limitation of a family's ability to commemorate its own members represented a powerful, and potentially ominous, method of social control.[19] Over time, a paradigm emerged whereby emperors who were seen as vicious were also represented as disruptive of the workings of social memory. The biographer Suetonius presents Caligula's wanton destruction of the statues of illustrious men in the Campus Martius as evidence of that emperor's cruelty, and Nero was said to have banished a descendent of Cassius Longinus, the assassin of Julius Caesar, for displaying the *imago* of his ancestor with the *titulus* "leader of the party."[20]

On the basis of this evidence, it is tempting to see the operation of memory during the Principate as rigidly controlled by omnipotent emperors who cynically manipulated all discourse about the past to serve their interests. Nevertheless, it would be inaccurate to describe the situation in such terms. Reformulations of public memory often occur for reasons other than the political self-interest of those in power, and we should

---

[17] Smith (1999: 208), cf. Bell (2003).

[18] Assmann (1992: 55), (2006: 7), cf. Trouillot (1995: 22–9), Fentress and Wickham (1992: 114–37), Connerton (1989: 7–13).

[19] Eck, Caballos, and Fernández (1996: ll. 75–82). Bodel (1999: 45–51), cf. Flower (1998: 155–87). See also Flower (2006: 115–48), Hedrick (2000: 89–130).

[20] Suet. *Calig.* 34.1. Tac. *Ann.* 16.7.2: *duci partium*, Suet. *Ner.* 37.1.

not overlook these alternative explanations when examining how memories change (or remain unaltered) over time. Because cultural memory, as defined by Assmann, is inscribed in monuments and texts, it often presents the rememberer with certain fixed points that are difficult to tamper with or redefine, however inconvenient they may be.[21] If anything, Cassius' continued reverence for his ancestor's portrait mask (and the public's ability to understand what this devotion may have signified) demonstrates how difficult it was for emperors to establish a monopoly over the institutions of memory in Roman culture. Unlike the rulers in modern totalitarian societies, who benefit from the power of centralized mass media, Roman emperors were not able to organize opinion through the coordinated workings of a state propaganda apparatus.[22] The more violent an emperor's attempts to repress memory, the more passionate the efforts to commemorate his victims became, as the record of repression by Caligula and Nero demonstrates. As a result, the nature of memory under the Principate was more complex and often more contentious than what the balance of power might suggest. In the end, as we shall see in the case of Domitian, emperors themselves could be subject to the kind of commemorative penalties that were imposed on Gnaeus Piso.[23]

In its broadest terms, this book is about the interaction of social memory and cultural identity in the face of profound historical change. It examines some of the ways in which the period we know as the Republic, during which Rome was ruled by magistrates operating under the authority of the senate and people, was remembered by Romans living in the era that followed the battle of Actium, when that whole system came under the absolute control of one man. Although the topic of the Republic's continuing impact on the Principate merits investigation in its own right, I hope to show that this problem provides a particularly useful heuristic for exploring the operation of memory within Roman culture.[24] The importance of this theme lies in the way it bridges two very different aspects of collective or social memory. On the one hand, the store of Roman cultural memory presented a record of events that made it easy to mark off the Republic as an era that was historically distinguishable from the present.

---

[21] Assmann (1988: 11). See also Kammen (1995: 329–30), Schudson (1995: 353–4).

[22] Levick (1982a), *pace* Syme (1939: 459–75). On the control of memory in the Soviet Union, cf. Hosking (1989), but note also the revealing anecdote about a visit to Bulgaria recounted by Burke (1989: 108).

[23] See Chapter 3. See also Flower (2006: 148–59, 197–233).

[24] Gowing (2005) pursues a similar approach, but touches only briefly on the period covered here. Other important studies include Castritius (1982), Sion-Jenkis (2000), and Eder (1990).

On the other hand, many Romans also clung to a notion of their identity that was predicated on the continuation of memories that stretched back into that distant era. The tension between these distinct but overlapping projects of remembering stands at the heart of the present study.

In the chapters that follow, I present a series of case studies, each of which centers on a particular set of circumstances in which the memory of the Republic was reactivated in some meaningful way. Because remembering as a social process (as opposed to "memory" as a concatenation of static representations) is historically contingent, each case will require a certain amount of thick description to account for the particularity of its context. Although my primary interest remains the frameworks of memory at work in each instance, I also of necessity depart at times from this central thread to go into more detail about various issues of Roman history and culture as they become relevant to the interpretation of how the Republic's memory was produced. Mindful not only of Nero's repression of Cassius but of the act of commemoration that gave rise to it as well, I have tried to organize the discussion in a way that calls attention to the complex and decentralized nature of memory within Roman culture. Competing memories of the Republican past, operating in a wide range of contexts and media, helped to shape – and were in turn shaped by – an ongoing process of negotiation and debate, through which the emperors and their subjects struggled to define Roman identity under the Principate.

The chronological limits of this discussion are relatively compressed, stretching from the last year of Nero's reign through the Principate of Trajan (AD 68–117). The decision to focus on this fifty-year span does not stem from any conviction about the unique importance of this period in the history of the memory of the Republic or for Roman cultural memory generally. Rather, I have chosen to restrict the time frame to investigate more fully and deeply the broad range of cultural contexts within which Imperial Romans remembered their Republican past. The era extending from the Flavian emperors through Trajan offers a wealth of material with which to examine the diversity of these processes. Although this half-century, which saw the successful establishment of two different dynasties, is generally viewed as occupying a central place in the story of the institutionalization of the power of the emperors, I do not wish to suggest that the issues discussed here were confined to the period in question. Just as there were important developments in the ways that the Republic was remembered before the fall of Nero, the story continued after the point at which this book leaves off.

With this caveat out of the way, the discussion begins roughly 100 years after Actium, by which time the reality of the break between the

Principate and the Republic that preceded it should have been well established. Conceptually, however, the nature of this change remained difficult to comprehend. Words, images, and even institutions that had been central to Roman self-definition during the Republic were taken over and reused by the emperors to justify their position within the new system of the Principate. Moreover, Republican commemorative practices (such as the display of family *imagines*) continued to play an important role in the formulation of elite identity. The Republic was thus both a discrete epoch of Roman history and a continuing part of the present: It had an end point, but it was not over. The opening chapter explores the nature of this ambiguity by examining how the concept of freedom (*libertas*) was deployed in the rebellion that brought an end to the Julio-Claudian dynasty in AD 68. Although *libertas* was tied to a particular conception of the Republic, the rebels of 68 were able to exploit the ambiguity of this concept to manipulate the memories that were associated with it, thus laying claim to the moral authority of the Republican past without doing anything to restore its political substance.

The second chapter moves from the ambiguity of political concepts as sites of memory to discuss the importance of public monuments and their multiplex associations with memory. Turning to the foundation of the Flavian dynasty by Vespasian, this chapter examines one of the first acts of that emperor's reign, the rebuilding of the temple of Jupiter Optimus Maximus, which had been destroyed by fire only a few days before the entry of Flavian armies into the city. The Capitoline temple was a quintessentially Roman *lieu de mémoire*, a place inscribed with a rich and well-known history. The importance of this temple for my discussion centers on its foundation narratives, which were closely linked with a particular, antimonarchical conception of freedom. The destruction of this temple in a context of civil war brought renewed attention to these narratives and to the overdetermined meaning that they gave to the term *libertas*. As a consequence, Vespasian had to be careful in how he proceeded with the project of rebuilding. I argue that the emperor negotiated this situation by involving the senate and people as much as possible in his work and by focusing public attention on a different set of memories, which connected the temple (and thus its rebuilding) with the stability of Roman imperial power. These mnemonic associations better suited the benefits that an emperor could provide.

Chapter 3 considers the plight of Vespasian's son Domitian, who was less successful at negotiating the ambiguities of Republican memory. Taking my starting point from the vivid description of the punishment of the chief Vestal virgin Cornelia in a letter composed by Pliny the Younger,

I examine this episode as a case in which the emperor's attempt to exploit Republican tradition failed to achieve the desired effect. For Domitian, the decision to bury Cornelia alive was part of a program of moral renewal intended to evoke the old-fashioned principles of ancient religious custom. In emphasizing strict discipline over rewards for virtue, however, Domitian failed to recognize the complexity of the tradition surrounding these priestesses. That complexity made it possible to challenge the emperor's manipulation of memory, and Cornelia proved herself to be adept at exploiting tradition to raise doubts about the legitimacy of the emperor's moral policies. I argue that her protests in the final moments before she was buried alive were intended to evoke the *exempla* of earlier Vestals who had proved their innocence with similar prayers. By presenting this alternate memory of the historical context for her fate, Cornelia exposed the arbitrariness of Domitian's attempts to exploit Republican tradition for contemporary political gain.

The problem of using the Republic to justify punishments meted out by the emperor is also the topic of Chapter 4. In a discussion that weaves together episodes from the reign of Nerva with Tacitus' accounts of Vespasian's reign, I focus on the role of senators in the administration of justice, and their use of models drawn from the Republic to justify their participation in (or retreat from) public life under the Principate. The bulk of this chapter focuses on the historical discussion presented in Tacitus' *Dialogus de Oratoribus*, a work that investigates another important turning point, the one that marked the end of the age of great orators. Tacitus offers many explanations of decline, but I suggest that he saw the most important break with the traditions of the Republic in the moral disillusionment of men such as the dialogue's host, Curiatius Maternus, who would rather write poetry than take part in the world of legal advocacy. The retirement of Maternus and others like him from public life left the way open for the *delatores* who saw to the unsavory business of prosecuting senators for treason and other offences. The issue, from Tacitus' perspective, was not so much that the scope for rhetorical accomplishments had diminished under the Principate, but rather that the moral status of a career in advocacy had been redefined.

Chapter 5 examines the works of two Flavian authors, Silius Italicus and Frontinus. Both wrote under Domitian, and both took Republican history as their subject matter. Their sensibilities stood at opposite extremes, however, as did their understanding of the relationship between the present and the past. Like the figure of Maternus in Tacitus' *Dialogus*, Silius withdrew from public life to write poetry. His epic poem on the Second Punic war, although not lacking in contemporary resonance, presents the Republic as an era of heroes in the Homeric mold, inaccessible to the humdrum realities of contemporary life. The other writer, Julius Frontinus, remained actively engaged in the administration of the empire throughout the Flavian period. The vision of Republican heritage that he puts forward in his *Strategemata*, in which the *exempla* of great feats of generalship are treated as object lessons in the principles of command, overlooks epochal distinctions like those found in Silius' work. Despite the differences in their approach, however, both writers reflect a way of thinking about Rome's past in which the *libertas* of the Republic was no longer a realistic alternative to the present system of government.

The concluding chapter returns to the perspective of the emperors to look at a final attempt to tame the memory of the Republic during the reign of Trajan. A series of *denarii* minted under that emperor reproduce in precise detail the types of various Republican coins (obverse and reverse), each with an encircling legend on the reverse that commemorates the "restoration" of these images by Trajan. I argue that the reissue of this numismatic set of Republican visual *exempla* was designed to call attention to the interconnections between the values advertised during the Republic and those of the current ruler. Many of the reverse types that were chosen for restoration can be read as establishing or reaffirming the Republican precedents for the iconography of other Trajanic coins and monuments. Although such continuities in the visual vocabulary of Roman public art had existed throughout the Principate, the ideological significance of this connection had never been articulated quite so explicitly before. Ultimately, the restoration of these coins suggests that the emperor himself had become the link between the two visions of the Republic discussed in Chapter 5. Trajan's self-presentation as a charismatic *princeps* who emulated Republican precedents invites the viewer to remember the Republic as a period of heroic exceptionality, while simultaneously sensing its continuity with the present. With Trajan, the emperor became the only Republican hero that Rome had left.

1

FREEDOM

In March of AD 68, the Roman governor of Gallia Lugdunensis, C. Julius Vindex, entered into open rebellion against the emperor Nero.[1] This was a dramatic step, but not in itself unprecedented. Although the relative tranquility of the empire under the Julio-Claudian emperors stood in marked contrast to the upheaval that had accompanied the final decades of the Republic, the Imperial *Pax Augusta* had been an imperfect peace. In the hundred-or-so years since the battle of Actium, Rome had witnessed numerous local uprisings and revolts by provincial commanders. Such disturbances were usually suppressed quickly, before they could pose a serious threat to the position of the emperor or to the stability of the empire as a whole.[2] The critical difference in the revolt of Vindex was that it had a chance to take hold and grow, eventually spreading beyond the boundaries of Gaul. What began as an isolated disturbance in an unarmed province developed into a wider rebellion involving the entire western portion of the empire, and it ultimately brought an end to the dynastic house that had dominated the Roman world since the rise of Augustus Caesar.

Much of the credit for this development probably should go to Vindex himself. In the months leading up to his open break with the emperor, the rebel leader began to lay the groundwork for a wider revolution by circulating secret letters encouraging other provincial governors – preferably those commanding legions – to throw off their allegiance to Nero.[3] Revolution is dangerous business, however, and enthusiasm for Vindex's

---

[1] Suet. *Nero* 40.1–4, *PIR*² I 628. See Urban (1999: 49–65), Raoss (1960), and Brunt (1959 = 1990: 9–32), also Wiedemann (1996), Flaig (1992: 240–92), Morgan (2006: 18–30), and Shotter (2008: 153–64).

[2] In 21, the Gallic uprising of Florus and Sacrovir was crushed before Tiberius even felt obliged to inform the senate of its outbreak: Tac. *Ann.* 3.47.1, *PIR*² I 315, I 539, Dyson (1975: 156–8), Urban (1999: 39–45). Similarly, in 42, Scribonianus' uprising against Claudius lasted only five days: Suet. *Claud.* 13.2, Dio 60.15.1–3, *PIR*² A 1140.

[3] Plut. *Galb.* 4.2.

plot appears to have been limited at first. The recent discovery (in 65) of a conspiracy to kill Nero and replace him with the aristocrat C. Calpurnius Piso had eliminated many of the men who were prepared to take this step.[4] For those who were left, the fate of those failed conspirators offered stark testimony to the risks involved in betraying a Roman emperor. Some commanders even forwarded Vindex's correspondence to Nero, hoping to win favor by exposing treason.[5] With his sedition forced into the open, persuasion became even more crucial to the survival of the rebellion and its author. Vindex then commenced a full-scale war of words, openly sending letters to the senate in Rome and to other provincial commanders in an effort to convince them to join him in opposition to Nero. Not since the conflict between Octavian and Mark Antony had political rhetoric been deployed so extensively as an instrument of civil war.[6]

In a few months, Vindex was dead, but the revolution he started lived on. The senate turned against Nero, whose suicide followed soon thereafter. Furthermore, the man Vindex had called on to lead his movement succeeded to the position of emperor. Although many factors contributed to this outcome, the importance of a clearly articulated political message should not be underestimated. Personal loyalties and calculations of self-interest certainly were operative at all levels, but these factors cannot be said to have predetermined the outcome of events.[7] The language of communal values also had a critical role to play in the successful usurpation that Vindex set in motion. This was particularly true with regard to the participation of members of the senatorial order, whose defection was essential to the overthrow of Nero. Although the depth or sincerity of personal convictions cannot be known, it is significant that the commanders who joined the revolution (and perhaps even some who did not) explained their actions, both to themselves and to posterity, in terms that matched the slogans that Vindex and his allies deployed.

This chapter will focus on the rebels' appeal to freedom (*libertas*) as the principal value that justified Nero's ouster. Like its modern analog, Roman *libertas* encompassed a complex range of legal, political, and historical associations, which made it a tricky concept to define.[8] As we

---

[4] Tac. *Ann.* 15.48–72, *PIR*² C 284. See Shotter (2008: 146–50), Griffin (1984: 166–70), Cizek (1982: 260–7), Rogers (1955: 207–11).

[5] Plut. *Galb.* 4.2.

[6] Suet. *Ner.* 41.1, Sutherland (1987: 105).

[7] Cf. the approach of Syme (1982a) and Cotta Ramosino (1999).

[8] The modern bibliography on freedom is impossibly vast. I have found the following useful: Cranston (1953: 3–62), Berlin (1969: 118–72), Patterson (1991), Pettit (1997: 21–50), and Skinner (1998).

shall see, the multiple valences of Roman *libertas* provide an analytically useful synecdoche for the conflicted nature of Imperial-era memories of Rome's Republican past. To an ancient audience, freedom was fundamentally the opposite of slavery. In political discourse, it denoted an absence of domination, whether by a king or some other unwelcome master. As the defining feature of the political order that had taken root at Rome after the expulsion of the kings, the concept of *libertas* acquired a substantial historical dimension in cultural memory as well. Under the Principate, the term became shorthand for the era of the Republic as a whole. This strong conceptual link with Republican history made discussions of *libertas* problematic under the emperors, but freedom nevertheless continued to occupy a central position in the constellation of Roman values. For the elites who formed the principal audience for Vindex's political rhetoric, freedom was simultaneously the defining feature of a lost Republican past and a value to be fought for and defended in the present. This ambiguity reflects the unresolved tensions inherent in the political compromise that had created the Principate, tensions that continued to play themselves out during the period under examination in this book.

C. JULIUS VINDEX

After formally entering into rebellion against the emperor, Vindex needed to raise an army as quickly as possible. In addition to soliciting the support of neighboring commanders, one of his first steps was to turn to the local population of his province, with which his family was well connected.[9] Vindex probably summoned an assembly of Gallic leaders and offered a thorough-going attack on the abuses of Nero's reign. His speech might have concluded with an exhortation for the Gauls to "come to the aid of themselves, come to the aid of the Romans, and set the whole world free" (Dio [Xiph.] 63.22.2–6: ἐπικουρήσατε μὲν ὑμῖν αὐτοῖς, ἐπικουρήσατε δὲ τοῖς Ῥωμαίοις, ἐλευθερώσατε δὲ πᾶσαν τὴν οἰκουμένην). Of course, it would be unreasonable to insist that these exact words, found in Xiphilinus' epitome of Cassius Dio's history, were actually spoken on that occasion. A well-known feature of ancient historiography – that speeches tend to represent "what the circumstances demanded" (rather than what was actually

---

[9] Dio (Xiph.) 63.22.1². Pace Dyson (1975: 158–61) and Schiller (1878: 261 ff.), the Gallic revolt of 68 was not primarily a nationalistic movement. Although descended from a royal line of the Aquitani (Dio [Xiph.] 63.22.12), Vindex had little reason to seek a break from Rome. See esp. Kraay (1949: 141–6), Brunt (1990: 19–27), and Urban (1999: 50).

said) – makes such a proposition unlikely.[10] In this case, however, other available evidence confirms that the promise of freedom was, in fact, a central article in the political manifesto of Vindex's rebellion.

Beyond the wording preserved by Dio's epitomator, the theme of *libertas* turns up repeatedly in the traces that have come down to us of the rhetoric employed during the political upheaval of 68. In particular, our sources suggest that the rebels revived a distinctively Roman political metaphor, which appropriates the legal terminology for the emancipation of slaves as a rallying cry for the oppressed. The Imperial biographer Suetonius summarizes a letter sent to the distinguished consular governor of Hispania Tarraconensis, Ser. Sulpicius Galba, whom Vindex invited to become "the *adsertor* and general for the human race" (*Galb.* 9.2: *ut humano generi assertorem ducemque se accommodaret*).[11] The phrase is echoed by the Elder Pliny, who described Vindex himself as an *adsertor* of freedom not long after the revolution that he began (*NH* 20.160: *adsertorem illum a Nerone libertatis*). The significance of this term is established by legal usage. Under Roman private law, slaves could be set free through a process known as *vindicatio in libertatem*, in which a third party – the *adsertor* – was required to touch the slave with a rod and testify to his status as a free person.[12] In this case, Galba is being asked to take a similar stand and assert the liberty of mankind, which had been "enslaved" by a tyrannical "master" – that is, Nero.

The principal legal context through which this metaphor operates signals an important aspect of Roman thinking about freedom, which cultural distance has nearly caused to fall out of modern understandings of political liberty. For a society in which the ownership of fellow human beings was both legally condoned and pervasive, *libertas* was always first and foremost a mark of personal legal status.[13] No matter your position on the

---

[10] Thuc. 1.22.1: τὰ δέοντα, cf. Plb. 12.25a.5, Walbank (1985: 151–2). On speeches in Dio, see Millar (1964: 42, 78–83). Extensive intervention by the epitomator probably can be ruled out (ibid. 2).

[11] Cf. Plut. *Galb.* 4.3: παρακαλῶν ἀναδέξασθαι τὴν ἡγεμονίαν καὶ παρασχεῖν ἑαυτὸν ἰσχυρῷ σώματι ζητοῦντι κεφαλήν, Ash (1997: 196–9). *PIR*[2] S 1003. Watson (1973) explains the shift to *adsertor* from the earlier catchword *vindex* by citing the legal nuance of the two terms, but it may simply have been an attempt to avoid the pun on Vindex's name: See Sutherland (1984: 30–1), also Baldwin (1975).

[12] Treggiari (1969: 21–5), Reggi (1973), Buckland (1963: 73), Mommsen (1881: 147–8). Slaves had no legal right to initiate such proceedings. Thus, an *adsertor* would typically bring the action on the slave's behalf.

[13] Brunt (1988: 283–91), Wirszubski (1950: 1–3), Connolly (2007: 158–61), see also Patterson (1991: 203–57) and Pettit (1997: 31–5). On the application of the metaphor of *vindicatio* to politics, see Wirszubski (1950, esp. 70–96), also Hellegouarc'h (1963: 550–9) and Scheer

ladder of the social hierarchy, the difference between slave and free status conjured vivid associations for every inhabitant of the Roman world. A lack of freedom implied slavery, which, in legal terms, was akin to death.[14] Conversely, a free person was someone who could expect to be protected from the indignities of being a slave. Appeals to the value of *libertas* thus had the potential to provoke an immediate and visceral subjective response from a wide range of audiences.

Like other fundamental concepts in Roman public life, Libertas was also revered as a goddess with anthropomorphic features. When depicted on coins or in other media, this personification can be recognized by the presence of a *pilleus*, the white woolen skullcap worn by emancipated freedmen, which is typically held out in her right hand. Sometimes she also holds a *vindicta*, the rod used in the manumission ceremony, in her other hand.[15] The use of these symbols in the religious iconography associated with the goddess Libertas further underscores the extent to which the concept of freedom was understood fundamentally as a mark of personal legal status in Roman culture.

Because of this connection between freedom and the status of the individual, terms such as *libertas*, *adsertor*, and *vindicatio* could mean different things to different people.[16] To the countless slaves who toiled away at the bottom of the social hierarchy, freedom was never a metaphorical abstraction. Emancipation offered the opportunity to be treated as a full-fledged human being and, if one's master was a Roman citizen, to participate in some of the advantages of civic life.[17] Nonslaves, on the other hand, could usually take such things for granted, so the promise of freedom for them

(1971). Following Cooper (1986), Roller (2001: 217–33) stresses the importance of the "parent domain" of meaning in the interpretation of metaphoric language. He goes too far, however, when he denies *libertas* the status of a political concept in its own right (ibid. 232). The use of the language of freedom to describe certain political conditions (on analogy with preexisting concepts of personal freedom) has been traced to the Greek experience in the aftermath of the Persian wars by Raaflaub (2004: 58–88) and Pohlenz (1966: 10–17), but the genesis of these concepts goes back even further: See von Dassow (2011), also Snell (2001).

[14] Ulpian *Dig.* 50.17.209: *servitutem mortalitati fere comparamus*, Buckland (1963: 72), Bradley (1994: 25).

[15] E.g., *RIC* I² 128 no. 97 (= *BMCRE* I 185 no. 145–8), 239 nos. 136–7, cf. *RRC* no. 392/1a–b. See, in general, Panvini Rosati (1996: 137), *LIMC* VI.1 278–85 s.v. "Libertas" [Vollkommer], also Livy 24.16.18–19, Koortbojian (2002).

[16] Indeed, the ambiguity of these terms is what made them so useful as political slogans: Hellegouarc'h (1963: 555). See also Brunt (1988: 283, 320–1), Roller (2001: 228), Raaflaub (2004: 266–7).

[17] Patterson (1991: 227–39), with further discussion by Millar (1995). If, as is likely, manumission was relatively rare, the prospect of freedom would be all the more delicious: See Wiedemann (1985).

had the potential to expand and encompass something more than what the minimal legal definition of the term implied. This is where the concept acquired its essential flexibility. Insofar as the *libertas* of the freeborn male represented a status quo of privileges and entitlements to be maintained, its substance as a metaphor could vary according to a person's social status.[18] As you moved up the social hierarchy, the number of visible constraints that might be placed on one's sense of freedom decreased. Consequently, the quality of the *libertas* that a Roman senator enjoyed was quite different from that of a merchant or a rural peasant. Within Roman society, different groups could even formulate contradictory understandings of the concept.[19]

Bearing in mind the role of the listener's subjectivity in decoding the meaning of freedom as a political concept, it is clear that Vindex's emphasis on *libertas* and his use of the term *adsertor* to refer to Galba's potential role in the revolution made it possible to speak to the concerns of multiple audiences simultaneously. However one defined the concept, liberty was a precious and therefore jealously guarded thing, the importance of which became more apparent when it was endangered. The abuse of power – by a landlord, a magistrate, or even the emperor – could be seen as a threat to freedom. For the subject populations of the Roman Empire, *libertas* might imply the overthrow of Rome's dominion or, less radically, the end of excessive interference by imperial administrators in local self-government. In this latter regard, Nero had introduced the divinity Jupiter *Liberator*, probably a Latin syncretism for Zeus *Eleutherios*, in advance of the remission of taxes that accompanied his celebrated tour of Greek festivals.[20]

In something of a paradox, the individuals who seem to have worried the most about the erosion of their *libertas* under the emperors were those

[18] Concepts such as *dignitas* are often brought to bear to explain this lack of uniformity: Bleicken (1972: 24–31), Stylow (1972: 23), cf. Brunt (1988: 337–8).
[19] Cf. MacCallum (1967: 313). It was no doubt galling to Cicero, who regarded himself as a champion of the freedom of the state, that Clodius had erected a shrine of Libertas on the site of his demolished house, but this seemed to be a legitimate statement to the voters in the popular assembly, who evidently were persuaded that Cicero's actions during the Catilinarian crisis undermined the sovereignty of law and thus constituted an attack on their freedom: Allen (1944), *LTUR* III 188–9 s.v. "Libertas (1)" [Papi], cf. Cic. *Sest.* 109, *Att.* 1.16.10, and other texts discussed by Wirszubski (1950: 60 n. 2).
[20] *RPC* I 1279, cf. *Syll*[3] 814 (= *ILS* 8794), Weinstock (1971: 144), Wissowa (1912: 106 n. 3). On freedom (*eleutheria*) of the subject peoples of the empire (particularly Greeks), Brunt (1988: 292–6), Ferrary (1988: 5–218), Jones (1939), Raaflaub (2004: 147–65), also Plut. *Mor.* 814E–815D, Momigliano (1996: 75–81), cf. Brunt (1990: 19–32).

who were furthest removed from any actual experience of the degradations of slavery. It was the Roman political elite, whose support Vindex
needed if his rebellion was going to have any chance at success, who
proved most receptive to his calls to assert mankind's freedom from Nero.
The emphasis that the nobility placed on their freedom is amply attested
throughout Rome's history, but the political circumstances of the Principate had done much to complicate elite attachments to this value. Serious
limitations were now imposed on magistrates' ability to do as they saw
fit in their performance of public duties, and officials sometimes chafed at
these restrictions. For example, the great commander Cn. Domitius Corbulo had been forced to abandon an invasion of Germany because it did
not fit with the strategic priorities of the emperor Claudius. His retreat
was said to have been marked by the lament, "blessed once were Roman
generals" (Tac. *Ann.* 11.20.1: *beatos quondam duces Romanos*).[21] More
recently, Corbulo's success at waging war in Armenia was thought to have
provoked the jealousy of Nero, and perhaps to have hastened the order to
commit suicide.[22]

It was not just the public careers of the nobility that were subjected
to restrictions and interference that felt degrading. Men's private affairs
could also suffer disruption from the arbitrary actions of an emperor.
Nero's friend and courtier M. Salvius Otho saw his wife Poppaea Sabina
taken from him by the emperor, who then went on to cause her death
by kicking her when she was pregnant – an act of cruelty also attributed
to the Corinthian tyrant Periander.[23] The emperor's third wife, Statilia
Messalina, was likewise stolen from another close associate, M. Julius
Vestinus, whom Suetonius says was executed for his trouble.[24] It goes
without saying that both women had already been seduced by Nero before
he married them. Divorce was nothing new, of course, and it cannot be
said that the Romans ever really married for love, but cases like these must
have caused men from noble families to feel like they were no longer secure
in their control of their own households. The threat of sexual abuse and a
lack of family stability were, of course, common features in the institution
of chattel slavery.[25]

---

[21] Cf. Dio (Xiph.) 60.30.5, Campbell (1984: 335).
[22] Dio (Xiph.) 63.17.5–6, cf. Tac. *Ann.* 15.25.2–30.2. *PIR²* D 141, Syme (1970b).
[23] Tac. *Ann.* 14.60.1–2, 16.6.1, Suet. *Otho* 3.1–2, *Ner.* 35.3, cf. Diog. Laert. 1.94, Mayer (1982). *PIR²* S 143, P 850, Griffin (1984: 45–6), also Cotta Ramosino (1999: 226–7).
[24] Suet. *Ner.* 35.1. *PIR²* S 866, I 624, Champlin (2003: 162–3), Shotter (2008: 151–2).
[25] Bradley (1984: 47–80), (1994: 28–9). Similar anxieties could be expressed about Augustus' marriage to Livia: Suet. *Aug.* 62.2, Flory (1988).

The situation confronting the Roman elite under the Principate is neatly encapsulated by the Stoic philosopher Epictetus, who, as a former slave, had much of interest to say on the subject of freedom in Roman society. In a key passage of the *Discourses* transmitted by his student Arrian, Epictetus explains the fraught nature of an Imperial senator's status, saying that the only honest advice for a powerful consular was to "recognize that, though you belong to a great house, you are still a slave" (*Disc.* 4.1.13: γίγνωσκε, ὅτι ἐκ μεγάλης οἰκίας, δοῦλος εἶ). It should be noted that this claim is used to support a philosophical (rather than a political) point. Even Epictetus does not assume that the underlying Stoic principle at work – that none but the true sage can ever be free – was widely acknowledged. In fact, the freedman philosopher warns that the most likely response to expect from a consular whose subservience has been pointed out is a beating.[26] Abuse of one's inferiors, it seems, was the most effective way to demonstrate one's freedom.

Theoretical absolutes aside, the reality was that Roman noblemen preferred not to think of themselves as slavish, even if the political realities of the Principate meant that they could not truly regard themselves as free. The problem facing these erstwhile masters of the world was that they could not fully enjoy the blessings of *libertas* so long as their ability to act was limited by the emperor's superior authority. The fact that Caesar's power was unlimited provided cold comfort to those who had to accept him as their master. This conflict between the actual circumstances in which these men found themselves and the self-image their pride demanded produced a situation akin to what social psychologists call "cognitive dissonance," which only deliberate reflection could break through.[27] For those who preferred either to ignore or to justify the compromised nature of their freedom, the emperor might help make things more bearable by downplaying the extent of his power and adopting the posture of a "first among equals," or *civilis princeps*.[28] Alternatively, as in Nero's case, the emperor's behavior could make matters worse. Writing a few generations after the event, Tacitus described the depressing string of elite suicides that marked the final years of Nero's reign as evidence of the nobles' "slavish endurance" (*Ann.* 16.16.1: *patientia servilis*). The historian construes this description as a rebuke, suggesting that the senators

---

[26] Epictet. *Disc.* 4.1.7: τὶ ἄλλο ἢ πληγάς σε δεῖ προσδοκᾶν; On the problem of freedom in Stoic philosophy, see Bobzien (1998, esp. 330–57), Long (1971). See esp. Sen. *Ep.* 47.17, also Shaw (1985: 38–43) and Bradley (1984: 113–37), (1994: 175–8).

[27] See Festinger, Riecken, and Schacter (1956, esp. 25–30) for the classic formulation.

[28] Wallace-Hadrill (1982a). The title of *princeps* itself suggests continuity with Republican norms: See (Wickert 1954: 2014), Drexler (1988: 100–20).

of Nero's day "took it" not like men, but like slaves who submitted to humiliation and even death without proper regard for their social status.[29] The implication is that Nero had reduced the senatorial order to the status of slaves, or at least made it so that they could no longer ignore the fact of their servitude.

These sentiments are also reflected in the rebels' argument that the freedom of the senatorial class was in need of restoration. The importance of this theme is most evident in the way that Galba announced his acceptance of Vindex's invitation to become an *adsertor*. When the Spanish governor finally made up his mind to join the cause, he embraced the central theme of Vindex's rhetoric, giving it an unmistakably aristocratic twist. In a clever bit of showmanship, Galba laid claim to the liberator's mantle by choosing a public ceremony for the manumission of slaves as the venue at which to announce that he was embracing the cause of liberty. According to Suetonius, "he mounted the tribunal, with as many official portraits (*imagines*) of those condemned or killed by Nero as possible displayed before him" (*Galb.* 10.1: *conscendisset tribunal, propositis ante se damnatorum occisorumque a Nerone quam plurimis imaginibus*). This staging recalls the spectacle of the public funeral of a nobleman at Rome, in which the *imagines* of ancestors were donned by actors who paraded through the Forum and gathered on the *Rostra* to listen to the laudation of the deceased. Such commemoration certainly had been denied to the men condemned by Nero, even though many of them had held high office and thus earned the right to be celebrated in this way.[30] The combination of these aristocratic symbols with a festival of manumission indicates that Galba wanted to signal a connection between asserting *libertas* from Nero and restoring the traditional prerogatives of members of his own class. To further underscore this link, he was accompanied on this occasion by a youth of noble family who had been banished by the emperor to the nearby Balaeric islands.[31] The message was clear: The Roman elite had suffered too long under an unjust and abusive "slavery," and Galba was offering to set them free.

---

[29] Cf. Tac. *Ann.* 15.73.2. Cizek (1972: 126–30), Rudich (1993, passim). On the socially contingent nature of what is suggested by *patientia*, see Kaster (2002). For Tacitus' sources in this part of the *Annales*, see Marx (1937), Syme (1958: 300–1).

[30] See esp. Plb. 6.53–4. Flower (1996: 53–9) offers a balanced treatment of the so-called *ius imaginum*. Galba probably used busts or other replicas rather than actual wax *imagines*, but the existence of recognizable portraits of these men certainly attests to their high status. On the denial of commemorative honors to condemned senators during the Principate, see Flower (2006: 132–8, 143–8).

[31] Suet. *Galb.* 10.1.

In a broader sense, Galba's mixing of ritual scenography suggests the extent to which the interpretation of concepts such as *libertas* was dependent on what Jan and Aleida Assmann describe as "connective memory" (*Bindungsgedächtnis*), which imposes itself on the members of a particular group.[32] Put simply, the Roman elite saw Nero as a threat to their freedom because they were culturally conditioned to do so. Their sense of what freedom should entail was wrapped up in how they understood their identity as members of a privileged social class. This meant that they had to reach beyond their unique experiences as individuals to come to a common understanding of what that status entailed. The nobles' sense of solidarity as a persecuted group depended not only on a shared experience of danger and/or suffering, but also on their access to a collective store of memory that produced certain expectations of how they were supposed to be treated. Galba's use of portrait *imagines*, which were themselves central to the transmission of cultural memory, underscores the importance of this connection.

M. Junius Brutus

Further evidence for the nature of the political rhetoric employed by the organizers of the rebellion in 68 can be found in the images and legends that appear on the coins they minted to pay the cost of raising and maintaining an army.[33] Although there has been some debate among historians and numismatists about the extent to which coins were actually useful as a means of conveying political messages in the ancient world, in this case it is profoundly clear that the design of the precious metal coinage issued by Galba and Vindex was both carefully considered and meant to reinforce ideas articulated more fully in other media. As the Roman governor of Gallia Lugdunensis, Vindex may have been more attuned than others to the communicative potential of coinage, since Lugdunum (Lyon) was also the primary site of the Imperial mint.[34]

The rebels' coins underline the importance of the theme of *libertas* in the political rhetoric deployed by Nero's opponents. The divine liberators *Hercules Adsertor* and *Iuppiter Liberator* appear on two of the silver

[32] Assmann (2000: 108–33), cf. (1992: 138–44).

[33] *RIC* I² 197–215 (= *BMCRE* I 288–308). The fundamental discussions are Kraay (1949) and Martin (1974), but see also Zehnacker (1987, esp. 337–45).

[34] Strabo 4.3.2, Metcalf (1989). Levick (1982a, 1999b: 41–6) provides a useful summary of the controversy, which goes back to Jones (1956) and Sutherland (1959). On the correlation between the messages on coins and those found in other media, see also Noreña (2001).

denarii ascribed to Vindex's mint.[35] These icons of supernatural support for freedom are connected (on the reverse side of each coin) with types that evoke the regenerative benefits of freedom, embodied as *Florente Fortuna P. R.* ("thriving Fortune of the Roman People") and *Roma Restituta* ("Rome restored"), respectively. Liberty and communal renewal are also brought together in the obverse legends *Pax et Libertas* ("Peace and Liberty") and *Salus et Libertas* ("Health and Liberty"), which appear on other coins issued by Vindex.[36] In light of the cumulative evidence of these coins and the pronouncements cited above, it is not difficult to credit Dio's description of Vindex as a "lover of freedom" (63.22.1²: φιλελεύθερος). Meanwhile, Galba (who had access to extensive supplies of silver in Spain) was toeing a similar line. The coins attributed to his mint operation also make explicit references to freedom. These legends advertise both Libertas and the restoration of liberty (*Libertas Restituta* or, more specifically, *Libertas P. R. Restituta*) that his uprising promised.[37]

Audience is again worth considering, but harder to assess in this case. As with the great majority of Roman specie, soldiers were the immediate recipients of these coins, which then circulated among the local population of the provinces.[38] But it would be reductive to suggest that the army was the only, or even the primary, audience for the messages contained in the decoration of these issues. It should not be overlooked that all but one of the coins mentioned above refer to the (Senate and) Roman People, represented by the letters P.R. or S.P.Q.R. Like the display of senatorial *imagines* at Galba's announcement of his rebellion, these abbreviations serve to clarify precisely whose liberty was being asserted. In fact, similar references to the authority of the *populus Romanus* appear on almost all of the rebels' coinage. Thus, despite coin legends that offer more expansive claims about the well-being of the human race (*Salus Generis Humani*) or specific references to the loyalty of the troops (*Fides Exercituum*) and the harmony of individual provinces (*Concordia Hispaniarum et Galliarum*), these themes are subordinated to a more essential claim about the authority of the Roman body politic.[39]

---

[35] *RIC* I² 207–8 nos. 49, 62.

[36] *RIC* I² 208 nos. 57–8, 64–6. On the linking of Salus and Libertas, see Sutherland (1984). For more on *Pax*, see Chapter 2.

[37] *RIC* I² 205 nos. 24–8. See also on *RIC* I² 214 nos. 132–3 (although the attribution of these coins to Galba and Vindex has been called into doubt because of their weight).

[38] On the importance of the legions to the circulation of coinage, see Hopkins (1980: 112–15), Duncan-Jones (1990: 30–47). In light of the reassessment of the array of the monetary instruments at the state's disposal by Harris (2006), the fact that soldiers were paid in cash becomes all the more significant for our understanding of how Roman coinage entered circulation.

[39] *RIC* I² 204–13 nos. 67–77 (*Salus*), nos. 118–22 (*Fides*), no. 15 (*Concordia*: cf. no. 119).

The rebels' assertion of rights on behalf of the Senate and Roman People invites further discussion of the multiple associations of *libertas*, because it raises the issue of the term's inevitable connection with a particular, historically defined phase in the development of the Roman polity. Starting with the Greeks, the idea that freedom was incompatible with the rule of one man had long been a touchstone in ancient political thought.[40] For the Romans, this concept was enshrined in one of the key foundation myths of their civic identity, that of the expulsion of the kings in 509 BC. Drawing on Greek models and analytical frameworks, the writers of Roman history portrayed Tarquinius Superbus, the last in the line of seven kings who had ruled Rome since its foundation, as a tyrant. The expulsion of Superbus by L. Junius Brutus consequently was regarded as the inauguration of *libertas* at Rome, in the same way that the overthrow of the Pisistratid tyrants marked the beginning of Athenian freedom (*eleutheria*).[41] Livy offers a typical expression of this view at the beginning of the second book of his history of Rome *Ab urbe condita*. Having described the fall of the Tarquins at the end of Book 1, Livy celebrates the fact that he now is able to relate the deeds of the Romans as a "free people," which were accompanied by "annual magistracies and the rule of law more powerful than that of men" (2.1.1: *liberi iam hinc populi Romani res pace belloque gestas, annuos magistratus, imperiaque legum potentiora quam hominum peragam*).[42]

In the Roman historical consciousness, therefore, the birth of political liberty was explicitly connected with the transition from a monarchy to the *respublica*, a form of government in which power was shared in common among several magistrates who held office for a limited period. Magistracies such as the consulship, which the orator Pliny the Younger described as an invention of "recovered liberty," continued to be filled after the battle of Actium, but the rise of Augustus to absolute power nevertheless introduced a new element into Roman thinking about how *libertas* related to the periodization of Roman history.[43] If the expulsion of the kings marked the beginning of Roman liberty, it follows that the return of de facto monarchy under the Principate might provide a terminus ante

---

[40] Raaflaub (2004: 89–101).

[41] Dion. Hal. *AR* 5.1.1. See esp. Ogilvie (1965: 195–219), also Gallia (2007).

[42] Cf. Dion. Hal. *AR* 4.73.1, Tränkle (1965).

[43] Plin. *Pan.* 78.3: *reciperata libertas*, cf. Tac. *Ann.* 1.1, Sion-Jenkis (2000: 27). Note also Pliny's hand wringing over whether the tribunate has become an *inanem umbram et sine honore nomen*: *Ep.* 1.23.1, Hoffer (1999: 195–209). See also Wirszubski (1950: 5), Bleicken (1975: 430), Brunt (1988: 330), Drexler (1988: 1–30), Hammond (1968: 131–42), Castritius (1982: 62–80).

quem for this condition as well.[44] In retrospect, the Imperial senator could recognize that the *libertas* of the Republic was incompatible in principle with the consolidation of power that Augustus institutionalized and passed on to his heirs.

Literary usage supports this conclusion. The poet Lucan, who also became a participant in the failed Pisonian conspiracy against Nero, provides a case in point. His epic treatment of the war between Pompey and Julius Caesar contains frequent references to the imperiled state of *libertas* at that time, and it is clear that the author wishes to suggest that this quality had disappeared in his own day.[45] Indeed, whenever writers of the Imperial period required a retronym with which to describe the nature of the Roman constitution before the imposition of the emperors' supreme authority, *libertas* was the inevitable choice. The historian Tacitus, for example, regularly employs this term to refer to the era that preceded Augustus' rise to sole power.[46] "Republic" might be our term, but *respublica* ("commonwealth") did not have the same temporal connotations for a Latin speaker. Technically speaking, the *respublica* continued to exist after Actium, even though it no longer could be regarded as the political embodiment of *libertas* in the same way that the old Republic, the *libera respublica*, had been.[47]

For *libertas* to return, therefore, it would appear to be necessary to recover the form of government that had existed before there were emperors. Such a conclusion is borne out by what took place following the assassination of Caligula, when there had been an abortive effort on the part of the senate and the consuls to take control of the city and govern the empire without a *princeps*. This doomed attempt to revive Republican principles of power sharing in government was said to be motivated by a desire to assert communal *libertas*.[48] Although it may be true that "Republicanism was no longer considered practical politics" a quarter of

---

[44] On the role of such periodization in the structure of historical memory, see Zerubavel (2003: 83–8).

[45] Lucan 1.669–72, 3.112–14, 145–7, 4.221–7, and especially 7.641–6. *PIR*² A 611, Ahl (1976: 35–56), MacMullen (1966: 23–7), Pecchiura (1965: 87–8), also Grimal (1992).

[46] See esp. Tac. *Agr.* 2.2–3, *Hist.* 1.1, *Ann.*1.1. Sion-Jenkis (2000: 27). Tacitus recognized that even the liberty enjoyed under the Republic was not absolute, but marked by brief periods of *dominatio*.

[47] Wirszubski (1950: 125), Brunt (1988: 323), Flower (2010: 19-20), also Wickert (1954: 2069–80). On the ambiguity of the term *respublica* under the Principate, Brunt (1988: 2), Gowing (2005: 4–5), Judge (1974: 280–7). See also Syme (1958: 548), Millar (2002: 51–4).

[48] Suet. *Claud.* 10.3: *consules… asserturi communem libertatem.* See also Joseph. *AJ* 19.161–89, where the byword ἐλευθερία is frequently mentioned, also Swan (1970), Goud (1996: 480), Sion-Jenkis (2000: 32–3).

a century later,[49] it nevertheless is important to bear in mind that the concept of political freedom continued to possess a significant historical dimension under Nero.

In the same way that the primary significance of *libertas* as a mark of individual legal status was essential to its meaning as a political value, the integration of this concept into one of the foundational narratives of Roman history meant that any promise to restore liberty was bound to conjure memories of a free Republic in which there was no room for the monarchal position of the emperor. As we have seen, concerns over political freedom arose naturally out of pervasive anxieties about social status within Roman culture. The further, historicized dimension of *libertas* meant that attention to this value had the potential to prompt inconvenient reflection about the origins of the Principate as a political institution and to tap into a latent sense of nostalgia for a lost past. It is clear that Galba and Vindex did not intend to shy away from these associations.

Apart from their frequent references to *libertas* in the abstract, the rebels' coins display certain features that call attention to the historical distance that separated the political conditions of the Principate from those of the Republic. Perhaps the most remarkable characteristic of the rebels' coinage is its overall lack of portrait images. Ever since the innovative honors that followed Julius Caesar's consolidation of political authority, it had become standard practice for his heirs to advertise their power by putting their portraits and titles on coins. Hence the admonition in the Gospels to "render unto Caesar" that which bears his name.[50] Although Galba ultimately became emperor and began to mint coins with his own likeness a few months later, he did not presume to present himself in the manner of a Caesar at the start of the rebellion. According to his biographers, Galba also refused the title *imperator* when it was offered by his troops, styling himself instead as a *"legatus* of the Senate and Roman People."[51] In the absence of an emperor's authority, there was no obvious place for the portrait "head" of a monarch that might have unified the message of these coins. The result is a chaotic mixing of obverse and reverse types that recalls the coinage of the Republic, before imperial portraits became an omnipresent feature of Roman coinage. Although the portrait

---

[49] Wirszubski 1950: 126 (with regard to the Pisonian conspiracy), cf. Joseph. *AJ* 19.224–5.

[50] Luke 20:24–5, see also Epictet. 3.3.3, Plin. *NH* 6.84, Wallace-Hadrill (1986), Crawford (1983: 55), Ando (2000: 222–7).

[51] Suet. *Galb.* 10.1: *consalutatusque imperator legatum se senatus ac populi R. professus est*; Plut. *Galb.* 5.2: οὔτε Καῖσαρ οὔτ᾽ αὐτοκράτωρ, στρατηγὸς δὲ συγκλήτου καὶ δήμου Ῥωμαίων ὀνομαζόμενος. Flaig (1992: 253–7), Hammond (1963: 99–110). Cf. also Zonar. 11.13, Reynolds and Ward Perkins (1952: 537).

Figure 1.1. *Denarius* of the Spanish Rebellion, AD 68. Obverse: bust of Libertas with legend LIBERTAS behind. Reverse: *pilleus* flanked by daggers, over legend RESTI-TUTA, letter P (of P · R) visible on left. (© Trustees of the British Museum, *BMCRE* I 290 no. 7)

of Augustus appears on some of the so-called anonymous Gallic coins, this nod to the extraordinary authority of the first *princeps* falls short of the threshold that would have been crossed if Galba had displaced the imperial image with his own.[52]

Further underscoring the old-fashioned character of this coinage was its general rejection of the numismatic iconography that had been deployed during the Julio-Claudian period in favor of older, Republican types. Roman coins are sturdy objects that could remain in circulation for many years, and so the users of these coins would have been able to notice the historical implications of such a change in style.[53] By far the most explicit reference to a connection between *libertas* and the bygone era of the Republic on these coins is the revival of a reverse type that was famil-iar from an earlier period of civil conflict (Fig. 1.1).[54] The meaning of the

[52] *RIC* I² 210–12 nos. 81–117. Comparison with the coins of Clodius Macer (*PIR²* C 1170), shows just how remarkable Galba's forbearance must have seemed: *RIC* I² 193–6, Zehnacker (1987: 334–7).

[53] Cf. Tac. *Germ.* 5.3, on the Germans' preference for (and hence recognition of) older coins. The coins, together with their Republican prototypes, are listed in the appendix to Wallace-Hadrill (1981a: 37–8). On the restoration of coin types as a method of appropriating "Republican" values, see further, Chapter 6.

[54] *RIC* I² 205 nos. 24–5 (= *BMCRE* I 290 nos. 7–8).

image is straightforward enough to decipher. It shows a *pilleus* flanked by two daggers, which suggests a form of freedom that must be obtained through violence. Such a message clearly was consonant with Vindex's call for Galba to become both the *adsertor* and *dux* for his rebellion. The source of the image was perhaps equally significant, however, as the circumstances in which this numismatic message was first promulgated were well known even in antiquity. The *pilleus* and daggers appeared on a *denarius* minted by the assassins of Julius Caesar during their flight from Rome in 43 BC. It is one of only a handful of coin types mentioned in an ancient historical source, and it was interpreted as a clear expression of the political views of the men responsible for its issue.[55] It is hard to imagine a scenario in which the person who revived so iconic an image could have been unaware of the historical circumstances in which this eloquent articulation of the necessary relationship between liberty and tyrannicide had first been deployed. Galba's coin can only be interpreted as a deliberate allusion to the political rhetoric of the opponents of Julius Caesar, and as an attempt to link Galba's appeals to *libertas* with the way that term had been used by the last champions of the Republican constitution.[56]

On the original coin, the legend *EID MAR* had been provided to assist the interpretation of the *pilleus* and daggers as a reference to the liberation of Rome that was supposed to have been accomplished on the Ides of March. The obverse displayed a portrait of the symbolic leader of the tyrannicides, M. Junius Brutus. On the coin from 68, however, both the reference to the Ides of March and the portrait image of Brutus have been omitted. The designer of this coin nonetheless kept the original significance of the borrowed image in mind, deploying on the obverse a labeled portrait of Libertas that was copied from a *denarius* produced by the same M. Brutus when he was moneyer.[57] On that prototype, the significance of the goddess had been explicated by a depiction of L. Junius Brutus, the original liberator of Rome and founder of the *respublica*, on the opposite face. This conscious and careful invocation on a single coin of two related exemplars that connected the Bruti with the theme of *libertas* could only bind this concept more closely to the life history of the Republic, from its foundation to its last defender. The word *RESTITUTA*, inserted below the field on the reverse of the new coin, can therefore be read as a promise to

---

[55] *RRC* no. 508/3. Dio 47.25.3, Price (1979: 278). Crawford (1983: 51) suggests that Dio's reference to the type derives from an earlier chronicle rather than from direct autopsy of the coin. The point to grasp is that the coin was well known, even if it did not circulate widely.

[56] Wirszubski (1950: 88–91).

[57] *RRC* 433/1.

restore the kind of liberty that had lapsed in the interval since M. Brutus'
famous deed.

This partly veiled but nevertheless deliberate reference to the intertwined
legacies of Lucius and Marcus Brutus brings us to an important crossroads
in the interpretation of *libertas* as a political ideal under the Principate.
Marcus Brutus was said to have been inspired by the example of his reputed
ancestor to join the plot against Caesar and free the Republic for a second
time.[58] He and his fellow assassins had hoped (however naively) that the
removal of Caesar's dominance would bring about a restoration of their
ideal of traditional Republican government. Given the restoration of this
coin and the general prominence of *libertas* in the political rhetoric of
the rebellion in 68, it might seem reasonable to conclude that Galba and
Vindex were pursuing a similar goal. Indeed, no less perceptive a historian
than Theodor Mommsen concluded that Vindex, at least, had intended
to abolish the Principate and restore the constitutional workings of the
Roman Republic.[59] This interpretation has since been rejected as unlikely
and will not be revived here. But it cannot simply be dismissed out of
hand. Like the assassins of Julius Caesar, the opponents of Nero promised
to restore *libertas* to the Senate and Roman People, and they did so in a
way that called attention to the special relationship between this value and
the historical conditions that defined the lost Republic. Whatever their real
political objectives, the architects of the revolution against Nero hoped for
their movement to be understood as "Republican" in some meaningful
way.

LIBERTAS AUGUSTA

Skeptics of the proposition that Vindex's revolt was an attempt to restore
the lost Republic can point to the fact that Galba made no attempt to
do this after Nero was out of the way. Instead, Galba became emperor
himself, preserving the essential administrative systems that had been put
in place since the founding of the Principate. The Republican form of government was not restored, and there is no indication that anyone seriously
considered restoring it. One can further argue, as Kraay has done, that
the interpretation offered in the previous section for the rebels' promise

---

[58] Plut. *Brut.* 10.6, cf. 9.5–7, Suet. *Caes.* 80.3. The ancient biographers suggest that Brutus had
a double heritage of tyrannicide, going back not just to L. Brutus but also to Servilius Ahala
on his mother's side: Plut. *Brut.* 1.5. MacMullen (1966: 7–10), Weinstock (1971: 146–7), also
Meier (1995: 479–82). On Brutus' posthumous reputation under the Principate, see Clarke
(1981: 79–84).

[59] Mommsen (1878), (1992: 180–1).

to restore *libertas* is mistaken, and that the controlling frame of reference for an interpretation of their coinage lay not in the Republican past, but rather in the age of Augustus.[60] As has been noted, a number of these "anonymous" coins in fact bear the portrait image of Augustus.[61] These coins emphasize the special religious authority of the first emperor, who is sometimes described as *DIVI F(ilius)* (the son of the deified Caesar), sometimes with his posthumous status as a *DIVVS* (god) in his own right. Other divinities closely associated with Augustus, such as Pax and Mars Ultor, also make frequent appearances on the rebels' coinage.[62] Because these coin types reflect the authority of the founder of the Principate, they appear to contradict the notion that the *libertas* promised by Vindex and Galba had anything to do with the lost political freedom of the Republic.

Furthermore, it is possible to identify *libertas* itself as one of the hallmarks of the Augustan program.[63] Co-opting the claims of Brutus and his fellow conspirators, the young Octavian/Augustus had used the language of liberation to characterize his own activities in the wake of Caesar's assassination. Writing toward the end of his life, Augustus began his *Res Gestae*, the public account of his career, with the following claim: "At the age of nineteen, on my own responsibility and at my own expense, I raised an army, with which I liberated (*in libertatem vindicavi*) the *respublica*, which was being oppressed by the despotism of a faction."[64] Similar language had been employed to characterize his role in the war against Antony and Cleopatra. Eastern *cistophori* of 28 BC label the portrait of Octavian with the Latin title *Libertatis P. R. Vindex* ("avenger of the Roman people's liberty" – *vindex* being an analogous term to *adsertor* in the Roman lexicon of manumission).[65] *Libertas* was thus one of the values that Augustus ostensibly embraced, despite a career that effectively brought an end

---

[60] Kraay (1949), also (Martin 1974: 68), Chilver (1957: 29), cf. Brunt (1990: 12).

[61] *RIC* I² 210–12 nos. 81–117. This is not in itself an altogether un-Republican move, because portraits of figures from the past (including kings) often appeared on Roman coinage. Cf. *RRC* nos. 425, 439/1, etc.

[62] *RIC* I² 203–12 nos. 2, 4–7, 9, 10, 34, 56–8, 113–15 (Pax), nos. 16–20, 23, 29, 43–4, 47–8, 53–5, 67 (Mars Ultor).

[63] Kraay (1949: 138–41), Hammond (1963: 95–6), also (1965).

[64] *RG* 1.1: *Annos undeviginti natus exercitum privato consilio et privata impensa comparavi, per quem rem publicam [a do]minatione factionis oppressam in libertatem vindic[avi] / . . .* τὰ κοινὰ πράγματα [ἐκ τῆ]ς τ[ῶ]ν συνο[μοσα]μένων δουλῆας [ἠλευ]θέ[ρωσα]. The *factio* in question was Antony's, and the formulation provided by Cic. *Phil.* 3.5: Galinsky (1996: 43–8), Cooley (2009: 108). Julius Caesar had said similar things to justify his own actions against Pompey: *BC* 1.22.5, cf. Dio 41.57.2. Weinstock (1971: 142–3), cf. Raaflaub (1974: 155–82) and (2003).

[65] *RPC* I no. 2203 (= *RIC* I² 79 no. 476, *BMCRE* I 112 nos. 691–3), with (Scheer 1971) and Sutherland (1970: 88–90), who notes that, with fifty known obverse dies, the issue "must have been of considerable size" (ibid. 13). See also Grant (1954: 22–4).

to the "freedom of the Republic" as the Romans traditionally understood that term.[66]

The letters SPQR, with their evocation of the traditional framework of Republican political authority, can also be read as a reflection of Augustan sloganeering. This is particularly evident because they are presented on the rebels' coins inside the oak wreath of the civic crown (*corona civica*).[67] This emblem, typically granted to soldiers who had saved a citizen's life in battle, was bestowed on Octavian by the senate and people in 27 BC, in conjunction with the title *Augustus* and the golden shield (*clupeus aureus*) enumerating his four most remarkable virtues.[68] The civic crown in particular served as a symbol of Augustus' claim to have rescued the Roman state (and thus all of its citizens) from destruction by putting an end to civil war. More importantly, this award was a convenient icon of the legitimacy the new *princeps* claimed for his position within the state. Because all of Augustus' honors were backed by the authority of the senate and people, the advertisement of awards like the civic crown could be used to suggest that Augustus' extraordinary powers were also consistent with traditional political principles – and thus with *libertas*.[69]

The assertion of *libertas* for the Senate and Roman People could thus be interpreted as an attempt to reclaim the legacy of Augustus. But if Augustus was a model of anything, it was of how to assert continuity with the past. As often happens at the beginning of a new regime, Rome's first emperor donned the cloak of traditionalism to disguise real innovation.[70] In the *Res Gestae*, he even went so far as to claim, "I handed over the *respublica* from my own power into the control of the Senate and Roman People" at the moment he received the oak crown, and similar claims were made in other contexts.[71] Such proclamations may have been less than sincere, but the

---

[66] Wirszubski (1950: 100–6), Walser (1955: 355–62), Mackie (1986: 304–24), Syme (1939: 313–30).

[67] *RIC* I² 203–12 nos. 26, 29, 31, 35, 46, 52–6, 58, 65–6, 68–9, 71–7, 104–10. Note also nos. 3, 21, 32–3, 102 (oak wreaths with the legend *Ob Civis Servatos*).

[68] *RG* 34.2, Val. Max. 2.8.7, Sen. *Clem.* 1.26, Strothmann (2000: 34–41), Zanker (1988: 92–7), Judge (1974: 291–6).

[69] The powers of the emperor would continue to be regarded as a legal grant from the Roman people: *Dig.* 1.4.1.*praef.*, Brunt (1977: 95), (1984), Millar (1988). Because laws were enacted by the will of the people, any legal grant of power could not be inconsistent with their political freedom: Brunt (1988: 319).

[70] Hobsbawm (1983). Eder (1990), cf. Meier (1990: 66–8).

[71] *RG* 34.1: *rem publicam ex mea potestate in senat[us populi]que R[om]ani [a]rbitrium transtuli/* ἐκ τῆς ἐμῆς ἐξουσίας εἰς τὴν τῆς συνκλήτου καὶ τοῦ δήμου τῶν Ῥωμαίων μετήνεγκα κυτιῆαν. Cf. *CIL* I².1 p. 231 (= *InscrIt* 13.2 p. 113), Jan. 13 or 14: *Corona quern[a uti super ianuam domus Imp. Caesaris] Augusti poner[etur senatus decrevit quod rem publicam] p(opulo) R(omano) restitui[t]* (it should be noted that *ius et leges* or, perhaps, *libertatem* might fit in the space

point remains that Augustus arranged matters so that his extraordinary powers were established in such a way as to reflect his own support for (and acquiescence to) the institutions of the free Republic.

Even as the *respublica* was taken over by a monarchy, the traditional political organs of government were preserved.[72] According to the official rhetoric, the new order was supposed to be indistinguishable from the old one. Even the constitutional power that Augustus kept for himself, the *tribunicia potestas*, was historically regarded as a "bulwark of *libertas*."[73] This posture may have helped the first *princeps* endear himself to his contemporaries, but it could only leave subsequent generations confused. As a result of Augustus' diplomatic regard for tradition, the radical shift in elite ideology that might have made it easier for posterity to accept the reality of life under a monarchy simply did not take place. There was no revolutionary break with the past; Augustan public ideals echoed those of the Republic, and the deliberate reinvigoration of the institutions through which those values were transmitted only encouraged their preservation. This fossilization of Roman culture at a moment of profound change explains why it was as difficult in antiquity as it is today to settle on a single event as the watershed that marked the break between Republic and Empire. It also provides some clue as to why senators continued to think of *libertas* in terms of its Republican associations long after that sort of freedom had ceased to represent a viable alternative to the monarchy that had replaced it.[74]

As has already been mentioned, *libertas* was the watchword of those who sought to restore the power of the senate and magistrates after Caligula's assassination. It is perhaps a sign of Claudius' conciliatory attitude to those disappointed idealists that he advertised a previously unattested *Libertas Augusta* on his coinage, and one of the many arches set up to celebrate his conquests in Britain records the inclusion of Vind(ex)

---

where "*rem publicam*" has been restored). A recently discovered *aureus* bears the legend *Leges et Iura PR Restituit*: Rich and Williams (1999), Abdy and Harling (2005).

72 The *comitia centuriata* would continue to convene on the Campus Martius to formally elect magistrates until as late as the third century: Dio 37.28.3, 53.21.6, cf. *RS* I # 37–8, p. 519–21, ll. 6–50, with Béranger (1973: 209–42) – a formality, perhaps, but not a mere formality. Note that competition for offices remained vigorous under the Principate: Hopkins and Burton (1983: 149–56). See also Flaig (2003: 155–80). The senate also continued to have an important role in the administration of the empire: Talbert (1984, esp. 372–487).

73 Livy 3.37.5: *tribuniciam potestatem, munimentum libertati*, cf. Sall. *Hist.* 3.48.12 Reynolds: *vis tribunicia, telum a maioribus libertati paratum.*

74 von Fritz (1957: 565), Sion-Jenkis (2000: 53–64), Várhelyi (2005), Flower (2010: 13–15, 149–53, 162–4), cf. Zerubavel (2003: 89–91).

Lib(ertatis) among his imperial titles.[75] It has also been noted that Nero promoted an association with Jupiter *Liberator* in a provincial context, and yet some of his political victims were said to have sacrificed to this very god before succumbing to their enforced suicides.[76] When the Pisonian conspiracy was revealed, the emperor made an offering to Jupiter *Vindex* on the Capitol, but Tacitus knowingly suggests that this would prove a portent of things to come (*Ann.* 15.74).

The evidence thus points not only to the continuing exploitation of *libertas* in the self-presentation of emperors down to the time of Galba, but also to its usefulness as a term with which to express dissatisfaction with the limitations of life under the Principate. There is a considerable difference, it seems, between the appropriation of traditional values for immediate political ends and the redefinition of those values to address the ideological needs of radically altered circumstances. It is true that Augustus had styled himself as a liberator, but this is simply another way of saying that he sought to vilify his rivals as tyrants. Despite the first *princeps'* success in associating himself with the term, *libertas* did not really become synonymous with *principatus*. As the reference to Marcus Brutus' vision of *libertas* on the coinage of 68 demonstrates, this value continued to be associated with the unique and increasingly distant political realities of the historical Republic.

L. VERGINIUS RUFUS

Given the nature of the Republic's hold on Imperial discourse, it was certainly to the emperors' advantage that the Roman concept of *libertas* was sufficiently ill-defined that they could present themselves as its champion while at the same time holding onto supreme power. But the emperors did not unilaterally control the interpretations to which this value might be subjected. To put the rhetoric of the emperors and would-be emperors in context, it will help to consider the statements of another important participant in the events of 68, one who emphatically refused to be considered for the position of *princeps*. L. Verginius Rufus was, at the time of Vindex's rebellion, Nero's commander on the southern Rhine, and he remains to this day one of the more enigmatic figures associated with these

---

[75] *RIC* I² 128 no. 97 (undated), *CIL* III 7061 (= *ILS* 217). Dio 60.3.5 says that Claudius actively honored those who had sought to restore τὴν δεμοκρατίαν after Gaius' assassination. It is also true that many of Claudius' policies reflected his own antiquarian interests in Republican history and institutions: See Momigliano (1934: 3–19), Levick (1978), Huzar (1984: 618–26).

[76] Tac. *Ann.* 15.64, 16.35, Dio (Xiph.) 62.26.4, cf. *RPC* I 1279. MacMullen (1966: 23).

events. After Vindex had begun to recruit an army from the local population, Verginius marched into Gaul with his three legions, but only after a
delay of some months. His objectives are not entirely clear, but the lapse
of time seems to suggest something less than complete loyalty to Nero's
interests.[77]

According to the account of Dio (Xiph. 63.24–5), a conference was held
near Vesontio (Besançon), where Verginius was supposed to have come to
an agreement with Vindex about the part that he and his legions could play
in the rebellion. Soon after this meeting of the minds, however, the discipline of the troops broke down and a battle erupted, apparently against
the will of both commanders. The makeshift Gallic army was crushed by
the better trained and better equipped Roman forces, and Vindex wound
up taking his own life. Following the conclusion of the battle, the Rhine
legions saluted their commander as *imperator*, but Verginius refused the
title. He stopped short, however, of calling this acclamation what it was:
treason against the authority of Nero. He thereby seems to have signaled
his support for the idea of revolution, so long as he was not to be its leader.
Verginius insisted that only the senate could name an emperor, echoing
Galba's modestly chosen title of *legatus* of the Senate and Roman People.[78]

Whether these actions demonstrate support for Galba's candidacy or
not, they certainly suggest an adherence to a set of principles very similar to those the rebels had been espousing. Verginius' refusal to let the
legions select an emperor would seem to reflect a strongly held position,
because he also avoided salutation by the troops after the demise of Otho
in the following year.[79] Doubts about his commitment to the overthrow
of Nero nevertheless began to surface soon after Vesontio. Galba appears
to have recalled Verginius from his command, although he did not send an
assassin to remove him, as he had done with more obvious threats such as
Clodius Macer in Africa and Fonteius Capito in Lower Germany.[80] After
the dust of civil war had settled enough for the histories to be written,
the judgment on Verginius remained mixed. Pliny the Younger, who had
benefited from this Milanese senator's hospitality and patronage from an

[77] *PIR*[1] V 284. Hainsworth (1962: 86–7), Brunt (1959: 536–8), *contra*, Levick (1985: 325–8).
For the chronology, see Shotter (1975: 64–9), also Syme (1991: 515).

[78] Dio (Xiph.) 63.24–5, cf. Plut. *Galb.* 6.2–4. The victory of Verginius' forces was celebrated with
a dedication to Jupiter in his native Transpadana, perhaps in the anticipation that he would
become emperor: *CIL* V 5702 (= *ILS* 982).

[79] Tac. *Hist.* 2.51. Much seems to hinge on the meaning of Tac. *Hist.* 1.8.2: *Germanici exerci-
tus…tarde a Nerone desciverant, nec statim pro Galba Verginius*. Urban (1999: 62–3),
cf. Hainsworth (1962: 93–6) and Daly (1975: 91–7).

[80] Tac. *Hist.* 1.8.2: *abducto Verginio per simulationem amicitiae*, cf. 1.7.1. *PIR*[2] C 1170, *PIR*[2]
F 468.

early age, described his refusal of the purple as "that divine and immortal deed" (*Ep.* 6.10.4: *divinum illud et immortale factum*), probably echoing a view espoused in his uncle's *Histories*. The consular historian Cluvius Rufus, on the other hand, appears to have been more critical.[81] After the publication of his work, Cluvius begged forgiveness if Verginius should find anything unpleasant in his version of events. In a letter recounting that exchange, the Younger Pliny says that his mentor simply replied with a question: "are you unaware, Cluvius, that I did what I did so that there might be freedom for you to write what you wish?" (*Ep.* 9.19.5: *tune ignoras, Cluvi, ideo me fecisse quod feci, ut esset liberum vobis scribere quae libuisset?*). Verginius points out that, if he had become emperor, Cluvius would have lost his freedom to criticize. The response is thus cleverly crafted to demonstrate Verginius' unwavering attachment to *libertas*.[82] Even if Verginius was directly implicated in the death of Vindex, he knew that his reputation could be redeemed if he could associate himself with this greater virtue.

More interesting still, Verginius' invocation of *libertas* closely echoes a riposte attributed to one of the greatest heroes of the Republic, P. Cornelius Scipio Africanus. When a tribune attempted to charge Scipio with misconduct in his handling of the peace settlement with Antiochus, the conqueror of Hannibal declared that the Roman people should not listen to anyone who would accuse him, because he had made it possible for the accuser to speak in the first place.[83] The resonance of this *exemplum* is all the more striking, given that Scipio, like Verginius, was admired in certain quarters for his refusal of monarchical powers.[84]

Verginius' role in what took place at Vesontio, a subject of controversy even during his own lifetime, has continued to provoke debate in modern scholarship. Indeed, it might be said that too much effort and ingenuity have been expended on efforts to uncover the underlying motivations of this particular character in the historical drama.[85] In attempting to isolate the precise moment at which Verginius became disloyal to Nero, however,

---

[81] *PIR²* C 1206. Syme (1958: 178–9), (1991: 517), Bardon (1956: 168). Pliny the Elder: Townend (1961: 339), Bardon (1956: 161).

[82] Urban (1999: 60), Ludolph (1997: 63–6).

[83] Plb. 23.14.3: οὐκ ἔφη δὲ πρέπον εἶναι τῷ δήμῳ τῶν Ῥωμαίων οὐθενὸς ἀκούειν κατηγοροῦντος Ποπλίου Κορνηλίου Σκιπίωνος, δι' ὃν αὐτὴν τὴν τοῦ λέγειν ἐξουσίαν ἔχουσιν οἱ κατηγοροῦντες, cf. Val. Max. 3.7.1g.

[84] Sen. *Ep.* 86.1–3, cf. Livy 38.56.12, Plb. 10.40.

[85] Verginius has been interpreted variously as a loyal supporter of Nero's interests (Syme 1958: 179, Levick 1985), an indecisive commander who lost his nerve in a moment of crisis (Shotter 1967, Morgan 2006: 23–5), an idealistic champion of the senate's prerogatives (Hainsworth 1962), and a faithful and important supporter of Galba (Daly 1975).

scholars risk losing sight of a more significant reflection of both the man and his age: namely, his own explanation of his actions. According to his friend and protégé, Verginius did not often discuss the part that he had played in the events of 68. He did, however, seek to explain himself in the elegiac couplet that he composed to serve as his epitaph:

> *Hic situs est Rufus, pulso qui Vindice quondam*
> *imperium adseruit non sibi, sed patriae.*

> Here lies Rufus, who, when Vindex was beaten,
> asserted power not for himself, but for the fatherland.
>
> *(Ep. 9.19.1)*

The phrase *imperium adseruit* further underscores the conceptual link that Verginius wanted his fellow Romans to draw between the deference he had shown to the authority of the Senate and Roman People and his role as a kind of liberator.[86] And yet, it also links the rhetoric of liberation to the disposition of imperial power, which continued to reside in the hands of a single man. In Verginius' case, the message was not that he had returned liberty to the fatherland by abolishing this power, but that he had respected the freedom of his fellow senators by avoiding it.

Even if these verses are deliberately misleading apologia, Verginius' epitaph has considerable value as evidence of the extent to which the vocabulary of liberation was employed by senators and emperors alike to justify their actions during and after the events of 68. A commander who, if only through his own incompetence, had dealt a serious blow to the rebellion of Galba and Vindex still sought to define himself by espousing the same basic commitment to *libertas* that they had advertised. Political freedom was necessarily associated with the old Republic, but such statements suggest that it could continue to exist under the Principate if the circumstances were right. A similar reasoning applies when Tacitus remarks on the unprecedented mixing of these previously incompatible conditions under Nerva (*Agr.* 3.1: *res olim dissociabiles miscuerit, principatum ac libertatem*), or when Pliny the Younger praises Trajan for making it so that "the rewards for virtue are the same under a *princeps* as they were in freedom" (*Pan.* 44.6: *eadem quippe sub principe virtutibus praemia quae in libertate*).[87]

---

[86] Shotter (2001), cf. Townend (1961: 339).

[87] Cf. *Pan.* 36.4, 58.3, Beutel (2000: 59–64). On Pliny's view of the Principate, see also Schowalter (1993: 33–5). Tacitus' use can be construed as referring to freedom of speech, or "the ability of senators in particular to criticize without endangering their lives" (Shotter 1978: 236). Cf. the admonition at *Dial.* 27.3: *utere antiqua libertate, a qua vel magis degeneravimus quam ab eloquentia*, discussed further, Chapter 4.

As will be discussed in more detail in the following chapter, the new Imperial arrangement offered stability under the rule of law, which was also a sine qua non for Roman conceptions of *libertas*.[88] Following the successive crises of the late Republic, the only way that anyone could devise to maintain order was to subordinate the ambitions of competing individuals and groups under the unifying control of a single ruler. This is what Julius Caesar, following Sulla, had accomplished briefly, and what Augustus institutionalized on more permanent foundations. Without an emperor, Rome and its far-flung empire risked chaos and a return of civil war. There were few who wanted freedom at such a cost.[89] The necessity of the Principate had finally been acknowledged, albeit grudgingly, after the assassination of Caligula, when the consuls' attempt to restore public *libertas* gave way to the praetorians' acclamation of Claudius. We can be reasonably certain that, twenty-seven years later, it was not the system of the Principate that Vindex and his potential supporters wanted to over-throw so much as the erratic young *princeps* many had come to fear.[90] Like the conspirators who had rallied around C. Piso a few years earlier, Vindex had a candidate in mind when he broke with Nero. But he also had the memory of Lucius and Marcus Brutus to contend with, and a pop-ular understanding of *libertas* that had little to do with any mechanical repetition of Augustan slogans.

Ser. Sulpicius Galba, Capax Imperii

Following Nero's suicide in June, Galba was again acclaimed *imperator*, this time by the praetorian forces in Rome. The senate quickly ratified the soldiers' choice, and Galba returned to the capital as *princeps*, apparently fulfilling various prophecies.[91] His reign was short lived, however, and was characterized by some astonishing political miscalculations. Tacitus would sum up Galba's character thus: "by common agreement, he was competent to rule, if only he had not ruled" (*Hist.* 1.49.4: *omnium consensu capax imperii, nisi imperasset*).[92] Like many Tacitean observations, this aphorism encapsulates an important insight into the nature of Roman political culture in the age of the Caesars. The fact that the expectations

---

[88] Cic. *Clu.* 146: *hoc fundamentum libertatis, hic fons aequitatis...legum denique idcirco omnes servi sumus, ut liberi esse possimus*, cf. Liv. 2.1.1. Arena (2007a: 54), Wirszubski (1950: 107–23), Hellegouarc'h (1963: 544–8). See also Pettit (1997: 35–41).

[89] See esp. *SCPP* ll. 45–7, Syme (1958: 250).

[90] Brunt (1990: 13), Vogel-Weidemann (1979: 98).

[91] Plut. *Galb.* 2.1–3, Suet. *Galb.* 4.1–3.

[92] Cf. Epictet. *Dis.* 3.15.14.

of so many proved faulty suggests that there was a significant disconnect between the realities of Imperial politics and the common understanding of what a successful *princeps* was supposed to be. Galba clearly possessed a repertoire of personal qualities that inspired other members of the ruling class to support his acclamation, even if these traits proved inadequate to ensure the success of his principate. Indeed, because of Galba's ultimate failure, the attributes that recommended him merit serious consideration. As we shall see, the nature of Galba's rise provides further insight into how the social institutions of memory made it possible for so self-contradictory a project as the restoration of *libertas* by a *princeps* to seem plausible.

The most extraordinary (and perhaps most important) of Galba's political assets was the nobility of his family lineage. Scion of an ancient and distinguished patrician *gens*, Galba could boast a heritage to rival any of the Claudii or Julii in the Imperial household.[93] Although he ultimately changed his name to reflect a posthumous adoption into the line of Caesar Augustus, Galba nevertheless remained fiercely proud of his natal ancestry. With great fanfare, he displayed his full stemma (no doubt accompanied by the ancestral *imagines* themselves) in the atrium of the Imperial palace.[94] All previous and subsequent emperors wore the signet ring that Augustus had used, but Galba preferred to keep the seal of his own family, which showed a dog looking over the prow of a ship.[95]

The emphasis that Galba placed on the achievements of his forebears both before and after he became *princeps* does much to illuminate the enduring importance, at the end of the Julio-Claudian regime, of a heritage that stretched back into the Republic. Galba's distinguished family history was not something that he had to wait until he became emperor to trumpet, but his deliberate emphasis on these ties as *princeps* suggests that his ancestry was thought to bolster his claim to represent a preferable alternative to Nero. For one thing, this noble lineage was important to the construction of the personal "authority" (*auctoritas*) that justified Galba's accession as *princeps*. Much like *libertas*, *auctoritas* was another essential yet

---

[93] Sancery (1983: 11–19). Galba could boast descent from two famous Republican generals, Ser. Sulpicius Galba (*RE* 58) and L. Mummius (*RE* 7a). The name of his great-grandfather, Q. Lutatius Catulus, could still be seen in the inscription of the temple of Jupiter Optimus Maximus on the Capitol: Tac. *Hist.* 3.72, see below. The monument proudly was advertised on Galba's coinage: *RIC* I² 207–14 nos. 42, 127–8, *RPC* I 5347, Kleiner (1989). Perhaps most relevant to his credentials as a restorer of *libertas* was the fact that his grandfather (*RE* Sulpicius 61) had been condemned under the *lex Pedia* for participating in the assassination of Julius Caesar: Suet. *Galb.* 3.2.

[94] Suet. *Galb.* 2, Flower (1996: 261).

[95] Dio 51.3.7, cf. Suet. *Aug.* 50.

conveniently malleable concept in the ideology of the Roman Principate.[96] Also a legal term, *auctoritas* denotes accountability and integrity, qualities that status-conscious Romans typically linked to social standing. As such, *auctoritas* could be used to describe a kind of influence or power that was customary rather than official and moral rather than political. Relying on his superior *auctoritas*, a charismatic Augustus had been able to claim that his official position was consistent with the Republican principle of *par potestas* (equal power shared among collegial magistrates), while at the same time transcending those limitations in practice.[97]

If the Tiberian author Velleius Paterculus is to be believed, some Romans initially did accept the argument that the *respublica* had been restored to its previous condition under the benign oversight of a uniquely gifted *princeps*.[98] Whereas tyrants ruled through brute strength and fear, it was theoretically possible for one man to surpass everyone in honor without compromising freedom. This, at least, is an ideal that Cicero attributes to Mark Antony's noble grandfather, whose definition of success was "to be equal to others in *libertas*, first (*princeps*) in distinction (*dignitas*)" (*Phil.* 1.34: *libertate esse parem ceteris, principem dignitate*).[99] In the eyes of a Roman senator, it might be possible to accept the emperor nominally as *primus inter pares*, whose exercise of power was consistent with *libertas* insofar as it was granted by virtue of the special aura of his individual *auctoritas*.

As time passed, however, it became increasingly difficult to maintain this view. Ideally, the emperor was supposed to act as if bound by the traditional limitations of his magistracies, but in reality, he was above the law – a fact made abundantly clear by the behavior of those "bad" emperors such as Caligula and Nero, who did as they liked without fear of consequences.[100] Legalistic distinctions between *potestas* and *auctoritas* are only part of this story. Although respect for constitutional niceties

---

[96] Heinze (1925), Béranger (1953: 114–31), Lind (1979: 29–34), also Wirzubski (1950: 34–6).

[97] *RG* 34.3: *post id tem[pus au]ctoritate [omnibus praestiti, potest]atis au[tem n]ihilo ampliu[s habu]i quam cet[eri qui m]ihi quoque in ma[gis]tra[t]u conlegae f[uerunt]*; ἀξιώμ[α]τι πάντων διήνεγκα, ἐξουσίας δὲ οὐδέν τι πλεῖον ἔσχον τῶν συναρξάντων μοι. See Adcock (1952), Brunt and Moore (1967: 78–9, 84–5), Hammond (1963: 96), Galinsky (1996: 10–41), Strothmann (2000: 39–40).

[98] Vell. Pat. 2.89.4: *prisca illa et antiqua rei publicae forma revocata*. See Gowing (2005: 34–41), Syme (1970a: 121).

[99] Cf. Cato *ap*. Fest. 408 Lindsay (= fr. 252 Malcovati).

[100] Sen. *ad Polyb*. 7.2: *Caesar . . . cui omnia licent*, cf. CIL VI 930 = ILS 244, ll. 22–5, Brunt (1977: 107–16). On the difficulty of reconciling *principatus* and *libertas* under Nero, see Shotter (1978: 244–7), also Wirzubski (1950: 135–6), Vogel-Weidemann (1979: 98–101), Toynbee (1944: 47).

clearly remained important, this issue does not in itself explain what Galba's emphasis on his distinguished Republican heritage had to do with his commitment to the broader theme of liberation. After all, the emperor that he proposed to replace did not suffer from a lack of impressive forebears. The critical issue lay elsewhere, in cultural expectations about what Galba's credentials might mean for the restoration of *libertas*.

Once again, Augustus provides a vital point of comparison, but this time not in his self-proclaimed role as a restorer of Republican political freedom. In spite of the considered opinion of authors such as Velleius and the tendentious claims of the *Res Gestae*, later writers looking back on the Augustan period regarded the return of political control to the senate and people as something that the emperor was rumored to have contemplated, but thought better of in the end.[101] In Book 52 of Cassius Dio's comprehensive history of Rome, we find what purports to be the record of the debate between two of Augustus' most trusted advisors, Agrippa and Maecenas, on the merits of *demokratia* and *monarkhia*, respectively. Modern scholars no doubt could dispute the use of these terms to describe the alternatives available to Caesar's heir in 27 BC, but this is an issue that does not appear to have troubled ancient authorities.[102] For the historian of the transition from the Republic to the Principate, this moment of decision offered an opportunity to reflect in Janus-like fashion on the relationship between the system that Augustus created and what came to be regarded as the previous status quo.[103]

Of particular interest for the present discussion is the connection that Dio has Agrippa draw between particular arrangements of political authority and the promotion of moral excellence. One of the primary concerns in his speech is the pernicious effect that monarchy would have on Roman virtue. According to a widely held view, kings are notoriously fearful of the best and most capable men in the state, because they are aware that "it does not happen that a worthy man is born without spirit, ... nor indeed can it be that someone who has spirit will not desire freedom and hate all who dominate him" (Dio 52.8.5: οὐ γὰρ ἔστιν οὔτ᾽ ἄνευ φρονήματος

---

[101] Suet. *Aug.* 28.1, cf. Virtr. *praef.* 1–2. Millar (1968: 265–6).

[102] Sion-Jenkis (2000: 43–6), Ruiz (1982: 59–101). The question of whether the Roman Republic can accurately be described as a "democracy" has excited much controversy for a while now: See North (1990), Millar (1998), Hölkeskamp (2010). For ancient perception of these issues, see Millar (2002, esp. 50–3), also Lintott (1999: 233–5).

[103] See Millar (1964: 102–18), Fechner (1986: 71–85). Far more space is given over to Maecenas' speech on kingship, essentially "a political pamphlet" aimed at influencing the policies of Caracalla. The idea of such an exchange can be traced back to the constitutional debate that precedes the accession of Darius to the Persian throne in Herodotus, 3.80–3.

ἀξιόλογον ἄνδρα φῦναι,... οὐ μὴν οὐδὲ φρονηματίαν γενόμενον μὴ οὐκ ἐλευθερίας ἐπιθυμῆσαι καὶ πᾶν τὸ δεσπόζον μισῆσαι). This statement, which is reminiscent of Aristotle's justification of the dominance of a master over his slaves, serves to remind us that, among ancient elites, the freedom-slavery binary involved not only political and legal status, but also moral valuation. The degradations inherent in the day-to-day operation of a slave economy tended to reinforce the perception that slaves are morally inferior to their masters, and thus deserving of their status. A worthy person – one with "spirit" (φρόνημα), to use Agrippa's term – was expected to be incapable of tolerating such abuse.[104] What this means in practice is that good men could not be trusted to serve under a monarch and would have to be persecuted to maintain such a constitution. This state of affairs contrasts with what Agrippa has to say about democracy, where, "as far as there are men who are wealthy and brave, so much more do they desire glory and expand the power of their state" (Dio 52.9.1: ὅσῳ ἂν πλείους καὶ πλουτῶσι καὶ ἀνδρίζωνται, τόσῳ μᾶλλον αὐτοί τε φιλοτιμοῦνται καὶ τὴν πόλιν αὔξουσι.).[105] The latter circumstance, because it encourages the exercise of noble qualities for the benefit of the community, is viewed as preferable.

These observations on the relationship between Republican (or "democratic") freedom and aristocratic excellence were not without precedent. The same basic principle finds expression in the work of the Late Republican historian Sallust, who warns that "kings are more suspicious of the good than the bad and the virtue of others is always frightening to them" (Cat. 7.2: nam regibus boni quam mali suspectiores sunt semperque iis aliena virtus formidulosa est). Dio's thinking also accords with a much older definition of libertas, reflected in a fragment from a tragedy by the second-century BC poet Ennius:

sed virum vera virtute vivere animatum addecet
fortiter innoxium vocare adversum adversarios:
ea libertas est, qui pectus purum et firmum gestitat;
aliae res obnoxiosae nocte in obscura latent.

but it is right for a man to live inspired by true virtue
and to stand flawless and bravely against enemies.

[104] Ar. Pol. 1253b2–1255b23, cf. Sen. Ep. 47, Patterson (1991: 10), Brunt (1988: 287). Compare also the reflections on the anxiety of tyrants in [Xen.] Hier. 6.3–6.

[105] Cf. Plb. 6.14.4, on the role of the demos as the authority (kurios) over honor (timê) and retribution (timôria) in the Republican constitution. Neither this nor the previous passage is accounted for adequately in the analysis of McKechnie (1981), who dismisses Agrippa as "advocating an un-Roman ideology."

This is liberty: he who maintains a pure and sturdy heart.
Other things are hateful and lie hidden in the obscurity of night.
(*Phoenix* fr. 126 Jocelyn = fr. 3 Vahlen, ap. Gell. *NA* 6.17.10)

Ennius' call to arms and equation of liberty with true courage are consistent with Dio's premise that an absence of freedom requires the suppression of valorous men. For generations, *libertas* was linked inextricably with manly *virtus*, the martial courage that formed an essential feature of Roman aristocratic identity.[106] Elite concerns about the incompatibility of the Principate and freedom were thus not purely a matter of political principles or constitutional categories. Their sense of moral value was involved as well. In the light of this more expansive framework for thinking about freedom and its opposites, it quickly becomes clear that the restoration of *libertas* implied not just the elimination of tyranny, but a return to an age in which individual excellence and the ability to earn honor through service to the state were both possible and encouraged.

Understanding *libertas* in this way does nothing to diminish its association with the era of the Republic. Quite the opposite, the term's moral dimension encouraged further reflection on the distance between Rome's past and its present. In the *Res Gestae*, Augustus boasted, "when new laws that I authored were passed, I restored many ancestral models (*exempla maiorum*) that were already disappearing in my day, and I myself handed down several models to be followed (*exempla imitanda*) by posterity."[107] This legislative program was part of a broader effort by the first *princeps* to promote himself as a moral reformer who had saved Rome by invigorating ancient traditions and restoring a sense of continuity with the past.[108] The revival of ancestral *exempla* necessarily brought with it a surge in the amount of attention paid to Republican history. New monuments, such as the inscribed lists of triumphant commanders and magistrates known today as the *Fasti Capitolini* and the gallery of "top men" (*summi viri*) in the Forum Augustum, reflect the emperor's drive to engage directly with the exemplary accomplishments of the Republic.[109] The same era also saw

---

[106] McDonnell (2006: 47), also Earl (1967: 20–1 and passim).

[107] *RG* 8.5: *legibus novi[s] m[e auctore l]atis m[ulta e]xempla maiorum exolescentia iam ex nostro [saecul]o red[uxi et ipse] multarum rer[um exe]mpla imitanda pos[teris tradidi]*; εἰσαγαγὼν καίνους νόμους πολλὰ ἤδη τῶν ἀρχαίων ἐθῶν καταλυόμενα διωρθωσάμην καὶ αὐτὸς πολλῶν πραγμάτων μείμημα ἐμαυτὸν τοῖς μετέπειτα παρέδωκα.

[108] Milnor (2007), Galinsky (1996: 58–64, 363–70), Wallace-Hadrill (1997, esp. 9–10), Eder (1990), Earl (1967: 59–79). The legal regulation of morals was a well-established feature of Republican politics, of course: See Levick (1982b), Edwards (1993).

[109] *Inscr. It.* 13.1 1–142, 13.3 1–36. Zanker (1988: 192–215), Luce (1990), Flower (1996: 224–36), Geiger (2008).

the creation of Livy's monumental *Ab urbe condita*, a 142-volume history of Rome composed with the express purpose of providing readers with *exempla* of behaviors that they should either imitate or avoid.[110] The idea that a *princeps* could arrest Rome's moral decay and restore ancient standards of conduct was thus part and parcel of any would-be emperor's self-advertisement as a restorer of Republican *libertas*. It was in this regard that Galba's emphasis on his own family heritage was so vital to his appeal.

Despite the influence of Greek ideas among certain segments of the Roman elite, virtue was not commonly regarded as a thing to be acquired through abstract philosophical speculation. There was a basic cultural assumption that moral principles originated in the distant past and were handed down from one generation to the next. To quote Ennius again, "the Roman state (*res Romana*) stands on its ancient customs and its men" (*moribus antiquis res stat Romana virisque*).[111] For a culture in which adherence to the "ancestral custom" (*mos maiorum*) was synonymous with appropriate behavior, the need to establish a sense of continuity with the past was central to any discourse about moral excellence. This belief was reinforced by such institutions as the aristocratic family, in which reverence for ancestors was regarded as a guarantee of *virtus*, and failure to live up to their achievements was treated as a mark of disgrace.[112]

As a nobleman, Galba was obliged to live up to the examples set by his ancestors. Their wax *imagines*, displayed so prominently in the atrium of the Imperial residence, functioned as a reminder to uphold family traditions of virtuous behavior. Galba's evident pride in these ancestors suggests that he had every intention of fulfilling these expectations. Before he was called on by Vindex to become an *adsertor*, Galba already had earned a reputation as a fair and thrifty administrator.[113] The two most famous commanders in his family tree, Galba and Mummius, were notable for their strictness (*severitas*), and Galba was also especially praised for this quality.[114] Another markedly old-fashioned feature of Galba's personality was his habit of meeting clients at a morning reception (*salutatio*) at his home, a custom of the Republican nobility that evidently had fallen into disuse

---

[110] Livy, *praef.* 10, Walter (2004: 421-6), Miles (1995: 15–20). On subsequent reception of Livy's work, see further, Chapter 5.

[111] Enn. *Ann.* fr. 156 Skutsch (ap. Cic. *Rep.* 5.1 ap. Aug. Civ. 2.21). On the relationship between *virtus* and liberty in the text in which this fragment was preserved, see Arena (2007a: 54–66).

[112] Earl (1967: 24–30), Blösel (2000), Flower (1996: 11–14), Walter (2004:42-6).

[113] Tac. *Hist.* 1.49, Plut. *Galb.* 3.2.

[114] Tac. *Hist.* 1.5.2, Suet. *Galb.* 6.2–3. On *severitas*, see further, Chapter 3. This ancestral trait would ultimately prove to be a liability in Galba's relationship with the legions and the praetorian guards: Dio (Xiph.) 64.3.

under the altered political conditions of the Principate.[115] By upholding such family traditions, Galba offered hope to his fellow senators that the moral traditions of the past could in fact continue under the Principate.

Galba encouraged similar conduct from other members of the aristocracy. His display of the portraits of Nero's noble victims at the start of the rebellion signaled a desire to revive the fortunes of his fellow aristocrats, particularly those with distinguished family histories. A preoccupation with noble lineage is also reflected in the decision to adopt L. Calpurnius Piso Licinianus as the heir apparent after Galba became *princeps*. In Tacitus' account of this event, Galba pointedly compliments Piso on his descent from men such as Pompey and Crassus, and congratulates him on acquiring the family glory of the Sulpicii and Lutatii in his adoptive lineage.[116] Given Piso's lack of military experience, the importance of family distinction in the emperor's choice must have been apparent to others besides the historian. Noble parentage was thought to sanction not only Galba's adoption of Piso, but also his appointment of A. Vitellius as commander of Lower Germany.[117]

This attention to ancestry should not be dismissed as mere snobbishness. From the point of view of aristocrats whose sense of identity was linked to their participation in an ancient moral tradition, the family and its institutions of memory were essential. In the next generation, Pliny the Younger (himself a "new man" in Roman politics) referred to the heirs of the old noble families as the "descendants of *libertas*" (*Pan.* 69.5: *illos posteros libertatis*). By cultivating elite families, Galba ensured the continuity of the *mos maiorum*, and thus of *libertas*. This policy toward the nobles represented a significant departure from the behavior of Nero, whose manifest hostility to the senatorial elite was taken as a sign of insecurity.[118] It seems that Agrippa's worst fears had been realized: The monarch had become hostile to virtue. In contrast, Galba held out the promise that the best citizens would receive the recognition they deserved, just as they had under the freedom of the Republic.

Age represents another inescapable difference between the two. Galba was in his seventies at the outbreak of the rebellion, whereas Nero was only 30. The decision to replace a charismatic young prince with a stern old man signals as much as anything that the remedy to the present crisis was thought to lie in a return to the ways of the past. Tacitus says that

[115] Tac. *Ann.* 3.55.2, Suet. *Galb.* 4.4, cf. *Claud.* 25, Sen. *Ep.* 19.11. Talbert (1984: 74–5), Winterling (1999: 138–42).

[116] Tac, *Hist.* 1.15.1, cf. Suet. *Galba* 17. PIR² C 300, Syme (1958: 151).

[117] Tac. *Hist.* 1.9.1, PIR¹ V 499.

[118] Dio (Xiph.) 63.15.1, Suet. *Ner.* 37, Rudich (1993: 137–52 and passim).

the urban populace, accustomed to Nero's youthful good looks, ridiculed Galba's age, but his own dismissive characterization of this superficiality as a "custom of the mob" (*Hist.* 1.7.3: *mos vulgi*) suggests that members of the senatorial elite felt differently.[119] Indeed, the so-called veristic portraiture of the Republican period indicates the moral value that attached to wrinkles and other marks of age in Roman culture.[120] In formulating *libertas* as an issue of adherence to the moral discipline of the past, Galba's relative maturity represented an extra advantage.

CONCLUSION

As things turned out, the message of Vindex's rebellion was extremely successful. Even the Roman plebs celebrated the news of Nero's death by wearing the freedman's *pilleus*. Galba continued to advertise his restoration of liberty on coins after taking the title of *Imperator*. In October of 68, the caretakers of the *imagines* of the imperial household set up a statue of *Libertas Restituta*, no doubt with Galba's approval.[121] The theme outlived his short reign and was invoked by other rivals during the long and destructive year of civil wars that followed. In the winter of 70–71, the new emperor Vespasian issued bronze *sestertii* with the Augustan oak wreath on the reverse, on which the phrase *Ob Cives Servatos* ("for saving citizens") had been replaced with the more emphatic *Adsertori Libertatis Public(ae)*.[122] The idea that old-fashioned liberty could coexist with the power of an emperor continued to be promoted from time to time well into the third century.

As contexts changed, however, so too did the formulation of what the coexistence of *libertas* and *principatus* was supposed to entail. Galba's age and family history gave added dimension to what otherwise might be regarded as a straightforward replaying of Augustan themes. Vespasian

---

[119] With the advantage of hindsight, Tacitus does criticize Galba as an *invalidus senis* (*Hist.* 1.6.1), unable to control the likes of T. Vinius (*PIR¹* V 450) and Cornelius Laco (*PIR²* C 1374).

[120] Nodelman (1975), Giuliani (1986: 190–7, 225–33). See also Lind (1979: 34–8), discussing the relationship between *gravitas* and *auctoritas*.

[121] Popular reaction: Suet. *Ner.* 57.1, Dio (Xiph.) 63.29.1; coins: *RIC I²* 233–54 nos. 22–3, 37–9, 56, 68–76, 136–9, 157–9, 237, 275–6, 293–6, 309, 318, 327–8, 346–9, 372–3, 387–91, 423–7, 436–43, 459–61, 479–80 (= *BMCRE I* 312–20 nos. 24, 65–75), Ramage (1983: 207); statue of *Libertas restituta*: *CIL* VI 471 (= *ILS* 238).

[122] Vespasian's coins: *RIC II²* 61 nos. 35, 121–4, 207–10, cf. 67–74 nos. 125–6, 211, 65–78 nos. 82–9, 170–4, 237, 272, Bianco (1968: 153–4, 156). *Libertas Restituta* appeared on the coinage of Vitellius: *RIC I²* 268–75 nos. 9–10, 43–4, 69, 80–1, 104–5, also *Libertas Augusti*: no. 128.

had different gifts, but he was able to present himself both as a liberator in the mold of Augustus and as an avenger of the fallen Galba.[123] With each stage in this progression, previous constructions of the value of freedom were reused, even as these older models were set within new frameworks. Ultimately, however, the Republican connection remained essential to any discussion of *libertas*. There was no such thing as a purely "Augustan" – or, for that matter, a "Galban" or "Vespasianic" – promise of freedom. Brutus' *libertas* would always have been visible somewhere in the frame as well.

The crisis of 68 provides a useful framework within which to observe the workings of the ideology of the Roman Principate. *Libertas* was invoked, and the memory of the Republican past along with it. As this discussion has shown, the use of such symbols was not the exclusive privilege of dissidents advocating the overthrow of the current political order. If these emblems continued to have broad appeal, it was because they remained part of the common currency of Imperial political discourse. By the same token, it is also inaccurate to suggest that the meaning of *libertas* "underwent a complete change" as the provision of peace and stability became the primary justification for the emperor's power.[124] What is perhaps most remarkable about the events of 68 is the way that values and sensibilities that emperors had exploited for generations to marshal assent could suddenly be used to undermine the authority of a sitting emperor. Although Augustus had provided later generations with one template for what freedom in a "restored" republic might look like, the ideological principles that underlie such a project remained part of a wider heritage that stretched back into the earliest history of the Roman community. It is therefore inadequate to suggest that the only legitimate, or even the principal, frame of reference for appeals to *libertas* in the rhetoric of Galba and Vindex must be sought in the political program of the Augustan Principate. Words do not change their meanings so easily.

The absence of a single, tightly controlled definition of *libertas* in Roman Imperial discourse underscores the importance of what might seem to be an obvious fact: Insofar as the Republican tradition existed before the establishment of the Principate, it remained external to it. When Roman emperors deployed the language of communal values derived from Republican experience, they were appealing to the authority of a tradition that was not of their own creation. As a result, the political principles of the Roman ruling class, which necessarily transcended any imposed notions

---

[123] Tac. *Hist.* 4.40.1. Gagé (1952), Bianco (1968: 185–200), Zimmermann (1995).

[124] *Pace* Wirszubski (1950: 167–71, quotation at 169), Bleicken (1975: 434). Cf. Walser (1955: 367), who speaks of a "Wandel des Vindexbegriffes" during the same period.

about the charismatic authority of the emperor, lay beyond Caesar's power to command.[125] The rebels of 68 drew on substantially the same sense of a shared Republican heritage to express their dissatisfaction with Nero that Augustus had deployed in founding the Principate. It was not the essence of these concepts that changed so much as the circumstances in which they were invoked.

As a value whose significance was deeply intertwined with one of the fundamental social institutions of ancient life (i.e., slavery), *libertas* could not easily be driven out of public discourse. Just as the legal and social implications of this term were essential to its meaning, the logic of a historical tradition that defined political freedom in terms of an antityrannical *respublica* and enshrined liberators such as Marcus and Lucius Brutus as exemplary figures was also inescapable. Emperors might attempt to co-opt *libertas* as one of the celebrated values of the Principate, but they could not prevent it from occupying ideological territory outside the boundaries they might have wished to establish for it. In the following chapter, we will see how Vespasian sought to get around these ambiguities by calling attention to other, more favorable, Republican memories.

---

[125] Charisma: Hopkins (1978: 203–5). As Champlin (2003) documents, Nero was an emperor with an overabundance of charismatic popular appeal, but nevertheless was overthrown by the Roman aristocracy.

2

REBUILDING

The rebellion of Vindex and Galba did little to settle the tensions that it exposed in the communal memory of Rome's Republican past. Nero's suicide was a dramatic turning point in many ways, not least in its impact on the principle of dynastic succession within the house of Augustus. But the ascent of Galba did not produce the meaningful changes in the nature of the Principate that some of his supporters might have hoped to see. What resulted instead was a series of civil wars that plunged the empire into turmoil, as four emperors replaced one another in quick succession. Romans and provincials alike discovered that the tranquility they had enjoyed since the rise of Augustus was suddenly at an end. This explosion of violence both prolonged and gave new intensity to the ongoing debate about the appropriate relationship between the Augustan Principate and the Republican institutions that had preceded it.

Originating for the most part in the provinces, these contests for dominance brought about the movement of troops from their posts around the perimeter of the empire inward, toward the seat of power in Rome. As a consequence, the municipalities of Italy experienced pitched combat for the first time in generations. The fate of Cremona – witness to two major battles in its outskirts before being sacked by the forces of Antonius Primus – was emblematic of the horrors of renewed civil war.[1] In the end, the centripetal pull of civil war culminated in armed combat through the streets of Rome itself, where the three-pronged assault by Vespasianic forces on December 20, 69, marked the devastating climax of a period that its survivors later described as "that one long year."[2]

However, the final coup de grâce was preceded by (and, in some accounts, precipitated by) an outbreak of fighting in the heart of the city

---

[1] Scott (1968: 95–9). *PIR*[2] A 866.

[2] Tac. *Dial.* 17.3: *illum . . . longum et unum annum.* See, in general, Wellesley (1975), Morgan (2006), also Tac. *Hist.* 1–3, Suet. *Galba, Otho, Vit.*, Plut. *Galba, Otho.*

two days earlier. Although less destructive when viewed in terms of the number of casualties involved, this tactically minor engagement exerted far more influence on subsequent assessments of the war than the decisive battle that followed. The reason for the prominence of the earlier conflict is that it inflicted a lasting wound on the heart of Rome's monumental landscape: In the course of the fighting, the great temple (*aedes*) of Jupiter Optimus Maximus on the Capitoline hill was attacked and burned to the ground. That calamity overshadowed anything that occurred during the actual battle for control of the city.

As a symbol of Roman sovereignty and imperial power, the Capitoline temple of Jupiter was a site with profound importance for the negotiation of Roman political and cultural identity. Perhaps most important for this discussion, the materiality of the building itself provided a tangible link between the city's present and its past. Like the concept of *libertas*, which had transcended the break between the Republic and the Principate in a different way, the meaning assigned to this temple was complex and polyvalent. The loss of any ancient monument is sure to have implications for the operation of cultural memory, but the destruction and subsequent rebuilding of the temple of Jupiter Optimus Maximus created a unique opportunity to redeploy the recursive frames of Roman cultural memory through which the ideals of the Republic continued to exert influence within the developing authoritarian culture of the Principate.

ARSERAT ET ANTE CAPITOLIUM

As the violence of civil war was careening toward the capital, the emperor of the moment, A. Vitellius, was in Rome, awaiting the inevitable. Vespasian's army had demolished the main Vitellian force at Cremona and was now unstoppable as it made its southward progress down the peninsula. In search of a graceful way out, Vitellius began private negotiations with the urban prefect T. Flavius Sabinus, the elder brother of his rival and inevitable successor Vespasian. Also present were Ti. Catius Asconius Silius Italicus, who had been consul *ordinarius* in the previous year, and the future historian Cluvius Rufus, another Neronian consular. According to Tacitus, terms were made for a peaceful surrender of power, to take place on December 18. But things did not go as planned when Vitellius entered the Forum to divest himself of the insignia of his office before an assembly of citizens and soldiers.[3]

---

[3] Tac. *Hist.* 3.65.2, 3.67.2–68.3, also Suet. *Vit.* 15.2. *PIR*[1] V 499, *PIR*[2] F 352. Yavetz (1969b: 568–9) reconstructs a different account of Vitellius' final days.

After delivering a brief speech explaining his decision to resign, Vitellius went to hand over his dagger, a symbol of the authority he would relinquish, to one of the consuls. This unprecedented and apparently unrehearsed bit of ceremony backfired terribly when the magistrate he approached refused to accept the weapon. The consul's insubordination fed the enthusiasm of the crowd of onlookers, who then began to make known their unwillingness to see the *princeps* they had just created resign his office. In the ensuing commotion, the hapless emperor was forced to give up on his abdication and returned, somewhat bewildered, to his residence on the Palatine.[4]

Meanwhile, Sabinus was at his own house on the Quirinal, meeting with a group of leading citizens to make arrangements for his brother's accession. When they heard what was happening in the Forum, these men decided to face down the unruly Vitellians with an armed force. On their way down from the ridge of the Quirinal, Sabinus and his faction encountered a contingent of Vitellian partisans in the neighborhood of the *lacus Fundani*. The Flavians got the worst of the ensuing struggle and fled to the fortified heights of the Capitoline hill. There they waited in the hope that things might calm down overnight. With the benefit of hindsight, Tacitus suggests they should have made an escape instead (Fig. 2.1).[5]

On the following day, soldiers from the Rhine frontier, who had marched into Rome with Vitellius just six months earlier, attacked the Capitol in the name of their unwilling emperor. The details of how the battle unfolded remain controversial, but its outcome is well known: The Flavians were overwhelmed by the much larger force of Vitellian troops. Among the defeated, some notable military commanders were killed in the fighting. Sabinus was taken alive, only to be murdered and have his body dragged back to the Capitol and thrown on the Gemonian steps – a post-mortem punishment that evoked the traditional penalty of a traitor or enemy of Rome. More fortunate was Vespasian's young son Domitian, who somehow had managed to join his uncle during the night, but then escaped to safety disguised among a throng of Isiac priests.[6]

---

[4] Tac. *Hist.* 3.68, cf. Dio (Xiph.) 65.16.6 and Suet. *Vit.* 15.3–4. On the symbolic significance of the dagger, see Shaw (2001: 72–3).

[5] Tac. *Hist.* 3.69.1–4: *arcem Capitolii insedit.* Wiseman (1978) would have the Flavians end up on the *Arx* proper, i.e., the northwest summit of the Capitoline, but Wellesley (1981, esp. 179–83) and Filippi (1998: 75–6) convincingly refute this claim. For the *lacus Fundani*, see Coarelli (1997: 151–2). The route taken from there is uncertain, but it seems plausible to suspect that the Flavians were driven down the slope of the Quirinal into the Pallacinae district (modern Piazza Venezia) before making their way southward to the Capitol.

[6] Tac. *Hist* 3.71–4, Dio (Xiph.) 65.17.3–4, Joseph. *BJ* 4.11.4, Suet. *Dom.* 1.2, Wellesley (1956: 211–14), *LTUR* III: 112–13 s.v. "Isis Capitolium" [Coarelli]. On the significance of exposing

Figure 2.1. Topography of Events in Rome, December 18–20, AD 69. 1: Forum Romanum; 2: Palatium; 3: Sabinus' house; 4: Lacus Fundani; 5: Capitolium. (plan by author)

The fact that we can say so much about the disposition of individual combatants suggests a great deal about the importance of this engagement in the Roman public imagination. Ultimately, however, the most significant outcome of the brief siege of the Capitol was the fire that broke out in the midst of the conflict. This conflagration destroyed many buildings, including the most important *aedes* of all, the temple of Jupiter Optimus Maximus Capitolinus.[7] More than any of the other acts of violence

corpses on the Gemonian steps, see Barry (2008), David (1984: 172–4). See also Sil. *Pun.* 3.609–10.

[7] Tac. *Hist.* 3.71.4, Dio (Xiph.) 65.17.3, Joseph. *BJ* 4.11.4, Suet. *Vit.* 15.3, cf. Plin. *NH* 34.38. All but Tacitus attribute the fire to a deliberate act of arson on the part of Vitellius' soldiers, and many blame Vitellius explicitly: Barzano (1984: 108–11), Briessmann (1955: 69–73), Darwall-Smith (1996: 42–3). See in general *LTUR* III 144–53 s.vv. "Iuppiter Optimus Maximus, Capitolinus, Aedes, Templum (fino all'A. 83 a. C.)" [Tagliamonte], "Iuppiter Optimus

witnessed during that "long year" of civil war, this was a disaster that resonated throughout the Mediterranean world. Poems were written about the "sacrilegious torches" that destroyed the Capitolium, and a later generation recounted stories about how the mystic sage Apollonius of Tyana knew of the temple's destruction on the following day, although he was in Alexandria with Vespasian at the time. In Gaul, Druid priests interpreted the fire as an omen of heaven's anger with the Romans and a harbinger of the end of Rome's empire. In less spiritually charged contexts, the expression "to burn down the Capitol" became a byword for committing a serious offense.[8]

Writing in the time of Trajan, Tacitus describes the burning of the Capitoline temple in 69 as "the most grievous and foulest crime to befall the *respublica* of the Roman People since the founding of the city" (*Hist.* 3.72.1: *id facinus post conditam urbem luctuosissimum foedissimumque rei publicae populi Romani accidit*).[9] He goes on to underscore the significance of this event by means of historical comparison, noting that the temple was "established under auspices by our ancestors as a guarantee of empire, which neither Porsenna when the city surrendered nor the Gauls when it was captured were able to desecrate" (*auspicato a maioribus pignus imperii conditam, quam non Porsenna dedita urbe neque Galli capta temerare potuissent*). According to received tradition, the temple had proved invulnerable to Rome's enemies. Tacitus notes that it had burned before, but this was also during a period of civil war, when Sulla and his armies were making their way across Italy to wrest control of the government back from his political opponents in 83 BC.[10] The similarity of the circumstances prompts the aphorism, "it stood, so long as we waged wars on behalf of the fatherland" (i.e., not against it: *stetit, <dum>pro patria bellavimus*).

Here Tacitus continues a pattern of analysis firmly established in the opening books of his *Histories*, in which he looks back to the civil wars of the Republic to comment on the crises of the year of four emperors.[11] This principle of viewing more recent events in the light of earlier

Maximus, Capitolinus, Aedes, Templum (fasi tardo-Repubblicane e di età Imperiale)" [De Angeli], also Danti (2001), Stamper (2005: 22–32).

[8] Epictet. 1.7.32–3: Καπιτώλιον κατέκαυσα . . . Καπιτώλιον ἐμπρῆσαι, cf. Plut. *Mor.* 379D. Poems: Stat. *Silv.* 5.3.197: *sacrilegis lucent Capitolia taedis*, Mart. 5.5.7–8, Bardon (1956: 229–30), cf. Coleman (1986: 3089–90). Apollonius: Philostr. *VA* 5.30 (cf. Plut. *Sull.* 27.6, Sall. *Cat.* 47.2). Druids: Tac. *Hist.* 4.54.2, cf. Dio (Xiph.) 65.8.2, Barzanò (1984: 117–18), Zecchini (1984).

[9] On Tacitus' account of the temple's destruction, see esp. Sailor (2008: 205–49).

[10] Cf. Plut. *Sull.* 27, App. *BC* 1.86.

[11] Scott (1968: 95–9), Sage (1991: 3398–3401), Keitel (1992).

catastrophes is set out in the introduction to the work, where Tacitus promises to describe "final moments equal to the celebrated deaths of the ancients" (*Hist.* 1.3: *laudatis antiquorum mortibus pares exitus*). Comparisons with the deeds of Republican *antiqui* are everywhere implied in the *Histories*. For example, after the account of Galba's assassination in Book 1, Tacitus suggests that the coming conflict between Otho and Vitellius evoked the memory of previous civil wars, as a fearful populace recalled their old misfortunes and drew unflattering comparisons between men such as Caesar and Pompey and the pair of rivals currently in contention (1.50.2–3). In Book 2, discussion of the military activities of Otho and Vitellius is broken up by an important digression in which Tacitus traces the development of "the ancient and long ingrained lust for power" (2.38.1: *vetus ac iam pridem insita mortalibus potentiae cupido*), which led first to the struggle of the orders, then to the civil wars of Marius and Sulla, and ultimately to the more secretive but no less sinister designs of Pompey, who transformed these conflicts once and for all into a contest for sole power. Later in Book 3 (3.83.3), he compares the battle for Rome that followed the destruction of the Capitol with the cruel precedents set by Sulla and Cinna.[12]

The list of examples is long, but Tacitus' technique of filtering the events of 69 through the lens of Republican civil war has a clear point. In nearly every case, the historian suggests that the moral circumstances of the civil war he is describing were more deplorable than those of the Republican precedents they evoke. Even the one-day consulship of Rosius Regulus at the end of October 69 comes off worse than Caninius Rebilus' equally brief tenure in that office during Caesar's dictatorship, because Vitellius failed to observe the proper legal forms in granting Regulus his office.[13] The difference between the burning of the Capitoline temple during the Republic and that under Vitellius was that the earlier fire had been set secretly, while in the latter case Roman troops "openly besieged and openly set fire" to the temple (3.72.1: *nunc palam obsessum, palam incensum*). Hence the superlative description of the Capitoline fire as "the most grievous and foulest crime to befall the *respublica* since the founding of the city."

In the end, however, Tacitus' judgment on the relative brazenness of the more recent incendiaries carries little conviction. His pessimism can be marked down to an immoderate application of the ancient historian's tendency to present his subject matter as unique and extraordinary.[14] As

---

[12] See Keitel (1992) for further discussion.

[13] *Hist.* 3.37.2, cf. Townend (1962: 116–17), Wellesley (1972: 129 ad loc).

[14] Cf. Virtr. 5.*praef*.1, Thuc. 1.1.2, with Dion. Hal. *Thuc.* 9 and Woodman (1988: 5–7), also Macleod (1983).

was common in Roman historiography, Tacitus focuses his energy on exposing unprecedented wickedness, a symptom of the inescapable logic of moral decline. The fire of AD 69 belongs to a later era than that of 83 BC, and as such it must reflect on the progressive degeneration of Roman values during the interval. The distinction that Tacitus draws between the two fires thus represents a commonplace of the intertwined historical rhetorics of unprecedentedness and decline.[15]

More interesting for our purposes is his acknowledgment of the underlying similarity between the two catastrophes. Setting aside Tacitus' obligation to treat his fire as the foulest crime ever to befall the Roman community, it was ultimately the shared context of civil war that made both incidents upsetting. The highly charged rhetorical questions "What military purpose could this serve? What benefit could be gained from such a catastrophe?" (*Hist.* 3.72.1: *quibus armorum causis? quo tantae cladis pretio?*) apply equally to both fires, as does the above-quoted *sententia* about the temple's security so long as Romans fought "on behalf of the fatherland" (*pro patria*). The burning of the Capitolium is therefore significant in the history of 69 not just as a single, uniquely horrible event, but as evidence of a recurrent phenomenon. Like the other calamities of that year, its association with a context of civil war raised the possibility that Rome was not in fact happier or more secure under the Principate than it had been during the Republic. For Tacitus, the destruction of the temple of Jupiter Optimus Maximus presented "a consummate image of the monstrousness of civil war," revealing the extent to which internal dissension continued to threaten Rome's stability.[16] This was a disaster of considerable ideological significance, which raised challenging questions about the nature of the Principate and its supposed continuities with Republican tradition.

PAX AUGUSTA

Before the upheavals of 68–69, the virtue of *pax* (peace) was regarded as one of the principal benefits of the era that followed Augustus' victory at

---

[15] Luce (1986) stresses the importance of not confusing such conventional rhetorical gestures for Tacitus' true opinions; compare Scott (1968: 64–70). On the underlying logic of decline narratives, see Zerubavel (2003: 16–18). The centrality of this trope has not been adequately accounted for in modern discussions of Roman historical thinking. See, however, Lintott (1972) and Levick (1982b).

[16] Scott (1968: 102). See also Edwards (1996: 79–80), Fontana (1993: 32), Rutledge (1998: 143–4). Cf. Tac. *Ann.* 15.41 and Dio 62.18.2, both comparing the Neronian fire in Rome with the devastation of the Gallic sack.

Actium. In the account of one contemporary witness, the establishment of peace throughout the world was linked explicitly with the restoration of the *respublica* and the benefits that came from the abolition of civil war.[17] Although Momigliano (1996: 33–43) correctly draws attention to the Near Eastern and Greek background for the Augustan rhetoric of peace, this was not an un-Roman pacifism. As Tacitus' comment on the Capitoline fire suggests, the commission of warfare on behalf of the fatherland (*pro patria bellare*) continued to be regarded as a central component of virtue. *Pax*, as offered by Augustus, was born instead of internal harmony (*concordia*). The celebration of this theme did not represent a shift in diplomatic or military priorities so much as a justification for the autocratic powers granted to the *princeps*, which many felt offered the only effective way to counterbalance the political instability and seemingly endless cycle of civil wars that had plagued the final years of the Republic.[18]

As welcome as this respite from violence and uncertainty must have been, it was not without its compromises. Cicero had said:

et nomen pacis dulce est et ipsa res salutaris; sed inter pacem et servitutem plurimum interest. pax est tranquilla libertas, servitus postremum malorum omnium, non modo bello sed morte etiam repellendum.

Both the name of peace is sweet and the thing itself is wholesome, but there is a great distinction between peace and servitude: Peace is tranquil *libertas*, while servitude is the worst of all evils and must be resisted not only with war but even with death. (*Phil.* 2.113)

Lucan invokes a similar reservation when he notes of the triumph of Caesarism, "that peace came with a master" (1.670: *cum domino pax ista venit*). Despite such worries and admonitions, most Romans proved willing to compromise the scope of their liberty in exchange for the blessings of peace. Poets, artists, and statesmen accepted and even celebrated the imposition of monarchy, embracing the values of a new era of peace and security in exchange for their old political freedoms.[19]

---

[17] Wistrand (1976) (= *ILS* 8393), col. 2, ll. 35–6: *Pacato orbe terrarum, res[titut]a republica quieta deinde n[obis et felicia] tempora contigerunt*. The same *cistophori* that label Octavian as *Vindex Libertatis* (*RPC* I no. 2203= *RIC* I² 79 no. 476, see Chapter 1, n. 65) were part of a larger series of coins, which features the representation of a personified Pax on the reverse.

[18] See Weinstock (1960: 45–6), Galinsky (1996: 84), Kuttner (1995: 22). Gruen (1985) rightly stresses the continued importance of conquest and militaristic themes in the ideology of Augustus, but somehow manages to ignore the relevance of *pax* to the issue of civil war. On the continuity of "Republican" expansionistic ambitions in the Imperial policy of Augustus, see Brunt (1963), (1990: 433–80), Whittaker (1994: 33–59), Eck (2003: 93–104).

[19] Raaflaub and Samons (1990). Poets: Little (1982). Artists: Zanker (1988, esp. 172–83). Statesmen: Syme (1939: 512–21). Even lowly pastoralists were enthusiastic: Verg. *Ecl.* 1, Millar (1984).

The renewed outbreak of civil war in 69 represented a serious stumbling block for this patriotic doctrine of *pax et princeps*, however.[20] In the shadow of the late Republican civil wars, obedience to the authority of one man might have seemed a small price to pay for lasting political stability. After the fall of the Julio-Claudian regime, however, when Rome was once again suffering the evils of civil war, the terms of this exchange could be called into question. Acquiescence to a powerful *princeps* had failed to prevent the return of uncertainty and violence. Worse still, the institution itself now provided the very cause of the fighting, as Tacitus' analysis of the Capitoline fire makes clear: "it was burned down by the rage of the *principes*" (*Hist.* 3.72.1: *furore principum excindi*).[21] The situation marked a return to a chaotic and violent era, when rival commanders fought one another for control of Rome. As a consequence, the man who sought to assume the position recently held by Nero, Galba, Otho, and Vitellius, would face new challenges in reassuring his subjects that peace was still possible under the Principate.

The fact that this return of civil war resulted in the destruction of the most important temple of Roman state religion would have been particularly troubling. As noted in the previous chapter, the formation of the monarchical *Pax Augusta* had been intimately linked to a program of moral renewal. This included an intensive revival of communal religious life. According to the ideological underpinnings of the new system, Rome's felicity under the benevolent guidance of the Caesars was the consequence of a *respublica* operating in harmony with divine will. The destruction of the Capitoline temple, on the other hand, signaled a crisis in Rome's relationship with the divine, what the Romans called the "peace of the gods" (*pax deum*).[22]

In the context of a renewed cycle of civil wars, the destruction of the temple of Jupiter Optimus Maximus was a prodigy of terrific significance, which shattered the illusion of the Principate's connection to *pax* in both its political and its cosmic sense.[23] When the flames of civil war finally died down, Vespasian worked hard to restore confidence in the stability of the Imperial system. Peace and cooperation became the hallmarks of

---

[20] Paladini (1985: 223).

[21] Sailor (2008: 209).

[22] Galinsky (1996: 288–312), Wallace-Hadrill (1982b), Weinstock (1960: 50). On *pax deum*, see, e.g., Livy 1.31.7, 3.5.14. Latte (1960: 40–1), Sordi (1985: 148–9).

[23] Dio (Xiph.) 65.8.2 reports that the appearance of footprints in the sanctuary and strange noises at night suggested that the gods had abandoned Rome during Vitellius' reign. Cf. Joseph. *BJ* 6.293–300 for similar omens in the Temple of Jerusalem. Barzano (1984: 117–18).

his cultural program.[24] Rebuilding the damaged city became a way to mark the return of a stable government and thus the renewal of *pax*. To make the message clear, the signature construction project of Vespasian's building program was the Temple of Peace (Templum Pacis), an enormous sacred precinct in the heart of the city with shops, libraries, and other public amenities, which Pliny the Elder describes as one of the wonders of the world.[25] In the winter of 69–70, however, that project still lay in the future. To fulfill his promise as a restorer of peace, Vespasian had to begin by rebuilding the Capitolium.

DECORA MAIORUM

It is clear that the destruction of the Capitolium was a devastating event for the continuity of Roman public memory. The accretion of monuments in and around the temple of Jupiter Optimus Maximus had created a richly layered *lieu de mémoire*, in which commemorative practice overlapped with religious ritual to create a public space that was at once the center of Rome's empire and a physical record of its growth.[26] A visit to the Capitol had the potential to elicit intense feelings of connection with the past. The monuments found there gave the space a unique evocative power. When these tangible markers of Rome's history were obliterated by the fire, their destruction invited reflection on the course of that history, just as they would for Gibbon centuries later, when he "sat musing amidst the ruins of the Capitol, while the bare-footed fryars were singing vespers in the temple of Jupiter."[27]

---

[24] Oros. 7.9.1: *tranquilla sub Vespasiano duce serenitas rediit*. Paladini (1985), Bianco (1968: 154–7), Levick (1999a: 70 and passim). *Pax Augusta* featured prominently on Vespasian's coinage, particularly in the early years of his reign: RIC II² 58–90 passim. Note also *Pax P. Romani* (RIC II² 73 nos. 187–9), and related themes, such as *Concordia Augusti* (RIC II² 79 nos. 291–8), *Salus* (RIC II² 67 nos. 111–12), *Securitas* (RIC II² 78 nos. 280–1), and *Tutela* (RIC II² 78 no. 282).

[25] Plin. *NH* 36.102: *pulcherrima operum, quae umquam vidit orbis*. See *LTUR* IV 67–70 s.v. "Pax, Templum" [Coarelli], V 285 [Santangeli Valenzani], Colini (1937), Anderson (1984: 101–18), Darwall-Smith (1996: 55–63).

[26] Hölkeskamp (2001: 99–111), Hölscher (2006), Purcell (2003, esp. 26–33). For the implications of the term *lieu de mémoire*, see Nora (1989). On the evocative power of places in general, see Casey (1987: 181–215), Halbwachs (1941), Assmann (1992: 59–60), Assmann (1999: 298–339), Walter (2004: 155–79), Huyssen (2003: 7).

[27] The quote is from a well-known passage of Gibbon's *Autobiography* (1869: 79), which establishes the date at which "the idea of writing the decline and fall of the city first started to my mind." See also Edwards (1996: 69–74). On Gibbon's successively improving recollections of this event, see R. Bufano, *TLS*, September 10, 1982: 973.

The most explicit examination by a Roman writer of the attachment to the past that monuments provide appears in the fifth book of Cicero's *On Ends*, in which the interlocutors begin by commenting on the special sense of history they experience while visiting the famous sites of Athens.[28] The conversation opens with a comment by Cicero's friend M. Piso, inspired by the group's arrival at the walkways of Academy:

> *"Naturane nobis hoc," inquit, "datum dicam an errore quodam, ut, cum ea loca videamus in quibus memoria dignos viros acceperimus multum esse versatos, magis moveamur quam si quando eorum ipsorum aut facta audiamus aut scriptum aliquod legamus? Velut ego nunc moveor. Venit enim mihi Platonis in mentem, quem accepimus primum hic disputare solitum; cuius etiam illi hortuli propinqui non memoriam solum mihi adferunt sed ipsum videntur in conspectu meo ponere. Hic Speusippus, hic Xenocrates, hic eius auditor Polemo, cuius illa ipsa sessio fuit quam videmus."*

Should I say that it is nature or some departure therefrom that gives us this faculty, that when we see the places that we remember noble men used to frequent, we are moved more than when we either hear their deeds or read one of their writings? I am now so moved. For Plato comes to my mind, who we remember was the first one to regularly discuss matters here; that nearby garden not only brings his memory to me, but seems to place the man himself before my eyes. Here (I see) Speusippus, here Xenocrates, here his student Polemo, on whose very seat we now gaze. (*Fin.* 5.2)

The question with which this passage begins seems incongruous at first, because it had long been accepted as "natural" that seeing something made a greater impact than hearing or reading about it.[29] In the event, however, Piso is not so much concerned with the primary act of looking as with a secondary, less organic, kind of sight. He observes that seeing a place triggers a mental image of a figure from the past, but he is also clear that this recognition only occurs when the individual's connection to the place has been established already through a separate process of remembering (*memoria . . . acceperimus*). Although the viewer's impression is deeply personal, the memory itself is a socially conditioned response, dependent on an external discourse of commemoration.[30]

---

[28] Cic. *Fin.* 5.1–6. See Vasaly (1993: 29–30), Assmann (1999: 312–13). Madvig (1876: 611) suggests that the sites each speaker finds appealing serve to establish his loyalty to a particular philosophical *magister*.

[29] Heraclit. *ap.* Plb. 12.27.1 (= frag. 101a Diels): ὀφθαλμοὶ γὰρ τῶν ὤτων ἀκριβέστεροι μάρτυρες, Hdt. 1.8.2: ὦτα γὰρ τυγχάνει ἀνθρώποισι ἐόντα ἀπιστότερα ὀφθαλμῶν. Hedrick (1993), Immerwahr (1960).

[30] Vasaly (1993: 31–2). On the social composition of personal remembrance, see Halbwachs (1925, esp. 273–96), Lowenthal (1985: 194–7).

Another notable feature of the mnemonic associations Piso describes is their specificity. It is not the space of the Academy as a whole that evokes the memory of past philosophers, but rather particular sites within it – the *hortulus* where Plato lectured, the *sessio* in which Polemo sat to listen to Xenocrates. These are discrete, tangible objects and locations that have lasted through the ages. To borrow Benjamin's term, the "aura" imparted to these monuments by their unique existence in time and space gives them a special commemorative authority, connecting the viewer to the great men who had been associated with them in the past.[31]

What Piso fails to notice is that the monumental landscape of the Academy that he and his companions have entered had changed substantially from how it was in Plato's day. At this point, one might seek to return to Halbwachs' claims about the subjectivity of memory when set against the positivist standards of the historian.[32] But Piso also makes it clear that, for those in the know, the alteration of a place from its original form was not incidental to the process of remembering. When he turns to talk about a more familiar place, he becomes more discriminating:

> *Equidem etiam curiam nostram (Hostiliam dico, non hanc novam, quae minor mihi esse videtur posteaquam est maior) solebam intuens Scipionem, Catonem, Laelium, nostrum vero in primis avum cogitare.*

> Similarly also when looking upon our Curia – I mean the Curia Hostilia, not this new one, which seems to me to be smaller now that it is larger – I was accustomed to think about Scipio, Cato, Laelius, and most of all my own grandfather. (*Fin.* 5.2)[33]

The speaker is at pains to specify that it was the *old* Curia, the one built by king Hostilius, that turned his thoughts to the great Roman statesmen

---

[31] Benjamin (1969: 222–3). A well-known Roman example of this is the statuette of Hercules Epitrapezios owned by Novius Vindex, discussed in Chapter 5. Gibbon (1869: 78) invites comparison again: "After a sleepless night, I trod, with a lofty step, the ruins of the Forum; each memorable spot where Romulus stood, or Tully spoke, or Caesar fell, was at once present to my eye." See also Roller (2004: 32–4) on the "temporal dislocation" accomplished by monuments in the Roman discourse of *exempla*.

[32] Halbwachs (1950). Cf. Assmann (1997a: 9–10), Lowenthal (1985: 326–31). A large gymnasium had been built on the sight in the late Hellenistic or early Roman period: See the brief summary of the site's archaeology in Travlos (1971: 42–3), also (Camp 2001: 64).

[33] Edwards (1996: 17–18). Piso alludes here to the enlargement of the senate house by the dictator Sulla in 81 or 80 BC, a project undertaken to accommodate the augmented size and majesty of the senate in his new constitutional arrangement: Dio 40.50.3, Madvig (1876: 606–7), Flower (2006: 93), *LTUR* I 331 s.v "Curia Hostilia" [Coarelli], *pace* Platner and Ashby (1926: 143), Richardson (1992: 102).

of the past. Sulla's rebuilt senate house, although enlarged, is nevertheless diminished in Piso's eyes, and we are left to the conclusion that the new building seemed less impressive because of the changes that Sulla had made. The new Curia lacked the powerful associations of the old one. For a Roman such as Cicero's Piso, rebuilding necessarily implied loss.[34]

We may assume that Piso had oratorical achievements in mind when he pictured such men in the Curia Hostilia, and imagine him thinking something like "Here is where Cato stood when he delivered his speech on the Rhodians," *et cetera*. But the Curia Hostilia, like the Capitolium, was also an important locus for monuments commemorating the historical conquests of the Roman people and their exemplary commanders.[35] The evocative character of these monuments is captured in the way that the consular poet Silius Italicus envisioned this building at the outbreak of the Second Punic war:

> *In foribus sacris primoque in limine templi*
> *captivi currus, belli decus, armaque rapta*
> *pugnantum ducibus saevaeque in Marte secures,*
> *perfossi clipei et servantia tela cruorem*
> *claustraque portarum pendent. hic Punica bella,*
> *Aegates, cernas, fusaque per aequora classe*
> *exactam ponto Libyen testantia rostra.*
> *hic galeae Senonum pensatique improbus auri*
> *arbiter ensis inest Gallisque ex arce fugatis*
> *arma revertentis pompa gestata Camilli,*
> *hic spolia Aeacidae, hic Epirotica signa*
> *et Ligurum horrentes coni parmaeque relatae*
> *Hispana de gente rudes Alpinaque gaesa.*

On the sacred doors and the ancient threshold of the temple
captive chariots, war's ornaments, and weapons confiscated
from belligerent chiefs, and battle-axes brutal in combat,
fractured shields and spears still stained with blood,
and the bolts of gates all hang. Here you might see
the Punic wars, Aegates, and how a fleet scattered over the waters
preceded the defeat of Libya at sea, to which the prows testify.
Here are the helmets of the Senones and the golden payment's unjust
arbiter, a sword, but after the Gauls had fled from the summit,
these arms were carried in the triumph of returning Camillus.

---

[34] Walter (2004: 136–7).
[35] Hölkeskamp (2001: 119–22). This association began when the first triumphal painting in Rome was set up by M'. Valerius in the Curia (Plin. *NH* 35.22).

Here are the weapons of Pyrrhus, here the Epirotic standards,
also the Ligures' shaggy headgear, crude little shields
taken from the Spaniards, and heavy Alpine javelins.

(Pun. 1.617–29)

The *enargeia* presented in this passage follows a pattern of conceptual linkage much like that of Piso's vivid imaginings at the Academy. The poet guides the viewer to see not only the monuments themselves but also the historical events they signify. Like the phantoms encountered by Piso in the Academy, each memory is tied to a specific site in the landscape: Here (*hic*) the *rostra* serve as mute witnesses to the disaster of the Punic fleet at the Aegates islands, while here (*hic*) Brennus' sword and other Gallic weapons call to mind both the ignominy of the senate's surrender and the elation of Camillus' triumphant return. Specific types of armor associated with particular enemies (Ligurian *coni*, Spanish *parmae*, Swiss *gaesa*) help to identify each conquest.[36]

Silius, of course, had never seen the Curia Hostilia that he describes in such detail. The only Curia he knew was the Curia Julia, a part of the Augustan building boom that made the Julian name omnipresent in the city's public spaces, which was neatly situated at the juncture between the old Forum Romanum and the portico of the new Forum Julium.[37] Like Piso, Silius will have been aware of the difference between the current Curia and the one in which debate took place during the Hannibalic war. His description is thus the representation of a missing monument, meant to evoke what Rome had been like in a bygone age.[38] The attention he pays to the significance of each triumphal dedication is a salutary illustration of what the Capitolium's destruction must have meant for memory in his own day.

As has already been noted, Silius was in Rome during the fateful events of 69.[39] Before that, he would have witnessed the destruction wrought during the famous Neronian fire of 64, the closest precedent to the conflagration on the Capitol. It was in the wake of this earlier fire that the inadequacy of replacement monuments had been felt most intensely. Suetonius observes:

tunc praeter immensum numerum insularum domus priscorum ducum arserunt hostilibus adhuc spoliis adornatae deorumque aedes ab regibus ac

---

[36] See Rawson (1990).

[37] Zanker (1988: 143–5), Favro (1996: 95–8, 199), Haselberger (2007: 73–5).

[38] Cf. Jaeger (1997: 32–3), Lowenthal (1985: 278–82).

[39] His presence in Rome on December 17 is attested by Tac. *Hist.* 3.65.2.

deinde Punicis et Gallicis bellis votae dedicataeque, et quidquid visendum atque memorabile ex antiquitate duraverat.

In addition to the enormous number of tenements, the houses of ancient generals, still adorned with their spoils, burned, as did temples of gods vowed and dedicated by the kings and then in the Punic and Gallic wars, along with much else worth seeing and memorable that had survived from antiquity. (*Ner.* 38.2)

It is difficult to ignore the way the biographer quickly passes over the destruction of so many *insulae*, in which the majority of the city's populace lived, to focus instead on the loss of ancient temples and elite housing. Such were Roman values, that he could overlook the suffering of the poor in this way.[40] For Suetonius, it was not the noble or divine status of their inhabitants that made the loss of particular structures significant, however, so much as their antiquity as monuments of past glory. Tacitus' comment in the *Annals* on the improvements to the city introduced by Nero after the fire reflects a similar concern: "although they recognized how beautiful the revitalized city was, the elders still remembered the things that could not be restored" (*Ann.* 15.41: *quamvis in tanta resurgentis urbis pulchritudine multa seniores meminerint quae reparari nequibant*).[41] Scattered apartment blocks could be rebuilt without the loss of anything culturally significant. The city might even be made more beautiful by their replacement. Ancient dedications of *prisci duces*, on the other hand, were "worth seeing and memorable" (*visendum atque memorabile*). The sense of history that such monuments provided was irreplaceable, and their destruction was consequently regarded as more regrettable. The burning of the Capitol in 69 was thus traumatic not just as a sign of the breakdown of the *pax deum*, but also for the destruction of the many tangible links to the past that had been established there.

Res Publica

In light of what has been said about how an individual's response to a monument was shaped by his prior familiarity with an external discourse of commemoration, it is important to note that, as one of the largest and most important public buildings in Rome, the Capitoline temple of Jupiter

---

[40] Not to mention the permanent displacements that resulted from Nero's plans for rebuilding: See the salutary observations of Newbold (1974: 858–63).

[41] Sailor (2008: 214–15). On the improvements in urban planning that accompanied Nero's rebuilding, see Phillips (1978), Champlin (2003: 198–209). Wiseman (1987: 393–6) discusses the importance of noble *domus* and religious *aedes* as sites for elite commemorative display.

Optimus Maximus had a well-documented (or at least a fully articulated) construction history. This narrative probably was given written form at an early date, although it continued to expand and develop over time. By the end of the Republic, Roman writers had begun to pay close attention to their city's built environment, which they studied for what it could tell them about the history of political and religious institutions. On the Capitoline temple, witness the *Mystagogica* (*Sacred Guide*) of a certain L. Cincius, whom Livy cites as a "painstaking authority about such monuments" (7.3.7: *diligens talium monumentorum auctor*). Cincius' work is now lost, but from what we can reconstruct of its contents, he gave particular notice to the inscriptions of the Capitol, offering useful commentary on the texts of the ancient laws and votive dedications located in and around the temple of Jupiter, Juno, and Minerva.[42] Drawing on conventional written sources as well as the specialized knowledge handed down within priestly colleges, these antiquarian scholars provided published accounts of some of the dedications they found in Rome's temples, together with the stories behind them.

Such books had an important role to play in the working of Roman cultural memory.[43] By writing about temples and the dedications they housed, historians and antiquarians provided the monuments they wrote about with a memorial permanence that transcended their durability as physical structures. For better or worse, authors such as Cincius took an erstwhile fragile and mutable tradition of meaning and imprinted it with a fixed form. Even as the monument itself changed, this tradition of antiquarian writing provided a stable point of contact between the present building and what was once known of its earlier history. Many of the Capitoline inscriptions discussed by Cincius must have been destroyed in the fire of 83 BC, but the survival of their texts in his work (and perhaps

---

[42] The antiquarian is probably not to be confused with the early annalist L. Cincius Alimentus: *RE* 3.2, 2555–6 s.v. "Cincius (3)" [Wissowa], cf. Peter *HRR* cviii–xii, Heurgon (1964), Chassignet (1996: 58 n. 9.1). *Contra*, Jacoby *FGrHist* 810 F 8, Verbrugghe (1982: 320), assigning the fragment associated with the quoted passage of Livy to the historian. Cincius the antiquarian is reckoned by Bardon (1956: 108) as an Augustan author, but the evidence is slim: See Verbrugghe (1982: 321 n. 12). Heurgon (1964: 434) counts him as a contemporary of Varro.
   Capitoline inscriptions discussed by Cincius included the *lex vetusta* regarding the ceremony of the *clavus annalis*, which had been affixed (*fixa fuit*) to the right side of the temple for many years before 363 BC (ap. Livy 7.3.5–7). He also copied the text that accompanied T. Quinctius' dedication *inter cellam Iovis ac Minervae* in 380 BC (Livy 6.29.9, Fest. 498 Lindsay). On Roman antiquarianism in the late Republic, see Rawson (1985: 235), (1990).

[43] Cf. Assmann (1999: 181–90). Winkler (2002) provides a helpful model for the interaction between monuments, texts, and individual consciousness.

in earlier written sources) ensured that they would not be forgotten.[44] Works such as the *Mystagogica* were thus an important part of the store of cultural memory, which helped to shape the broader significance of the Capitoline temple for subsequent generations.

The relatively stable nature of this tradition would prove significant when it came time for Vespasian to rebuild the temple of Jupiter Optimus Maximus. Before any work of restoration could begin, educated Romans had an opportunity to reflect on well-established narratives relating to the construction and dedication of both the original edifice and the one that burned to the ground in 69. As defined by this tradition, these buildings were connected inextricably with a particular formulation of Republican *libertas* – one that had the potential to create problems for Vespasian as he took on the role of *princeps*. Because he did not control this tradition, the new emperor could not simply ignore these associations as he sought to restore peace and rebuilt the temple. As we shall see, Vespasian's actions and the senate's response to him reflect a delicate negotiation over the definition of these memories and of the meaning they imparted to public space.

The clearest glimpse of the literary tradition that attached to the Capitoline temple can be found in the potted construction history that follows the account of its destruction in Tacitus' *Histories*. The passage reads in full:

> *voverat Tarquinius Priscus rex bello Sabino ieceratque fundamenta spe magis futurae magnitudinis quam quo modicae adhuc populi Romani res sufficerent. mox Servius Tullius sociorum studio, dein Tarquinius Superbus capta Suessa Pometia hostium spoliis exstruxere. sed gloria operis libertati reservata: pulsis regibus Horatius Pulvillus iterum consul dedicavit ea magnificentia quam immensae postea populi Romani opes ornarent potius quam augerent. isdem rursus vestigiis situm est, postquam interiecto quadringentorum quindecim annorum spatio L. Scipione C. Norbano consulibus flagraverat. curam victor Sulla suscepit, neque tamen dedicavit: hoc solum felicitati eius negatum. Lutatii Catuli nomen inter <tan>ta Caesarum opera usque ad Vitellium mansit. ea tunc aedes cremabatur.*

King Tarquinius Priscus had vowed the temple in the Sabine war and laid foundations of a size that accorded with hopes of future greatness rather

---

[44] In assessing the significance of Cincius' familiarity with such ancient inscriptions, much depends on chronology. There are three possibilities: (a) Cincius saw the inscriptions himself before 83 BC and his *Mystagogica* should be dated accordingly, (b) he was able to consult some archival or literary source that preserved their texts, or (c) the texts were reinscribed on the Capitol after 83 BC – an action that also presupposes the underlying conditions of (b). Livy 6.4.1 associates the disappearance of three gold *paterae* inscribed with the name of Camillus with this fire.

than with the modest means of the Roman People available at that time. Soon Servius Tullius worked to build it with help from allies, followed by Tarquinius Superbus with enemy spoils after the capture of Suessa Pometia. But the glory of the work was saved for liberty: when the kings were driven out, Horatius Pulvillus in his second consulship dedicated an enormous structure, which the subsequently vast resources of the Roman People would decorate rather than enlarge. It was laid out again on the same footprint, four hundred and fifty years later, after it burned when L. Scipio and C. Norbanus were consuls. The victor Sulla undertook the work of rebuilding, but still he did not dedicate it: this alone was denied to his good luck. The name of Lutatius Catulus remained among so many works of the Caesars until Vitellius. Then this temple burned. (*Hist.* 3.72.2)

There is a somewhat fuller, but remarkably similar, account of the temple's history in Plutarch's *Life of Publicola*, which also includes a brief discussion of Vespasian's temple as well as the fourth phase of construction, an opulent structure built by Domitian following another fire in AD 80.[45] The similarities may point to the use of a common source by the two authors – perhaps an account of the temple's history compiled under Domitian. More importantly, the overlap between Tacitus' and Plutarch's versions indicates that a common stock of information about the temple was circulating among the intelligentsia of the Mediterranean in the generation that followed the civil wars of 69. As the material out of which cultural memory was produced, these narratives set the stage for Vespasian's rebuilding efforts and the public response that they produced.

As the above-quoted summary makes clear, the central message in the narrative of the construction of the first Capitoline temple is that it was planned and built by the kings but was not dedicated until after the establishment of the free Republic. Tacitus is explicit: "the glory of the work was saved for liberty" (*gloria operis libertati reservata*). This postponement fits with the general pattern of the tradition about the expulsion of the kings, according to which the property of the Tarquins became a public possession (literally, *res publica*) when the royal family was sent into exile. Although kings had laid the foundations and done most of the construction, they ultimately were denied the honor of dedicating the temple, which consequentially was stripped of its monarchical associations and

---

[45] Plut. *Popl.* 14–16. Similarities between Plutarch's and Tacitus' accounts of the events of 69–70 have long been noted, leading to speculation about the use of a common source: See Mommsen (1870), Groag (1897: 733–65), Syme (1958: 674–6). To my knowledge, no one has suggested that the lost source may be responsible for the similarities in their digressions on the history of the Capitolium.

became instead a symbol of the freedom of the *respublica*.[46] This connection between the dedication of the temple and the era of the Republic was reinforced by Roman historians, who computed a date for the founding of the Republic by counting back the number of nails that had been hammered into the wall of Minerva's chamber in an annual ritual performed by the state's chief magistrate.[47]

This association with public *libertas* was given expression in the sacred precinct that surrounded the temple as well. Statues of the kings stood somewhere in the forecourt, probably toward the southwest corner of the Area Capitolina. Like that of the temple itself, the meaning of these ostensible monuments of Rome's regal history was redefined by the addition of an image of Lucius Brutus with sword unsheathed, defending Rome's freedom against the aggression of tyrants.[48] Furthermore, on the slope of the hill facing the Forum, the carefully preserved open space of the Aequimelium was thought to mark the spot where the house of the would-be tyrant Sp. Maelius had been destroyed, while, on the other summit of the hill, the temple of Juno Moneta literally warned of the threat of tyranny by marking the spot where the same fate had befallen the house of M. Manlius.[49] These topographical features, together with the aetiological stories that attached to them, served to reinforce the associations that identified the Capitolium as a key site in the ceaseless struggle to preserve Roman *libertas*.

The importance of the public status of the temple and its association with the founding of the Republic was further underscored by the story of its inauguration, which Plutarch and others record.[50] According to this well-known legend, the *pontifex* Horatius Pulvillus was interrupted in the

---

[46] Beard, North, and Price (1998: 59), Stamper (2005: 10). See also Livy 2.5.2, Zevi (1995: 301–3), Gallia (2007: 63–4), cf. Oros. 5.18.27, Wirszubski (1950: 121). On the significance of public authority over the dedication of temples during the Republic, see Orlin (1997: 162–71).

[47] Fears (1980: 100): "In republican political mythology, it was no coincidence that Jupiter's Capitoline temple was coeval with the establishment of Roman *Libertas*, the creation of the *respublica* and the expulsion of Tarquin the tyrant." The significance of the *clavus annalis* as a measure of the age of the Republic is discussed by Feeney (2007: 104–5), Purcell (2003: 29–30), Momigliano (1969: 8–9), Alföldi (1963: 78–84).

[48] Plut. *Brut.* 1.1, Dio 43.45.4, cf. Plin. *Pan.* 55.6–7. Evans (1990), Sehlmeyer (1999: 68–74), Walter (2004: 144-6), Weinstock (1971: 145–6), *LTUR* IV 368–9 s.v. "Statuae Regum Romanorum" [Coarelli]. The liberative message of this grouping was reinforced by the nearby introduction of replicas of the famous Athenian tyrant slayers: See Coarelli (1969), Flower (2006: 70–6).

[49] Livy 4.16.1, 6.20.13, Cic. *Dom.* 101, Val. Max. 6.3.1, 1c, Varro *Ling.* 5.157. *LTUR* I 20–1 s.v. "Aequimelium" [Pisani Sartorio], *LTUR* III 123 s.v. "Iuno Moneta, aedes" [Giannelli], Flower (2006: 48–9), cf. Walter (2004: 161). See also Jaeger (1997: 80–8), Meadows and Williams (2001).

[50] Plut. *Popl.* 14, also Livy 2.8.6–8, Val. Max. 5.10.1, Cic. *Dom.* 139.

middle of the dedicatory sacrifices by a false report that his son had died. Undeterred, he completed the ceremony without showing any signs of grief, "lest he seem to perform the role of a father more than that of a *pontifex*" (Val. Max. 5.10.1: *ne patris magis quam pontificis partes egisse videretur*). This *exemplum*, which is typical of the selfless ethos ascribed to many of the heroes of the early Republic, demonstrates that private concerns (*res privata*) must be subordinated to one's duty to the community in a free *respublica*.[51] It also suggests how deeply concerns about public *libertas* were interwoven into the narrative of the temple of Jupiter Optimus Maximus. No wonder, then, that the assassins of Julius Caesar proclaimed their restoration of Rome's freedom with a speech delivered by Marcus Brutus on the Capitol, or that the consuls convened the senate there for the same purpose following the assassination of Caligula.[52]

This association between the Capitoline temple and Republican *libertas* did not end with the story of Horatius Pulvillus. Both Plutarch and Tacitus point out that the construction of the second temple, like that of the first, was begun by one person and completed by another. Plutarch explains:

Ἔοικε δὲ καὶ περὶ τὸν δεύτερον ναὸν ὁμοία τύχη γενέσθαι τῆς καθιερώσεως. τὸν μὲν γὰρ πρῶτον, ὡς εἴρηται, Ταρκυνίου κατασκευάσαντος, Ὡρατίου δὲ καθιερώσαντος, ἐν τοῖς ἐμφυλίοις πολέμοις πῦρ ἀπώλεσε· τὸν δὲ δεύτερον ἀνέστησε μὲν Σύλλας, ἐπεγράφη δὲ τῇ καθιερώσει Κάτουλος Σύλλα προαποθανόντος.

It seems that a similar fate also befell the dedication of the second temple. The first one – which, as I said, Tarquinius had built but Horatius dedicated – was destroyed by fire in the civil wars. Then Sulla established the second, but after his death the inscription for its dedication was that of Catulus. (*Popl.* 15.1)

The similarity is superficially obvious, but the comparison between Sulla and Tarquinius also points to a deeper meaning. As Plutarch's comment indicates, similar issues were raised by the Republican-era rebuilding of the temple. The parallels between the two circumstances helped to reinforce the association of the temple with *libertas*.

As multiple sources confirm, Sulla had taken a particular interest in the reconstruction of the Capitoline temple, both during and after his dictatorship.[53] Indeed, his determination to build a magnificent temple was so fervent that it seems to have contributed to his death. Valerius

---

[51] Flower (2010: 12).
[52] Cic. *Att.* 15.1a.2, App. *BC* 2.137–42, Suet. *Calig.* 60, cf. Joseph. *BJ* 19.248.
[53] Thein (2002: 222–43).

Maximus (9.3.8, cf. Plut. *Sull.* 37.3) records that Sulla died after suffering a hemorrhage while in the midst of a tirade against one of the leading citizens of Puteoli who had been dilatory in coming up with that town's contribution to the rebuilding effort. The fact that Sulla's passion for the project deprived him of the chance to see the work completed was regarded as a clear instance where the dictator's proverbial good fortune (*felicitas*) failed him, as Tacitus notes ironically (*Hist.* 3.72.3: *hoc solum felicitati eius negatum*, "this alone was denied to his good fortune").[54]

Like the account of Pulvillus' determination, Sulla's failure to dedicate the temple reinforced the monument's association with a Republican concept of political liberty. The connection with Sulla's *felicitas* also suggests that this narrative may have been tied in with a larger discourse about tyrants, who were often the focus of paradoxical disquisitions on the true nature of happiness.[55] The dictator, whom Tacitus ominously styles as *victor* in his discussion of the Capitolium's history, would have been an inviting subject for such reflections, because his title "Lucky" (Felix) had been adopted in the midst of the proscriptions − an otherwise unhappy time for Rome. Echoing what appears to have become a commonplace of the declamation halls, Valerius Maximus opens his chapter *On Cruelty* with a litany of Sulla's crimes, culminating in the *sententia*, "mark my words, with these accomplishments he thought he should lay a claim to the name of *felicitas*" (9.2.1: *en quibus actis felicitatis nomen adserendum putavit*).[56] The point is also made by the Elder Pliny, who expresses it in such a way as to invite comparison with the descriptive nickname applied to Tarquinius Superbus ("the Proud"): "and even so he added to this glory the proud cognomen Felix" (*NH* 22.12: *addat etiamnum huic gloriae superbum cognomen Felicem*). Sulla's failure to live long enough to complete his ambitious plans for the Capitoline temple squares nicely with this moral, even as it provides a further point of contact between the dictator and the hated king.

Like the expulsion of Tarquinius Superbus, the death of Sulla Felix spared the temple from the unhappy fate of being dedicated by a person

---

[54] The phrase echoes a sentiment that the elder Pliny attributes to Sulla himself at the moment of his death: *NH* 7.138: *hoc tamen nempe felicitati suae defuisse confessus est quod Capitolium non dedicavisset*. Sulla was also regarded as *infelix* in some quarters owing to the skin condition (φθειρίασις) that plagued him at the time of his death: Quintus Serenus, *Liber Medicinalis* 62–3, quoted in Thein (2002: 145 n 16).

[55] Hdt. 1.30–3, 86, cf. Sen. *Contr.* 1.praef.23, *Suas.* 1.9.

[56] Cf. Sen. *Prov.* 3.7–8 (quoting the contemporary exile P. Rutilius Rufus): *"viderint," inquit "isti quos Romae deprehendit felicitas tua."* The cognomen *Felix* was formally conferred in 82 BC: Plut. *Sull.* 34.2, cf. 6.4–7, Sall. *Iug.* 95.3–4, Balsdon (1951).

whom many considered to hold an unjust *dominatio* over his fellow Romans.[57] The man who ultimately dedicated Sulla's temple, the *pontifex* Lutatius Catulus, was, like Horatius Pulvillus before him, remembered in this context as an *exemplum* of civic *pietas*.[58] In a speech written to reflect the contemporary atmosphere surrounding the temple's rededication, Cicero appeals directly to Catulus, who happened to be one of the jurors in the case, saying, "by the kindness of the senate and Roman people, your honor and the eternal memory of your name is consecrated along with that temple" (*Verr.* 2.4.69: *tuus enim honos illo templo senatus populique Romani beneficio, tui nominis aeterna memoria simul cum templo illo consecratur*).[59] The honor of having his name displayed in the most conspicuous inscription in Rome brought Catulus lasting glory, but Cicero stresses the authority of the Republican community in conferring these honors. More importantly, as Cicero points out later in the same text, Catulus ensured that the temple was rebuilt publicly (*publice*), "just as was done by our ancestors" (*Verr.* 2.5.48: *sicut apud maiores nostros factum est*).[60]

It is significant that Tacitus twice mentions the *populus Romanus* in his brief history of the temple. Unlike the privately financed, self-glorifying monuments constructed by triumphal generals during the second and first centuries BC, the temple of Jupiter Optimus Maximus was, from its original foundation, a public rather than a private sanctuary.[61] Had Sulla lived to finish its reconstruction, he might have undermined this distinction, but Catulus' intervention ensured that the work was carried out and completed using public funds. The temple's inscription, to which Cicero refers, is itself likely to have recorded the senatorial authority that enabled Catulus' work. Some idea of its wording can be gleaned, mutatis mutandis, from an inscription found in the nearby Tabularium, another structure rebuilt after the fire of 83 BC:

```
Q · LVTATIVS · Q · F · Q · N CATVLVS · COS
SUBSTRVCTIONEM    ·    ET    ·    TABVLARIVM
DE · S · S · FACIVNDVM · COERAVIT · EIDEMQVE
```

---

[57] Cf. Quint. *Inst.* 5.10.30, Sen. *Clem.* 1.12.1–2. Flower (2010: 93–5).

[58] Dio 37.46.3–4: καὶ ὁ μὲν διφανέστατα τῶν πώποτε τὸ δημόσιον ἀεὶ πρὸ παντὸς προτιμήσας, cf. Plut. *Pomp.* 16.1, *Caes.* 6.3. *RE* 13.2, 2082–94 s.v. "Lutatius (8)" [Münzer]. Tradition linked Catulus with the Sullan cause (e.g., Flor. 4.11.6), but apparently not with its excesses.

[59] Cf. Val. Max. 6.9.5, Suet. *Galb.* 2

[60] Cf. Palombi (1997). Caesar later tried to prosecute Catulus for malfeasance in the use of public monies for rebuilding the temple: Dio 37.44.1–2, Suet. *Iul.* 15, cf. Plin. *NH* 33.57.

[61] On manubial temples, see Orlin (1997: 130–5), Shatzman (1972), Ziolkowski (1992: 235–58).

PROB[AVIT]
The consul Q. Lutatius Catulus, son of Quintus, grandson of Quintus,
by a vote of the senate oversaw the building of this substructure and the
    Tabularium
and approved the same.

(*CIL* I² 737 = *ILS* 35, *ILLRP* 368)

The language, like that of most Latin inscriptions, is highly formulaic. But adherence to formula can be telling in itself. In his role as *curator restituendi Capitolii*, Catulus is represented as following the traditional role (and the traditional limitations) of a Republican magistrate.[62] His authority is explicitly subordinate to the collective will and interests of the senate and thus is consistent with the interpretation given to public *libertas* by most elite Romans.

Tacitus' observation, "the name of Lutatius Catulus remained among so many works of the Caesars up to Vitellius" (*Hist.* 3.72.3: *Lutatii Catuli nomen inter <tan>ta Caesarum opera usque ad Vitellium mansit*), resonates within this context. Even as the institutions of monarchy began to form at Rome, Catulus' temple had been carefully preserved as a symbol of prior liberty. In the turbulent years that followed the temple's rededication in 70 BC, various attempts were made to replace Catulus' name and thereby lay an individual claim over the Capitolium, but these were without effect. When Augustus performed major repairs to the temple, he famously refrained from replacing the original dedicatory inscription. So long as the temple and its inscription stood, it represented one of the few remaining vestiges of the pre-Caesarian Republic.[63]

Although Augustus boasted about transforming Rome from a city of brick to one of marble, there were certain buildings, such as the temple of Jupiter Optimus Maximus and Pompey's enormous theater complex, that he could take credit in the *Res Gestae* for rebuilding, but on which he dared not impose his name. This sort of modesty and reverence for tradition remained the ideal practice for many of Augustus' successors,

---

[62] Varr. *ap.* Gell. 2.10.2. The construction and dedication of public temples could be administered by censors or aediles, but sometimes was entrusted to specially created *duumviri*: See Orlin (1997: 140–58, 172–8). The Capitolium evidently was a special case.

[63] Sailor (2008: 212–13). On Augustus' interventions on the Capitol, *RG* 20.1: *sine ulla inscriptione nominis mei*; ἄνευ ἐπιγραφῆς τοῦ ἐμοῦ ὀνόματος, cf. Suet. *Aug.* 30.2. See Rea (2007: 54–6), Gros (1976: 16, 34), cf. Strothmann (2000: 29). Earlier attempts to erase Catulus' name: Suet. *Iul.* 15, cf. 7.1, Cic. *Att.* 2.24.3, Dio 37.44.1–2, 43.14.6, Weinstock (1971: 85), Flower (2006: 106).

enshrined most famously in the architrave of the Hadrianic Pantheon.[64] In Zonaras' epitome of Cassius Dio, we find the following statement about Vespasian:

Ἐλθὼν δ' ἐς τὴν Ῥώμην καὶ τοῖς στρατιώταις καὶ τῷ δήμῳ παρέσχηκε δωρεάς, καὶ τὰ τεμένη καὶ τὰ δημόσια ἔργα τὰ πεπονηκότα ἀνελάμβανε καὶ τὰ ἤδη ἐφθαρμένα ἐπανεσκεύαζε, καὶ συντελουμένοις αὐτοῖς οὐ τὸ ἑαυτοῦ ἐπέγραφεν ὄνομα, ἀλλὰ τὸ τῶν πρώτως δομησαμένων.

Upon coming into Rome he gave gifts to both the soldiers and the people, and he restored the temples and public buildings that were worn down and rebuilt those that had been destroyed. When these were finished, he did not inscribe his own name, but the names of those who had first built them. (Dio (Zon.) 66.10.1[a])

This generalization, taken from a late and sometimes unreliable source, attests to the persistence of the Augustan ideal, but it does not necessarily tell us anything about Vespasian's actual practice in rebuilding the Capitolium. The wording of Tacitus, "the name of Lutatius Catulus remained... until Vitellius" (*Hist.* 3.72.3: *Lutatii Catuli nomen... usque ad Vitellium mansit*), suggests that Vespasian's piety did not extend to the reinscription of the original builder's name in this case. Unlike the restoration and improvement projects undertaken by Augustus, in this case the temple had been destroyed entirely. With the complete reconstruction of a building from the ground up, it would not have been necessary to preserve the original dedicatory inscription.[65] After all, Catulus had put his own name on the temple he constructed.

When the rebuilding of the temple of Jupiter Optimus Maximus was complete, the name it bore would be that of an emperor. Within the framework of cultural memory provided by the narratives discussed above, this change implied profound repercussions for the relationship between the Capitoline temple and *libertas* under the Principate. Like King Tarquin and the dictator Sulla before him, Vespasian began the construction of this temple as a holder of sole power. Unlike these archetypal figures, however, he survived to see the work completed and to dedicate the temple in his

---

[64] *CIL* VI 896 (= *ILS* 129), *LTUR* IV 54 s.v. "Pantheon" [Ziolkowski]. Suet. *Aug.* 28.3, 31.5, cf. Dio 53.2.4–5, Haselberger (2007: 97), Wardman (1982: 71). Cf. Suetonius' criticism of Domitian on this count, *Dom.* 5: *plurima et amplissima opera incendio absumpta restituit,... sed omnia sub titulo tantum suo ac sine ulla pristini auctoris memoria.*

[65] This rule applied even to the pious Augustus: See Stuart (1905). For example, Augustus put his name on the completely rebuilt temple of Magna Mater on the Palatine: Ov. *Fast.* 4.347–8, Haselberger (2007: 209). Still, Sailor (2008: 227) suggests that Vespasian did not put his name on the temple.

own name. No Horatius or Catulus intervened on behalf of the communal interests of the *respublica*.

This rewriting of the script for the dedication of a temple to Capitoline Jupiter represented a potential problem for an emperor who styled himself as both a bringer of peace and a restorer of Roman liberty. Vespasian claimed to have entered the civil wars as a rightful successor to Galba, taking up his message of *libertas restituta* as a promise to reassert senatorial freedom against the tyranny of illegitimate usurpers such as Otho and Vitellius. But there was also a salvation narrative that went with his rise to power, and Vespasian openly celebrated the role of *Fortuna* in his family's success and sought to associate himself with public *Felicitas*.[66] In the context of rebuilding the Capitolium, the latter message can only have invited an unwelcome comparison with Sulla. Plutarch appears to make this connection explicit when he notes that "Vespasian rebuilt the third structure from start to finish, with the good fortune that attended everything he did" (*Popl.* 15.2: τὸν τρίτον τῇ πρὸς τἆλλα καὶ τοῦτο χρησάμενος εὐποτμίᾳ Οὐεσπασιανὸς ἐξ ἀρχῆς ἄχρι τέλους ἀναγαγὼν). Although the interpretation Plutarch gives is positive, such luck was not an unproblematic blessing. The new emperor might wish to stress the peace and good fortune that his Principate promised to provide, but it would not be appropriate to let the reconstruction of the temple call attention to the restriction of *libertas* that made these benefits possible.

The sensitivity of the situation quickly became apparent. At the first senate meeting to be held following the death of Vitellius, a motion was put forward by the consul designate Valerius Asiaticus regarding the restoration of the Capitolium (Tac. *Hist.* 4.4.2). As Vespasian was still en route to Rome from settling affairs in Egypt, debate was perhaps more lively that day than it might otherwise have been. Asiaticus' motion passed unaltered, but in the course of the discussion the praetor designate Helvidius Priscus expressed his view "that the Capitolium should be restored at public expense, and that Vespasian should assist" (ibid. 4.9.2: *ut Capitolium publice restitueretur, adiuvaret Vespasianus*). It is not entirely clear what Helvidius meant for the emperor's assistance to entail, but the context in which Tacitus mentions this opinion suggests that a monetary contribution was not envisioned. Perhaps Helvidius was suggesting that Vespasian be granted a responsibility more limited than what Asiaticus had proposed,

---

[66] Tac. *Hist.* 2.1.1–2, 4.40.1, *RIC* II² 61–80 nos. 35, 82–9, 121–4, 171–4, 207–10, 237, 272, 309–10 (= *BMCRE* II 118 no. 549 etc.), 59–87 nos. 11, 33, 50, 73–7, 157–8, 230–1, 270, 302, 373–4, 421, etc., 64–86 nos. 62, 133, 268–9, 299, 392, 400–1, 413, etc. Bianco (1968: 172–3), Levick (1999a: 67–73), also Scott (1968: 70–84).

along the lines of the role performed by Catulus a century and a half earlier. The point was to preserve the temple's association with liberty as a *res publica*.[67]

In the event, Helvidius' amendment was passed over as impractical. The public treasury was in a financial crisis at the time, so the reconstruction work had to be funded out of the greater resources of the emperor's fisc. Tacitus nevertheless sounds an ominous note when recording Helvidius' proposal: "the most moderate individuals passed over this statement in silence and then forgot it, but there were also those who remembered" (ibid.: *eam sententiam modestissimus quisque silentio, deinde oblivio transmisit: fuere qui et meminissent*). In this formulation, the role assigned to memory is that of holding a grudge, with the implication that Helvidius' words would be used to harm him at some point in the future. Discussion of the subsequent exile and execution of Helvidius must wait for a later chapter, but it is appropriate at this point to consider why such comments might have been regarded as dangerous. As necessary as it may have been, the rebuilding of the Capitolium by Vespasian meant that the central cult site of Roman state religion became what it had never been before: a privately financed monument, built and dedicated under the direction of a single, uniquely powerful individual. The radical nature of this change, together with its potentially serious legal and religious implications, suggests why moderates may have felt that Helvidius' proposal was best forgotten. The praetor's insistence on a public role in the temple's reconstruction called unwanted attention to an inconvenient truth about the balance of power during a sensitive moment in the new emperor's relationship with the senate.[68]

Once aired, however, Helvidius' proposal could not be entirely overlooked. Following the initial meeting of the senate, Vespasian took affirmative steps to engage the senate in tasks related to the reconstruction. This was in all likelihood an attempt to mollify public anxieties about the temple's loss of its public status. In light of his delicate position, it behooved the new emperor to choose carefully the issues that might be raised by

---

[67] Malitz (1985: 236), cf. Galimberti (2000: 220–1).

[68] Sailor (2008: 224–6), Darwall-Smith (1996: 43–4). Note the distinction drawn by Festus 284 Lindsay: *publica sacra, quae publico sumptu pro populo fiunt...at privata, quae pro singulis hominibus, familiis, gentibus fiunt.* Property was legally regarded as *sacra* only if it was dedicated at public expense, according to *Digest* 1.8.6.3: *sacrae autem res sunt hae, quae publice consecratae sunt, non private.* The site (*locus*) of a public temple remained *sacer* even if the *aedes* itself was destroyed, however. On the relationship between *aerarium publicum* and emperor's private *fiscus* at this time, see Plin. *Pan.* 6.3, Millar (1963), (1977: 189–201), also Jones (1950), Brunt (1966).

the senate's participation. We can be sure the work Vespasian delegated to the senate was designed to turn discussion away from memories of the *libertas* embedded in the foundation narratives of the temple itself. By confining their efforts to the recovery of a particular set of public inscriptions, Vespasian attempted to divert the senators' attention to a different set of mnemonic associations, which centered on Jupiter's status as the protector of Roman imperial power. This redirection of public attention from uncomfortable questions about political authority within the Roman state onto an issue of external power was, of course, made easier by the unique character and complexity of the Capitolium as a site of public memory.

INSTRUMENTUM IMPERII

Although it happened more by accident than through any deliberate choice or policy, Vespasian would transform the Capitolium from a symbol of Roman public *libertas* into a dynastic possession of the Imperial house. Because of the need to rebuild after the fire, the new emperor had no choice but to look for alternate meanings in the temple that were more amenable to this arrangement. The connection he arrived on, which also ran deep in the memory of the site, was the temple's status as the center of Rome's empire and guarantee of world rule. As an emperor who emerged from a military career and was currently wrapping up a successful campaign in Judaea, Vespasian was in a much better position to confront these associations.[69]

As has already been discussed, Vespasian made sure that the proposal providing for the reconstruction of the Capitolium was among the first business taken up by the senate on the day his proclamation as emperor became official.[70] Because he was still occupied in the East at the time, he arranged for the preliminary planning of the reconstruction work to be handled by L. Julius Vestinus, whom Tacitus describes as "a man of the equestrian order, but among the nobles in *auctoritas* and reputation" (*Hist.* 4.53.1: *curam restituendi Capitolii in Lucium Vestinum confert, equestris ordinis virum, sed auctoritate famaque inter proceres*).[71] The first thing Vestinus did according to Tacitus was to consult the ancient college of Etruscan seers, or *haruspices*. This should be seen not only as an

---

[69] Fears (1981a: 79–81) assigns the formulation of a "Jovian theology" of imperial power to the Flavian period. See, however, the important critique of Schowalter (1993: 13–27).

[70] Tac. *Hist.* 4.4.2. See above.

[71] *PIR*[2] I 622. Vestinus' role was perhaps analogous to (but probably more extensive than) that of the equestrian functionary L. Cornelius, who had served Catulus as *praefectus fabrum* and later as *architectus* (*AE* 1971: 61).

act of piety, but also as an attempt by Vespasian's agent to steer attention away from the memory of Horatius Pulvillus and Catulus and onto a different constellation of narratives relating to the temple's construction. According to tradition, Etruscan divinatory arts had been used in the original foundation of the temple, going back to the days of the immigrant king Tarquinius Priscus, whom Tacitus credits with laying the temple's enormous foundations. This work was said to have involved a number of favorable omens foretelling the growth of Rome's empire – that "future greatness" (*futura magnitudo*) to which Tacitus alludes.[72] The first of these omens was the refusal by the god Terminus to yield his place when the site was being cleared. Terminus' obstinacy necessitated the incorporation of that god's shrine within the temple and was taken as a signal that Roman borders would always remain firm.[73] Another story involved the discovery of a human head (*caput*) during the digging of the foundations themselves, the event that was generally thought to have given the Capitolium its name. This omen also was referred to Etruscan seers, who interpreted it as a sign that Rome was destined to become the political "head" of Italy, and eventually the world.[74]

Vestinus' consultation of the *haruspices* would have served to reactivate public interest in these narratives, which commemorate the Capitolium's association with the growth and strength of Rome's empire. According to Tacitus, the terms of their advice were that, after the rubble had been cleared, "the temple should be erected on the same footprint, (since) the gods do not want the old form to be changed" (*Hist.* 4.53.1: *ut ... templum isdem vestigiis sisteretur: nolle deos mutari veterem formam*). When set in context with the omens that appeared during the laying of the original foundations, this response could be read as a sign that the Capitolium still might be rebuilt in such a way as to preserve its significance as a guarantee of empire. The association with *libertas* could not be preserved unchanged, and so the restoration of the original floor plan at least ensured that its implications for *imperium* remained part of the Capitolium's enduring meaning. In the present circumstances, this was an aspect of the temple's history that the new emperor would have benefited from highlighting.

The role of Jupiter Capitolinus as a guardian of the empire would be emphasized in other aspects of the restoration as well. As the governing

---

[72] *Hist.* 3.72.2. Simonelli (1990: 71–5), Rea (2007: 49–50). On the special position of *haruspices* in Roman state religion, see Latte (1960: 157–60), MacBain (1982: 43–59).

[73] Dion. Hal. 3.69.3–6, Ov. *Fast.* 2.667–84, cf. Livy 1.38.7, 55.2–4.

[74] Dion. Hal. 4.59–61: κεφαλὴν ... συμπάσης Ἰταλίας, Livy 1.55.5–6: *caput rerum*, cf. Plin. *NH* 28.15, Serv. *Aen.* 8.345, Borgeaud (1987).

deity of the Roman empire, Jupiter Optimus Maximus was the principal recipient of two types of gifts. The first were triumphal dedications, which might be set up by victorious generals to commemorate their moment of glory and supplement the laurel branch typically offered to Jupiter at the conclusion of a triumph. Trophies and other tokens of military glory could be found in temples and private houses throughout the city, but the Capitol was favored for its prominence.[75] Another category of gifts for which Jupiter Optimus Maximus was the most suitable recipient were the offerings sent by kings, cities, and wealthy foreigners "to decorate the Capitolium in the way that the importance of the temple and the name of (Rome's) empire demand" (Cic. *Ver.* 2.4.68: *Capitolium sic ornare ut templi dignitas imperiique nostri nomen desiderat*).[76] Together with the triumphal dedications set up by the commanders themselves, these monuments documented the diplomatic underpinnings of Rome's relentless expansion alongside its more obvious military aspect.

As the Roman Empire grew, dedications of both varieties multiplied. Already in 179 BC, the Capitoline precinct was so crowded that the censor M. Aemilius Lepidus had a number of statues removed and, to clean the building's columns, took down the jumble of shields and military standards that had become affixed to the temple itself.[77] Religious scruples forbade the destruction of these dedications, however, so instead of being discarded they were placed in special underground pits, called *favissae*. The Capitolium thus became something akin to a Roman Imperial War Museum, complete with its own moldering storerooms for items not on public display.[78] Comparison might be made to the Forum of Augustus and its portrait gallery of the "top men" (*summi viri*) from Roman history.

---

[75] Hölscher (2006), Hölkeskamp (2001: 108–11), Edwards (1996: 71), Stamper (2005: 12). On the display of spoils, see Wiseman (1987), Rawson (1990), also Beard (2007, esp. 143–86), Brilliant (1999), and Künzl (1988) on the triumph. The tradition of dedicating the arms of a defeated foe (*spolia*) to Jupiter on the Capitoline could be traced back to Romulus (Livy 1.10.5–7, Flower (2000)), but dedications also took the form of valuable works of art: See, e.g., Strab. 6.3.1, Plin. *NH* 34.40, 35.22, Val. Max. 3.6.2, Sehlmeyer (1999: 144–5, 112–29, 159–61).

[76] When given by a polity, these donatives typically took the form of a gold crown: See, e.g., Livy 2.22.3, 43.6.5–9, Strab. 4.5.3, but note esp. the statue group given by king Bocchus to celebrate his role in Sulla's capture of Jugurtha: Plut. *Sull.* 6.1, *Mar.* 32.4, *LTUR* IV 306 s.v. "Statuae: C. Cornelius Sulla, Bocchus, Iugurtha" [Sehlmeyer], cf. Plin. *NH* 34.32.

[77] Livy 40.51.3, cf. Plin. *NH* 35.14. Augustus also cleared dedications from the Area Capitolina, removing several *statuas virorum inlustrium* to the Campus Martius to make room (Suet. *Calig.* 34.1).

[78] Varr. *ap.* Gell. *NA* 2.10, Fest. 78 Lindsay, cf. Flower (2006: 213–15). On the museological function of public spaces in Rome, see Stambaugh (1978: 586–7), Strong (1994), Kuttner (1999).

There, as on the Capitol, an accumulation of monuments commemorating individuals and their achievements created an impression of the collective greatness of the Roman community.[79] But whereas the neat rows of statues in the porticoes of the Forum Augustum provided a beautiful and well-ordered representation of the Republic, the Capitolium, with its chaotic agglomeration of ancient dedications, felt closer to the Republic itself.

This richly textured *lieu de mémoire* is what was consumed in the fire of 69, and its loss was deeply felt. In his encyclopedic *Natural History*, Pliny the Elder occasionally discusses works of art that once stood in or near the temple of Jupiter Optimus Maximus but had disappeared. Some of these losses are signaled indirectly through the use of the perfect tense (*fuit*) to describe paintings that no longer existed, but Pliny is more explicit about the fate of a Hellenistic bronze of a dog licking its wounds, of which he says, "our era saw [it] on the Capitolium, before it recently was set on fire by the Vitellians and burned down, in the *cella* of Juno" (*NH* 34.38: *aetas nostra vidit in Capitolio, priusquam id novissime conflagraret a Vitellianis incensum, in cella Iunonis*).[80] After the precinct's destruction, antiquarian guidebooks no longer provided inventories of what might be seen there. Instead, they became the basis for a memory of what had disappeared.[81]

It bears repeating that the question of guilt probably should be left open. Tacitus reports that Sabinus also overturned several "ancestral honors" (*Hist.* 3.71.2: *decora maiorum*) to form makeshift barricades during the siege of the Capitolium. In the end, the fact that Pliny and other Flavian partisans were so eager to assign the blame to Vitellius is proof that these monuments (and the valuable connection to the past they provided) were dearly missed once peace was finally reestablished.[82] When assessing the impact of the events of 69 on Roman memory, therefore, it is important to bear in mind that the regression into civil war was to blame not only for the destruction of a temple, but for the loss of countless smaller monuments on the Capitoline as well. Inevitably, Vespasian's rebuilt Capitolium would

---

[79] See now Geiger (2008).

[80] Plin. *NH* 35.69: *quae Romae in Capitolio fuit*, followed by another painting, *quae est Rhodi*, ibid. 35.108: *quae tabula fuit in Capitolio in Minervae delubro supra aediculam Iuventatis*. See also 33.154. It is not clear whether these works were destroyed in the fire of 69 or in 83 BC. de Angeli, *LTUR* III 149 s.v. "Iuppiter Optimus Maximus, Capitolinus, Aedes, Templum (fasi tardo-Repubblicane e di età Imperiale)," opts for the earlier date.

[81] Cf. Cic. *Verr.* 2.4.132, on the *mystagogoi* of Syracuse, who show the places where things had been before Verres' peculations: *nam ut ante demonstrabant quid ubique esset, item nunc quid undique ablatum sit ostendunt*.

[82] Cf. the way that Nero was blamed for the fire of 64: Yavetz (1975: 187–8), Johnstone (1992: 63–8).

be judged in comparison with what stood there previously, just as Sulla's Curia and the neighborhoods rebuilt by Nero had been. For this reason, it was important to recover and restore as much as possible.[83]

Triumphal spoils and famous works of art might be irreplaceable, but there also stood on the Capitol an important collection of legal documents in the form of inscribed bronze tablets. As a rule, official enactments of the Roman people and decisions of the senate (*leges, senatus consulta*) were engraved on bronze and set up in the space of inaugurated *templa*.[84] These could be found throughout the city, but because of the special association between Jupiter Optimus Maximus and Rome's *imperium*, the Capitoline precinct seems to have been the preferred location for the posting of those tablets that recorded the written apparatus of Roman foreign policy. These included treaties and alliances between Rome and other states, as well as special grants of privileges to official friends (*amici*) of the Roman People.[85]

From an administrative point of view, it is unlikely that these bronze plaques served any practical function. With respect to the diplomatic and administrative documents posted on the Capitolium, copies of these texts were typically sent to the individual or community in whose interest the original law or decree had been passed, so that they could be published epigraphically, kept in a local archive, or both.[86] In such a diffusive documentary culture, however, it was important to be able to establish the

---

[83] Instructive comparison may be made to the rebuilding of central Warsaw following World War II, discussed by Tung (2001: 73–95). Every effort was made to recreate the historic cityscape exactly as it had been. The government even went so far as to institute special ateliers of workers who revived outmoded construction techniques so that the new buildings would have the same "authentic" hand-made feel as the old ones. It goes without saying, of course, that the rebuilt city reflected more a myth of the past than the dilapidated reality of what Warsaw had been like before the ravages of the occupation. See also Huyssen (2003: 49–84) on post-unification Berlin.

[84] Williamson (1987), Meyer (2004: 27). Crawford, *RS* 25–6 presents a list of literary *testimonia* for the inscribed publication of *leges*.

[85] Plb. 3.26.1, Joseph. *AJ* 14.188, *CIL* I² 588 (= *RDGE* 22), *CIL* I² 589 (= *RS* 19). Mellor (1978: 328–9), Pucci ben Zeev (1996), cf. Meyer (2004: 95–7). See also Appian's comment on the Peace of Apamaea, 11.39: ταῦτα συγγραψάμενοι τε καὶ ἐς τὸ Καπιτώλιον ἐς δέλτους χαλκᾶς ἀναθέντες, οὗ καὶ τὰς ἄλλας συνθήκας ἀνατιθέασιν. By the same logic, the *lex Icilia*, an agrarian law benefiting plebeians, was set up in Diana's temple on the Aventine, a shrine with strong plebeian associations: Dion. Hal. *AR* 10.31–2.

[86] Sherk in *RDGE* 12–13, Ando (2000: 90–6). On the practice of setting up inscribed archives in Greek *poleis*, see also Sherwin-White (1985: 74). Compare the "*gnomon*" of the Egyptian *idios logos*: Riccobono (1950). Although archival texts of all statutes and *senatus consulta* were lodged among the *tabulae publicae* in the Aerarium at Rome, the inadequacies of Roman archival procedure made it difficult to consult these records: Culham (1989: 102–3, 112–14), cf. Williamson (2005: 394–7).

authenticity of those locally curated copies. For this purpose, reference was often made to the bronze inscription on the Capitol, as the diplomas awarded to auxiliary soldiers on their release from military service demonstrate.[87] These sealed diptych tablets provided the bearer with a copy of the imperial decree in which citizenship and other privileges had been granted, specifying the units and the names of the individual veterans to whom the grant applied. The record of this information is always followed by a formula worded along the following lines:

> descript(um) et recognit(um) ex tabula aenea quae fixa est
> Romae in Capitolio post aedem Iovis O(ptimi) M(aximi) in
> basi Q. Marci Regis pr(aetoris)

transcribed and certified from the bronze tablet that is set up at Rome on the Capitolium behind the temple of Jupiter Optimus Maximus on the base of the statue of the praetor Q. Marcus Rex. (*CIL* XVI 5 ll. 13–15)

Although the precise location of the "original" inscription varies for each grant, such imperial *constitutiones* were typically set up somewhere in the Capitoline precinct (*in Capitolio*), until the rebuilding of the site under Domitian caused them to be moved elsewhere. Similar appeals to the authority of the bronze tablets set up on the Capitol can be found in other contexts throughout the empire.[88]

Despite the proverbial indestructibility of bronze, these tablets did not escape destruction in the fire of 69.[89] Unlike the *spolia* and priceless works of art that had been lost, however, these monuments could be recovered.

---

[87] Williamson (1987), cf. Rhodes (2001, esp. 145–8), Nicolet (1991: 124–5). As Ando (2000: 82 n. 28) points out, "mere posting of a text inscribed on bronze did not make law." Nevertheless, it is the *perceived* authority of the bronze tablets that is at issue here. On diplomas, see Nesselhauf in *CIL* XVI (1936: 147–50), see also Maxfield (1984: 37–43). Meyer (2004: 136–7) discusses Neronian tablets of similar form and function found at Herculanium. A Republican-era bronze inscription (or perhaps the Vespasianic copy of one, see below) recording Pompey's enfranchisement of certain Spanish horsemen *virtutis caussa* (*sic*) has survived in Rome (*CIL* I² 709 = *ILS* 8888, unprovenanced but likely from the Capitol). A list of the locations on the Capitol mentioned in military diplomas before AD 90 appears in Roxan and Holder (2003: 617). See also, with caution, Dušanić (1984).

[88] *AE* 1976: 678. A similar appeal occurs in the prescript of the *Monumentum Ancyranum* (*RG praef.*: *rerum gestarum divi Augusti ... et impensarum ... incisarum in duabus aheneis pilis, quae su[n]t Romae positae, exemplar sub[i]ectum*; πράξεις τε καὶ δωρεαὶ Σεβαστοῦ θεοῦ, ἃς ἀπέλιπεν ἐπὶ Ῥώμης ἐνκεχαραγμένας χαλκαῖς στήλαις δυσίν).

[89] Williamson (1987) argues convincingly for the significance of bronze's durability (famously attested by Hor. *Carm.* 3.30.1–5, also Plin. *NH* 34.99) for its status as the material of choice for inscribed legal texts in the Roman West. Cf. Meyer (2004: 30–6) on the finality and permanence of all *tabulae*, regardless of material.

Suetonius records this important aspect of Vespasian's restoration of the Capitolium:

> aerearumque tabularum tria milia, quae simul conflagraverant, restituenda suscepit undique investigatis exemplaribus: instrumentum imperii pulcherrimum ac vetustissimum, quo continebantur paene ab exordio urbis senatus consulta, plebiscita de societate et foedere ac privilegio cuicumque concessis.

> Searching everywhere for copies, he undertook to restore three thousand bronze tablets, the most beautiful and ancient trappings of empire, which had burned up together with the temple and in which were recorded decisions of the senate and enactments by the people going back almost to the creation of the city, concerning alliances and treaties as well as privileges granted to individuals. (*Vesp.* 8.5)

The language of this passage betrays the scholar's enthusiasm for old documents, but there was more to Vespasian's decision to restore these thousands of tablets than a commitment to preserving the heritage it represented.

Like the other monuments that stood on the Capitol, its bronze inscriptions were a vital part of Roman historical memory. Beyond the historical and antiquarian interest that attached to such documents, the restoration of these inscriptions may also have been necessitated by other more practical considerations. The bronze tablets of the Capitolium were not just relics of the past, they were also functionally and symbolically necessary for the continued stability of Rome's relationship with the subject peoples of the empire. As the monumental proofs on which the authority of much of the written apparatus of imperial law was based, they constituted an *instrumentum imperii* through which the status quo of Roman power was legitimized and maintained. The recovery of these tablets ensured that the same decisions and laws that had applied to provincial subjects in the past continued to be valid. Rebuilding the temple with its bronze inscriptions was thus an important symbolic step not only in restoring peace and order throughout the empire after the turbulence of the civil wars but also in reasserting the authority of law and legal precedent.

Just as the destruction of the Capitolium in the fires of civil war signaled the fragility of the *pax* that the Principate was supposed to provide, the violence of the previous year also made it clear that the emperor owed his position more to military might than to the legal niceties of things such as civil *tribunicia potestas* and *auctoritas*. Perhaps embarrassed by the revelation of this "secret of power" (Tac. *Hist.* 1.4.2: *evolgato imperii arcano*), Vespasian sought to establish a clear legal basis for the legitimacy of his rule. To that end, a formal piece of comitial legislation was enacted and duly inscribed in bronze, which clearly set out the powers and responsibilities of the new emperor. It happens that the first rubric in the portion of the inscription that has come down to us contains the following grant of authority to Vespasian:

> FOEDVSVE CVM QVIBVS VOLET FACERE LICEAT ITA VTI LICVIT DIVO AVG
>
> TI IVLIO CAESARI AVG TIBERIOQVE CLAVDIO CAESARI AVG GERMANICO
>
> He may make [some diplomatic arrangement] or a treaty with whomever he wishes, as it was granted to the divine Augustus, Tiberius Julius Caesar Augustus (= Tiberius), and Tiberius Claudius Caesar Augustus Germanicus (= Claudius). (*CIL* VI 930 = *ILS* 244, *RS* I 39 ll. 1–2)

Such powers were clearly Vespasian's for the taking, but under the polite pretenses of the new regime, it was necessary for the people to bestow this authority on their chosen *princeps*. Although many years of tradition had established the emperors' de facto control over Rome's foreign policy, the negotiation of treaties, alliances, and special grants of privileges to foreigners was still represented as the de jure responsibility of the senate and people. The Vespasianic law thus marks an effort to reaffirm the political principle of continuing *libertas* under an acceptable and accountable *princeps*, whose exercise of power was authorized by the Senate and Roman People.[90]

Modesty and respect for tradition were an integral part of this program. Tacitus notes that the tone of Vespasian's first dispatch to the senate was appropriate for a *princeps*, "civil with regard to himself and effusive toward the *respublica*" (Tac. *Hist.* 4.3.4: *ceterum ut princeps loquebatur, civilia de se et rei publicae egregia*). Although Vespasian was officially authorized to alter the terms of the treaties contained in the bronze tablets of the Capitolium, he chose instead to reestablish both the form and the substance of these documents, which stretched back to the earliest days of Roman imperial expansion. There seems to have been ample precedent for this sort of restoration. The bronze tablets of the Capitol are known to have attracted occasional lightning strikes, and it would have been necessary to replace the melted texts afterwards.[91] There was probably an

---

[90] On the so-called *lex de imperio Vespasiani*, see esp. Brunt (1977), Hurlet (1993: 265–8), cf. Millar (1988).

[91] The omen of lightning striking bronze inscriptions was almost commonplace in the records for the final years of the Republic: Dio 37.9.12, 41.14.3, 42.26.3, 45.17.2, etc. Cf. Rea (2007: 52–3).

ad hoc procedure for dealing with these situations, although we do not have any direct evidence for it.

More concretely, fate has preserved an analogous series of dedicatory inscriptions honoring Jupiter and the Roman People, which Mellor associates with the Sullan-era restoration of the Capitol.[92] The (usually bilingual) texts of these dedications, which range in date from the mid-second century BC to the Sullan period, appear to have been collected and reinscribed together on an enormous travertine base set up on the Capitol following the fire of 83 BC. The texts testify to the gratitude of various Asian cities, leagues, and kings for benefits received at the hands of the Roman people, a theme worth emphasizing in the aftermath of the First Mithridatic war. Like Vespasian's efforts to recover and reinscribe thousands of bronze tablets after the turmoil of 68–69, this monument suggests an attempt to reaffirm Rome's benevolent influence throughout the Mediterranean following a turbulent period of upheaval and civil war.

The issue of *libertas* was not entirely submerged, however, and the way in which the tablets' restoration came about signaled Vespasian's careful regard for Republican tradition. Although Suetonius attributes the restoration of the Capitoline tablets entirely to the initiative of his biographical subject, the process of collecting copies of these texts was, in fact, begun under the auspices of the senate, long before the emperor had returned to Rome. On the first day of the year AD 70, not long after the senate had conferred sole responsibility for rebuilding the Capitolium on Vespasian, that body met again to take up some of the more pressing matters of state. Commissions were established by lot to deal with a variety of projects. As Tacitus reports, one of these was charged "to look into and reestablish the bronze tablets of the laws that had deteriorated with age" (*Hist.* 4.40.2: *quique aera legum vetustate delapsa noscerent figerentque*). The odd wording of this passage suggests that Tacitus is paraphrasing from the recorded *acta* of the senate. Although the claim that tablets made of durable bronze "had deteriorated with age" (*vetustate delapsa*) appears incongruous, this appears to be a common idiom used to mark the restoration of derelict structures of various kinds, including inscriptions in need of republication.[93] Clearly, the *aera delapsa* mentioned here must be the texts that were destroyed in the conflagration on the Capitol.

---

[92] *CIL* I² 725–32 and *AE* 1956: 70–1 (= *ILLRP* 174–81b), Mellor (1978), Degrassi (1952), with photographs in *ILLRP: Imagines* (1965: 85–90). See also Lintott (1978), Badian (1968: 247–9).

[93] Wellesley dryly remarks in a note to his Penguin translation (1964: 239 n. 1), "bronze does not decay with the passage of time." For *vetustate delapsa*, cf. Livy 4.20.7, *CIL* VI 981, 1257 (= *ILS* 218), 31554, IX 4116, XIV 3485 (= *ILS* 3813), and note esp. Dio 57.16.2. For Tacitus'

Once again, a close precedent for establishing a special commission to recopy and restore a large corpus of damaged texts can be found in the aftermath of the Sullan fire, when the senate appointed three envoys to travel throughout the Mediterranean in search of copies of the Sibyl's prophecies, from which the Sibylline books, which had been destroyed in the burning of the temple, might be reconstructed.[94] In light of this procedure, Vespasian's deference to a senatorial commission in the restoration of the bronze tablets suggests a deliberate effort to show respect for the traditional prerogatives of the senate. There were certainly enough scribes on the emperor's staff to accomplish this task, but Vespasian ceded responsibility to the senate so that it might exercise its authority, and thus its *libertas*, as the final guardian of laws and other sacred texts. Not only was this assignment flattering to the senators' sense of their own importance, the unique nature of the legal texts they were asked to investigate served to distract them from the historical issues raised by the emperor's rebuilding of the temple itself and to refocus their attention on the imperial associations of the sanctuary and the stable power that its restoration was designed to reassert.

CONCLUSION: παλαιὸν πάτριον

After the initial clearing of debris from the site had been accomplished, a procession of priests and magistrates mounted the Capitol on June 21. They were led by soldiers who had lucky names carrying magical branches, followed by the Vestal virgins and children who sprinkled the site with holy water. The significance of much of this ritual, which was suggested by the *haruspices*, is now obscure, but it does not seem unreasonable to suggest that the soldiers with auspicious names were there to represent the military and imperial associations of the Capitoline cult.[95] They no doubt signified the Romans' hope for continued good fortune in their military operations, particularly with regard to the ongoing siege of Jerusalem, which had been left in the hands of the emperor's son Titus. There followed the sacrifice of a *suovetaurilia* and prayers to the Capitoline triad. Plautius Aelianus presided on behalf of the pontifical college, because Vespasian as *pontifex*

---

use of the *acta senatus*, see Groag (1897: 711–29, esp. 728), Syme (1958: 271–86), (1982b: 76–80). See also Chilver and Townend (1985: 52–3).

[94] Dion. Hal. 4.62.5–6, Tac. *Ann.* 6.12. Parke (1988: 137–40). The names of the three envoys are recorded by Fenestella *ap.* Lact. *Inst.* 1.6.14 (= frag. 18 Peter). A committee of three was also appointed under Tiberius, when inscriptions destroyed by a fire were recovered (Dio 57.16.2).

[95] Tac. *Hist.* 4.53.2–4. The date has no known significance in the Roman calendar: Chilver and Townend (1985: 64).

maximus had not yet returned to Rome, and the prayers themselves were offered by none other than Helvidius Priscus, who, as praetor, was officially the ranking magistrate in the city.[96]

The ceremony culminated with Helvidius taking hold of the fillets that had been wrapped around a stone (*lapis*) and leading the assembled group of magistrates, priests, senators, knights, and citizens as they collectively dragged this "giant rock" (*saxum ingens*) into position using a harness of ropes (Tac. *Hist.* 4.53.3). Townend has identified the boulder in question as the *lapidem... informem et rudem* (Lact. *Inst.* 1.20.37), which the Romans worshipped as Terminus.[97] This god of boundaries, whose fixity was essential to its purpose, apparently had been dislodged during the destruction of the enormous *aedes* that housed it. In accordance with the *haruspices*' instructions to preserve the temple's ancient form, the populace of Rome was enlisted to help return the Terminus stone to its proper situation. By arranging for this ritual act to take place in his absence and by engaging the senate and people in its performance, the new emperor (aided by his agent Vestinus and the Etruscan *haruspices*) worked to mollify any concerns about the public status of the temple, by encouraging the participants to remember the site's imperial associations instead. The restoration of the stone recalled the original foundation of the temple, in which Etruscan augury had indicated that Terminus could not be relocated.

The final stages in the process of reconstruction were carried out under the direction of the *princeps* himself. Vespasian returned to Rome in October of 70 and immediately set to work on the restoration of the Capitol. He literally dug right in, carrying off a load of rubble on his own back, and gestured for others to join in the work as well. Although he arranged the funding of the project from his own private fisc, the emperor seems to have continued to involve the Roman people in the work as much as possible.[98] We do not know the details of the actual dedication ceremony

---

[96] As a holder of two priesthoods, Aelianus was a figure of great religious authority: *PIR*² P 480. He also was a fitting person to stress the triumphal and imperial associations of the Capitol, because he would be rewarded by Vespasian with the *ornamenta triumphalia* for military achievements that had gone unrecognized by Nero: *CIL* XIV 3608 (= *ILS* 986). In light of Helvidius' earlier proposal about the financing of the reconstruction, Darwall-Smith (1996: 44) regards his participation in this ceremony as "ironic," but it is more likely evidence of Vespasian's conciliatory attitude toward the senate at this point in his reign. See also Sailor (2008: 221–3). The suggestion of Townend (1987: 247), followed by Wardle (1996: 213–17) that Helvidius, as some sort of protest, arranged for this ceremony to take place in the emperor's absence also seems implausible.

[97] Townend (1987: 245).

[98] Dio (Xiph.) 66.10.2, Suet. *Vesp.* 8.5, Keaveney (1987). Note also Suet. *Vesp.* 18, and the debate between Casson (1978) and Brunt (1980b) about the significance of this passage.

for the rebuilt temple, but it was customary to mark such an event with a banquet and elaborate public games. Catulus' dedicatory games for his rebuilt Capitolium had been notable for their opulence – they were the first Roman spectacles at which *velaria* were used to provide the audience with shade.[99] As the man responsible for the conception of the great Flavian Amphitheater, Vespasian can be expected to have followed this model.

The critical moment, however, came in June of 71, when the emperor's son Titus arrived back in Rome to celebrate the completion of the Roman reconquest of Judaea. Their triumph was a powerful unifying spectacle, which brought before the eyes of the inhabitants of the city the results of a war that had all but restored tranquility to a turbulent region of the empire. Like every Roman triumph before and since, the Flavian celebration culminated in a procession up the Capitol.[100] Before sacrifices were made to Jupiter Optimus Maximus, however, the two *imperatores* waited, in accordance with what the historian Josephus describes as "an ancient custom" (*BJ* 7.153: παλαιὸν πάτριον), for the signal that their star captive, the rebel leader Simon ben Gioras, had been killed and laid out on the Gemonian steps. With this final act of violence, the peace and security of the Roman empire was restored to its ancient balance.[101]

The emperor's triumphal ascent of the Capitol marked the culmination of an ongoing effort to create a more suitable place for the temple of Jupiter Optimus Maximus in Roman memory. The burning of the temple just eighteen months earlier had created an inauspicious circumstance in which to begin the reign of a new emperor. Not only did its destruction raise doubts about the reliability of the Imperial *pax* established by Augustus, but the necessity of rebuilding the temple also conjured up the memory of unfortunate Republican parallels that, if followed through, could have prompted difficult questions about the nature of liberty in Augustus' (and thus Vespasian's) restored *respublica*. Just as the second burning of the temple drew people's attention to the recurrent circumstance of civil war, so too did its second rebuilding occasion memories of an association with Republican *libertas*. Vespasian was faced with a stark dilemma: He could

---

[99] Val. Max. 2.4.6, Plin. *NH* 19.23, cf. Stambaugh (1978: 567).

[100] Elements of triumphal ritual had been doubled and attached to the temple of Mars Ultor in the Forum of Augustus, but the Capitol remained the customary focus of the ritual: Bonneford (1987: 252–62), cf. Plin. *Pan.* 5.2–3.

[101] On the importance of the Judaean victory to the justification of Flavian ascendency, see Overman (2002), also Brilliant (1999). Beard (2003: 554) notes that Josephus describes everything about this triumph as "customary" or "traditional." She also argues (2007: 129–32) that executions did not in fact constitute a clearly defined element of triumphal ritual.

not shirk his responsibility to rebuild the Capitolium, but to do so would call attention to the problematic nature of his position vis-à-vis *libertas*.

Happily for Vespasian, the temple was not only a focal point in Roman discussions about their public freedom, it was also the symbolic center of their imperial power. The rebuilding of the Capitol offered an opportunity to reshape memory by reassessing the nature of this tradition in a way that called attention to something the Principate, and especially the Flavian dynasty, could claim to do well – the propagation and maintenance of Rome's military dominance throughout the Mediterranean. Vespasian did not so much redefine what the Capitolium signified as reemphasize particular aspects of the tradition and encourage certain memories to form instead of others. When the senators voted in January of 70 to appoint a commission to see to the restoration of the bronze documents that had been destroyed on the Capitol, they were operating in accordance with established Republican precedents. More importantly, they were also helping to further Vespasian's efforts to highlight the temple's status as the seat of Rome's imperial majesty. This message was underscored by the initial ceremony of restoration, at which the Terminus stone was reinstalled, and in the celebration of the Judaean triumph, when the Roman community gave thanks for the favor that Jupiter continued to bestow on their *imperium*.

The theme of *libertas* was not entirely ignored, however. In showing so much respect for the prerogatives of the senate as the official organ through which the ritual and legal administration of the Roman empire continued to function, Vespasian may have hoped to suggest that liberty could still exist under the right sort of *princeps*. Senators were employed to recopy and restore the bronze tablets on which the legal machinery of the empire was based, and there was even a dramatic ceremony in which one of the loudest advocates for the prerogatives of this order was appointed to lead the populace in returning the Terminus stone to its proper position as the guardian of Rome's boundaries. Ultimately, however, these rituals and policies served only to reinforce a vision of Roman tradition that served the emperor's claim to power. In the end, even the most skeptical of senators fulfilled their roles, accepting what liberty their sovereign was ready to grant them. But the sense of continuity with the Republic that these rituals were supposed to enact remained unstable, as it continued to stir up new conflicts about how best to remember this receding past.

3

CONTROL

An inscription set up by the *sodales Titi* to honor Vespasian in 78 includes among that emperor's titles the remarkable designation "preserver of public rites and restorer of sacred temples" (*CIL* VI 934 = *ILS* 252: *conservatori caerimoniarum publicarum et restitutori aedium sacrarum*). These epithets reflect a confluence of values – religious scruple, commitment to tradition, and concern for the preservation of public spaces – that first came to prominence in Vespasian's efforts to rebuild the Capitolium. The importance of urban renewal in Flavian self-presentation is also suggested by Suetonius, who describes Rome as being "in a wretched condition from old fires and cave-ins" (*Vesp.* 8.5: *deformis urbs veteribus incendiis ac ruinis erat*) at the start of Vespasian's reign and lists some of the steps the emperor took to encourage rebuilding.[1] For reasons discussed at the end of the previous chapter, much of this new construction went hand-in-hand with a celebration of the emperor's military accomplishments. The golden implements of the Temple of Jerusalem, which had been paraded through the streets of Rome in the shared triumph of Vespasian and Titus in 71, were put on permanent display in the Temple of Peace.[2] Likewise, the construction of the enormous stone amphitheater that was destined to become the most iconic monument of the Flavian dynasty was also evidently connected to the Judean conquest. It has been identified as a manubial dedication, explicitly funded out of the commander's share of the Jewish spoils.[3]

---

[1] Darwall-Smith (1996: 41), Levick (1999a: 124–9). Most of the damage was due to the fire of 64. Cf. *CIL* VI 931 (= *ILS* 245), 1257 (= *ILS* 218), *RIC* II² 67–157 nos. 109–10, 194–5, 382, 1360, Castagnoli (1981).

[2] Joseph. *BJ* 7.148–9, 161. Beard (2007: 152), Millar (2005), Anderson (1984: 101–13), Darwall-Smith (1996: 58–65).

[3] Alföldy (1995), Millar (2005: 113–19). See also Gunderson (2003).

The link between Rome's renewal and imperial conquest was perhaps most evident in 75, when Vespasian exercised the privilege of enlarging the sacred boundary of the city, or *pomerium*. This religious ritual, which was thought to derive from an ancient Etruscan practice, suggested a refounding of the city. The honor of performing it was said to be reserved for those who had added to the territory of the Roman people through conquest and was likely justified in this case by the seizure of Jewish lands and the imposition of veteran settlements at sites such as Caesarea and Emmaus.[4] The four-year interval between the triumph and the expansion of the *pomerium* suggests that the latter step was not undertaken lightly, even though the privilege of conducting this ceremony was already listed among the special powers of the emperor in the law that formally established Vespasian as *princeps* in December of 69.[5] The immediate precedent, mentioned in that same legal grant, was an extension of the *pomerium* by Claudius in 49, an enlargement of the city that had been justified by the conquest of Britain, a campaign in which Vespasian also participated as commander of the legion II Augusta.[6] By repeating Claudius' ritual act, Vespasian showed regard for tradition while also calling attention to his own military accomplishments. It was not the last time that a member of the Flavian dynasty would emulate the policies of the antiquarian-minded Claudius.

Perhaps less visible, but more profound in its long-term repercussions, was the procedure whereby the rebuilding of the temple of Jupiter Optimus Maximus was itself connected to Vespasian's triumph over the Jews. Following the destruction of the Jewish Temple of Jerusalem, the tithe that had been offered by the faithful for its maintenance was converted by the emperor into an official tax to be levied annually on all Jews throughout the empire. The revenue thus generated went to pay for the restoration of the Capitolium. This intervention by the emperor into an alien custom prevented the Jews from fulfilling their traditional obligations to the temple while simultaneously forcing them to subsidize a pagan cult. It was a harsh penalty, but one that many Romans are likely to have regarded as just.[7]

---

[4] Gell. *NA* 13.14.3: *habebat autem ius proferendi pomerii, qui populum Romanum agro de hostibus capto auxerant,* cf. Tac. *Ann.* 12.23.2, Varr. *LL* 5.143. *CIL* VI 31538a–c (b = *ILS* 248), 40854 (= *MW* 51), Castagnoli (1981: 264), *LTUR* IV 103 s.v. "Pomerium" [Andreussi]. For probable numismatic commemorations of the ritual, see *RIC* II² 127 nos. 943–5, 951–2. Jewish lands and Emmaus: Joseph. *BJ* 7.216–17, Caesarea: Goodman (2007: 438–9).

[5] *CIL* VI 930 (= *ILS* 244 = *RS* I 39) ll. 14–16.

[6] Tac. *Ann.* 12.24, *CIL* VI 31537a–d (a = *ILS* 213), 37022–4, 40852. Levick (1999a: 71), Huzar (1984: 649). Boatwright (1984: 37–40). For Vespasian's service in Britain, see Suet. *Vesp.* 4.1, Tac. *Agr.* 13.3, *Hist.* 3.44, Birley (2005: 232–3).

[7] Joseph. *BJ* 7.218, Dio (Xiph.) 66.7.2, Goodman (2007: 433–42), Rives (2005).

Something changed, however, after another fire destroyed Vespasian's Capitolium during the brief but disaster-plagued reign of his elder son Titus.[8] When Domitian became *princeps* following the death of his brother in 81, he spared no expense in rebuilding the temple of Jupiter Optimus Maximus. The new temple was an extraordinarily opulent construction, with a golden roof worth 12,000 talents and columns of Pentelic marble imported from Attica.[9] Domitian's own experience as a survivor of the siege of 69 no doubt encouraged a special attachment to the Capitoline cult. To celebrate the rededication, elaborate games were instituted in honor of the Capitoline triad, with lavish prizes for the victors.[10] All of this, presumably, was paid for out of the *fiscus Iudaicus*, a fund that Domitian is said to have administered "with extreme severity" (*acerbissime*). Apparently his agents sought to extract the tax from all Jews, regardless of whether they continued to openly confess themselves as practitioners of the Jewish religion. Suetonius recounts his own experience as a boy during Domitian's reign witnessing the humiliation of a ninety-year-old man who was examined in open court to see if he had been circumcised.[11] Although overt hostility toward Jews was not uncommon in Roman society at the time, these actions appear to have crossed a line. Following Domitian's death, his successor Nerva immediately suspended the aggressive prosecutions and issued coins to mark the remission of the *calumnia* associated with the Jewish tax.[12]

Whether Domitian's excessive zeal in the administration of the *fiscus Iudaicus* reflects a change in official policy or simply a shift in public perception is difficult to know with certainty. Part of the problem is that the surviving criticisms of Domitian were all written after he was assassinated by his wife's steward.[13] The posthumous nature of these criticisms makes them suspicious, especially because (as Nerva's coinage testifies) the next

---

[8] Dio (Xiph.) 66.24.2. Cf. Fredrick (2003: 199–200).

[9] Plut. *Popl.* 15.3–4, Suet. *Dom.* 5, cf. Mart. 9.3.7–8, Sil. *Pun.* 3.622–4. For Domitian's Capitolium, see Darwall-Smith (1996: 105–10), *LTUR* III 151 [De Angeli], Packer (2003: 174). The precinct was decorated with statues of the emperor fashioned in precious metals: Plin. *Pan.* 52.3, Suet. *Dom.* 13.2, but this is to be expected, because there were many such statues throughout the city: cf. Mart. 1.70.5–6, Scott (1936: 98–9).

[10] Suet. *Dom.* 4.4, Coleman (1986: 3097–8), Jones (1992: 103–4).

[11] Suet. *Dom.* 12.2, Thompson (1982).

[12] *RIC* II 227–8 nos. 58, 72, 82: FISCI IVDAICI CALVMNIA SVBLATA. For Roman attitudes toward Jewish custom, see, e.g., Tac. *Hist.* 5.4–5, Mart. 7.82, Isaac (2004: 446–84), also Goodman (1989) and (2005).

[13] There were various accounts of how Domitian met his end: See Suet. *Dom.* 16.2–17.3, Dio (Zon.) 67.14.5–15.6, (Xiph.) 67.17. For the most part, the sources agree that the assassination was the result of a palace plot. We can discount the suggestion that Nerva was somehow involved: Syme (1958: 3), Jones (1992: 193–6).

regime encouraged negative portrayals of Domitian to benefit from the contrast they provided. In light of these concerns, scholarship of the past two generations has done much to complicate our picture of Domitian and his accomplishments. K. H. Waters, one of the pioneers in this effort, has demonstrated that the much-celebrated "rebirth of liberty" under Nerva and his successor Trajan did not in fact correlate with any substantive changes in imperial policy.[14] If anything, it seems that Trajan did more to consolidate the power of the *princeps*, expanding many of the authoritarian policies for which Domitian is supposed to have been reviled. In light of this inconsistency, it is possible to conclude that the real difference between Domitian and Trajan was that one had the misfortune to be the last member of his dynastic line, whereas the other could rely on successive generations of "good emperors" to burnish his reputation as the "best" (*optimus*) *princeps* of all.[15]

To assess the role of the Republican tradition in public memory during Domitian's reign, therefore, we must confront the additional screen of memory distortion that these posthumous attacks create. On one hand, it is clear from Domitian's own actions and from the characterizations of him in contemporary sources that this emperor displayed an active dedication to the cults of Roman state religion, and especially to Jupiter in his manifold guises.[16] Yet despite his own displays of piety and efforts to encourage good behavior in others, Domitian's public commitment to moral and religious renewal was ultimately overshadowed by hostile rumors and charges of clandestine immorality. Under different circumstances, the strict discipline that Domitian imposed in matters of religion might have been greeted as a welcome display of moral rigor. Instead, his policies only fed into the atmosphere of resentment and mistrust that circulated around him. Assuming that Domitian did not set out to earn a reputation as an insincere and brutal villain, the question we must ask is what, if anything, he did to bring this failure on himself.

It is not the aim of this chapter to exonerate Domitian by exposing the bias of the posthumous sources, however. The attacks of later writers are not simply distortions to be discredited and replaced with some "fairer" version of events. What they offer, in fact, is an opportunity to

---

[14] Waters 1969, followed by Jones (1992: 163). See also Ramage (1983), Rogers (1960), Pleket (1961), Waters (1964), Evans (1976). Recognition of the need to "mitigate the influence of Tacitus and Pliny and redeem the memory of Domitian from infamy and oblivion" can be traced back to Syme (1930).

[15] Vinson (1989: 339): "Domitian's only real crime was to be the last Flavian." See also Jones (1992: 160–1).

[16] Scott (1936: 90–2).

see the official policy of an emperor from an oppositional point of view. By considering the full range of responses to Domitian's moral policies, both sympathetic to skeptical, we can better understand how and why an emperor's attempts to exploit Republican tradition might go awry. For the purposes of this discussion, I will take as emblematic of Domitian's failure to manage Republican memory the fate of the chief Vestal virgin Cornelia, who was convicted in or around 91 of having violated the chastity required by her priesthood.[17] Ostensibly, this was a case of immorality exposed and justice rendered. Cornelia was buried alive as punishment for her crimes, following the ancient custom. But Domitian's detractors were able to see a different narrative.

An examination of this episode and the reactions it provoked reveals two major stumbling blocks that Domitian encountered in his effort to associate himself with the restoration of ancient religious discipline. The first difficulty had its roots in the personalization of authority that takes place under a monarchical system. In response to the severity of Domitian's policies, many of his critics leveled their own accusations of immorality, complaining that the emperor did not hold himself to the same standards as his subjects. Although emotionally effective, this line of attack offers a rather limited critique of the Principate as an institution. By focusing on rumor and innuendo, the posthumous critics of Domitian who took this tack avoided any direct consideration of the underlying realities of power that enabled the emperors to appropriate the Republican moral inheritance for their own ends.

The other, more essential, problem facing Domitian lay in the ambiguity of the Republican tradition itself.[18] The complex history of Roman religion was such that it also gave rise to memories that could be used to call into question Domitian's punitive approach to moral reform. Direct criticism of the emperor did not come easily, however, and it was left to the condemned Vestal herself to challenge the legitimacy of her punishment on these terms. Taking advantage of the public venue provided by her own execution, Cornelia was able to put forward an alternative vision of her place within the history of her priesthood. Although it could not save her life, this strategy of direct confrontation enabled Cornelia to expose the arbitrary

---

[17] *PIR*² C 1481, *FOS* 275, *FS* 248. The date derives from Jerome (*Chron.* 2.161 Schöne), accepted also by Grelle (1980: 347). In contrast, Gsell (1894: 80–1) and Vinson (1989: 436) follow the Armenian version of Eusebius (*Chron.* 2.160 Schöne), placing the punishment of Cornelia in late 89. Their preference for this date seems to rest on a misinterpretation of the reference to Vesta in Stat. *Silv.* 1.1.36, however (see below, n. 45).

[18] Cf. Gordon (1990: 188–90).

served only his cruelty and lust for self-aggrandizement certainly involves elements of distortion and caricature, but even tendentious fiction can be useful if it helps us to understand the conceptual framework within which a vicious *princeps* was defined.

Turning to the structure of the letter itself, it is clear that the news with which Pliny begins his discussion is presented so as to elicit as much sympathy for the exiled Licinianus as possible (§1–4). The fact that a once-promising Roman aristocrat has turned up in Sicily wearing Greek clothes, employed in a traditionally Greek occupation (as a professor of rhetoric), gives reason to reflect on the extremity of his tragic reversal. Pliny introduces Licinianus' own musings about the fickleness of fortune (§2) with observations that suggest the extent to which Pliny was able to identify with his subject's plight. Not only has a senator become an exile, but a fellow orator has been reduced to the status of a mere rhetor (§1). This loss of status was tied up with the issues of moral value already discussed in Chapter 1.[24]

Although the nature of Licinianus' crime was evidently well known, it is significant that the author waits to mention this aspect of his biography until the pathos of his circumstance has been fully established. Lest the reader dismiss this suffering as "what that man deserves, who sullied these very pursuits with the crime of *incestum*" (§4: *dignum tamen illum qui haec ipsa studia incesti scelere macularit*), Pliny proceeds immediately to raise doubts about the official story of Licinianus' guilt. Following good rhetorical practice, Pliny supports this exculpatory proposition with a detailed narrative of events. The move is perhaps more suited to the courtroom than to a friendly letter, but apparently it can be justified by the author's selection of C. Cornelius Minicianus, an equestrian dependent from Pliny's native region north of the Po, as his addressee.[25] As Pliny says near the close of the letter, "rumor presents the outcomes rather than the full sequence of events" (§15: *summam enim rerum nuntiat fama, non ordinem*).

Although Licinianus' reemergence as a lecturer in Sicily provides an opportunity to revisit these events from a new perspective, Pliny's account of the trial and punishment of the *Vestalis maxima* Cornelia (§6–9) is by far the most compelling part of the letter. This story is relevant to the question of Licinianus' guilt insofar as it raises the possibility of Cornelia's own innocence (which, in turn, would obviously exonerate anyone implicated in her supposed corruption). As Pliny describes things (§11), the arrest and forced confession of Licinianus were essentially an exercise in damage

---

[24] Hoffer (1999: 164).
[25] *PIR²* C 1406, Sherwin-White (1966: 14).

control, undertaken to counteract the public resentment that the punishments of Cornelia and her supposed corruptor, the equestrian Celer, had stirred up. The emperor was beside himself, it seems, because these brutal executions, which he hoped would stand as shining examples of the revival of ancient Roman moral restraint, had not gone as planned. The objects of his disciplinary fervor had provoked popular discontent by objecting to their fate. It therefore became necessary for someone to confess to an involvement in their crimes and vindicate the justice of those punishments. In exchange for his cooperation with this plan, Pliny claims that Licinianus was allowed to escape with his life and withdraw into a "soft exile" (§13: *exsilium molle*).

Modern defenders of Domitian's reputation call attention to the fact that Licinianus remained an exile at the time of Pliny's writing, which they cite as evidence of his "manifest guilt" in the matter.[26] For all his *clementia*, Nerva permitted Licinianus only to relocate to Sicily; he did not restore him to the senate or even remove the interdiction of fire and water that kept him from returning to Italy (§14). This might indicate that there was further evidence of his guilt, but it could also mean that the nature of the crime in which Licinianus had admitted complicity (§5: *confessus est quidem incestum*) was so grave that no emperor could grant him a pardon without provoking outrage. The question of Licinianus' guilt is not really the issue, however, and by engaging in this debate one risks missing the larger significance of Pliny's letter. In fact, Pliny concedes the possibility of Licinianus' guilt, thereby shifting the terms of the discussion so as to evade the trap that modern commentators would like to set for him. As Pliny presents it, the case is not simply about what Licinianus did or did not do; it is about the public perception of the legitimacy of the process by which justice was administered. As the successful advocate must have realized, the guilt of the condemned matters less if the judge can be shown to be a tyrant.

The importance of this insight becomes clearer when we consider Pliny's account of the original conviction and punishment of Cornelia. The vividness with which her final moments are described underscores the impression that the real topic of Pliny's letter is not the fate of a former praetor but rather the tyrannical cruelty of (the now defunct) Domitian. However much the reader might feel sorry for a Roman senator reduced to scraping out his living as a rhetor in the provinces, most will find the prospect of being buried alive a great deal more terrifying. The implicit horror of this

---

[26] Vinson (1989: 434). See also Sherwin-White (1966: 282), Pleket (1961), Jones (1992: 101–2), Carlon (2009: 200).

event, to which Pliny may have been an eyewitness, forms the backdrop against which all of Domitian's subsequent behavior will be judged.[27] It is also at this moment, however, that the task of interpreting the emperor's actions becomes most fraught with ambiguity. Regarding Cornelia's noble death, Pliny admits, "I do not know whether she was innocent, but she certainly at least was held to be innocent" (§8: *nescio an innocens, certe tamquam innocens ducta est*). He does not need to deny her guilt – the fact that she behaved as if she were innocent is enough to raise doubts about the legitimacy of the conviction. Given the ambiguity of the emperor's position and that of the tradition he was trying to exploit, these doubts are sufficient to undermine the moral authority that Domitian had hoped to enhance with the punishment of Cornelia's supposed crime.

SAECULUM SUUM

According to the ancient stereotype, a defining characteristic of the tyrant was his turbulent emotional state. This preconception is reflected in the language of Pliny's letter, where verbs such as *fremebat, aestuabat*, and *ardebat* suggest that Domitian was ruled by violent passions. Pliny also says that Domitian "longed to bury Cornelia... alive" (§6: *Corneliam... defodere vivam concupisset*), further associating the emperor's actions with an underlying passionate irrationality.[28] Whether or not this is a fair characterization of Domitian's state of mind, it is not too difficult to see how such an impression might have been formed in this case. What Pliny does not mention, but perhaps assumes general knowledge of, is that this was not the first time Cornelia had been tried for *incestum* under Domitian. We owe most of our information about the earlier trial to Suetonius, who records that Domitian punished unchastity among the Vestals on two separate occasions. In the earlier trial, which we can assign to the winter of 82–3, three priestesses, a Varonilla and two Oculatae, were condemned,

---

[27] The precise chronology of Pliny's early career is uncertain, but in 91 he would have had much to gain by remaining active in Rome. Sherwin-White (1966: 74) dates Pliny's service as *quaestor imperatoris* (*ILS* 2927) to 90 (cf. *PIR*² P 490). But it might be that this came a year earlier and that 91 was the year of his tribunate: Syme (1958: 653). In either case, a new senator was likely to stay in the capital during the interval between his quaestorship and praetorship: Eck (1997: 75).

[28] Dunkle (1967: 153–5). Domitian's ruddy complexion also contributed to this assessment of his inner psyche: Suet. *Dom.* 18, Tac. *Agr.* 45.2, Plin. *Pan.* 48.4, cf. Sen. *Ira* 1.1.4, ps.-Arist. *Physiognomonika* 812a. Sulla too was noted for this condition: Sen. *Ep.* 11.4; recall too the fit of rage that precipitated his death, as noted in Chapter 2.

but Cornelia was acquitted of any involvement in their crimes.[29] It did not take much imagination to interpret the emperor's insistence on a second trial, after the passage of what Suetonius describes as "a lengthy interval" (*Dom.* 8.4: *longo intervallo*), as a sign of pathological fixation with the case. Also, the inconsistency in the nature of Cornelia's punishment could suggest vindictive reprisal. Whereas the Vestals condemned in the earlier proceedings had been allowed to choose the manner of their deaths, Domitian ordered that Cornelia and her seducers be punished "according to the ancient custom" (Suet. *Dom.* 8.3: *more veteri*) in the sequel. Pliny describes for us in detail what that meant (§7–10).[30]

Beyond his speculative and unflattering characterization of Domitian's tyrannical psychology, Pliny also suggests a more rational justification for Cornelia's execution. In Pliny's words, the purpose of the emperor's desire to bury her was "so that he might be thought to have enlightened his age with examples of this sort" (§6: *ut qui inlustrari saeculum suum eiusmodi exemplis arbitraretur*). Taken on its own, this explanation is probably much closer to the truth. As was discussed in Chapter 1, the provision of moral *exempla* had been an integral part of Augustus' restoration of freedom to the *respublica* and continued to represent one of the primary obligations of the Roman *principes* thereafter.[31] This responsibility for moral leadership was thoroughly intertwined with the emperor's unique position in the state religion. Since the time of Augustus, the *auctoritas* of the *princeps* had been bolstered by his responsibilities as Rome's chief priest (*pontifex maximus*) and a member of all the major priestly colleges.[32] It was in this role that Domitian's oversight of Cornelia's punishment provided another opportunity to revive Roman morals.

Of particular interest to Domitian was his status as one of the *quindecimviri sacris faciundis*, the board of fifteen priests responsible for

---

[29] Suet. *Dom.* 8.3–4, Philostr. *VA* 7.6. FOS n. 275, PIR² C 1481, PIR¹ V 197, PIR² A 303. Once again, the evidence of the chronographers is unclear. The Armenian version of Eusebius (*Chron.* 2.160 Schöne) places the first prosecution in 2098 Abr. (= October 81–September 82), but Jerome (2.161 Schöne) puts it in the following year. According to Dio (Xiph.) 67.3.3–4.1, these trials took place before Domitian set out on his first German campaign. See Gsell (1894: 80), Grelle (1980: 345). In the interval between trials, Cornelia rose to the position of *Vestalis maxima*, which likely means she was the oldest serving member of the priesthood, who acted as its chief representative (Ov. *Fast.* 4.639: *quae natu maxima virgo est*, cf. Tac. *Ann.* 11.32.2). See also Pigoń (1999)

[30] Bauman (1996: 94–6).

[31] See also Baltrusch (1989: 133–89, esp. 180–3).

[32] Aug. *RG* 8.5, 67, Taylor (1931: 183–4), Strothmann (2000: 42–5), Bowersock (1990), Beard, North, and Price (1998: 186–92), Wardman (1982: 73–4), Schumacher (2006). See also Orlin (2007).

organizing the *ludi Saeculares*. This festival, which was supposed to be celebrated once every century, marked both the emergence of a new generation and the cyclical return of a renewed sense of communal morality. The secular games had been produced to much fanfare by Augustus in 17 BC, to mark the dawning of a new era of peace, prosperity, and "upright morals" (*probos mores*).[33] Following this example, the emperor Claudius seized an opportunity to demonstrate the blessings of his own reign by celebrating the secular games again in AD 47, although he had to do a fair amount of tinkering with the calendar to justify repeating the celebration, which was supposed to be a once-in-a-lifetime event, so soon. Tacitus, who was himself a proud member of the college of *quindecemviri*, confirms that there was uncertainty about the calculations. He was involved as both a priest and a praetor in AD 88, when Domitian resolved this dispute by hosting the *ludi Saeculares* yet again, apparently correcting the arithmetic of both of his deified predecessors.[34] Whether by chance or because of the official condemnation of this emperor's memory, the epigraphic record of Domitian's games does not survive, but other archaeological and numismatic traces do exist, including a *sestertius* with a depiction of the emperor standing in front of the temple of Jupiter Optimus Maximus, leading three kneeling matrons in prayer (Fig. 3.1).[35] It seems likely that Pliny has this bold assertion of authority in matters of state religion in mind when he says that Domitian hoped that the execution of Cornelia would provide an example for "his age" (§6 *saeculum suum*).

CORRECTIO MORUM

By all accounts, Domitian appeared to take his responsibility as Rome's moral guardian quite seriously. The pursuit of a deliberate policy was apparent to Suetonius, who lists the trials of the Vestals under the rubric of Domitian's "correction of morals" (*Dom.* 8.3: *correctio morum*).[36]

---

[33] Hor. *Saec.* 45, Strothmann (2000: 49–56), Wardman (1982: 72), Zanker (1988: 167–72), also Edwards (1993: 58–9). See Beard, North, and Price (1998: 71–2, 201–6), Pighi (1965), also *CIL* VI 32323–35 (excerpted in *ILS* 5050, 5050ᵃ), Liberman (1998), Boyce (1938).

[34] Tac. *Ann.* 11.11.1. Censorinus, *Nat.* 17.11, Kienast (1996) 115, cf. *Inscr. It.* XIII.1, p. 63 (= MW 61): *a(nno) p(ost) R(omam) c(onditam) DCCCXLI . . . ex s.c. ludi saeculares facti.* Suet. *Claud.* 21.2, Momigliano (1934: 27), Huzar (1984: 648), Bengtson (1979: 271). Suet. *Dom.* 4.3 suggests (inaccurately) that Domitian simply followed Augustus' original calculations: cf. Syme (1958: 65 n. 6).

[35] *RIC* II² 307 nos. 610–11 (= *BMCRE* II 393 no. 424), cf. Ryberg (1955: 174–7), Hill (1965). See also *RIC* II² 307–9 nos. 606–31, *LTUR* IV: 341–3 s.v. "Stadium Domitiani," [Virgili], Suet. *Dom.* 4.3. On the condemnation of Domitian's memory, Flower (2006: 240–62).

[36] Grelle (1980: 348–52), Bauman (1996: 94).

Figure 3.1. *Sestertius* Commemorating the *Ludi Saeculares* of AD 88. Reverse: Domitian leads three Roman matrons in prayer. (© Trustees of the British Museum, *BMCRE* II 393 no. 424)

Among other things, the emperor showed his commitment to fostering an era of moral renewal by outlawing the practice of male castration and encouraging prosecutions under the *lex Scantinia*, a somewhat obscure law that criminalized sodomy.[37] In 85, he revived and reinvented the office of censor, a powerful Republican magistracy that had fallen into general disuse under the Principate. Through their control of the census rolls, which recorded the social rank (*ordo*) of every Roman citizen, the censors were in a unique position to exercise oversight over moral conduct. They were expected not only to evaluate property qualifications, but also to take note of (*notare*) shameful behavior by stripping individual senators and knights of their rank when they misbehaved. This aspect of the censor's power had been deployed with particular effectiveness by M. Porcius Cato, the Republican icon who came to be known by the epithet "the Censor" for his unprecedented strictness during his tenure of this office in 184 BC.[38]

Although the census was carried out on numerous occasions during Augustus' reign, the first *princeps* never bothered to add this particular

[37] Prohibition of castration: Suet. *Dom.* 7.1, Stat. *Silv.* 3.4.73–6, 4.3.13, Mart. 6.2.2. *Lex Scantinia*: Suet. *Dom.* 8.3. For the possible terms of this law, see Mommsen (1899: 703–4).

[38] Among the sources listed in Broughton *MRR* I 374, note esp. Val. Max. 2.9.3: *et censor et Cato, duplex severitatis exemplum*, also Livy 39.42.5–43.5, Astin (1978: 78–80). On the censor's moral oversight, which Livy 4.8.2 terms *morum disciplinaeque regimen*, see Dion. Hal. *AR* 20.13.3, Astin (1988), Baltrusch (1989: 7–30), Fantham (1977: 46–8), Nicolet (1980: 73–88). More generally, Kunkel and Wittmann (1995: 391–471), Lintott (1999: 115–20).

title to his long list of public offices. Following the brief and contentious censorship of Paullus Aemilius Lepidus and L. Munatius Plancus in 22 BC, the office was occupied only twice, by Claudius and L. Vitellius in AD 47–8, followed by Vespasian and Titus in 73–4. On each occasion, the revival of this Republican institution brought with it an expectation for renewed emphasis on issues of moral conduct.[39] This expectation would have been particularly appropriate when Domitian revived the office in 85. Unlike Claudius, whose censorship was noted for its mildness, Domitian seems to have tried to follow the Catonian model. Suetonius records that he removed one senator from the rolls for taking up pantomime and that he disqualified a knight from serving in the courts who had reconciled with his wife after accusing her of adultery.[40]

Because our information is limited to isolated anecdotes, we cannot assess the full extent to which Domitian exercised his power of *notatio*. The actual frequency of its use is irrelevant, however, because ancient perceptions of imperial policy need not line up with what modern scholars might determine to be its true significance. Even a limited application of this power could seem excessive to those on the receiving end of Domitian's censorial surveillance. During the Republic, the threat of expulsion from the senate was statistically quite remote, but the *nota* nevertheless continued to be regarded as a potent tool for moral control. The same would hold true for Domitian, but he discovered that the exercise of such power had become more problematic in the Imperial context.[41] The Republican heritage of the institution may have made the censorship an attractive vehicle for launching a moral crusade, but it did not exempt Domitian from the resentment of members of the ruling class when his tenure in this office came to be regarded as a pretext for unwarranted and arbitrary interference in their lives.

It did not help matters that there were certain noticeable divergences between Domitian's conduct as censor and Republican precedent. Under the carefully balanced political arrangement of the Republic, every regular magistracy was supposed to be subject to the principle of collegiality. With a pair of censors, one official was able to act as a check on the power of

---

[39] Suolahti (1963: 501–15). Note Syme (1939: 339), on the censorship of 22 BC: "The appointment of a pair of censors…announced a return to Republican practices and a beginning of social and moral reform." See also Nicolet (1991: 126–39), Hammond (1959: 85), Astin (1963).

[40] Suet. *Dom.* 8.3, cf. *Claud.* 16.1, Tac. *Ann.* 11.25, Ryan (1993), also Momigliano (1934: 44).

[41] Fredrick 2003: 220–1, cf. Jones (1979: 28), Astin (1988: 29–30). On the anecdotal nature of our evidence, see Saller (1980). For the importance of perception, Benario (1979).

the other.[42] In keeping with Augustan claims about the *princeps'* reliance on inherent *auctoritas* rather than extraordinary official *potestas*, this rule continued to be upheld, even on the two previous occasions when one of the censors was also the *princeps*.[43] But Domitian did not see fit to share his censorial power with a colleague, and the duration of his sole censorship represented an even more radical departure from tradition. Rather than hold the office for a limited term, Domitian extended his power to regulate morals indefinitely, creating the unprecedented position of *censor perpetuus* for himself. This innovation, which all previous emperors had avoided, may have been presented as the renewal of a Republican magistracy, but in practice it meant that the emperor's oversight of public morals was no longer confined to authoring laws, expressing his views, and setting a good example. It was now a formal police power, enforced through his censorial control over the senatorial and equestrian lists.[44] The prospect of constant official scrutiny must have made many members of the Roman elite uncomfortable, even those who might claim in principle to favor moral reform.

Literature written during Domitian's reign suggests the kind of response the emperor wanted his efforts to receive. Referring to the punishment of Varonilla and the Oculatae that Domitian undertook in his role as *pontifex maximus*, Statius describes the Roman Forum as a place where "Vesta applauds her servants now that they have been examined" (*Silv.* 1.1.36: *exploratas iam laudet Vesta ministras*).[45] Incorporating a topical allusion into his epic on the Hannibalic war, Silius Italicus characterizes the gruesome torture visited on the shade of an unchaste Vestal in the underworld as "still not equal to her crime" (*Pun.* 13.848: *nec par poena tamen sceleri*). Quintilian, who was rewarded with the trappings of consular status for his contributions to Roman culture, speaks with pride of

---

[42] Siber (1951), Astin (1988: 30), cf. Mommsen (1887: 41–4), Kunkel and Wittmann (1995: 8–10). A case in point is the censorship of 142 BC, when the zeal of Scipio Aemilianus was impeded by his colleague L. Mummius: Val. Max. 6.4.2a.

[43] Claudius bestowed great honor on L. Vitellius (*PIR*[1] V 500), the father of the future emperor, by taking him as a colleague in his censorship: Suet. *Vit.* 2.4, Plin. *NH* 15.83, *RIC*[2] I 268–72 nos. 7, 94. Note also *CIL* VI.1232 (= *ILS* 248), which mentions the censorship in the titulature of both Vespasian and Titus in conjunction with the extension of the Pomerium in 75.

[44] Dio (Xiph.) 7.4.4, Buttrey (1975), Hammond (1959: 86–7). *Pace* Jones (1973b), Domitian was not simply perpetuating a "Flavian attitude" to the censorship by assuming the title in perpetuity.

[45] This is clearly a reference to the first trial, which, unlike Cornelia's, took place in the Forum. The decisive factor in determining the poem's date is the absence of Julia, who died before the second trial, from the list of deified Flavians (1.1.97–98). While correctly noting this fact, Vinson (1989: 436) still misinterprets this line as a reference to Cornelia.

the special honor that Domitian, the "most sacred censor" (*Inst.* 4.pr.3: *sanctissimus censor*), had paid him by entrusting him with the tutelage of his niece Domitilla's children. In an epigram published closer to the date of Cornelia's execution, Martial addresses the emperor as *censor maxime* (6.4.1), neatly combining his religious and moral interests. He goes on to say that, out of all the emperor's accomplishments, his greatest gift to Rome was the restoration of its chastity (6.4.5: *plus debet tibi Roma quod pudica est*).

If taken at face value, these contemporary tributes suggest that there was broad public support for Domitian's efforts to reinvigorate Rome's religious and moral traditions. On the other hand, Pliny's letter and other posthumous sources paint a very different picture of this emperor. One way for scholars to resolve this conflict has been to assume some kind of mendacity on the part of time-serving writers who were unable to tell the truth about Domitian while he was alive.[46] Another approach is to interpret Pliny and Suetonius as participating in a smear campaign directed against the final member of a superseded dynastic line.[47] As a means to understanding the cultural and political realities of the Roman Principate, however, these approaches achieve only partial success. The contradiction in our sources might be appreciated in itself as a reflection of something more profound. If we can defer our concerns about the narrow contexts and motivations of the individual authors and simply read their testimony as discrepant reflections of a common reality, these accounts reveal the continuing reverberations of the dissonance that was inherent in the ideology of a "restored republic" under the Principate.

As was noted in Chapter 1 with regard to the publicity of Galba and Vindex, a good way to allay concerns about the loss of ancestral *libertas* under the Principate was to emphasize the emperor's role in restoring the ancient moral virtue that was thought to underpin much of freedom's essential social value. What made Domitian's participation in this project remarkable is the way in which it ultimately failed to improve the emperor's public image. The disagreement of our sources about the justice of Domitian's reform efforts shows that an emphasis on restoring traditional morals was not in itself sufficient to counteract elite anxiety about their diminishing freedoms. The problem he encountered was that the enforcement of

---

[46] See Garthwaite (1990), Langlands (2006: 360–2). Neither mentions Quintilian's praise of Domitian, though Ahl (1984), on whom both heavily rely, discusses his rhetorical theory at length. Clarke (1967: 35–6) detects sincerity in that compliment, and McDermott and Orentzel (1979: 13–15) regard it as a heartfelt expression of gratitude. See Newlands (2002: 18–26), who outlines a more profitable approach to these sources.

[47] Ramage (1983).

these values required an exercise of power that necessarily led to further questions about the sustainability of *libertas* under a *princeps*. With the whole system of Imperial ideology balanced on such a tightrope, it is little surprise that Domitian managed to succeed and fail simultaneously in his role as Rome's moral censor.

NEC MINORE SCELERE QUAM QUOD ULCISCI

One of the most striking features of Pliny's letter to Minicianus is its emphasis on doubt. For example, Pliny repeatedly calls attention to the instability of social roles. This concept is introduced in Licinianus' bitter *sententia* about how Fortune "make[s] senators out of professors, professors out of senators" (§2: *facis enim ex senatoribus professores, ex professoribus senatores*), which Pliny himself reworks in his explanation of the circumstances in which this line was delivered. The same verbal trope returns at the end of Pliny's narrative, with Herennius Senecio's laconic statement at Licinianus' trial that he has been transformed from an advocate into a messenger (§12: *ex advocato nuntius factus sum*). The constant redefinition of people's identities is obviously relevant to Pliny's uncertainty about the question of Cornelia's guilt or innocence (§9), but the heart of the issue lies in the anxiety over social status that was also fundamental to the obsession with *libertas* in Roman society. This pervasive sense of instability even applies to the emperor, in Pliny's efforts to remake Domitian from a *pontifex maximus*, whose actions are legitimate, into a tyrant and licentious master (§6: *pontificis maximi iure, seu potius immanitate tyranni licentia domini*). The mask finally slips completely when Domitian's intemperate response to Senecio's presentation reveals his need to be exonerated by another man's confession of guilt (§13: *"absolvit nos Licinianus"*). Although he sits in judgment over others, the emperor acknowledges that he is really the one on trial.

In a manner reminiscent of the historical works of his friend Tacitus, Pliny draws a distinction between the publicly offered justifications for Domitian's actions and his true motivations, which he assumes to be more sinister.[48] He begins from the assumption that Domitian was by nature a despotic ruler, and then concludes that any outward signs of respect for the ancient traditions of Roman religion must be disingenuous. To prove that Domitian was insincere in his pursuit of moral reform, Pliny insists that he was a hypocrite as well. The tyrant was guilty of "no less of a crime than the one he appeared to be punishing" because he himself had

---

[48] Ryberg (1942: 384–6).

engaged in a form of *incestum* with his niece Julia (§6: *nec minore scelere quam quod ulcisci videbatur*).⁴⁹ As someone who engaged in the same behavior he claimed to censure, Domitian lacked the moral authority that was required of a *princeps*, particularly one who presented himself as a *corrector morum*.⁵⁰

This hoisting of Domitian with his own petard is not simply a literary technique deployed to discredit the praiseworthy deeds of a supposedly "bad emperor."⁵¹ More fundamentally, the accusation of hypocrisy can be seen as a useful conceptual strategy for navigating the conflict between *libertas* and the *mos maiorum* that Domitian's religious initiatives exposed. As a proponent of conformity and the status quo, Pliny did not question the legitimacy of the moral principles that Domitian publicly claimed to uphold.⁵² Instead, he simply redeployed the same normative terms of value and reproach, turning them back on an emperor he disliked. Although the shift in the application of these terms is superficially intriguing, the underlying continuity between the moral outlook of this member of the Roman ruling class and that promoted by the ruler he sought to delegitimize is perhaps a more significant reflection of the power of their shared culture and ideology.⁵³ It is not that Pliny found the objective of restoring old-fashioned virtue illegitimate. He simply felt that a particular ruler who claimed to be pursuing this goal was actually an impediment to its attainment.

It is perhaps only natural that Domitian's strict enforcement of public morality brought about parallel scrutiny of his own private life. We may note that the grounds on which Domitian was said to have expelled an unnamed *eques* from the courts – the fact that he had separated from but then reconciled with his wife – mirror what was said about his own relationship with Domitia Longina.⁵⁴ Domitian was also rumored to have had sexual relationships with Nerva and Clodius Pollio as a youth, although

---

⁴⁹ The ambiguity of the term *incestum*, used by Pliny to denote both the loss of a Vestal's chastity and intrafamilial sex, led Koch (1960: 4) to conclude that the Vestals were originally supposed to represent the symbolic kin of each individual Roman. There is not space here to pursue the various other theories that have been presented to account for the Vestals' chastity: See, inter alia, Beard (1980), (1995), Cancik-Lindemaier (1990), Parker (2004).

⁵⁰ Cf. Wallace-Hadrill (1997: 12): "without moral authority, there can be no political authority."

⁵¹ *Pace* Waters (1964: 51–2). Domitian is vigorously defended against the charge of incest by Vinson (1989: 432–8) and Jones (1992: 38–40).

⁵² Andrews (1938), also Riggsby (1998), who employs a different idiom to make the same point.

⁵³ Cf. Bartsch (1994: 162–6), where continuity in the normative language of praise and blame is linked to the dominant power's need for a "public transcript."

⁵⁴ Suet. *Dom.* 8.3, 3.1. Vinson (1989: 444–5).

as emperor he renewed the enforcement of the *lex Scantinia*.[55] For members of the elite who chafed under the emperor's censorial surveillance, the charge of hypocrisy provided a way to rationalize their outrage at the effects of a repressive policy without having to abandon the moral principles by which that repression was sanctioned.

The legitimacy of these charges is unknowable, and for our purposes beside the point. Although it is impossible to determine whether Domitian did in fact engage in an incestuous relationship with his brother's daughter, the prevalence of this charge in post-Flavian literature and the offhand way that Pliny refers to the incident seem to suggest that rumors of an inappropriate relationship between Domitian and his niece were already in currency before his assassination.[56] Gossip often circulates about the private lives of those in power, and it is not difficult to imagine that the circumstances of Julia's death gave rise to prurient speculation about the use of an abortifacient at the time.[57] When Domitian presided over the conviction and execution of Cornelia a few years later, rumors of incest and poisoning within the imperial palace took on an added significance.

One way to explain the intensity of the reaction Domitian faced is to see it as a consequence of his failure to negotiate the tension between the conflicting values of justice and mercy – or, more precisely, *severitas* and *clementia*.[58] In many ways, *severitas* was the quintessential virtue of the old-fashioned Republic. It was what the early Romans displayed in punishing would-be tyrants such as Manlius, Spurius Cassius, and Maelius, and what Cicero called for when pursuing harsh punishments for Verres or the Catilinarian conspirators.[59] Under the Principate, however, when

---

[55] Suet. *Dom.* 1.1, *PIR*² C 1176.

[56] Garthwaite (1990). Other sources: Plin. *Pan.* 52.3, Juv. 2.29–33, Suet. *Dom.* 22.

[57] Waters (1964: 60). Vinson (1989: 436–7) fails to prove that Julia's death had nothing to do with a pregnancy, or to explain why such a conclusion would be necessary. For abortion and contraception among the Roman elite, see Kapparis (2002: 7–22), Dixon (2001: 59–65), Hopkins (1965, esp. 136–40).

[58] Although Seneca insists that "no virtue can be opposed to virtue" (*Clem.* 2.4.1: *sed nulla virtus virtuti contraria est*), these traits were clearly incompatible. In linguistic usage, *clementia* is closely associated with terms like *benignitas*, *mansuetudo*, and *misericordia*, which are given as antonyms for *severitas*. Compare the fuller lists at *RAC* III 207 s.v. "Clementia" [Winkler] and Bernardo (2000: 14). It is worth noting that in the *Panegyricus* Pliny praises Trajan for possessing both qualities, but in moderation: *quam mitis severitas, quam non dissoluta clementia* (80.1, cf. 34.2, 35.1), cf. Rees (2001).

[59] Cic. *Verr.* 2.5.45–6, *Cat.* 4.4, 7, Val. Max. 6.3.1a-c. *Severitas* is often characterized as *prisca* (Cic. *Har.* 27), *vetus* (Cic. *Fam.* 9.10.2, *Verr.* 2.5.46, *Phil.* 7.14), or *pristina* (Cic. *Att.* 1.16.8, *Cael.* 40). Note also that it is also associated with disapproving old men (as in Catullus 5.2): Bernardo (2000: 30–1).

public authority was diminished and collective responsibility for such punishments was more attenuated, *severitas* was more readily praised in a private citizen or a philosopher than in a *princeps*. The emperor Galba was closely associated with this virtue, which had been displayed by such ancestors as L. Mummius, but as Tacitus wryly observes, "he was harmed by his ancient inflexibility and excessive *severitas*, to which we are no longer equal" (*Hist.* 1.18.3: *nocuit antiquus rigor et nimia severitas, cui iam pares non sumus*).[60]

Clementia, on the other hand, was a more contemporary virtue, and one more useful for autocratic rulers. It was closely associated with Julius Caesar and the forgiveness shown to his enemies after the civil wars, and was among the four charismatic virtues inscribed on the *clupeus aureus* that the senate dedicated in Augustus' honor in 27 BC. In their public response to the death of Germanicus, the senate invoked *clementia* as a value they had not just inherited from their ancestors, but also been taught by their *principes*. The virtue's association with monarchy is made clear in a treatise on the topic that Seneca addressed to Nero. As an adjunct to the philosophical ideal of *humanitas*, clemency was particularly desirable in a *princeps*, whose unique position of authority brought special attention to his personal qualities.[61] By holding to the impersonal standards of Republican *severitas*, Domitian neglected the virtue that was more appropriate to the realities of his position.

The quality of mercy is not strained, however, and insincere clemency could rankle as well. Tacitus is often (although not always) sarcastic when attributing this virtue to an emperor, and Suetonius says that Domitian kept everyone off kilter by prefacing the announcement of grim penalties with a declaration of his *clementia*.[62] But if the advertisement of a ruler's clemency served "to call attention ... to the fact that one did have the power to bestow it," a preference for *severitas* only indicated his unwillingness to employ his powers humanely.[63] When it came to the renewal of Republican virtues under the Principate, therefore, wise policy required that the emperor show some leniency toward those who failed to live

---

[60] Cf. *Hist.* 5.3, Suet. *Galb.* 6.2–3, also Plin. *Ep.* 1.10.7, 1.14.6. On Galba's ancestry, see Chapter 1, n. 93.

[61] Sen. *Clem.* 1.3.3: *nullum tamen clementia ex omnibus magis quam regem aut principem decet.* RAC XVI 680 s.v. "Humanität" [Chadwick], Classen (1988: 300), Griffin (2003: 165–77), Bauman (1996: 78–80), Trapp (2007: 177–80), Adam (1970). On Caesar's *clementia*, see esp. Konstan (2005), *contra* Earl (1967: 60–1), also Weinstock (1971: 237–43), Yavetz (1983: 96–7, 174–6). Clupeus: RG 34.2, cf. Sen. *Clem.* 1.9–11. Senate: SCPP ll. 90–2.

[62] Suet. *Dom.* 11.2: *numquam tristiorem sententiam sine praefatione clementiae pronuntiavit.* Tac. *Ann.* 15.35.3, cf. 12.52.2, 3.24.2, Syme (1958: 414–15).

[63] Burgess (1972: 340). Cf. Sen. *Clem.* 1.5.7: *servare proprium est excellentis fortunae*, 2.3.

up to the ancient standard. Tacitus provides the apposite maxim in his *Annals* when he explains how simple dining habits became fashionable again under a modest ruler such as Vespasian. The historian notes, "obedience toward the *princeps* and love of emulation are stronger than legal penalties and fear" (*Ann.* 3.55.4: *obsequium inde in principem et aemulandi amor validior quam poena ex legibus et metus*).[64] Paradoxically, it seems, ancient Roman *mores* were better served by an emperor with the proper temperament than by the strict implementation of measures that might have the appearance of being more Republican.

PONTIFICIS MAXIMI IURE

Although the severity of Domitian's moral censorship is essential to understanding the reaction we find in Pliny's letter, it does not in itself explain the specific problems raised by Cornelia's condemnation. The Vestal priesthood was an ancient institution with a long and storied tradition, and the unique nature of this religious history must be accounted for in the unfolding saga of Cornelia's two trials and eventual execution. To be sure, the taboos associated with the Vestal virgins and their special place within the Romans' historical consciousness provided a clear rationale for the actions taken by Domitian. By reenacting the ritual execution of an unchaste Vestal, the emperor sought to harness the authority of this ancient tradition. However, the history of the Vestal college was itself shaped by an ongoing conflict about the proper balance between severity and mildness, one that ran parallel to what we have detected in the hostile reactions to Domitian's moral censorship. By attempting to selectively revive elements of the Vestal tradition, Domitian inevitably provoked others – most notably Cornelia herself – to take up the other side of this debate.

As the keepers of the sacred flame of the public hearth, the Vestal virgins enjoyed a position of remarkable privilege in Roman society.[65] Cult activity is a powerful engine in the workings of cultural memory, and the cult of Vesta had such a central role in the formation of Roman identity that in many ways the Vestals could be said to represent Rome itself.[66] This synecdochic quality explains the priestesses' participation in the rituals that marked the initial restoration of the Capitoline temple in 70, and Rome's renewal at the beginning of Vespasian's reign also coincided with

---

[64] Cf. Plin. *Pan.* 45.6: *nec tam imperio nobis opus est quam exemplo*. Similarly, when Tacitus recounts the history of moral legislation, he concludes, *corruptissima re publica plurimae leges* (*Ann.* 3.27.3): Milnor (2005: 144–5).

[65] Dion. Hal. *AR* 2.67.3, Plut. *Numa* 10.3, Beard (1980: 17), cf. Ryberg (1955: 51).

[66] Assmann (1992: 56–9).

Figure 3.2. Cancelleria Relief, Panel B. Domitian, accompanied by Vestal virgins (on left), greets Vespasian on his return to Rome in AD 70. (Vatican Museum, DAIR negative 2007.0010)

the reappearance of Vesta on the official coinage.[67] The chance rediscovery of a monumental relief set up by Domitian to commemorate his father's return to the city in the summer of 70 further demonstrates the importance of the Vestals' role in promoting the restoration of *pax* in the opening days of the Flavian dynasty (Fig. 3.2). The scene is fragmentary, but it is clear that five Vestals are in attendance, while the sixth has been left behind at the shrine in the Forum to tend the sacred fire. Although the priestesses dominate the left side of the frame, they have not been given recognizable portrait features in the same way that their counterparts Vespasian and the young Domitian have. Given the scandal that later attached to some of these women, it is not surprising that they are represented not as individual personalities so much as the embodiment of an abstract ideal. Their function in the relief is similar to that of the divine personifications and anonymous attendants who also populate the scene, in that they help to fill out a visual shorthand for the Roman community as a whole.[68]

The Vestal's special symbolic status, like that of the *princeps*, came at the price of intense public scrutiny. In addition to their other responsibilities,

[67] *RIC* II² 95–100 nos. 515–16, 524, 530, 548–50, 557–8 (= *BMCRE* II 21 nos. 107–9), Bianco (1968: 157–8). Nero had restored the temple of Vesta after it was destroyed in the fire of 64 (Tac. *Ann.* 15.41.1); it was the only monument so restored to appear on his coinage: *RIC²* I 153 nos. 61–2 (= *BMCRE* I 213 nos. 101–6), cf. Champlin (2003: 188–91). Magi (1945: 37–54). For the Capitoline restoration (Tac. *Hist.* 4.53.2), see Chapter 2.

[68] Magi (1945: 3–4, 90–3), Toynbee (1957: 5–7). On the removal of the friezes and their reworking as part of the posthumous attack on Domitian's memory (which ultimately explains their survival) see Varner (2004: 118–20). The novelty of the Vestal's prominence in this scene is stressed by Ghedini (1986: 297), but this may be an accident of survival: cf. Ryberg (1955: 41, 71–3).

the unique requirement of sexual abstinence, which was a central part
of the Vestals' religious identity since time immemorial, could give rise
to suspicion and anxiety. In the history of the Republic, the discovery of
incestum among the Vestals was invariably linked to the appearance of
other signs (*prodigia*) indicating a breakdown in the *pax deum*. Livy's
account of a case from 215 BC, when Rome was in the throes of religious
panic stirred up by Hannibal's invasion of Italy, is typical:

> *territi etiam super tantas clades cum ceteris prodigiis, tum quod duae
> Vestales eo anno, Opimia atque Floronia, stupri compertae et altera sub
> terra, uti mos est, ad portam Collinam necata fuerat, altera sibimet ipsa
> mortem consciverat; L. Cantilius scriba pontificius, quos nunc minores pon-
> tifices appellant, qui cum Floronia stuprum fecerat, a pontifice maximo eo
> usque virgis in comitio caesus erat ut inter verbera exspiraret.*

In addition to these military disasters, the people were terrified by other
prodigies, and by the fact that in that year two Vestals, Opimia and Floronia,
were discovered to have been defiled. One met her death underground, as
is the custom, at the Colline gate; the other immediately took her own life.
Because he had taken part in the defilement of Floronia, L. Cantilius, one of
the pontifical secretaries that they now call *pontifices minores*, was lashed
with rods in the Comitium by the *pontifex maximus* himself until he died.
(Livy 22.57.2–3)

Such episodes appear with some regularity in the annalistic histories of the
Republic, which placed special emphasis on recording prodigies and their
expiation. The pattern of association between *prodigia* and the punishment
of Vestals for *incestum* is so well established, in fact, that it has led some
scholars to suppose that the very purpose of the Vestal priesthood was to
provide a reserve store of scapegoats, who might be sacrificed as expiation
whenever a religious crisis arose. Although these arguments in their fullest
form are probably untenable, the evident connection between the burial of
unchaste Vestals and moments of religious crisis does suggest a context in
which the investigation and punishment of Cornelia's supposed *incestum*
can be understood.[69]

At the beginning of Domitian's reign, there must have been a tremendous sense of foreboding. The death of Titus had been a sudden and
unexpected blow, following a brief reign that saw an outbreak of plague,

---

[69] See, most recently, Parker (2004), drawing on the ideas of Girard (1977) and Douglas
(1966). But note also Radke (1972: 428–33), (1987: 264–86), followed by Lovisi (1998: 733),
cf. Takács (2008: 86–9). The importance of *incestum* in defining the place of the Vestals in the
ancient literary tradition is noted (but not explained) by Beard (1995: 172). See also Cornell
(1981: 31), Fraschetti (1984: 102–9), Mustakallio (1992), Scheid (1981: 152–3).

another great fire in the heart of Rome, and the devastating eruption of Vesuvius on the bay of Naples. Domitian came to power in the aftermath of these calamitous events, and he soon had to confront the threat of conspiracy, whether real or imagined, involving one or more members of his family. Once the succession was assured, external dangers quickly presented themselves on the Rhine frontier. In such perplexing circumstances, an inquiry into the status of the Vestals' sacred chastity would have made a great deal of sense. As *pontifex maximus*, Domitian had the opportunity to allay public anxiety by reviving an ancient religious stricture. The discovery of an explanation for these crises would be reassuring, while the punishment of the wrongdoers offered a way to bring about the return of the gods' favor.[70]

In this case, remarkably, a measure of clemency was shown. Ancient custom dictated that unchaste Vestals be buried alive in a special chamber near the Porta Collina, at the northern corner of the Servian wall, and that the male participants in their crime be whipped to death in the Comitium.[71] Although these were the fates of Cornelia and Celer several years later, Suetonius reports that Varonilla and the Oculatae were allowed to select the manner of their death, while their *corruptores* were simply banished. The abrogation of the famous and long-standing penalty shows that Domitian was acting deliberately, selecting which elements of the tradition to implement and which to leave aside. If the *mos maiorum* dictated a particularly grim form of punishment, the "free choice of one's death" (*liberum mortis arbitrium*) could be offered as a gesture of the emperor's *clementia*.[72] This need not be misconstrued as an arbitrary display of mercy by an arrogant young *princeps* who wished to demonstrate his power to shape the implementation of religious law. It is also possible that Domitian's decision was a concession to the sentiments of the other members of the pontifical college, many of whom probably shared the view of writers such as Livy and Plutarch that a ritual in which human beings were buried alive was barbaric.[73] Despite its emphasis on formula, Roman religion was never so rigid as to preclude adaptation. Unchaste Vestals were usually buried alive, but a regular practice need not be mandatory. Even in the "typical"

---

[70] Suet. *Dom.* 8.4, 10.4, Philostr. *VA* 7.7, Dio (Xiph.) 67.3.3–4.1, Frontin. *Strat.* 1.8.1, cf. Suet. *Dom.* 6.1. *PIR*² F 355, Jones (1992: 45–6), Southern (1997: 43–4, cf. 37, which paints a rosier picture), *contra* Gsell (1894: 248). On the dating of the war, see Evans (1975), *contra* Jones (1973a), also Southern (1997: 79–81), Fraschetti (1984: 119).

[71] See, e.g., Livy 22.57.2–3: *uti mos est.* Note also Dion. Hal. *AR* 2.67.4.

[72] Suet. *Dom.* 11.3 (quoting the exact language of Domitian's intercession in a different case), cf. Tac. *Ann.* 11.3.1 (of Claudius). Vestals' choice: Suet. *Dom.* 8.4, Fraschetti (1984: 118).

[73] Livy 22.57.6: *minime Romano sacro*, Plut. *Mor.* 284B–C, cf. Fraschetti (1981).

case cited above, it was not possible to prevent one of the guilty Vestals from taking her own life before the "traditional" punishment could be imposed.[74]

More to the point, the exercise of discretion (and even clemency) was entirely in keeping with the established authority of the pontifical college in the investigation and punishment of Vestal misbehavior. If these priests determined that a Vestal had simply been negligent in the performance of her duties but was not guilty of *incestum*, the *pontifex maximus* was supposed to administer a public beating, after which the offending priestess was allowed to return to her sacerdotal duties.[75] Other, more lenient sentences could also be handed down, even when the Vestal's behavior was not above reproach. The earliest example is that of Postumia, a priestess who provoked popular suspicion on account of what was regarded as her luxurious manner of dress and overly spirited behavior. Although acquitted on the charge of *incestum*, she was nevertheless judged to have acted improperly. No punishment was imposed, but Postumia did receive a public reprimand from the *pontifex maximus*, who warned her that she needed to conduct herself with more decorum and dress in an appropriate manner.[76]

Domitian and his fellow *pontifices* were thus acting more or less within the traditional boundaries of their authority in moderating the nature of the penalty imposed on the condemned Vestals in 83. Because Cornelia was acquitted in these proceedings, she was ineligible to benefit from this display of clemency. As her case suggests, it also continued to be possible for a Vestal to prove her innocence when accused of *incestum*, at least at this point in Domitian's reign. Some of the Republican precedents for her acquittal will be discussed in detail below, but it should be noted that this is where the tradition began to fragment into multiple, competing memories regarding the appropriate balance between *clementia* and *severitas*. It is clear from the historical tradition that pontifical leniency was not always met with popular approval. In 114 BC, the priests' inquiry into alleged improprieties involving several Vestals and members of the equestrian

---

[74] Other examples of Vestals or their lovers who escaped the traditional punishment through suicide: Oros. 4.5.9, Dion. Hal. *AR* 9.40.4, Fraschetti (1984: 98), Saquete (2000: 96). See esp. North (1976).

[75] Val. Max. 1.1.6, Dion Hal. *AR* 2.67.3, Plut. *Num.* 10.4, cf. 9.5, Fest. 200 Lindsay: *pontifex maximus, quod iudex atque arbiter habetur rerum divinarum humanarumque*, Guizzi (1968), Cornell (1981: 29–30), Lovisi (1998: 715–19), Beard (1980: 14).

[76] Livy 4.44.11–12, Plut. *Mor.* 89 F. Ogilvie (1965: 602) discusses the potential political context for her accusation.

order resulted in only one conviction. The following year, the tribune
Sextus Peducaeus called for the case to be reopened on the grounds that
the *pontifices* had decided improperly. The presiding magistrate at the second trial, L. Cassius Longinus Ravilla, was so severe in his judgments that
his tribunal, at which two more Vestals were convicted, became known
as the rock on which defendants' ships were dashed (Val. Max. 3.7.9:
scopulus reorum).[77]

Although the parallel is not precise, the similarities between Cornelia's
fate and that of the Vestals condemned under Peducaeus' law are illuminat-
ing. The events of 113 BC stand as part of a broader trend in Republican
religious history, whereby the Roman people gradually impinged on what
had long been the guarded preserve of aristocratic, primarily patrician,
priesthoods. An anxious populace became suspicious of the priests' verdict and decided to make sure that the guilty Vestals (who, as members of
the same social stratum as the *pontifices* responsible for overseeing their
behavior, appeared to have benefited from favoritism) were subjected to
the strictest discipline possible.[78] Similar antagonism between popular and
elite conceptions of religious justice may have prevailed under the Principate as well, although this is more difficult to trace in our sources.[79]
Because Domitian presided over both of Cornelia's trials in his position
as *pontifex maximus*, the second inquiry cannot have been intended as a
repudiation of the earlier verdict. Given the amount of time that elapsed
between her two trials, it is far from certain that public outrage played a
direct role in the decision to try Cornelia again. Nevertheless, her reversal
of fortune, together with the decision to impose the ancient, more brutal
punishment, suggests a shift not just in the emperor's disposition, but in
the public mood as well. No longer constrained by his earlier concern
for sophisticated sensibilities, Domitian decided to provide his age with
an *exemplum* that he hoped would resonate more fully with stern traditionalists and perhaps the more vengeful sentiments of the urban plebs as
well.[80]

---

[77] See also Dio fr. 87.3–5, Livy *Per.* 63, Plut. *Mor.* 284A–B, Oros. 5.15.20, Obseq. 37, Ascon.
46–7 Clark, cf. Cic. *ND* 3.74. *MRR* 1.537, Gruen (1968b).

[78] Rawson (1974: 207–8), Cornell (1981: 37), Scheid (1981: 146), McDougall (1992: 12), see
also Staples (1998: 137–8), Flower (2010: 69–70). Cf. Gruen (1968a: 127–31), who focuses
on the competition between rival aristocratic groups.

[79] Cf. Yavetz (1969a: 114–16, 139).

[80] Grelle (1980: 362), also Bengtson (1979: 190–2), cf. MacMullen (1986: 147–51). Contrast the
popular demands for clemency as the senate considered the case of the condemned slaves of
Pedanius Secundus in 61: Tac. *Ann.* 14.42, Yavetz (1969a: 29–36).

ABSENTEM INAUDITAMQUE DAMNAVIT

In addition to the change in the nature of the penalty imposed, there was also an important difference in the way that Cornelia's conviction was accomplished. The trial in which Varonilla and the Oculatae were condemned had been an elaborate public spectacle, but Cornelia was tried in private. Republican tradition provided that inquiries into the behavior of Vestals be performed at the Regia, the traditional residence of the *pontifex maximus* in the heart of the Forum Romanum. Though it no longer served this purpose under the Principate, the Regia nevertheless remained the logical place to carry out disciplinary oversight of the Vestal college, because it stood beside Vesta's temple and the residence of her priestesses.[81] In this central location, the proceedings of 82 were sure to draw a crowd, as the scope of the scandal that was uncovered no doubt also heightened the notoriety of the case. Cassius Dio records that one of the *pontifices*, Helvius Agrippa, was so overwhelmed by the number of people condemned that he collapsed in the midst of the proceedings and died in the nearby Curia.[82]

In contrast, Cornelia's second trial was conducted far from public view at Domitian's Alban villa, which lay about 25 kilometers (15 miles) to the south of Rome along the Via Appia.[83] Pliny calls attention to this change in venue to support his claim that the emperor was not acting in his capacity as a *pontifex maximus* but instead was behaving as a tyrant when Cornelia was condemned (§6). In fact, Domitian appears to have made a habit of holding deliberative councils at his Alban villa. The special association between Alba Longa and the Trojan Vesta may have been enough to justify convening Cornelia's tribunal at the emperor's suburban residence, but this nevertheless could be construed as a problematic break with convention.[84] It is difficult to escape from the conclusion that the real significance of

---

[81] Dion. Hal. *AR* 2.67.3, Cornell (1981: 29–30). Coarelli (1983: 64–72), *LTUR* I: 138–9 s.v. "Atrium Vestae," IV: 189–92 s.v. "Regia" [Scott], cf. Wardman (1982: 69), Beard, North and Price (1998: 189–91). As Lovisi (1998: 715–17) makes clear, *incestum* trials were public hearings, similar to any other judicial proceeding. Cf. Stat. *Silv.* 1.1.36.

[82] *PIR*² H 64, Dio (Xiph.) 67.3.3²: ἐν τῷ συνεδρίῳ. I assume that Helvius had gone (or was taken) to the Curia to recover, but it might be that the trials were actually conducted there. In either case, the critical point is that the trial was conducted in the public spaces of the Forum.

[83] On the site, see Hesberg (2006), Crescenzi (1979), also Ashby (1927: 191).

[84] Sherwin-White (1966: 283), followed by Carlon (2009: 198), argues that "Roman jurisdiction was not tied to places," but Roman religion, which depended so much on augury, was deeply tied to place: See Beard, North, and Price (1998: 167–8). Alban Vesta: *CIL* 6.2171 (= *ILS* 5011), Juv. 4. 60–61, Serv. *Aen.* 1.273, cf. Dion. Hal. *AR* 2.65.1, Latte (1960: 405), Granino Cecere (1996: 308–14), also Stewart (1994: 323–4). Tribunals: *CIL* 9.5420, Jones (1992: 27–8), Courtney (1980: 195–9), Anderson (1982: 70–7).

the change in location was the secrecy it afforded. Unlike in the previous trial, at which Cornelia had been allowed to mount her own defense and secure an acquittal, this time she was condemned "absent and unheard" (§6: *absentem inauditamque*).

We may assume that Domitian did not need or want the excitement that might come with a public trial. His aim was to demonstrate swift and decisive action, which meant getting directly to the punishment of Cornelia's supposed crimes unimpeded by the legalistic ambiguities that might emerge from an investigation. In this case, the central spectacle was not the trial, but rather the ritual imposition of the traditional penalty for these offenses. For better or worse, the focus of public attention was on the procession that took Cornelia from the Vestals' residence in the Forum to the Campus Sceleratus, where the entrance to the underground chamber stood.[85] Here, at a site imbued with grim and fearsome memories, Domitian hoped to reassert the continuity of one of the most ancient forms of Roman moral severity.

The intended significance of Cornelia's punishment as a public spectacle that recalled the moral rigor and unflinching justice of an earlier era seems to be confirmed by the iconography of the so-called Forum Transitorium, which like other monuments in Rome was conceived and built under Domitian but subsequently dedicated by Nerva. The central feature of this monumental passageway, which stood on the site where the street of the Argiletum passed between the Forum Augustum and Vespasian's Temple of Peace, was a temple of Minerva – another chaste goddess to whom Domitian showed particular devotion.[86] In keeping with Minerva's status as a patroness of handicrafts, the entablature that ran along the walls of this narrow forum was decorated with figural panels depicting women engaged in the spinning and weaving of wool, the paradigmatic activity of a chaste Roman matron, whose care of the household was comparable to the responsibilities of the Vestal virgins.[87] Amid scenes of virtuous female behavior, the most prominent image in the program seems to have been the

---

[85] Hinard (1987: 112–13). The repetition of this rite in Domitian's day disproves the claim of Palmer (1975) that the construction of the Sullan temple of Bellona in the vicinity had obscured the area known as the Campus Sceleratus. On the location of the chamber, see *LTUR* I 225 s.v. "Campus Sceleratus" [Coarelli]. Celer's execution under whips in the Comitium was likewise a dramatic public demonstration of the strict enforcement of religious law.

[86] Suet. *Dom.* 5.1, Tortorici (1991: 32–7), Anderson (1982), (1984: 119–32), Platner and Ashby (1926: 228). For Domitian's special relationship with Minerva, see Suet. *Dom.* 15.3, Scott (1936: 166–86), Girard (1981), D'Ambra (1993: 10–11).

[87] D'Ambra (1991), (1993: 51–8), Fredrick (2003: 223–7). Weaving: Wissowa (1912: 158–61), Latte (1960: 108–10), also Wildfang (2001: 229–30).

representation of an act of retribution. The panel located above the gateway to the Subura has been interpreted as a representation of the mythical punishment of Arachne, who transgressed the limits imposed on female piety (and chastity) by challenging Minerva's supremacy in weaving. As D'Ambra explains, "the scene of the punishment of Arachne forms a central *emblema* surrounded by other contrasting motifs, moralizing exempla of virtue."[88] The interplay of these images rearticulates the logic that had been enacted during Cornelia's execution, which held that female virtue had to be maintained by the imposition (or at least the threat) of violent punishments.

Moreover, the corridor along which this forum stood was an ideal place in which to articulate the importance of retributive justice in Domitian's moral program (Fig. 3.3). The street of the Argiletum was itself the most likely route by which Cornelia was carried out of the Forum Romanum in the morbid procession that led through the crowded valley of the Subura and thence up the Quirinal to the Porta Collina, where her burial took place in an area known as the Campus Sceleratus. In an enigmatic poem written before the forum's construction, Martial associates this location with the bloody whips of torturers, which suggests that public executions not unlike Celer's were performed nearby.[89] Given these topographical associations, it is perhaps unsurprising that Domitian and his architects chose to combine the theme of feminine virtue with a representation of the threat of violence that they regarded as necessary to its maintenance in the design of the forum that gave this passageway its monumental form. They could be confident that the memories associated with this site would reinforce the message the new monument was intended to convey.

Like the arch of Titus, which commemorated Flavian military accomplishment on the very spot where the triumph it depicts had entered the Sacra Via, the Forum Transitorium presents a document of Domitian's moral severity along the route of the procession that provided the most spectacular demonstration of this virtue.[90] There is no evidence of any explicit reference to Cornelia or the punishment of Roman Vestals in the iconographic program of this monument, but the metaphorical language of myth was perhaps a more appropriate way to elucidate these issues. Minerva's wrath can stand in for the religious principles that Domitian

[88] D'Ambra (1993: 47), citing Ovid *Met.* 6.1–145, also *LTUR* II 309 s.v. "Forum Nervae" [Bauer–Morselli].

[89] Mart. 2.17.1–3: *tonstrix Suburae faucibus sedet primis, / cruenta pendent qua flagella tortorum/ Argique Letum multus obsidet sutor.* See Williams (2004, ad loc.) and *LTUR* IV 379 s.v. "Subura" [Welch], also Anderson (1984: 139), D'Ambra (1993: 30).

[90] *LTUR* I 110 s.v. "Arcus Titi (via sacra)" [Arce]. Millar (2005: 123), cf. Beard (2007: 92–105).

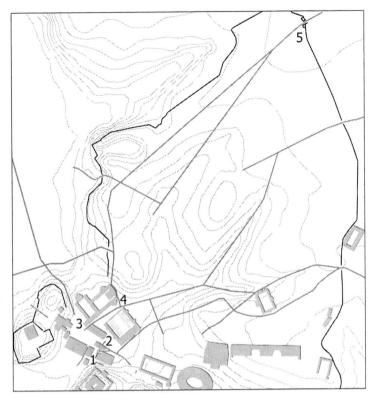

Figure 3.3. Topography of Punishments in Rome, AD 91. 1: Temple of Vesta; 2: Regia; 3: Comitium; 4: Argiletum; 5: Porta Collina (Campus Sceleratus). (plan by author)

claimed to be upholding by burying Cornelia alive, while elsewhere in the frieze, the personification of *Aequitas* attests to the implicit fairness of such punishments.[91] The use of these mythological touchstones also provides a more cosmic perspective on Domitian's moral program, suggesting that the punishment of Cornelia was not simply a reenactment of an ancient but specifically Republican ritual, but was rather the manifestation of a more fundamental, and universal, religious principle.

Despite the official effort to justify these actions, the secretive nature of Cornelia's second trial left some questions about the fairness of her punishment. The protests of the condemned, which played on this uncertainty, clearly did not fit with the message that Domitian and his supporters intended to convey. If Pliny is to be believed, Cornelia and Celer actually

---

[91] *Aequitas*: D'Ambra (1993: 58–9).

succeeded in turning public opinion against the emperor (§11). Here we should note that Cornelia's protests were quickly cut short, because she was in fact physically muzzled as she was carried to her doom. Although the evidence is far from certain, we should consider the likelihood that this too was an adaptation of the tradition, undertaken as a response to the objections that Cornelia had been voicing about her condemnation to inhibit her ability to arouse popular sympathy further or to raise further questions about her fate.

According to Plutarch, who may also have been a witness to the events of 91, Cornelia was not only deprived of the right to speak for herself at her own trial, she was also silenced again in the course of her punishment. He describes the punishment for unchaste Vestals as follows:

ἡ δὲ τὴν παρθενίαν καταισχύνασα ζῶσα κατορύττεται παρὰ τὴν Κολλίνην λεγομένην πύλην... αὐτὴν δὲ τὴν κολαζομένην εἰς φορεῖον ἐνθέμενοι καὶ καταστεγάσαντες ἔξωθεν καὶ καταλαβόντες ἱμᾶσιν, ὡς μηδὲ φωνὴν ἐξάκουστον γενέσθαι, κομίζουσι δὶ ἀγορᾶς. ἐξίστανται δὲ πάντες σιωπῇ καὶ παραπέμπουσιν ἄφθογγοι μετά τινος δεινᾶς κατηφείας· οὐδ᾽ ἐστὶν ἕτερον θέαμα φρικτότερον, οὐδ᾽ ἡμέραν ἡ πόλις ἄλλην ἄγει στυγνοτέραν ἐκείνης.

But one who has polluted her virginity is buried alive near the so-called Colline gate.... Having set the one being punished on a litter, placing covers over her and tying her down with straps so that no audible sound can be produced, they carry her though the forum. Everyone stands aside in silence as the speechless attendants escort her with an awesome sense of grief. No other spectacle is more horrible, and the city does not observe any holiday more miserable than this. (*Num.* 10.8–11)[92]

Compare, however, the account of Dionysius of Halicarnassus, who must have based his description of the procession on preexisting Republican accounts of the ritual:

ζῶσαι γὰρ ἔτι πομπεύουσιν ἐπὶ κλίνης φερόμεναι τὴν ἀποδεδειγμένην τοῖς νεκροῖς ἐκφοράν, ἀνακλαιομένων αὐτὰς καὶ προπεμπόντων φίλων τε καὶ συγγενῶν, κομισθεῖσαι δὲ μέχρι τῆς Κολλίνης πύλης, ἐντὸς τείχους εἰς σηκὸν ὑπὸ γῆς κατεσκευασμένον ἅμα τοῖς ἐνταφίοις κόσμοις τίθενται.

Though living, they are carried on a processional couch with all the pomp that is accorded to the dead, with friends and family weeping for them and following along. Once conveyed as far as the Colline gate, wearing their funeral attire, they immediately are placed into an underground cell prepared within the walls. (*AR* 2.67.4)

---

[92] Sherwin-White (1966: 283): "Plutarch may have witnessed the scene," cf. Barrow (1967: 37–9).

Both authors describe the same essential mise en scène, but their accounts differ significantly in tone. In Plutarch's version the attendants are speechless (ἄφθογγοι), and the whole city watches on in silence (σιωπῇ). Dionysius, on the other hand, stresses the ceremony's similarity to a public funeral and focuses on the commotion caused by the antiphonal wailing associated with such events. The attendants in his account weep openly (ἀνακλαιομένων).[93]

Plutarch also includes a detail that is missing from other accounts of the ritual: the binding of the victim under blankets to muffle any cries she might make. It could be that covering the Vestal to suppress her cries was an act of profound religious significance and an essential part of the rite, but it is also possible that Plutarch's description of the silent procession reflects the unique conditions of Cornelia's punishment and special measures that were instituted to limit her capacity for vociferous protest.[94] Such a conclusion would fit the pattern of what we know about the circumstances of Cornelia's execution. Domitian wanted to impose a narrow interpretation on his intervention into the Vestal tradition, one that emphasized retribution and the strict punishment of sexual misconduct. By keeping the trial out of the public eye and later monumentalizing the course of the procession as he did, the emperor sought to control memory in ways that defined his actions as an ideal guardian of public morality. Cornelia's insistence on her innocence, on the other hand, represented a challenge to this message, and as such could not be tolerated. It is thus quite possible that Domitian directed his fellow *pontifices* to interpose the blankets and silence this critic for whom the fear of death was no longer a deterrent, if they did not do so on their own initiative.

CERTE TAMQUAM INNOCENS DUCTA EST

With the emperor deploying such wide-ranging justifications for the central place of punishment in his moral program, the meaning of Cornelia's execution might appear to have been overdetermined. But, in fact, all of the effort that went into stage-managing these proceedings only called attention to the instability of the situation. The slightest slip could undermine Domitian's message of moral and religious reform, and we have already

---

93 On Roman funerals, see Flower (1996: 125). The similarity between the two rituals is also stressed in the interpretation of Fraschetti (1984: 121–4).

94 Fraschetti (1984: 122–3) suggests that the coverings were intended to prevent the contamination of the ritual by the corrupted Vestal, and points to an injunction prohibiting the *pontifex maximus* from viewing a corpse. Beard (2007) offers a strong corrective to synchronic interpretations of Roman ritual.

examined the charges of hypocrisy that his actions provoked. Another such moment took place at the Campus Sceleratus, where Cornelia was interred in the underground chamber. Again, Plutarch describes what he regarded as the essential elements of the ceremony:

ὅταν δὲ πρὸς τὸν τόπον κομισθῇ τὸ φορεῖον, οἱ μὲν ὑπηρέται τοὺς δεσμοὺς ἐξέλυσαν, ὁ δὲ τῶν ἱερέων ἔξαρχος εὐχάς τινας ἀπορρήτους ποιησάμενος, καὶ χεῖρας ἀνατείνας θεοῖς πρὸ τῆς ἀνάγκης, ἐξάγει συγκεκαλυμμένην καὶ καθίστησιν ἐπὶ κλίμακος, εἰς τὸ οἴκημα κάτω φερούσης. εἶτ᾿ αὐτὸς μὲν ἀποτρέπεται μετὰ τῶν ἄλλων ἱερέων. τῆς δὲ καταβάσης ἥ τε κλίμαξ ἀναιρεῖται καὶ κατακρύπτεται τὸ οἴκημα γῆς πολλῆς ἄνωθεν ἐπιφορουμένης.

When the litter has been brought to this place, the attendants release the straps. The chief priest [*pontifex maximus*], having offered some secret prayers and stretched his hands to the gods before the punishment, brings forth the woman, still completely wrapped up, and places her at the ladder leading down into the chamber. Then he turns away along with the other priests, and when she has descended, the ladder is pulled up and the chamber is covered over and a mound of earth is piled on top of it. (*Numa* 10.12–13)

Because this is intended as a generalized account, the author does not mention the specific problem that Domitian as *pontifex maximus* encountered as he led Cornelia to the entrance of the underground chamber. No doubt because of the heavy wrappings that had been imposed on her, Cornelia had difficulty descending the ladder, and her stola became entangled. According to Pliny, "although the executioner offered his hand, she turned away and with a final display of holiness repelled that shameful contact as though from an obviously pure and chaste body" (§9: *cumque ei manum carnifex daret, aversata est et resiluit foedumque contactum quasi plane a casto puroque corpore novissima sanctitate reiecit*). Because an "executioner" (*carnifex*) was not called for in this context (Cornelia was being buried alive, not dispatched), Pliny is likely using the term to refer to Domitian. Thus it seems that it was not the *pontifex maximus* who turned away from the condemned Vestal in this instance, but vice versa.[95]

The significance of Cornelia's act, as Pliny explains, is that it helped her make the case for her innocence, which in turn threatened to unravel the moral logic of her punishment. Moreover, Cornelia's rejection of the emperor's touch as "shameful" (*foedum*) was also an implicit challenge to Domitian's authority as an enforcer of sacred law. As her reaction demonstrates, it was not simply the purity of her body that had to be protected,

---

[95] McDermott (1969: 331–2). Domitian is also described as a *carnifex* in Plin. *Pan.* 90.5.

but that of her garment as well. The stola that the Vestals wore was itself a symbol of sexual purity, which only they and married women (whose status also depended on their chastity) were allowed to wear. Indeed, Valerius Maximus records the terms of an ancient law, the purpose of which was "that the stola be left unsullied by the touch of a strange hand" (2.1.5a: *ut inviolata manus alienae tactu stola relinqueretur*).[96] Cornelia's narrow escape from the outstretched reach of the *carnifex* thus could be interpreted as a rebuke to Domitian's apparent ignorance of (or disregard for) the taboos surrounding the Vestals' sacred costume. Although not as grave an error as Vitellius assuming his priesthood on the anniversary of the disaster at Allia, Domitian's apparent lack of respect for the Vestal stola was nevertheless a potentially embarrassing blunder for a *pontifex maximus* to commit.[97] As Cornelia fell "decorously" (εὐσχήμων) into the chamber, some of the other *pontifices* may well have turned away in horror.

But more than its potential to undermine Domitian's religious authority by making him look foolish, this incident underscores the more fundamental weakness in Domitian's policy of *severitas*: his failure to acknowledge the substantive value of a Vestal's virginity as anything more than a restriction to be punished in its transgression. By insisting on Cornelia's punishment, Domitian promotes an essentially negative view of her status, which implies that the only way for her to participate in the renewal of Roman morals was as a cautionary *exemplum*. Like Arachne, Vestals were able to achieve prominence only for their misdeeds. From the Vestal's point of view, however, chastity was a virtue that she actively embodied. Whether involuntary or deliberate, Cornelia's reflex to the outstretched hand reaching for her stola called attention to the incorporated habits of bodily practice through which members of her priesthood preserved the memory of this fundamental aspect of their identity.[98] Moreover, for those who were prepared to admit the possibility that Cornelia might be innocent of the crimes lodged against her, the history of the Vestal priesthood offered a very different framework within which to interpret the questions raised about her chastity. The precautions of moving the pontifical tribunal to Alba Longa and muffling Cornelia's cries could not eliminate the fundamental ambiguity of the situation.

Although we do not know the nature of the crisis that prompted the reopening of *incestum* trials in 91, it should be noted that Cornelia's own

---

[96] Sebesta (1997: 535–7), Wildfang (2006: 13–4). See Mart. 1.35.8–9, Fest. 112 Lindsay, Staples (1998: 69–70), also Beard (1980: 16), Milnor (2005: 150–3), and Noreña (2007: 297–301).

[97] Tac. *Hist.* 2.91.1.

[98] See Connerton (1989: 72–104).

testimony implies that there was no serious prodigy or threat to justify her condemnation.[99] Before the *pontifices* arrived to bind her under the heavy covers that would mute her cries as they carried her through the city, Cornelia protested the fact that the same Caesar who had earned triumphs while she was performing sacrifices could now think she was unchaste (§7). Pliny is unable to decide whether this was derision or flattery. In fact, Cornelia's words place the emperor in an untenable ideological position no matter how they are interpreted. If it was true that Rome was flourishing under Domitian's leadership, it follows that the *pax deum* was still intact, which means that the punishment of a Vestal was unnecessary.[100] If, on the other hand, Cornelia was guilty, then the emperor's celebrated military accomplishments must have been illegitimate, because Rome cannot have enjoyed the gods' favor while she was performing sacrifices.[101] From Domitian's perspective, neither conclusion was favorable.

Because obtaining clemency was already out of the question at this point, Cornelia instead tried to redefine what was happening to her. By calling attention to the emperor's role in her execution, she exposed the fact that her condemnation was not the product of the impersonal workings of an ancient and ineluctable religious law, but was instead further proof of this Caesar's unrestrained and arbitrary power. Whether Cornelia was innocent or not, her protest reflects a deep engagement with the history of her priestly college, which enabled her to promote an alternative reading of her own role within it. By deftly invoking the memory of innocent Vestals, she was able to turn the tables on Domitian and call attention to his efforts to manipulate Rome's religious traditions for his own political advantage.

Alongside those Vestals whose names entered the annals because of their condemnations for *incestum* stood another, equally important group of women who had acquired fame by disproving malicious accusations of misconduct. Virtuous Vestals such as Tuccia and Aemilia, as well as the matron Claudia Quinta, provided a template that Cornelia was able to invoke as she sought to protest the injustice of her treatment. Because the trials of Tuccia and Aemilia belong to the period covered in the missing second decade of Livy's *Ab urbe condita*, it is difficult to reconstruct the historical context in which they belong. Instead, each stands as a discrete *exemplum* of virtue rewarded, which is how they were probably

---

[99] *Pace* Fraschetti (1984: 119), who sees a connection with the Dacian war. If we accept the date of 91 for Cornelia's punishment (above, n. 17), this is more likely what she has in mind when she refers to Caesar's triumph (§7): Sherwin-White (1966: 283).

[100] Fraschetti (1984: 111).

[101] Cf. Juv. 4.146–9, with Stewart (1994: 326).

best known in any event.[102] Of Tuccia, Valerius Maximus provides the following account:

> *quae conscientia certa sinceritatis suae spem salutis ancipiti argumento ausa petere est: arrepto enim cribro "Vesta" inquit, "si sacris tuis castas semper admovi manus, effice ut hoc hauriam e Tiberi aquam et in aedem tuam perferam." audaciter et temere iactis uotis sacerdotis rerum ipsa natura cessit.*

She, secure in the knowledge of her integrity, dared to pursue her hope of safety with an uncertain argument. Taking up the sieve, she said "Vesta, if I have always applied chaste hands in your rites, make it so that I can draw water from the Tiber with this and carry it to your temple." The nature of things itself gave way to the prayers of the priestess, which were boldly and impetuously offered. (8.1.absol.5)[103]

According to Dionysius of Halicarnassus, she returned with the water in her sieve and poured it out at the feet of the *pontifices*, who were assembled in the Forum for her trial (*AR* 2.69.2). This was interpreted as a dramatic public proof of the goddess' continued favor for a loyal and chaste priestess.

Dionysius also provides a strikingly similar account of the miracle performed by Aemilia, who, like Cornelia, was *virgo Vestalis maxima* when she fell under suspicion:

> ἔνθα δή φασι τὴν Αἰμιλίαν ἀναίτιον μὲν οὖσαν, ἀπορουμένην δ' ἐπὶ τῷ συμβεβηκότι παρόντων τῶν ἱερέων καὶ τῶν ἄλλων παρθένων τὰς χεῖρας ἐπὶ τὸν βωμὸν ἐκτείνασαν εἰπεῖν· "Ἑστία, τῆς Ῥωμαίων πόλεως φύλαξ, εἰ μὲν ὁσίως καὶ δικαίως ἐπιτετέλεκά σοι τὰ ἱερὰ χρόνον ὀλίγου δέοντα τριακονταετοῦς καὶ ψυχὴν ἔχουσα καθαρὰν καὶ σῶμα ἁγνόν, ἐπιφάνηθί μοι καὶ βοήθησον καὶ μὴ περιίδῃς τὴν σεαυτῆς ἱέρειαν τὸν οἴκτιστον μόρον ἀποθανοῦσαν· εἰ δὲ ἀνόσιόν τι πέπρακταί μοι, ταῖς ἐμαῖς τιμωρίαις τὸ τῆς πόλεως ἄγος ἀφάγνισον." ταῦτ' εἰποῦσαν καὶ περιρρήξασαν ἀπὸ τῆς καρπασίνης ἐσθῆτος, ἣν ἔτυχεν ἐνδεδυκυῖα, βαλεῖν τὸν τελαμῶνα ἐπὶ τὸν βωμὸν μετὰ τὴν εὐχὴν λέγουσι καὶ ἐκ τῆς κατεψυγμένης πρὸ πολλοῦ καὶ οὐδένα φυλαττούσης σπινθῆρα τέφρας ἀναλάμψαι φλόγα πολλὴν διὰ τῆς καρπάσου.

Then, they say that Aemilia, who though innocent was nevertheless bewildered, stretched out her hands to the altar in the presence of the priests who were there and the other virgins, and said, "Hestia [= Vesta], protector of the Romans' city, if I have discharged your rites with piety and justice and have kept my spirit pure and my body chaste for almost thirty years, then

---

[102] The accusation of this Aemilia cannot be dated with any certainty. Tuccia's exoneration probably belongs in 230 BC, but the strange notice in *Per.* 20: *Tuccia, virgo Vestalis, incesti damnata est*, cannot be an accurate reflection of the original text: Münzer (1937–38: 199–203).

[103] Mueller (2002: 50–2).

reveal yourself to me, come to my aid, and do not allow your own priestess to be put to death in the most shameful fashion. But if any offence has been committed by me, then let me purify the city's guilt with my punishment." As she said these things, she tore off the band from the linen garment she happened to be wearing and threw it on the altar. They say it was in the midst of her prayer that from the ashes, which had long been cold and had no spark left, the linen burst into flames. (AR 2.68.3–4, cf. Val. Max. 1.1.7, Prop. 4.11.53–4)

Although more prolix in this telling, the structure of Aemilia's prayer closely parallels that of Tuccia's in Valerius' account. Both Vestals deploy a conditional framework to establish a causal relationship between their chaste service and Vesta's willingness to intervene on their behalf. Unlike a typical votive prayer, in which a divinity is asked to provide some benefit in exchange for a sacrifice that is currently being performed or soon to be fulfilled, Tuccia and Aemilia instead emphasize their past good deeds and point to the obligation that Vesta already owes to them.[104] Furthermore, both miracles were accomplished using some element of the Vestals' costume or ritual apparatus, which further underscores the connection between the priestess' chaste performance of her religious duties and the divine favor revealed in the miracle.[105]

A similar conditional framework also underpins the prayer offered in Ovid's account of the arrival of the Idaean mother, when Claudia Quinta came forward to fulfill the requirement that the goddess be received with "chaste hands" (Fast. 4.260: casta est accipienda manu).[106] In Ovid's account, Claudia is a matron whose beauty had made her the subject of vicious rumors, but it is interesting to note that other versions of this story, including one attributed to Seneca, suggest that she was a Vestal virgin. It is difficult to make sense of this claim, because a Vestal who was under suspicion of incestum would not ordinarily have been allowed to participate in any religious ritual, but the idea nevertheless appears to have taken hold in later tradition, where Claudia's miracle is also paired with that of Tuccia.[107] The link was evidently already present in Ovid's mind,

---

[104] See Appel (1909: 152–7), also Pulleyn (1997: 16–38), Hickson (1993).

[105] The Vestals used a bronze cribrum to carry burning coals into the temple: Fest. 94 Lindsay. Aemilia's inflammable piece of linen was probably the fibula (or perhaps the infula) with which she bound her white veil, or suffibulum: Fest. 474 Lindsay.

[106] Fast. 4.319–24: "supplicis, alma, tuae, genetrix fecunda deorum, / accipe sub certa condicione preces. / casta negor: si tu damnas, meruisse fatebor; / morte luam poenas iudice victa dea; / sed si crimen abest, tu nostrae pignora vitae / re dabis, et castas casta sequere manus." cf. Livy 29.14.12.

[107] Tertul. Apol. 22.12, August. Civ. D. 10.16. Sen. ap. Hier. adv. Iov. 41 (= fr. 80 Haase), Lact. Inst. Div. 27, Scheid (2001: 24–5).

as Claudia explicitly (but incongruously) expresses her willingness to offer her life as forfeit if she has been unchaste (321–2: *si tu damnas, meruisse fatebor; / morte luam poenas iudice victa dea*).

The slippage in Claudia's status from matron to Vestal can be explained by the overwhelming importance of chastity in the religious identity of the Vestal virgins. This virtue was not simply a base requirement of their priesthood, but was itself also regarded as a positive source of numinous power. As Pliny the Elder explains, the Vestals were known for their powerful incantations (*NH* 28.13). He refers not only to Tuccia's miracle, but also to a contemporary belief that these priestesses could prevent fugitive slaves from leaving the city by uttering a prayer. Thus, more than any other class of Roman women, the Vestals provided a model of chastity that could be verified through the miraculous intervention of divine forces in human affairs.[108]

The memory of women such as Tuccia, Aemilia, and Claudia Quinta represented an important strand in Roman discourse of gender and religion. The popularity of these stories can be inferred from the fact that the exact language of Tuccia's prayer was preserved in written sources, and Claudia Quinta was the subject of at least one play.[109] Clearly, the *exemplum* of an acquitted Vestal could make as much of an impact as that of a priestess who was executed for her transgressions. What this means is that there was already an alternative in place to Domitian's use of punishment and surveillance in the restoration of contemporary morals. From Pliny's brief description of Cornelia's protest, it seems likely she was attempting to associate herself with this particular strand of the Vestal tradition. The significance of her statements, which Pliny reads as ambiguous, becomes clearer when viewed in the context of the memory of miracle-working Vestals.

Like Aemilia, Cornelia stretched out her hands to Vesta and other gods in a gesture of supplication. According to Pliny, "she... cried out many things, but this most often: 'Caesar thinks that I am unchaste, though he has conquered and triumphed when I perform the rites!'" (§7: *multa sed hoc frequentissime clamitabat: "Me Caesar incestam putat, qua sacra faciente vicit triumphavit!"*) Although the words of this protest do not follow the precise conditional formula found in the earlier prayers, there is a parallel emphasis on the blameless manner in which she had carried out her duties, along with the implication that benefits would continue to accrue

---

[108] Dion. Hal. 2.68.2.
[109] Plin. *NH* 28.12: *extat Tucciae Vestalis incesti deprecatio.* Ov. *Fast.* 4.326: *mira, sed et scaena testificata loquar.* Scheid (2001: 26).

from her chaste behavior. In effect, Vesta has already testified to Cornelia's chastity by providing Domitian with military glory. By maintaining absolute confidence in her own innocence, Cornelia raised the expectation that she too should be saved by some act of divine intervention. But no miracle occurred, and she was not spared. In the end, she was powerless to overcome the historical distance that separated her from the innocent Vestals she took as her models.

Lurking beneath the surface of this protest, of course, was the issue of the divinity of the Roman emperor.[110] Like other aspects of Imperial authority that have already been discussed, this concept operated on multiple levels. In the provinces, the worship of the emperors, like that of the goddess Roma, was an essential element in the interface between local communities and the institutions of Imperial government. Closer to the center of power (and more within the purview of the present discussion), the senate came to accept the posthumous deification of individual Caesars as a means of passing final judgment on their memory. Although Pliny might impugn Domitian's motives in securing these honors for his father and brother, the policy differed little from that of Augustus, who had actively publicized his own status as the son of a god (*divi filius*).[111]

Nevertheless, the principle of the *civilis princeps* required that a clear distinction be drawn between the living emperor and the gods of Roman state religion. Tiberius had made a point of refusing the divine honors offered him by the people of Gytheum in Laconia, saying that he was content with honors that were "more modest, and suitable for men" (*SEG* 11 923 = EJ 102b, l. 20: ταῖς μετριωτέραις τε καὶ ἀνθρωπείοις).[112] Domitian was not so rigorously self-effacing, it seems, and later tradition held that he was the first emperor to adopt the title "master and god" (*dominus et deus*) for himself.[113] A lack of epigraphic testimony suggests that this collocation was not, in fact, an official title, but Suetonius was able to cite official correspondence in which imperial procurators employed the formula "our master and god orders that this be done" (*Dom.* 13.2: *dominus et deus*

---

[110] The subject is obviously great in scope. See, *inter alia*, Taylor (1931), Hopkins (1978: 197–242), Price (1984), Fishwick (1987), (1991), Veyne (1990: 306–21), Schowalter (1993), Gradel (2002).

[111] Plin. *Pan.* 11.1, cf. Buttrey (1976). See Scott (1936: 62–7), Jones (1992: 87–8), *LTUR* V: 124–5 s.v. "Vespasianus, Divus, templum" [De Angeli], II: 19–20 s.v. "Divorum, porticus, templum" [Coarelli], II: 368–9 s.v. "Gens Flavia, templum" [Coarelli].

[112] Cf. Tac. *Ann.* 4.38. Charlesworth (1939), Gradel (2002: 143), Price (1984: 72).

[113] Eutrop. 7.23, cf. Oros. 7.10.2, Aur. Vict. *Caes.* 11.2. Jerome (*Chron.* 2.161 Schöne) dates the adoption of this "title" to 85/6. The reliability of this tradition has been much debated: See Thompson (1984), Jones (1992: 108–9) for the revisionist views, also Scott (1936: 102–12), Bengtson (1979: 219–20), Gradel (2002: 160).

noster hoc fieri iubet). The terms also appear together in Martial's poetry, which provides the clearest contemporary evidence for the use of these titles in combination (5.8.1, cf. 7.5).

Although it was accepted as a polite form of address for subordinates to use with their betters, the first of these appellatives would have been particularly unsettling to members of the Roman elite for reasons outlined in the opening chapter of this book.[114] The traditional attitude is reflected by the poet Statius, who compliments Domitian for refusing to allow grateful dinner guests to refer to him as *dominus* (*Silv.* 1.6.83–4). That refusal does not seem to have been part of a steadfast policy, however, because Statius himself refers to the emperor as "the powerful master of the world" in a later poem (*Silv.* 3.4.19–20: *potenti terrarum domino*). He also speaks of the "nearby god" (*Silv.* 5.2.170: *proximus ille deus*) who looked down on Rome from Alba. By referring to Domitian not only as a master but as a god as well, contemporary writers signaled the degree to which the emperor was elevated above his fellow citizens.[115]

In retrospect, the religious adoration bestowed on Domitian in his lifetime was regarded as excessive. In the *Panegyricus*, Pliny expresses outrage over the fact that cattle were sacrificed before the statue of "the cruelest master," which should have been offered to Jupiter Optimus Maximus instead (*Pan.* 52.7: *saevissimi domini atrocissima effigies*). Even if he did not explicitly demand divine honors, Domitian's apparent receptiveness to this kind of flattery was regarded as a symptom of his despotic character. Martial had honored Domitian in precisely these terms, but he was able to praise Trajan for denying that he was master and god (10.72.3: *dicturus dominum deumque non sum*). When Pliny discusses the appropriate way to honor Trajan, he says, "nowhere will we flatter him as a god, nowhere as a deity: for we are not speaking of a tyrant, but of a citizen, not of a master, but a parent" (*Pan.* 2.3: *nusquam ut deo, nusquam ut numini blandiamur: non enim de tyranno sed de cive, non de domino sed de parente loquimur*). The implication is clear: Domitian had been treated like a *deus*, but only because he behaved as a *dominus*.[116]

This imputation of divine arrogance to Domitian may be reflected in the replacement of Vesta's name with that of Caesar in the recorded version of Cornelia's "prayer," which stands out as its most striking departure from

---

[114] Cf. Suet. *Aug.* 53.1, also Roller (2001: 254–61).

[115] Scott (1936: 106–8). Cf. Stat. *Silv.* 4.praef., 1.1.62, Mart. 8.praef.1, 6.64.14, 8.1.1, 7.8.2, 7.60, 8.8.6, 13.74.

[116] Dio (Xiph) 67.13.3–4 tells the story of Juventius Celsus (*PIR*² I 880), who escaped a charge of treason by performing *proskynesis* and calling Domitian δεσπότης τε καὶ θεός. Schowalter (1993: 71–4).

the Republican precedents that she was invoking. Even as her protests recalled the ancient models of Tuccia, Aemilia, and Claudia Quinta, Cornelia also acknowledged the fact that, under the Principate, religious life had been restructured just as radically as political authority had been. Whereas the Vestals' prayers once were concerned with well-being of the community as a whole, Cornelia describes herself as presiding over rites that resulted in the success and glory of a single individual. This shift in ritual can be traced to changes instituted after Actium, when Augustus' name was introduced into the Salian hymn.[117] Clearly, Domitian's incipient divinity altered the political and religious dynamics of the suspect Vestal's predicament. Not only was the emperor able to tip the balance between aristocratic *clementia* and a more populist impulse for *severitas*, his judgment also had the force of divine will. By comparing the memory of virtuous Republican Vestals with Cornelia's attempt to reenact their proofs of innocence, the essential incompatibility of the two eras became clearer. Instead of offering prayers to the gods, those in peril now appealed directly to the emperor for salvation.

CONCLUSION

It is difficult to judge the impact that Cornelia's invocation of Republican precedent had on the public perception of Domitian's oversight of religion and morality. If Pliny's indecisive assessment is any guide (§8: *blandiens haec an inridens, ex fiducia sui an ex contemptu principis dixerit, dubium est*), much of the subtlety of her protest went unnoticed or was deliberately overlooked by the majority of her audience. Contemporary writers, who had an interest in flattering the emperor, suggest that the strict discipline he imposed on the Vestals was regarded as a welcome display of moral rigor and a reaffirmation of the sanctity of one of Rome's most ancient religious traditions. From Domitian's point of view, the punishment of Cornelia was part of a larger narrative about the restoration of traditional values – and of sexual chastity in particular – under his supervision. The *severitas* he displayed in this case was sanctioned by religious tradition as a necessary element in the struggle to arrest moral decline. His approach to moral oversight received validation from the actions of earlier generations of *pontifices*, the justice handed down by Cassius Ravilla, and even the wrath shown by Minerva in the myth that provided the inspiration for the decoration of the Forum Transitorium.

---

[117] *RG* 10.1, cf. Dio 51.19.7–20.3, Beard, North, and Price (1998: 206–10).

After Domitian's death, however, the execution of Cornelia was remembered as an emblem of this emperor's tyrannical cruelty. Although a posthumous critic such as Pliny the Younger continued to accept the essential justice of the principles that underlay Domitian's approach to moral reform, he rejects the legitimacy of any action undertaken by a ruler whose own supposed immorality should have debarred him from sitting in judgment of others. For all the power he enjoyed, Domitian was unable to control how his policing of his subjects' behavior was received. In light of this reversal, it is interesting to note that Pliny leaves undefined the "examples of this sort" (§6: *eiusmodi exemplis*) with which he says Domitian wished to enlighten his age. Depending on one's point of view, these *exempla* might be either models of righteousness or crimes to avoid. The ambiguity of the phrase mirrors the ambiguity of the situation being described.

In the end, however, Cornelia's reaction to her fate offers the most direct challenge to the assumptions underpinning Domitian's (or any emperor's) assertion of authority as a protector of Roman morals. Domitian sought to impose a restrictive interpretation of ancient moral virtue that could be maintained only by strict discipline, but the peculiarity of his position in political and religious life ultimately destabilized any attempt to use magistracies or priesthoods as ostensibly traditional sources of authority for the imposition of such severe measures. Cornelia's claims of innocence, and particularly the way that they were staged, called attention to this instability. By emphasizing the complexity of the tradition in which moral behavior was fostered, she shifted the framework in which the *pontifex maximus'* imposition of severe penalties might be viewed. Although the benefit of a public inquiry was denied to her, Cornelia nevertheless did all she could to demonstrate an alternate vision of how positive belief in her chastity might have benefited the Roman community. Like Domitian, she employed memories of the Republican past in support of her position. But just as the emperor's attempts to control the historical framework in which this exercise of power was viewed resulted in failure, Cornelia's prayers for salvation also landed on deaf ears.

4

PERSUASION

INTER CLAROS MAGIS QUAM INTER BONOS

Two years after Cornelia's execution, Domitian gave further proof of the *severitas* of his regime. In the autumn of 93, at a time when philosophers were being expelled from Rome, the younger Pliny reports that seven friends of senatorial rank were either condemned or exiled.[1] All were connected to each other through their association with the Patavian consular and Stoic P. Clodius Thrasea Paetus and his equally eminent son-in-law Helvidius Priscus, the troublesome praetor of 70.[2] The new political order had proved destructive to both men. Thrasea took his own life after being condemned under Nero, and Helvidius met a similar fate during Vespasian's reign. In death as in life, these men remained central figures in the ongoing struggle to understand the role of the senate in the administration of the empire and the *respublica* under a *princeps*. For subsequent generations, their memory became yet another contested element in the interpretation of the Republic's significance for contemporary life. Like the controversies about Domitian's moral oversight discussed in the previous chapter, these debates filtered persistent concerns about the balance of political authority in the present through competing claims about how best to preserve continuity with the Republican past. Although the discussion so far has centered on the efforts of emperors (and would-be emperors) to frame the memory of the Republic in ways favorable to themselves,

---

[1] Plin. *Ep.* 3.11.3, cf. Dio (Xiph.) 67.13, MacMullen (1966: 65–7), Bengtson (1979: 235–8). The date is confirmed by both Jerome and the Armenian chronicle (160–1 Schöne), and provides a year for Pliny's praetorship: Syme (1958: 76), (1991: 561–4), Sherwin-White (1966: 763–71). Furthermore, it was shortly after the death of Tacitus' father-in-law, in August of that year: *Agr.* 44.1, 45.1.

[2] *PIR²* C 1187, *PIR²* H 59 (appears in Chapter 2). Syme (1991: 568–87) examines the connections among this group in detail. See also the diagram in MacMullen (1966: 43).

this chapter takes a wider view of this process to examine debates that were taking place not only between the *princeps* and potentially dissident subjects, but within the ranks of the elite itself.

It was not simply proximity to Thrasea and Helvidius that brought Pliny's group of nobles into peril. The three who met with death – Herennius Senecio, Q. Arulenus Junius Rusticus, and the praetor's son C. Helvidius Priscus – were all convicted of literary crimes. Following the condemnation of the first two men, copies of their works were burnt in the Forum. As Tacitus notes, "wrath was visited not just on the authors themselves, but on their books as well" (*Agr.* 2.1: *neque in ipsos modo auctores, sed in libros quoque eorum saevitum*).[3] The nature of these prosecutions is interesting, because verbal treason was, at root, a religious crime (*impietas*), stemming from the emperor's special position in Roman state religion.[4] The importance of this connection is underscored by the fact that Rusticus had written a biography of Thrasea, describing him as "holy" (ἱερός).[5] At Fannia's request, Senecio had written the life of her husband Helvidius, presumably in a similar vein.[6] The charge against the younger Helvidius was comparable, although his work belonged to a different genre. According to Suetonius (*Dom.* 10.4), he had written a play about the ill-fated love of Paris and Oenone, which was taken as an insulting reference to Domitian's brief divorce from Domitia Longina.[7] In light of the issues investigated in the previous chapter, it is easy to see why the emperor chose not to tolerate these forms of dissident expression.

[3] Cramer (1945). *PIR*[2] H 128, I 730 (but note Syme [1991: 582–3] on the nomenclature), H 60. Those exiled included Rusticus' brother, Junius Mauricus (*PIR*[2] I 771), Verulana Gratilla (*PIR*[1] V 289, perhaps Rusticus' wife), Thrasea's widow Arria (*PIR*[2] A 1114), and their daughter Fannia, the wife of the elder Helvidius (*PIR*[2] F 118). See esp. Bauman (1974: 160–2) *contra* Rogers (1960), whose approach is criticized, with good reason, by Chilton (1955). On Tacitus' reflections and the implications of these events for memory in Roman Imperial culture, see Hedrick (2000: 153–70), Sailor (2008: 51–73).

[4] Bauman (1974: 2–19). Cf. Dio 57.9.1–2, cf. Tac. *Ann.* 4.37.1–38.5, Taylor (1929).

[5] Dio (Xiph.) 67.13.2, cf. Tac. *Agr.* 2.1, Suet. *Dom.* 10.3. On the significance of Rusticus' biography for later tradition, see Murray (1965: 56–9).

[6] Plin. *Ep.* 7.19.5, Dio (Xiph.) 67.13.2. Senecio had also failed to pursue any office beyond the quaestorship and so may have been suspected for a sullen quietude, as Thrasea had been: cf. Tac. *Ann.* 16.21.1–22.5, Murray (1965: 54–6). Senecio's abandonment of the *cursus* does not seem to have involved a complete retirement from public life, because shortly before his conviction he can be found alongside Pliny in the prosecution of Baebius Massa (*PIR*[2] B 26) for *repetundae* in his native Baetica: Plin. *Ep.* 7.33.

[7] Jones (1992: 187). It is generally assumed that Domitian was portrayed as Paris, whose rejection of Oenone led to trouble: Syme (1991: 575), Rutledge (2001: 134). A different connection might have been intended, however, given the hostile rumors about Domitia's passion for an actor named Paris: Suet. *Dom.* 3.1, Dio (Xiph.) 67.3.1, *PIR*[2] P 128, cf. Vinson (1989: 439–40).

The prosecutions of these authors cast a long shadow. In some quarters, the elation that followed the death of Domitian was tempered by a sense of shame. Tacitus evokes the feeling of collective guilt that stemmed from the senate's complicity in the emperor's cruelty: "our hands led Helvidius to prison, the sight of Mauricus and Rusticus ruined us, and Senecio soaked us with his innocent blood" (*Agr.* 45.1: *mox nostrae duxere Helvidium in carcerem manus; nos Maurici Rusticique visus <afflixit,>nos innocenti sanguine Senecio perfudit*). Pliny, whose letters generally eschew this sort of melancholic self-reflection, saw instead an opportunity to make things right: "When Domitian was killed, I consulted with myself and decided that here was a substantial matter ideal for attacking the guilty, avenging the unfortunate, and promoting oneself" (*Ep.* 9.13.2: *occiso Domitiano statui mecum ac deliberavi, esse magnam pulchramque materiam insectandi nocentes, miseros vindicandi, se proferendi*). The matter in question was the basis for his public denunciation of Publicius Certus, a speech he later published under the title *On the Avenging of Helvidius* (*de ultione Helvidii*).[8]

What, precisely, Certus had done is unclear. Pliny refers to an incident where "in the senate, a senator laid hands on a senator, a praetorian on a consul, a judge on the accused" (*Ep.* 9.13.2: *in senatu senator senatori, praetorius consulari, reo iudex manus intulisset*). Perhaps Certus was one of those who physically dragged Helvidius to the prison in Tacitus' account, but here the contrast between the two authors is stark. Whereas Tacitus speaks of using "our hands" against Helvidius, Pliny prefers to fix blame on the actions of a single individual. Overlooking his own complicity in these events, Pliny uses the accusation of Certus to further his effort to reconfigure the memory of his own position under Domitian. Despite his claim that thunderbolts were crashing all around him in 93, his connection to the condemned does not seem to have been as close as his belated support for their cause might imply. In fact, Pliny's career continued to flourish after the crisis that claimed Helvidius, Rusticus, and the others.[9]

Nevertheless, the decision to vindicate the interests of Helvidius' family after Domitian's assassination was a relatively bold stroke. Owing to

---

[8] Plin. *Ep.* 9.13.1, *PIR*² P 1040, cf. *Ep.* 4.21.3, 7.30.4, also 1.2. It may be significant that this speech is being studied by the young C. Ummidius Quadratus, under whose great-grandfather Helvidius senior had served when he was a legate in Syria: *PIR*¹ V 603, cf. Syme (1968: 84–9).

[9] *Ep.* 3.11.3: *tot circa me iactis fulminibus quasi ambustus.* Giovannini (1987: 232–4), Syme (1991: 564), Flower (2006: 267).

Nerva's age and the absence of a clear successor, there must have been a great deal of anxiety at the start of this emperor's reign.[10] If a young senator antagonized the wrong people, good intentions might become a liability when power changed hands again. Glory seeking entailed risk in those days, and caution forbade bold gestures. After Pliny entered the meeting and declared his intention to pursue the question of Certus' responsibility for what had been done to Helvidius, Pliny says that consular friends came over to admonish his temerity. "You have made yourself conspicuous to future emperors" (*Ep.* 9.13.10: *notabilem te futuris princibus fecisti*), one said. Another pointed out, "you have assaulted a man who is already prefect of the treasury and soon to be consul, and furthermore one supported by such influence and such friends" (*lacessis hominem iam praefectum aerarii et brevi consulem, praeterea qua gratia quibus amicitiis fultum*). Pliny boasts of the courage and youthful idealism with which he shook off the older men's objections, but he does not suggest that their caution was unwarranted.[11]

When Pliny first raised the matter at a meeting of the senate, he was met with various objections, including the shouted appeal, "let those of us who have survived remain unharmed." (9.13.7: *salvi simus, qui supersumus*). It was thought that little would be gained from another condemnation, especially when so many had been complicit in the crime Pliny was seeking to prosecute. The mood of the chamber was acknowledged by C. Julius Cornutus Tertullus, a friend of Pliny's and the custodian of Helvidius' daughter.[12] Speaking on behalf of the family, Cornutus offered a compromise: "if the punishment for such an obvious crime is to be set aside, he should at least be branded with something like the censor's mark" (9.13.16: "*si poena flagitii manifestissimi remittatur, nota certe quasi censoria inuratur*"). It is worth reflecting on the unacknowledged irony in the continuity between the moral vocabulary favored by Domitian and

---

[10] Syme (1958: 8–11), Grainger (2003: 66–102). Much has been made of the unnamed "somebody" *qui tunc ad orientem amplissimum exercitum non sine magnis dubiisque rumoribus obtinebat* who was named as one of Publicius' powerful friends (*Ep.* 9.13.11). Alföldy and Halfmann (1973: 363–9) identify him as M. Nigrinus Curiatius Maternus, discussed briefly below. This identification is accepted by Grainger (2003: 92–4), but Berriman and Todd (2001: 317–23) reopen the case for identifying this *ignotus* with L. Javolenus Priscus (*PIR*[2] I 14), proposed by Gsell (1894: 332 n. 2), once credited, but later dubbed "not very likely" by Syme (1958: 632).

[11] Pliny also suggests (*Ep.* 9.13.6) that this impetuosity explained why he did not seek the advice of Corellius Rufus (*PIR*[2] C 1294), which he would have been compelled to follow. See Hoffer (1999: 156).

[12] *PIR*[2] I 273.

that used by those who eventually objected to the severity imposed by his regime. As things turned out, the question of public censure quickly became moot. Certus escaped formal condemnation, but Pliny could still claim to have gotten what he was aiming for (*Ep.* 9.13.22: *obtinui tamen quod intenderam*): The man was removed from his post as prefect of the treasury and lost his anticipated nomination for the consulship. He died of an illness shortly thereafter. Pliny acceded to the position vacated in the *aerarium Saturni*, and thence to the consulship in his own right, with Cornutus as his colleague in both posts. One might say that the bold gamble of denouncing Certus paid off rather well.[13]

In this atmosphere of retaliations, feared retaliations, and excuses, the old general Verginius Rufus was made consul for a third time, as a colleague to the new emperor. He died in office, leaving instructions for his tomb and the epitaph that articulated the values of patriotism and liberty that were embraced as the hallmarks of the new regime. A public funeral for Verginius offered Nerva a grand opportunity to celebrate these principles while also reviving the ancient custom of commemorating the deeds and habits of a famous man. The eulogy delivered by the consul Cornelius Tacitus, whom Pliny praises as a *laudator eloquentissimus*, would have glorified Verginius' self-sacrificing service to his *patria* and held him up as an example of the kind of glory that could be achieved in the present.[14]

It was not long before Tacitus took the opportunity to reflect further on the new era inaugurated by Nerva, in which freedom and the Principate could finally coexist (*Agr.* 3.1: *res olim dissociabiles miscuerit*), by composing his own biography of a figure with whom he was intimately associated, his father-in-law Cn. Julius Agricola.[15] Although the sinister imprint the historian puts on his account of the treatment Agricola received from Domitian and his court is comparable to the claims Pliny makes about the perils of his own early career, Tacitus also concludes his work with a muted criticism of figures such as Rusticus and Helvidius, whose persecution had made them famous. He offers Agricola's life of cooperation and achievement as proof that an illustrious death was not the only way to earn glory, and that great men could still emerge even under bad emperors (*Agr.* 42.4: *sciant, quibus moris est inlicita mirari, posse etiam sub malis*

---

[13] Sherwin-White (1966: 75–8), Syme (1991: 565). It is perhaps to mitigate the impression of a self-serving campaign that Pliny stresses the uncertainty of the situation and calls attention to his consultations with Helvidius' widow Anteia (*PIR*² A 732), along with Arria and Fannia, in the letter that describes his decision to take up the case (9.13.4–5).

[14] Plin. *Ep.* 2.1.5–6, Dio (Xiph.) 68.2.4. Grainger (2003: 41), Syme (1958: 129–30).

[15] Tac. *Agr.* 3.1: *nunc demum redit animus.* Syme (1991: 519): "From Verginius a straight swift line leads to Agricola," see also Syme (1958: 121).

principibus magnos viros esse). This argument may have offered some cover for senators such as himself, who had failed to take positive steps to curb the abuses of Domitian's reign, but it does not address the problem of what to do about bad men such as Publicius Certus, who had amplified the suffering inflicted by a vicious emperor.

For Tacitus' views on this issue, we must turn to the opening books of the *Histories*, which are germane to many of the issues that emerged in the years that followed Domitian's assassination.[16] His account of the outrage directed against certain Neronian prosecutors (*delatores*) in the aftermath of Galba's rebellion offers certain parallels to the impulse for retribution chronicled in Pliny's discussion of the circumstances surrounding his *de Helvidii ultione*. As with the reflections on the recurrence of civil war in 69 discussed in Chapter 2, Tacitus' treatment of these parliamentary conflicts casts stark light on the ambiguities of Imperial ideology, particularly the uneasiness that characterized the embrace of Republican traditions within the system of the Principate.

Early in Galba's reign, a *senatus consultum* was adopted, which called for an investigation into the activities of informers under the previous regime.[17] This decree remained in effect after Otho seized power, when further steps were taken against individual *delatores*. At this point in Tacitus' narrative, Vibius Crispus, whom the historian describes as a figure whose money, power, and ability ranked him "among the notable rather than the good" (*Hist.* 2.10.1: *pecunia potentia ingenio inter claros magis quam inter bonos*), took the opportunity to exact revenge on a personal enemy. He initiated proceedings against the equestrian prosecutor Annius Faustus, who had once leveled a charge against Crispus' brother.[18] Noting the mixed public reaction to Faustus' swift condemnation, the historian remarks that the people "certainly remembered that Crispus himself had engaged in the very same accusations for profit" under Nero (*Hist.* 2.10.3: *quippe ipsum Crispum easdem accusationes cum praemio exercuisse meminerant*).

This irony was linked to a more disturbing issue – the extent to which success or failure in such cases reflected the preexisting balance of power between accuser and accused. Tacitus explains:

> *id senatus consultum varie iactatum et, prout potens vel inops reus inciderat, infirmum aut validum, retinebat adhuc terroris.*

---

[16] Note esp. Syme (1957a), (1958: 130).
[17] Tac. *Hist.* 2.10.1, cf. Dio (Zon.) 64.3.4ᵃ, id. (Xiph.) 68.1.2. Rutledge (2001: 121–6).
[18] *PIR*¹ V 379, *PIR*² A 645, Rutledge (2001: 278–82).

The senate's decree was variously interpreted: it was ineffective or forceful, depending on whether the defendant happened to be powerful or unprotected, weak or strong, and still it preserved some fear. (*Hist.* 2.10.1)

The equestrian Faustus was outmatched by the consular Crispus, making the outcome all but predetermined.[19] A similar concern also impinges on Pliny's description of the indictments that were undertaken at the start of Nerva's reign. In those turbulent first days of liberty, Pliny says, "each man on his own account went after and destroyed his enemies, so long as they were lesser" (*Ep.* 9.13.4: *pro se quisque inimicos suos, dumtaxat minores . . . postulaverat simul et oppresserat*). In the weighing of who was *minor*, one could conclude that these prosecutions did not reflect true justice, but were simply a continuation of the vengeful power plays that they were supposed to rectify.

"EGO IUGULUM STATIM VIDEO, HUNC PREMO"

As the parallel from Tacitus' *Histories* suggests, Pliny's actions in 98 were not an isolated occurrence. Moments of transition at the top of a political system tend to destabilize relationships throughout the power structure, providing opportunities for individuals to act on grudges and bring down old foes. By Pliny's own admission, much of this was going on at the opening of Nerva's reign, although he insists that he acted on principle, not out of personal animus, in attacking Certus (*Ep.* 9.13.4).[20] In a previously published letter (*Ep.* 1.5), however, Pliny records his sincere delight at the discomfiture of M. Aquilius Regulus, an old foe who may have played a role in the prosecution of Arulenus Rusticus, and certainly registered his hostility to the Helvidian group by publishing a work in which he attacked Rusticus as the "Stoics' ape."[21] Once Domitian was dead, Regulus was exposed to the possibility of retribution, just as Publicius Certus had been. Worse still, he also had attempted to embarrass (and perhaps endanger) Pliny under cross-examination in a civil trial, by pressing him about his reliance on the legal analysis of the jurist Mettius Modestus, who was in exile at the time.[22] This personal history placed Regulus in a difficult

---

[19] On the significance of the term *potens* in this context, see Gallia (2009).

[20] Cf. Dio (Xiph.) 68.1.2–3, Grainger (2003: 40).

[21] *Ep.* 1.5.2: *in quo Rusticum insectatur atque etiam "Stoicorum simiam" adpellat. PIR²* A 1005. It is not clear whether the *liber* in question was a prosecutorial speech or some other defamatory work. See Rutledge (2001: 131–2), Rogers (1960: 20). Hostility toward Regulus is also registered at *Ep.* 2.11.22, 2.20, 4.2, 4.7, and 6.2.4. See Hoffer (1999: 55–92), Rutledge (2001: 192–8).

[22] *Ep* 1.5.4–7, *PIR²* M 565.

position, and Pliny takes evident pleasure in describing the deference now on display, as Regulus sent emissaries to conciliate with him.[23]

Then, at a chance meeting, Regulus took the opportunity to apologize for a previous offense, which he worried had stuck in the younger man's mind. To Pliny's surprise, however, it was not the rough questioning about Mettius Modestus that Regulus regretted. Instead, the apology concerned a different exchange in the centumviral court, in which Regulus had referred to Pliny's co-counsel in a particular case as "Satrius Rufus, who has no competition with Cicero and who is satisfied with the eloquence of our era" (*Ep.* 1.5.11: *Satrius Rufus, cui non est cum Cicerone aemulatio et qui contentus est eloquentia saeculi nostri*).[24] This comment was evidently intended as an insult to Pliny, although he claims to have regarded it as a compliment. Indeed, Pliny made no secret of his *aemulatio* with Cicero, which expressed itself most notably in the Demosthenic fulsomeness of his argumentation. This was an aspect of Pliny's rhetorical style that he once set out to justify in a self-consciously overlong letter to Tacitus, wherein he quotes yet another exchange with Regulus, which gives an even more stark impression of the difference between their approaches. According to Pliny, Regulus once told him, "you think that everything that is in a case must be explored; I see the throat immediately, and throttle it" (*Ep.* 1.20.14: "*tu omnia quae sunt in causa putas exsequenda; ego iugulum statim video, hunc premo*").[25]

Pliny and his rival clearly disagreed about the merits of a Ciceronian style, although it remains to be seen why an admiration for Cicero and the sense that contemporary eloquence had fallen short of that standard should be positions that Regulus might want to apologize for having pointed out.[26] Pliny was hardly alone in seeking to return Roman oratory to the standard Cicero had established, after all. Already at the end of the Augustan era, it was generally agreed that Cicero's speeches represented the highest accomplishments of Roman oratory. Quintilian, a teacher of rhetoric particularly favored by the Flavians, proclaimed, "among his successors, 'Cicero' is no longer regarded as the name of a man but of eloquence

---

[23] *Ep.* 1.5.8–12. The peace envoys were Caecilius Celer (*PIR²* C 28, unknown beyond Pliny's correspondence), L. Fabius Justus (*PIR²* F 41, discussed below), and later the aged Vestricius Spurinna (*PIR* V 308). See Hoffer (1999: 76–82).

[24] *PIR²* S 197, cf. *Ep.* 9.13.17. Rutledge (2001: 195) misconstrues the significance of the insult, and its target.

[25] Williams (1978: 213–32), Cugusi (2003), and Riggsby (1995). See also *Ep.* 9.26, 6.2.5.

[26] Winterbottom (1964: 94). For a different view, see also Rutledge (1999: 562), although he misses the significance of *Ep.* 1.2.11–12 in this context.

itself" (*Inst.* 10.1.112: *apud posteros vero id consecutus ut Cicero iam non hominis nomen sed eloquentiae habeatur*).[27]

Cicero's status as a classic was not without its ambiguities, however. The great orator's death, as a victim of the proscription lists drawn up by the second triumvirate, gave him the potential to represent something more than a purely aesthetic model. In his account of this event, the Tiberian historian Velleius Paterculus does what he can to exculpate Octavian and fix the blame on Antony, but an apostrophe makes clear the importance of Cicero's death to his subsequent reputation: "you [Antony] did not so much rob him of the fame and glory of his deeds and sayings as increase them. He lives, and he will live on in the memory of all ages" (2.66: *famam vero gloriamque factorum atque dictorum adeo non abstulisti, ut auxeris: vivit, vivetque per omnem saeculorum memoriam*).[28] In the same schools of rhetoric where Cicero's speeches were recommended for *imitatio*, students were assigned declamation exercises that dealt with the circumstances of his murder. The elder Annaeus Seneca provides examples of the topics discussed (*Controv.* 7.2, *Suas.* 6, 7): Should Cicero have offered to burn his speeches to spare his life? Was his executioner guilty of ingratitude, if the great orator had previously defended him in court?[29] The utilitarian focus of rhetorical training and the banality of these themes helped to render most schoolroom denunciations of tyranny innocuous. But it is also true that the rhetor Albucius Silus had gotten into trouble under Augustus for calling M. Brutus "the author and avenger of laws and liberty" (Suet. *Rhet.* 6: *legum ac libertatis auctorem et vindicem*).[30] By engaging students directly in a consideration of the historical circumstances that led to the creation of the Principate, these exercises served to fix Cicero's identity as a champion of *libertas* and to establish a "Republican" interpretation of this virtue as an integral part of the memory of his eloquence.

Although admirers such as Velleius and Quintilian (and Pliny, for that matter) posed no threat to the status quo of the Principate, regard for Cicero's oratory had the potential to suggest an enthusiasm for political sentiments of the kind displayed in the much-admired "divine *Philippic*,"

---

[27] Winterbottom (1982: 241–4), (1975: 79–80), Richter (1968: 186), *PIR*² F 59. See also Kennedy (1962), Fantham (1978b: 111–14).

[28] Schmitzer (2000: 184–8), cf. Gowing (2005: 44–8), also Winterbottom (1982: 238–40). On the tradition generally, see Richter (1968, esp. 169–77). Emphasis on Antony's guilt was typical: Roller (1997: 116).

[29] See Roller (1997), Wright (2001), also Winterbottom (1982: 252). On the importance of declamation for the inculcation of values, see Friend (1999), Imber (2001).

[30] *PIR*² A 489. Cf. MacMullen (1966: 35–6), Caplan (1970: 164–5).

which denounced Antony and the threat to freedom he represented.[31] If Regulus' comment about Pliny's *aemulatio* with Cicero had been construed along these lines, it might have become a serious matter indeed. Pliny could boast about how he took Regulus' aggressive words as a compliment, but his account of their subsequent exchange demonstrates how important it was that one's affinity with a Republican icon not be misinterpreted in an era when men continued to pay the ultimate price for such outspokenness.

"ULTERIORA MIRARI, PRAESENTIA SEQUI"

The ambiguity of Cicero's status as a rhetorical model ran parallel to that of a more notorious Republican hero, M. Porcius Cato "Uticensis," the recalcitrant Stoic and opponent of Julius Caesar. The politicization of Cato's memory can be traced back to Cicero, who published an encomium of his friend that provoked Caesar to respond with an *Anticato*.[32] The poet Lucan, who was executed for involvement in the Pisonian conspiracy, expressed special admiration for Cato in his poem on the civil wars, although the epic as we have it breaks off before the final stand at Utica.[33] Thrasea Paetus, whose own life ended similarly, composed a biography of Cato, expounding the Stoic principles that guided his actions.[34] This interest apparently contributed to the impression that Thrasea and his fellow Stoics harbored a dangerous devotion to *libertas*. In time, Thrasea became associated with the memory of Brutus and Cassius as well, presumably in the belief that Cato's opposition to Caesar had formed the basis of his appeal.[35]

It is unlikely, however, that Cato's political attachments were a central issue in the way his memory was cultivated by later adherents of his philosophical school. The noted Stoic Seneca saw Cato's suicide as an exemplary act of liberation, identifying the sword he used as his *adsertor libertatis*, but

---

[31] Juv. 10.125, cf. Vell. 2.64.3. Hammond (1963: 94), Kraus (2000: 439–44).

[32] Cic. *Att.* 12.4.2, 12.5.2, *Top.* 94, Tac. *Ann.* 4.34, Kierdorf (1978), Pecchiura (1965: 25–35), Bardon (1952: 280–1). On the complexity of Cato's posthumous reputation, see Pecchiura (1965), Goar (1987), Gowing (2005: 76–9).

[33] See esp. Luc. 9.601–4. Ahl (1976: 254–79), George (1991: 245–6), Morford (2002: 200).

[34] Plut. *Cato Min.* 25.2, 37.1, cf. Mart. 1.8.1–2. Geiger (1979). Cf. Syme (1958: 557–61), who discounts the importance of philosophy as a motivation for the group that surrounded Thrasea.

[35] Juv. 5.36–7, Sedley (1997). Note esp. the accusations put in the mouth of Cossutianus Capito (*PIR*² C 1543) by Tacitus, *Ann.* 16.22.2–5, cf. Murray (1965: 55). The charge is often repeated in modern scholarship: Wistrand (1979: 95), MacMullen (1966: 21–30), Toynbee (1944: 49–51).

he also refutes the perception that the Stoics were fundamentally obstructionist or opposed to those in power.[36] Rather than promote a particular political agenda, the teachings of this philosophical school (which would eventually claim emperors among its adherents) tended to stress the link between freedom and moral character. The premise that only the wise can understand what is good and that only the good are truly free can be traced to Zeno's *Politics* and was evidently the most significant contribution made by this work to later Stoic doctrine.[37] Moreover, the classical formulation of Stoic thought held that the practical details of political life are among the "indifferent goods" that should not impair the wise man's ability to act in accordance with virtue.[38] As we saw in Chapter 1, a focus on freedom's moral dimension could make it easier to reconcile this value with life under the Principate. In this regard, it is worth noting that Helvidius Priscus was said to have recovered Galba's body for burial after his assassination.[39]

According to the precepts of his philosophical successors, therefore, Cato's suicide was not really admired as a political act, but was viewed instead as a demonstration of the personal freedom that only the truly wise person could achieve. Like Socrates, Cato did not fear death, and his suicide proved that he was neither enslaved by circumstance nor by his own emotions.[40] Seneca therefore could reject the political implications of Cato's defiance, while still admiring the courage he displayed in refusing to

---

[36] Sen. *Ep.* 13.14, cf. *Ep.* 73.1: *errare mihi videntur qui existimant philosophiae fideliter deditos contumaces esse ac refractarios, contemptores magistratuum aut regum eorumve per quos publica administrantur.* Griffin (1989: 22).

[37] Zeno ap. Diog. Laert. 7.33 (= Arnim *SVF* I 222): παρισάντα πολίτας καὶ φίλους καὶ οἰκείους καὶ ἐλευθέρους τοὺς σπουδαίους μόνον, cf. Stob. *Ecl.* 2.99, 3–5 Wachsmuth (= Arnim *SVF* I 216). Schofield (1991: 95–7). The principle is stated most starkly in the *Acro scholia* to Hor. *Ep.* 1.19.19: *negant Stoici quemquam liberum esse praeter sapientem* (= Arnim *SVF* III 597). For fuller articulations, see Cic. *Fin.* 3.75 and Stob. *Ecl.* 2.101, 15–16 Wachsmuth (= Arnim *SVF* III 591, 593), Manning (1989: 1521–2).

[38] The problem of "indifferent goods" (ἀδιάφορα) was central to Stoic ethics: See Zeno ap. Stob. *Ecl.* 2.57–8 Wachsmuth (= Arnim *SVF* 1.190), Long (1986: 189–99). The ideal Stoic *politeia* was one in which all men were sages: Devine (1970), cf. Brunt (1975: 16–18), also Schofield (1991). Zeno held that the wise were not only the only truly free men, but also kings, ap. Diog. Laert. 7.122 (= *SVF* 3.617). Panaetius, it is true, seems to have recommended the mixed constitution (Cic. *Rep.* 1.34) as a practical matter, and this was thought to reflect a general principle of the later Stoa (Diog. Laert. 7.131 = *SVF* 3.700). There was no objection to monarchy in principle, however, but rather an underlying concern with moral stability, given the tendency of unmixed constitutional types (such as kingship) to degenerate into morally pernicious forms (such as tyranny): cf. Cic. *Off.* 2.41–2.

[39] Plut. *Galb.* 28.3. Compare the evident loyalty, but equivocal postmortem judgment, of Musonius Rufus (*PIR²* M 753), quoted in Epictet. *Dis.* 3.15.14.

[40] Sen. *Ep.* 24.6–8, 104.28–9, cf. Diog. Laert. 7.130, (= *SVF* 3.757), also *SVF* 3.759, 768. On the importance of Socrates' example in Stoicism, see Long (1988: 160–71). It is certainly significant

submit to Caesar's clemency.[41] The circumstances of Thrasea's death suggests a devotion to similar principles, but the fact that it was accomplished while he was under indictment for treason pointed to other associations as well. Because the quarrel with Caesar remained the central feature of Cato's image within the culture at large, it was difficult to divorce philosophical admiration of Cato's *exemplum* from the political undercurrents of the Republican narrative to which it also belonged.[42]

This ambiguity of Cato as both a Stoic *exemplum* and a political icon hangs over Tacitus' account of the senate meeting at which the elder Helvidius Priscus expressed the opinion about the funding for the Capitolium, which Tacitus indicated would be remembered by certain sinister figures (*Hist.* 4.9.2: *fuere qui et meminissent*). What Tacitus says about that session is revealing: "this day in particular was for him (Helvidius) the start of a great offense and of great glory" (*Hist.* 4.4.3: *isque praecipuus illi dies magnae offensae intitium et magnae gloriae fuit*). Like Pliny a generation later, Helvidius increased his reputation by antagonizing a personal enemy at the start of a new regime. That man, who we can assume became the unnamed agent of memory who eventually turned Helvidius' words against him, was T. Clodius Eprius Marcellus. Another notorious Neronian *delator* like Crispus and Regulus, Marcellus had taken part in the prosecution of Helvidius' father-in-law Thrasea under Nero.[43]

Relying on the same *senatus consultum* that provided the grounds for Vibius Crispus' prosecution of Annius Faustus, Helvidius attacked Marcellus for wrongful prosecution during Galba's reign, but failed to secure a conviction. Then, at the meeting that marked the start of Vespasian's Principate, their feud reopened in a dispute over whether the envoys sent to inform Vespasian about the senate's decree regarding his *imperium* should be selected by lot or nominated by the magistrates.[44] As Tacitus reports the exchange, both speakers suggest a role for memory in determining how the senate should proceed. The focus of these competing memories, particularly in the role they give to the Republican past, merits close consideration. For his part, Helvidius objects to the selection of envoys by

---

that Cato had prepared for his suicide by rereading Plato's *Phaedo*: Plut. *Cat. Min.* 68.2, Griffin (1986: 195–6). See also Wilson (2007: 127–30).

[41] Sen. *Ep.* 14.12–13, Griffin (1968), (1989: 10), Brunt (1975: 11), Morford (2002: 171–3), Inwood (2005: 306–11). It is worth noting that Stoics were faulted not for their opposition to bad emperors, but rather for the celebration of deaths that accomplished nothing: Tac. *Agr.* 42.3–4, Mart. 1.8, Wistrand (1979: 100).

[42] Zecchini (1980), Fantham (2003: 105–6), Leigh (2000: 468–70).

[43] Tac. *Ann.* 16.27–9, PIR² E 84. Syme (1958: 212), Galimberti (2000: 219–23), Malitz (1985: 234–6), Rutledge (2001: 225–8), Sailor (2008: 225–6).

[44] Tac. *Hist.* 4.6.1–3, Melmoux (1975: 31–2), Galimberti (2000: 216–17).

lot because it implies an unwillingness to acknowledge the differences in men's characters (*Hist.* 4.7.1: *sorte et urna mores non discerni*). If Marcellus were excluded from the embassy, it would send a message, he feels.[45] Helvidius therefore focuses narrowly on the memory of Marcellus' bad acts under Nero. Reflecting a Stoic's disdain for "indifferent goods," he asks sarcastically why Marcellus feared the magistrate's decision, "since he had money and eloquence and would surpass many others, if he were not burdened by the memory of his crimes" (*Hist.* 4.7.1: *esse illi pecuniam et eloquentiam, quis multos anteiret, ni memoria flagitiorum urgeretur*).[46] The question takes on added significance, because in Marcellus, these qualities were linked to one another in a particularly disreputable way: The *delator* had earned a reward of 5,000,000 HS for his role in the prosecution of Thrasea.[47] Like Pliny and Cornutus a generation later, Helvidius asks the senate to take a moral stand against the vicious prosecutors of the previous regime and to redefine their status for posterity.

In response, Marcellus points out that selection of the embassy by lot was not his idea, but was proposed by the consul-designate Valerius Asiaticus. Moreover, it was "in keeping with longstanding precedents," and "nothing had occurred to explain why something established since antiquity should have come to the end of its usefulness, or why an honor for a *princeps* should be twisted into a rebuke of anyone" (*Hist.* 4.8.1: *secundum vetera exempla... nihil evenisse cur antiquitus instituta exolescerent aut principis honor in cuiusquam contumeliam verteretur*). As Tacitus presents the matter, both official authority and historical precedent were on Marcellus' side. It is he, not Helvidius, who expands the framework of remembering to include Republican precedent.[48] More striking still, Marcellus is the one to call attention to the Stoics' regard for Republican heroes, saying that Helvidius has sought "to match the determination and fortitude of the Catones and the Bruti" (4.8.3: *denique constantia fortitudine Catonibus et Brutis aequaretur*). Marcellus, in contrast, "remembers the times in which he was born, what kind of state their fathers and grandfathers had established. While he admires those more distant examples, he follows the present ones" (*Hist.* 4.8.2: *se meminisse temporum quibus*

---

[45] Tac. *Hist.* 4.7.3: *hoc senatus iudicio velut admoneri principem quos probet, quos reformidet.* See Pigoń (1992: 236–40).

[46] Tacitus calls particular attention to this aspect of Stoic doctrine in his introduction of Helvidius at *Hist.* 4.5.2.

[47] Tac. *Ann.* 16.33.2. Rutledge (2001: 36–7) argues unconvincingly that such a reward was not exceptional.

[48] Pigoń (1992: 243). Chilver (1985: 28) notes the existence of Republican precedent for Helvidius' position, but the important point is that these are not acknowledged in Tacitus' account.

natus sit, quam civitatis formam patres avique instituerint; ulteriora mirari, praesentia sequi). Not only did Republican tradition sanction the selection of envoys by lot, it also provided the context in which the activities of a *delator* could be justified. By mocking his antagonist's emulation of Cato and Brutus, Marcellus calls attention to the necessary compromise of liberty that came with the emergence of the Principate.

Marcellus won this argument. The senate voted to select envoys by lot, as was the custom. But outrage against the Neronian *delatores* continued.[49] First, the Stoic Musonius Rufus accused P. Egnatius Celer, a onetime philosopher who had betrayed his friends by testifying against his teacher, Barea Soranus.[50] When the senate reconvened on the first day of the new year, Curtius Montanus (another member of Thrasea's group) launched a famous but futile attack on Regulus, whose activities as a *delator* went back to the time of Nero.[51] Then, inevitably, Helvidius Priscus rose to speak and began praising Cluvius Rufus, "who was eminent for wealth and eloquence but never endangered anyone under Nero" (*Hist.* 4.43: *dives et eloquentia clarus nulli umquam sub Nerone periculum facessisset*), before turning to compare this example with the activities of Eprius Marcellus. Anticipating where his enemy was headed, Marcellus angrily stormed out of the senate, accompanied by his powerful and eloquent colleague Vibius Crispus: "'We go,' he said, 'and leave your senate to you, Priscus, though a Caesar presides in person'" (4.43: *"imus" inquit, "Prisce, et relinquimus tibi senatum tuum: regna praesente Caesare"*). Marcellus refers to the young Domitian, who had been made praetor in the place of Sex. Julius Frontinus at the start of this session so that he could preside over the senate and represent the interests of his father. The point of mentioning his presence was to remind his fellow senators once again of the era in which they lived.

In the end, the calls for vengeance that marked the beginning of the Flavian era were largely a disaster. Despite the objections of Helvidius and others, powerful *delatores* such as Regulus, Crispus, and Marcellus managed to maintain their power under the new regime. Shortly after his encounters with Helvidius, Marcellus was appointed to an extended tenure as proconsul of Asia. He also became an augur and a priest of

---

[49] See esp. Syme (1958: 187–9) on Tacitus' representation of these events, also Rutledge (2001: 124–6), Rogers (1949).

[50] Tac. *Hist.* 4.10, 40.3, cf. *Ann.* 16.32.2, Juv. 3.116–18, *PIR*² M 753, E 19, B 55. Evans (1979).

[51] Tac. *Hist.* 4.42, *PIR*² C 1615. Analysis of Montanus' speech by Martin (1967) reveals its distinctly Ciceronian flavor. Syme (1991: 576) suggests that it may have been modeled on the *de ultione Helvidii*. Regulus' activities under Nero are also discussed by Pliny, who says that his crimes under Domitian were *non minora . . . quam sub Nerone sed tectiora* (*Ep.* 1.5.1). See also Rutledge (2001: 192–4).

the imperial cult. Crispus, meanwhile, became proconsul of Africa in 72 and was entrusted with taking the census in Spain not long thereafter. Both men were granted second consulships in 74 (but not together), and Crispus went on to become consul for a third time, early in Domitian's reign.[52] Although he was a less prominent figure in 70, Regulus survived Montanus' attack, thanks in part to the defense offered by his young half-brother Vipstanus Messala. Little is known about the course of his public career, but Regulus' prominence in Pliny's letters surely reflects an elevated social position during the period of Flavian rule.[53]

More unsettling than the offices and honors granted to these men was the continuation of what some perceived to be their pernicious influence with the emperor. At its core, Helvidius' hostility toward Marcellus is motivated by a belief that those who helped to formulate and enforce the oppressive policies of Nero should be held accountable for their actions. As Tacitus frames the argument, his concern about the method of selecting the members of the embassy arose from a belief that "there is no greater instrument of good rule than good friends" (*Hist.* 4.7.3: *nullum maius boni imperii instrumentum quam bonos amicos esse*). It is not just the emperor himself, but also the members of his court, who are responsible for the character of a regime.[54] Personal accountability requires personal freedom, however, and the historical perspective that Tacitus bestows on Marcellus allows him to upend the moral certainties of his opponent. From his perspective, the Imperial-era senator can only pray for good rulers, but he must endure whatever comes.[55] He argues that he was only doing what he had been compelled to do, and points out that he was not alone in doing so. As "a member of the senate that submitted to slavery at that time" (*Hist.* 4.8.3: *se unum esse ex illo senatu, qui simul servierit*), Marcellus was no more responsible for Thrasea's condemnation than any

---

[52] Consulships: *CIL* 16.20 (= MW 299), Equini (1967: 14–16), Gallivan (1981: 188, 210). Bradley (1978: 177) suggests this year as the dramatic date of the *Dialogus*. For Marcellus' three years in Asia, *CIL* 10.3853 (= *ILS* 992), Eck (1970: 83), Bradley (1978: 177). Townend (1961: 54) suggests the special honor shown him was the result of his role in the repression of Helvidius. On Crispus' tenure in Africa, Plin. *NH* 19.4, with Syme (1969), Eck (1970: 91); his post as *leg. Aug. pro pr.* in Hispania citerior: *AE* 1939 60, Eck (1970: 225–6). See also Juv. 4.81–93, Stat. ap. Schol ad Juv. 4.94.

[53] Tac. *Hist.* 4.42.1–2, *PIR* V 468. Syme (1953: 161), see also Hoffer (1999: 87–9), Rutledge (2001: 194–5). Martial's description (1.12) of the massive arcade that collapsed while he was racing a chariot through it suggests something of Regulus' wealth, if nothing else. On Messala, see below.

[54] Cf. Frede (2003, esp. 201–5).

[55] Tac. *Hist.* 4.8.2: *bonos imperatores voto expetere, qualescumque tolerare.*

other member of that body, which collectively acquiesced to whatever the emperor demanded.[56]

Helvidius' concerns appear to have been well founded, however. One consequence of the *delatores*' continued influence under Vespasian was that Marcellus had the opportunity to exact revenge for the offense that marked the beginning of Helvidius' glory. Although Tacitus' account has been lost and the rest of the evidence is ambivalent, we are able to conclude that Helvidius was arrested during his praetorship or shortly thereafter, apparently for insulting remarks about the dynastic intentions of the emperor. He was exiled and eventually killed, but according to what seems to be the official version of events, his execution was carried out against Vespasian's wishes.[57] Whatever motivations and secret machinations contributed to Helvidius' death, the exile of a praetorian senator is sure to have required a public trial. From the exchanges described above, it does not seem unreasonable to conclude that the *delator* responsible for this initial prosecution (and perhaps the sequel as well) was Eprius Marcellus.

Looking back as a witness to the reprisals that followed the fall of Domitian, Tacitus was able to present the beginning of Vespasian's reign as an object lesson in the workings of the nexus of Imperial repression, senatorial factionalism, and Republican precedent that continued to weave through public life in his own day. Although the outcomes of the two proceedings were radically different, there are important similarities between Helvidius' accusation of Marcellus and Pliny's account of the stand he took against Publicius Certus. In both cases, a moment of transition provided the opportunity for an aggrieved minority to avenge itself on the individuals who had participated in the persecution of someone to whom they were close under the previous emperor. This personal outrage inevitably came up against the inertia of the status quo and the realities of power in the Imperial era. Although the emperor did not participate in either senatorial debate, a consideration of his authority hangs over both conflicts. Whatever judgment the senate decided to pass against individual *delatores* would ultimately become irrelevant if it was not supported by will of the *princeps*.

Tacitus is more explicit than Pliny in tying these conflicts to the ambiguity of the Republican past as a source of authority under the Principate.

---

[56] Pigoń (1992: 241–2), *Hist.* 4.8.3: *non magis sua oratione Thraseam quam iudicio senatus adflictum*, cf. Dio 59.16.2–4.

[57] Suet. *Vesp.* 15, Dio (Xiph.) 66.12.1–3. Around the same time, Mucianus used his influence with Vespasian to expel philosophers from Rome: id. 66.13.1. The chronology suggested by these notices is uncertain: Murison (1999: 158).

In his account, Marcellus is able to invoke Republican precedent for his position in contemporary politics while simultaneously pointing to the tyrannical conditions of the more recent past as a way to exculpate himself (and the rest of the senate) for the injustices that took place under Nero. The point of this episode seems to be that the formal continuity of senatorial procedure was not enough to ensure a continuity of moral principles. Helvidius was linked with Cato, just as Pliny was with Cicero, but his primary focus is on issues of contemporary relevance. The uneasy fit between these present concerns and a devotion to a Republican hero is apparent only to someone such as Marcellus, who uses it to discredit his opponent. Tacitus acknowledges that instruments such as the censor's mark no longer meant what they once did. Pliny may have resented Regulus' insulting treatment of Arulenus Rusticus, but it was also reported that Domitian's nightmares were haunted by Rusticus' ghost.[58] When the ultimate responsibility for all public actions lay with the emperor himself, individual accountability became a treacherous concept to define.

VIX NOMEN IPSUM ORATORIS RETINEAT

Further reflection on the nature of the conflict between men such as Helvidius Priscus and Eprius Marcellus and its significance for the continuity of Republican traditions under the Principate can be found in Tacitus' *Dialogus de oratoribus* (*Dialogue on Orators*), a work composed perhaps a few years after Pliny had delivered his *de ultione Helvidii*. This difficult and enigmatic work, the interpretation of which is further complicated by problems with the manuscripts, offers a wide-ranging account of the changes that had occurred in the profession of oratory since the end of the Republic. In a discussion that explores both the form and the content of Roman rhetoric, Tacitus presents three distinct perspectives on the applicability of Republican precedent to the conduct of public life under the Principate. Because the issues are framed within the context of a debate, the *Dialogus* is particularly successful in exploring the ambiguities of issues that could not easily be resolved. By the end of the work, the reader is left to consider the prospect that the continuities that persisted in the practice of oratory represented more of a problem than the acknowledged differences between past and present.[59]

---

[58] Dio (Xiph.) 67.16.1.

[59] Gowing (2005: 111): "the text questions the value of remembering the Republic at all." See also Luce (1993), Williams (1978: 45), Häussler (1969: 42). The question of the *Dialogus'* date has been reexamined in detail by Brink (1994), who finds a date somewhere in the range 100–103

The *Dialogus* is dedicated to L. Fabius Justus, a career soldier like Tacitus' father-in-law, who was also coincidentally one of the men Regulus asked to intervene with Pliny in the anxious days that followed Domitian's assassination.[60] Fabius seems to have taken an interest in the issues that marked the greatest rift between Regulus and Pliny – their disagreements about Cicero's relevance as a model for the contemporary practice of oratory. Tacitus ascribes the impetus for his work to a question posed by his dedicatee:

> *Saepe ex me requiris, Iuste Fabi, cur, cum priora saecula tot eminentium oratorum ingeniis gloriaque floruerint, nostra potissimum aetas deserta et laude eloquentiae orbata vix nomen ipsum oratoris retineat. neque enim ita appellamus nisi antiquos, horum autem temporum diserti causidici et advocati et patroni et quidvis potius quam oratores vocantur.*

> You often ask me, Fabius Justus, why, whereas earlier generations were overgrown with the genius and renown of so many distinguished orators, our age in particular is barren of them, such that, deprived of the praise of eloquence, scarcely the name itself of orator remains. For there are none whom we describe in this way, except for the ancients. Instead, the skilled speakers of these days are called "pleaders" and "advocates" and "patrons" and anything besides "orators." (*Dial.* 1.1)[61]

As the principal statement of the topic of the *Dialogus*, this passage merits consideration on its own terms. Although it touches on issues of talent (*ingenium*) and public esteem for eloquence (*gloria, laus*), the central problem raised by Fabius' question is the disappearance of a particular kind of speaker, the orator. The pointed contrast between the *oratores* of the past and the *causidici, advocati,* and *patroni* of the present suggests that everything turns on an issue of definitions, just as the reference to "the very name of *orator*" signals that the proper application of terms will be central to the investigation that follows.[62]

---

most likely; cf. Syme (1957b), (1958: 112, 670–3), *contra* Murgia (1980) and Barnes (1986: 229–32). For discussion of the manuscript history and other textual problems, see Bo (1993), also Barnes (1986: 226–8), Merklin (1991: 280–3), and Brink (1994). With one exception, I rely here on the text of the Oxford Classical Text, ed. Winterbottom (1975).

[60] Plin. *Ep.* 1.5.8, *PIR²* F 41, Syme (1957b). It may be out of respect for Fabius' friendship with Regulus that the latter is only alluded to briefly in this text (*Dial.* 15.1), although his half-brother Vipstanus Messala appears as one of the primary interlocutors in the discussion: cf. Williams (1978: 29).

[61] The device of presenting one's work as the author's response to a question or request was conventional: cf. *ad Her.* 1, Cic. *Orat.* 1–3, *Top* 4, Quint. *Ep. ad Tryph.* 1.

[62] Cicero had been similarly careful about the application of the term orator: cf. *Brut.* 176, *de Or.* 1.64.

The key to understanding the significance of this term may lie in a maxim of Cato the Elder, who defined an orator as "a good man, skilled in speaking" (frag. 14 Jordan: *vir bonus dicendi peritus*).[63] This definition, with its emphasis on moral character, took on renewed significance under the Principate (and under the Flavians especially), apparently in response to the perceived rise of disreputable *delatores* to positions of prominence.[64] According to Pliny, Herennius Senecio had played on the phrase, using its inverse to discredit Regulus as "a bad man unskilled in speaking."[65] Quintilian also took special note of Cato's formulation, placing emphasis on the first part of the definition (*vir bonus*). In the final book of his extensive guide for rhetorical education, he goes so far as to specify, "I am not simply saying that he who would be an orator ought to be a good man, but rather that no one can become an orator unless he is a good man" (*Inst.* 12.1.3: *neque enim tantum id dico, eum qui sit orator virum bonum esse oportere, sed ne futurum quidem oratorem nisi virum bonum*).

This interpretation of the term has obvious relevance to the meaning of the *Dialogus* as a whole. If it is appropriate to assume that the elder Cato's definition of the *orator* is operative in Fabius' question, we can conclude that the *Dialogus* is not concerned with the decline of rhetoric per se. Tacitus' own career, like those of Pliny and Regulus, confirms the vitality of forensic oratory as a vehicle for elite self-promotion. Furthermore, each of the interlocutors in the *Dialogus* was a successful advocate in his own right, and, in the course of the discussion, they repeatedly compliment each other's eloquence.[66] Instead, the issue that Tacitus has set out to address in his response to Fabius' request is the disappearance of a particular kind of speaker, whose combination of eloquence and virtue merit the designation *orator*. This distinction suggests that this profession, with its roots in the tradition of Cato and Cicero, has undergone a loss of moral authority.

With a modesty that is perhaps meant to suggest his own complicity in Fabius' claim about the absence of true *oratores* among contemporary *diserti*, Tacitus declines to offer his own views on such an important matter. Rather than rely on his own talents of argumentation, he prefers instead to

---

[63] Cited by both the elder Seneca (*Contr.* 1.*praef.*9) and Quintilian (*Inst.* 12.1.1). The idea has affinities with Stoic teaching: cf. Walzer (2003), Morr (1926), but also had wider application in a Roman context: See also Austin (1948: 51–3).

[64] Winterbottom (1964).

[65] Plin. *Ep.* 4.7.5: *itaque Herennius Senecio mirifice Catonis illud de oratore in hunc e contrario vertit: "Orator est vir malus dicendi imperitus."*

[66] Tac. *Dial.* 2.1, 9.3, 14.3, 15.1, 23.5–24.1. Cf. Plin. *Ep.* 2.1.6, 2.11.17, Crook (1995, esp. 174–87).

retrace the lines of a conversation he claims to have overheard in his youth. This task of explanation will be easier, he says, because "it requires memory and recollection, not talent" (*Dial.* 1.3: *ita non ingenio, sed memoria et recordatione opus est*). Deference to the authority of an external group of speakers is, of course, a literary device typical of dialogues in which the author is not represented as one of the interlocutors.[67] In this case, however, it also allows Tacitus to provide his work with a necessary historical dimension. Because orators have ceased to exist in the present, it is logical for Tacitus to seek the causes of their disappearance in the past. Once again, he chooses to explain a contemporary circumstance by looking back to the early years of Vespasian's reign.

It quickly becomes apparent that the ranks of those who deserved the title of *orator* had already begun to dwindle by the era in which Tacitus lays his scene. The historian recalls how as a boy he used to tag along with Marcus Aper and Julius Secundus, two of "the most celebrated talents of the forum at that time" (*Dial.* 2.1: *celeberrima tum ingenia fori nostri*).[68] Despite their eminence, neither man's eloquence was beyond criticism: Secundus was said to lack a ready facility with language, whereas Aper seemed to rely too much on natural talent, owing to a lack of education and refinement. Tacitus loyally goes on to dispute these widely held opinions, but he does not directly contradict the accepted view so much as seek to modify it and render it a bit less damning. He says that Secundus' words were fluent "so far as was necessary" and that Aper was not so much lacking in refinement as simply contemptuous of it – faint praise indeed.[69]

As it turns out, Aper and Secundus are not the only potential orators featured in the *Dialogus*. Perhaps the most important character in the work is Curiatius Maternus, the man whose career in literature and politics provides the impetus for the conversation that Tacitus claims to remember. Maternus had recited a tragedy entitled *Cato*, and on the next day "it was going around that he had offended the sensibilities of the powerful" (2.1: *cum offendisse potentium animos diceretur*).[70] Not only does the selection

---

[67] Hirzel (1895: 50–1). See also Brink (1993: 337–8), Goldberg (1999: 226).

[68] *PIR*[2] A 910, I 559. Later in the discussion, Messala will call them *viri optimi et temporum nostrorum oratores* (14.3), but it is clear that the chronological qualification in this phrase is sharply pointed: See Mayer (2001: 134).

[69] Tac. *Dial.* 2.2: *Secundo purus et pressus et, in quantum satis erat, profluens sermo non defuit, et Aper omni eruditione inbutus contemnebat potius litteras quam nesciebat.* Cf. Ryberg (1942) on Tacitus' use of *innuendo* to introduce opinions for which he does not wish to take responsibility.

[70] *PIR*[2] C 1604. On Maternus' importance in the *Dialogus*, see esp. Barnes (1986: 238). On the language used here, Gallia (2009).

of Cato as the subject of Maternus' drama suggest a connection with the Stoics, but the registration of an offense also recalls Tacitus' description of the fateful senate meeting at which Helvidius began to acquire glory.

Alarmed by the predicament facing Maternus, Secundus and Aper visit him in his chambers, with the young Tacitus in tow. They find the playwright at work revising the text of his *Cato*, and Secundus encourages him to produce "perhaps not a better Cato, but at least a safer one" (*Dial.* 3.2: *emitteres Catonem non quidem meliorem sed tamen securiorem*), but his solicitude is met with a stubborn refusal: "You will read what Maternus owes to himself, and you will recognize what you have heard" (3.3: *leges tu quid Maternus sibi debuerit, et agnosces quae audisti*). Maternus continues, "And if the *Cato* left out anything, Thyestes will say it in the next reading" (*quod si qua omisit Cato, sequenti recitatione Thyestes dicet*). He evidently has a new play in mind and is rushing the *Cato* to press to begin work on it as soon as possible. These preoccupations elicit a complaint from Maternus' other visitor, M. Flavius Aper:

> Adeo te tragoediae istae non satiant . . . quo minus omissis orationum et causarum studiis omne tempus modo circa Medeam, ecce nunc circa Thyesten consumas, cum te tot amicorum causae, tot coloniarum et municipiorum clientelae in forum vocent, quibus vix suffeceris, etiam si non novum tibi ipse negotium inportasses, <ut>Domitium et Catonem, id est nostras quoque historias et Romana nomina Graeculorum fabulis adgregares.

> Are those tragedies so unfulfilling to you . . . that, as your attention to oratory and your law cases slides, you might stop wasting all your time with not just *Medea* but now indeed with *Thyestes*? Meanwhile, as the cases of so many friends and the *clientela* of so many colonies and towns call you into the Forum (for which you would scarcely have enough time even if you did not take on any new work) you are herding your *Domitius* and your *Cato* (which are at least Roman names and about our history) together with plays about trivial Greeks. (*Dial.* 3.4)

Aper puts the situation in stark contrast: Maternus, a man of character and ability, has abandoned the practice of forensic oratory to compose plays on historical and mythical themes. To Aper, this is unacceptable behavior for a man of Maternus' social position. A little culture is one thing, but Maternus has responsibilities to consider; his literary output threatens to interfere with the real business of public advocacy.

As the only character in the *Dialogus* who refuses to acknowledge the basic premise of Fabius' question, Aper is an important figure in the discussion.[71] He believes that there can still be orators in the present, but his objection to the trajectory of Maternus' career also points to a plausible explanation for their disappearance. In his unwillingness to yield to the unnamed powerful figures who were offended by his tragedy, Maternus shows himself to be brave and honorable. Indeed, at one point in the conversation, he equates the ability to say something that might be regarded as offensive with the "ancient liberty" (*antiqua libertate*, 27.3) from which contemporary standards had declined. This attitude suggests a similarity not only to Helvidius, but also to the main character of his most recent play.[72] Maternus could be regarded as a *vir bonus*, who had the potential to become a true *orator*. If Aper's interpretation of the circumstances in which the *Dialogus* takes place can be taken as an answer to Fabius' question, it seems that the absence of orators in the present was to be explained by the fact that good men such as Maternus would rather write dramatic poetry than deliver speeches.

"AB AUDITORIIS ET THEATRIS IN FORUM ET AD CAUSAS ET AD VERA PROELIA VOCO"

Aper's objection strikes an unexpected chord with Maternus, who admits that he has been wanting to abandon "the confines of forensic pleading" and devote himself to the "more sacred and august eloquence" of poetry for a long time (*Dial.* 4.2: *quod iam pridem opto… ut omissis forensium causarum angustiis… sanctiorem illam et augustiorem eloquentiam colam*). He offers to debate Aper, with Secundus as the judge, about the appropriateness of such a choice. A mock trial ensues, in which Aper takes the part of the prosecution, Maternus that of defendant. The stakes are high: If Maternus succeeds, he plans to give up his career at the bar, thus depriving Roman eloquence of what might have been its last true *orator*. Such a decision would mark a break with the ethical traditions of the past, in which the practice of forensic oratory was held to be a defining responsibility of the elite Roman male.

---

[71] *Dial.* 1.4: *neque enim defuit qui diversam quoque partem susciperet*, Goldberg (1999). Although established in such terms, Aper's role is more complex than that of a simple devil's advocate: Champion (1994: 161).

[72] Cato was admired for his willingness to provoke Pompey and Caesar simultaneously, which demonstrated his fearlessness in the face of power: Sen. *Ep.* 104.33. Cf. Luc. *BC* 2.315–23.

Aper begins his case by discussing the utility of oratory, which consists in the power it provides to skilled practitioners.[73] Eloquence, he says, acts as "a defense as well as a weapon with which you have the ability to protect and intervene equally, whether in court or in the senate or before the *princeps*" (*Dial.* 5.6: *praesidium simul ac telum quo propugnare pariter et incessere sive in iudicio sive in senatu sive apud principem possis*). The talented speaker is "constantly armed" and "protected by virtually continuous power and authority" (5.5: *semper armatus . . . velut quadam perpetua potentia ac potestate munitus*). The sustained reliance on metaphors of martial valor serves to forge a link between Aper's outlook and the moral traditions of the past, in which oratory was treated as the extension of an aristocratic *virtus* that was intertwined with the Ennian concept *libertas* discussed in Chapter 1.[74]

To Aper's way of thinking, Maternus neglects his duty to his clients to commit himself entirely to an endeavor that should not become more than a passing hobby for a senator in his prime. Maternus' social position entails a certain sense of propriety, which prescribes the kind of activities that are appropriate for him to pursue. Poetry might be an acceptable pursuit for Maternus if he had been born in Greece, but as a Roman citizen, he was "born for manly eloquence and oratory" (*Dial.* 5.4: *natus ad eloquentiam virilem et oratoriam*).[75] Because Aper regards active engagement in public life as the proper role for a Roman aristocrat, he cannot understand why someone would waste his time writing tragedies of any kind, much less ones that deal with Greek mythology. The construction of these cultural differences depends on a type of social memory that is somewhat different in character from the cultural forms of remembering elicited by the monuments and religious institutions discussed in the previous two chapters. Aper's complaints about Maternus' poetic interests reflect a traditional bias that stretched back into the Republic, but he does not explicitly invoke the model of someone such as Cato the Elder to justify his disdain for Greeks and Greek culture.[76] Instead, his perspective is tied to the "common understanding" of such issues handed down from

---

[73] *Dial.* 5.5, cf. Cic. *Inv.* 2.169.

[74] The metaphor was pervasive in Roman discussions of the role of oratory: Güngerich (1980: 20), also Gallia (2009: 175–6). On Republican aristocratic *virtus*, see McDonnell (2006), also Earl (1967: 20–3) and Oakley (1985).

[75] Cf. *Dial.* 10.5. The charge represents a leitmotif in Aper's criticism of Maternus: Heldmann (1982: 259). See also Goldberg (1999: 229–30), Hershkowitz (1995).

[76] See esp. Plut. *Cat. mai.* 12.7, 23.1, Plin. *NH* 7.113, also Plb. 39.1.1. In fact, Cato's response to Hellenism was more complicated than simple reactionary hostility: Astin (1978: 157–81), Gruen (1992: 52–83), but image is what would have counted here.

one generation to the next without conscious examination. Likewise, his sense of what it means to be an orator is personal and immediate, as he goes into a detailed description of the thrill of appearing before a crowd to speak (6.4–6) but does not explicitly imagine himself to be reenacting the deeds of Cicero.[77]

Despite the conventional cast of his thinking, Aper is also an unrepentant modernist, and this contradiction will lead him into difficulties in his debate with Maternus. The only evidence he provides for the usefulness of the orator's weapons is the recent success of Eprius Marcellus, who deployed eloquence to defeat the "accomplished but inexperienced wisdom of Helvidius, which was not refined for this kind of struggle" (5.7: *qua accinctus et minax disertam quidem sed inexercitatam et eius modi certaminum rudem Helvidi sapientiam elusit*). Blatantly disregarding the potential significance of this conflict for his friend's recent interest in the theme of Cato, Aper concludes this section of his speech with an unwarranted expression of self-assurance: "I will not say more about utility, since I think my dear Maternus will scarcely contradict me on this point" (5.7: *plura de utilitate non dico, cui parti minime contra dicturum Maternum meum arbitror*). In due course, Maternus will offer his own, very critical perspective on the uses to which Marcellus' brand of *eloquentia virilis* is put.

Unlike Marcellus, who in Tacitus' account was able to call attention to long-standing precedent in support of his views, Aper does not invoke Republican authorities to demonstrate the importance of engagement in public affairs for a man of Maternus' position. He also neglects the philosophical arguments that might persuade his Cato-admiring friend of this proposition. Pliny could cite a maxim of Thrasea Paetus, related to him by their mutual friend Avidius Quietus, to the effect that "one should undertake the cases of friends, hopeless ones, or those which might provide *exempla*" (*Ep.* 6.29.1: *praecipere solitum suscipiendas esse causas aut amicorum aut destitutas aut ad exemplum pertinentes*). There is an obvious overlap between this list of ethical obligations and the ones that prompted Aper's objection to Maternus' literary activities, but the *Dialogus* contains no explicit reference to Stoic ideals, or to Zeno's principle that "one should render service to the *respublica* unless something prevents it" (Sen. *de Otio* 3.2 = *SVF* 1.271: *accedet ad rem publicam, nisi si quid impedierit*).[78]

---

[77] Cf. Connerton (1989: 72–104) on "habitual memory" and the connection between social memory and bodily practices.

[78] Cf. Sen. *Ep.* 8, 55. The idea is also found in Chrysippus (*SVF* 3.695–9 cf. Cic. *Off.* 1.71). As the context of this citation makes clear, allowances were made by later adherents of the stoa

If anything, Aper's argument acquires something of a paradoxically Epicurean tone as he moves from the public usefulness of oratory to focus more extensively on the pleasure it brings. He goes on at length about this aspect, citing the satisfaction experienced by those who have gained social prominence from their eloquence. Noting his own success as a new man who has overcome obscure birth to rise through the ranks of a public career, Aper even claims that his rhetorical accomplishments are more dear to him than any public office (*Dial.* 7.1–2). These personal reflections lead Aper back to Eprius Marcellus, whom he celebrates together with Vibius Crispus as contemporary examples of men who were able to rise from obscurity to acquire vast wealth "through the rewards of eloquence" (8.2: *eloquentiae beneficio*).[79]

According to Aper, the recentness of these men's success gives greater weight to their *exempla*, just as the meanness of their origins makes them "more brilliant and illustrious examples for showing the usefulness of oratorical eloquence" (8.3: *eo clariora et ad demonstrandam oratoriae eloquentiae utilitatem inlustriora exempla sunt*). Republican *exempla* were available, but Aper regards them as less persuasive. More remarkable still, he notes:

> *sine commendatione natalium, sine substantia facultatum, neuter moribus egregius, alter habitu quoque corporis contemptus, per multos iam annos potentissimi sunt civitatis ac, donec libuit, principes fori, nunc principes in Caesaris amicitia agunt feruntque cuncta.*

> Without the recommendation of birth, without the advantages of property, neither one remarkable in his conduct, the one even despicable for the appearance of his body, they have been for many years the most powerful men in the state and, so far as is permissible, the chief men (*principes*) of the Forum, and now as the *principes* in Caesar's friendship, they propose and deal with everything. (*Dial.* 8.3)

The two most successful speakers of the present day are, by Aper's own admission, not the most appealing characters. Nevertheless, their eloquence has earned them the wealth, status, and power that comes with the emperor's friendship. Aper goes so far as to compare their position to

---

for circumstances that might inhibit the sage's participation in public life: See Grilli (2002: 90–107, 247–55), Reydams-Schils (2005: 83–113), also Wistrand (1979: 98–100). The only references to Stoic philosophy in the *Dialogus* occur in Messala's descriptions of the orator's broad training (30.3, cf. 31.7).

[79] Marcellus' fortune is said to be on the order of 200 million HS (cf. Schol. ad Juv. 4.81), and Crispus possessed 300 million. *AE* 1956 186 (= Sm. 242a) provides valuable information on Marcellus' early career: See Bradley (1978: 171–6).

that of the *princeps* himself. One cannot say that oratory has ceased to flourish under the Principate, but it is also clear that the top ranks of the profession do not belong to men one might describe as orators.[80]

Returning to the terms of his debate, Aper proceeds to compare the position of the advocate with the impotence and relative obscurity of the poet. Saleius Bassus, a friend of Julius Secundus, may have earned the honorific title of "most celebrated bard" (9.2: *plaeclarissimum vatem*), but no one pays him very much attention. Aper acknowledges the largess that Vespasian had recently bestowed on Bassus but regards this gift as essentially inferior to the rewards that Marcellus and Crispus derive from their friendship with the *princeps*.[81] The difference lies in the fact that eloquent speakers do not rely on the emperor's *indulgentia* but possess benefits that are uniquely their own: "Vespasian well understands... that Marcellus and Crispus bring to his friendship something that they did not and cannot acquire from a *princeps*" (8.3: *Vespasianus... bene intellegit... Marcellum autem et Crispum attulisse ad amicitiam suam quod non a principe acceperint nec accipi possit*).

Aper's first speech in the *Dialogus* provides the reader with a clear impression of the values that motivate his character.[82] He does not overlook the moral failings of successful *delatores* such as Marcellus and Crispus, but he does not condemn them either. The portraits, statues, and inscriptions that signal their elevated position are no more to be scorned than their wealth and resources. Aper dismisses the philosophical devaluation of such benefits, saying, "you more easily find someone to disparage [these] than despise them" (8.4: *quas facilius invenies qui vituperet quam qui fastidiat*). But Aper's values are not simply to be dismissed as bourgeois and mercenary. The appeal of oratory for him lies not just in the access it provides to such rewards, but also in the fact that he regards this activity as an independent source of power, a way of "taking care of oneself" (9.5: *se ipsum colere*).[83] According to Aper, contemporary advocates are responsible for their own success, while poets are passively dependent on the emperor's good will.

---

[80] Heldmann (1982: 258). On the significance of the reference to their position *in Caesaris amicitia*, see Crook (1955: 21–30), Winterling (1999: 161–94), Paterson (2007: 143).

[81] *Dial.* 9.5. The gift was 500,000 HS, a figure that invites comparison with the 5 million HS received by Marcellus for his role in the destruction of Thrasea. Cf. Woodside (1942: 125–6).

[82] For sympathetic discussion of Aper's position, see Luce (1993: 34–6), Champion (1994: 155–8), Goldberg (1999: 230–30), Dominik (1997: 60). More critical appraisals: Syme (1958: 109–9), Williams (1978: 27–8), Barnes (1986: 237–8).

[83] See Gudeman (1914: 247), also Gallia (2009: 176–9).

MUTARI CUM TEMPORIBUS FORMAS QUOQUE ET GENERA DICENDI

Aper concludes this opening speech with a final exhortation for Maternus to give up his dalliance with poetry and return to the substantive business of legal advocacy. His objection to Maternus' interest in poetry is essentially the same that Quintilian offered against philosophy, which is that it involves a retreat from the responsibilities of public life. Whether one seeks serene contemplation of the nature of the universe or the "groves and glades" of poetic retreat, retirement is not regarded as a worthwhile option.[84] Leaving aside for now the question of whether Maternus' poetry is really as disengaged and inconsequential as Aper makes it out to be, this overlap between Aper's position and Quintilian's critique of philosophy is worth noting, because Aper will soon face criticism along similar lines when confronted by a character whose views are much more closely aligned with those of the Flavian teacher of rhetoric.

After Maternus completes his defense of poetry (discussed below), the conversation is interrupted by the arrival of another visitor, the young nobleman Vipstanus Messala. Messala expresses his pleasure that "the best men and the orators of our times" (14.3: *viri optimi et temporum nostrorum oratores*) are not so preoccupied with public business that they do not have time to discuss issues of literature and learning:

> *itaque hercule non minus probari video in te, Secunde, quod Iuli Africani vitam componendo spem hominibus fecisti plurium eius modi librorum, quam in Apro <improbari>quod nondum ab scholasticis controversiis recessit et otium suum mavult novorum rhetorum more quam veterum oratorum consumere.*

> And so indeed I see that there is no less approval for you, Secundus, who by composing a *Life of Julius Africanus* has given men hope for more books of this sort, as there is for Aper, on account of the fact that he no longer retires from school-room debates, preferring to occupy his leisure in the manner of the new rhetors rather than in that of the old orators. (*Dial.* 14.4)

It appears that Messala does not share Aper's concern that Maternus' interest in poetry represents a waste of time. In fact, he reveals the manufactured nature of the choice that his two friends are contemplating. Although the

---

[84] *Dial.* 9.6, 10.3–8, Quint. *Inst.* 11.1.35, cf. 12.2.6–7, Kennedy (1962: 135–6), Clarke (1967: 36), see also MacMullen (1966: 58–60). Antipathy between rhetors and philosophers can be traced back in the Greek tradition to Gorgias and the sophists. See Manzoni (1990), Bowersock (1969: 11–14).

two fields of cultural activity were traditionally opposed to one another (witness the denigration of Cicero's poetic abilities), there was nothing to prevent an orator from engaging in a variety of literary pursuits in his time away from handling public business.[85]

Although Messala's remark is couched as a compliment to Secundus' interest in biography, it ultimately has more impact for its implied criticism of Aper as someone who acts more like a *rhetor* than an *orator*. Here Fabius Justus' initial distinction between modern practitioners of rhetoric and the *oratores* of the past reasserts itself, but in a way that focuses explicitly on the activities to which their talents are applied. In this framework, the significance of Pliny's sympathy for Licinianus, who had been transformed "from an orator into a rhetor" (*Ep.* 4.11.1: *rhetor de oratore fieret*) becomes clearer. Like Aper's objection to a play about Thyestes, Messala's dismissal of Greek *rhetores* is founded in basic prejudices about social status and ethnic identity. He denigrates the scholastic declamations that occupy the *rhetores* of the present as an unworthy pursuit for the great Roman orators whom they have displaced.[86]

Piqued by this disparagement of the rhetorical accomplishments that bolster his reputation, Aper attempts to turn the tables on Messala:

> *nam hunc tuum sermonem saepe excepi, cum oblitus et tuae et fratris tui eloquentiae neminem hoc tempore oratorem esse contenderes [antiquis], eo (credo) audacius, quod malignitatis opinionem non verebaris, cum eam gloriam, quam tibi alii concedunt ipse tibi denegares.*

> I have often gotten this sort of sentiment from you. Forgetting both your own eloquence and that of your brother, as you argue that no one of this era is an orator, I find you braver because you do not fear acquiring a reputation for mean-spiritedness, since you deny to yourself the glory that others grant you. (*Dial.* 15.1)

Aper refuses to accept the idea that the occupation he has just defended against poetry has declined to such an extent that there are no longer any orators. Messala's disparagement of contemporary oratory is either a sign of rudeness or of excessive insecurity. If things are really as decadent as Messala suggests, his own eloquence would not deserve the compliment that Aper pays it.

---

[85] Quint. *Inst.* 9.4.41, Juv. 10.122, cf. [Sall.] *in Cic.* 3.5. See Chapter 5.

[86] See Chapter 3. On the emergence of declamation in the Imperial period, see Kraus (2000: 445-8), Parks (1945: 62-9), Caplan (1970: 162-6), Bloomer (1997).

Having brought the discussion to a more explicit connection with the terms of Fabius' question, Messala asks the others to turn their attention to "the causes of this vast difference" (15.2: *causas huius infinitae differentiae*). Secundus, in his role as the discussion's arbiter, agrees that this is an interesting topic and asks Messala to open the conversation by sharing his own views. But, first, Maternus gives Aper the opportunity to dispute their common estimation of "the ancients" (16.3: *hanc nostram pro antiquorum laude concordiam*). This Aper proceeds to do, beginning with his own definitional issue. He asks, "Whom do you call ancients, what age of orators do you indicate with that designation?" (16.4: *quos vocetis antiquos, quam oratorum aetatem significatione ista determinetis*). It would seem that the most eloquent heroes of the Homeric epics, Ulysses and Nestor, are truly ancient, but the only Greeks Messala and the others have mentioned are figures such as Demosthenes and Hyperides, whose era Aper claims (inaccurately) was not much more than 300 years distant from their own day. Invoking the cosmic "great and true year" of 12,954 terrestrial years discussed in Cicero's *Hortensius*, he suggests that these exemplary Greeks are not really very ancient at all.[87]

Aper applies a similar logic to the received chronology of Roman orators. It is not the primitive oratory of Menenius Agrippa that the others prefer to the present, but rather Cicero, Caesar, Calvus, Brutus, Asinius, and Messala [Corvinus] (17.1). Aper calculates (again inaccurately?) that 120 years have passed since Cicero's death in the consulship of Hirtius and Pansa.[88] This is the length of one man's life, as personal experience demonstrates. Aper claims to have met an old man in Britain who remembered Caesar's invasion of that island. At a recent distribution of imperial largess, the others had seen men who remembered receiving similar gifts from Augustus. The Briton might have heard Cicero speak, if only he had

---

[87] *Dial.* 16.5–7: *non multo plures quam trecentos annos* (the real figure was much closer to 400 years). The exemplars Messala cited at 15.3 were Demosthenes and Aeschines. Demosthenes, Hyperides, and Lysias were mentioned by Maternus (12.5). For discussion of Cicero's philosophical dabblings into the concept of the *magnus et verus annus*, see Callataÿ (1996: 42–58).

[88] *Dial.* 17.2–4. This is the most specific, but also the most confusing, indication of the dialogue's dramatic date. One hundred and twenty years from Cicero's death would place the discussion in 77, but Aper's own arithmetic may point to a date earlier than that. Much depends on the interpretation of the phrase *sextam iam felicis huius principatus stationem* (17.3), which has been taken as an indication of the year of Vespasian's reign in which the *Dialogus* is set: Gudeman (1914: 56–62), Mayer (2001: 143), also Letta (1985). More probably, it refers to the fact that Vespasian's Principate occupies the sixth position in his list: Köstermann (1932), Beck (2001). This conclusion does not necessarily validate the accuracy of Aper's calculations, however.

been brought to Rome as a slave, and the Romans could have witnessed the oratory of Asinius Pollio and Messala Corvinus, the most recent members of Messala's cannon.[89]

There is an undeniable element of playfulness in the way that Tacitus provides Aper with this opportunity to demonstrate, however carelessly, the kind of erudition that he supposedly possessed but held in contempt (*Dial.* 2.2, cf. 24.1). Messala will dismiss this portion of Aper's speech as "a dispute over a name" (25.2),[90] but these considerations of personal longevity and time frames are essential to Aper's argument. He recognizes that Cicero's career defined the era universally regarded as the high point of Latin oratory. Velleius Paterculus testifies to the perception that this moment of glory had already come to a close by the end of Augustus' reign.[91] Rather than accept this historical break from the era of Cicero, Calvus, et al., Aper uses his generational framework to suggest an alternative perspective. He objects, "why you assign these men to ancient times rather than to our own, I cannot see" (17.1: *quos quid antiquis temporibus potius adscribatis quam nostris non video*). To keep open the possibility that great talents can still emerge in the present, it is essential that Aper destabilize the logic that critics have used to establish boundaries between different historical periods.[92]

And yet, the very arithmetic that Aper employs to make his point about the proximity of the "ancients" only calls attention to the difficulties he must overcome if he truly intends to claim Cicero for the current era. Although the great orator's death is reckoned by its consular year, Aper proceeds to catalog the number of years each emperor had ruled since then:

statue sex et quinquaginta annos, quibus mox divus Augustus rem publicam rexit; adice Tiberi tres et viginti, et prope quadriennium Gai, ac bis quaternos denos Claudi et Neronis annos, atque illum Galbae et Othonis et Vitellii longum et unum annum, ac sextam iam felicis huius principatus stationem, qua Vespasianus rem publicam fovet.

Set fifty-six years, in which divine Augustus ruled the *respublica*, add the twenty-three of Tiberius, nearly four years of Gaius, the fourteen of both

---

[89] *Dial.* 17.4–5. See esp. Zerubavel (2003: 56–60). Cf. Plin. *NH* 7.153–65 for comparable interest in centenarians, as culled from the census rolls. Aper's position in Britain is not otherwise attested: Syme (1958: 104). For the dates of Vespasian's attested *congiaria*, see Levick (1999: 125).

[90] Cf. Cic. *de Or.* 1.107, Barnes (1986: 237).

[91] Vell. 1.17.3, cf. 2.66.1–5, Schmitzer (2000: 81–5), Fantham (1978a: 15–16). See also Heldmann (1982: 146–62). Cf. Quint. *Inst.* 12.10.11, who is more sanguine about the merits of contemporary age.

[92] Cf. Flower (2010: 1-9), Zerubavel (2003: 58–9, 83).

Claudius and Nero, that one long year of Galba, Otho, and Vitellius, and the sixth post of this happy Principate, with which Vespasian favors the *respublica*. (*Dial.* 17.3)

Without acknowledging the significance of this change, Aper shifts from the traditional measure of Republican chronology (the consular year) to a monarchical standard (the ruler era) in the middle of his computation. Moreover, by equating the death of Cicero with the beginning of Augustus' rule, he makes the connection between Cicero's death and the end of the Republic more explicit than it might otherwise appear to be.[93] The use of this evidence tends to reinforce, rather than undermine, the sense that Cicero belonged to a different and distant era of Roman history.

Aper's inability to acknowledge the connection between the perceived decline in rhetorical standards since Cicero's death and the political change that coincided with this event becomes more incredible when we come to his next point, which is that "the forms and styles of speaking change with the times" (18.2: *mutari cum temporibus formas quoque et genera dicendi*). The philosopher Seneca, whose prose style was sometimes linked to the perceived "corruption" of eloquence under the Principate, had made a similar observation, noting that "style of speaking often imitates public morals" (*Ep.* 114.2: *genus dicendi aliquando imitatur publicos mores*).[94] Seneca's point had been a moral one, however, emerging from the more essential Socratic maxim that "as men's speech is, so too is their life" (*Ep.* 114.1: *talis hominibus fuit oratio qualis vita*).[95] In the same way that Maecenas' lax oratory was a manifestation of his effeminate character, public appetites for novelties of expression reflect the spirit of an age corrupted by luxury. Although the underlying concepts are similar, Aper does not follow Seneca in drawing a connection between rhetorical style and public morality.

Just as he was able to overlook the importance of personal character in his evaluation of Eprius Marcellus and Vibius Crispus, Aper also leaves moral questions out of his historical analysis. Instead, his sole focus is on what will bring success. As Aper sees things, the contemporary orator is defined by his ability to hold the attention of an increasingly sophisticated audience. Familiarity with the precepts of rhetorical handbooks and a smattering of philosophy may have been impressive when speakers addressed an "inexperienced and unrefined" populace, but now everyone has at least some familiarity with these things (*Dial.* 19.2–5). To

[93] Sailor (2008: 131–2).
[94] Dominik (1997: 50–5, 65, Williams (1978: 12–14).
[95] Cf. Cic. *Tusc.* 5.47.

make an impact, one's oratory must be striking and ornate, replete with novel *sententiae* and poetic phrasing.[96] Aper criticizes the ancients for a variety of flaws, but his analysis ultimately rests on the argument that imitation of their sparse and restrained style renders the modern advocate ineffective. As he puts it, "those who carry on before a judge in the old-fashioned style are not followed by their listeners, go unheard by the people, and are scarcely endured by the client himself" (23.3: *quos more prisco apud iudicem fabulantes non auditores sequuntur, non populus audit, vix denique litigator perpetitur*).

In summary, Aper acknowledges that times have changed (and with them the styles of speaking), but he refuses to equate this change with decline. In so doing, he deliberately overlooks both the political and the moral implications of the changes he describes. Aper's aesthetics are determined not by abstract principles, but by whatever achieves the best results. The paradox of this so-called modernism, however, is that it is rooted in a more fundamental sense of tradition.[97] Aper criticizes the past, but only to put the present on a more equal footing. In both of the speeches given to him in the *Dialogus*, Aper is consistent in his belief that advocates continue to play an essential role in Roman public life. He refuses to acknowledge the authority of a remote, closed canon of "ancient orators" because he sees his own oratory and that of his contemporaries as part of an unbroken continuum of progress that stretches back, via Cicero and others, to the hallowed traditions of the Republic.

"NON PUGNAT SED RIXATUR"

At one point in his justification of contemporary eloquence, Aper explains the departure from old standards in the following terms:

> *novis et exquisitis eloquentiae itineribus opus est, per quae orator fastidium aurium effugiat, utique apud eos iudices qui vi et potestate, non iure et legibus cognoscunt, nec accipiunt tempora sed constituunt nec expectandum habent oratorem dum illi libeat de ipso negotio dicere, sed saepe ultro admonent atque alio transgredientem revocant et festinare se testantur.*

There must be new and unusual paths for eloquence, through which the orator can avoid what is distasteful to the ear, especially in front of those judges who determine everything not by laws and justice but according to force and authority, who do not accept the times but set them, and feel that

---

[96] *Dial.* 20.4–5. Aper's speeches in the *Dialogus* are themselves a model of the style he advocates: Mayer (2001: 45–6).

[97] *Pace* Gowing (2005: 114–15), who describes Aper as "the arch-enemy of memory."

they should not wait while an orator is allowed to speak about his business, but often admonish him and call him back from digressing into other issues and claim that they are in a hurry. (*Dial.* 19.5)

This passage accords well with the image of public rhetoric that emerges from other Imperial-era sources. As the result of legal efficiencies put in place under the Principate, the majority of civil litigation was conducted before private judges, who were granted a great deal of discretion in the conduct of their inquiries. Even in the more formal circumstances of the centumviral courts, strict time limits were imposed on speakers, and cases often hinged on technicalities.[98] Aper's recognition of these limitations sits uneasily with his earlier claim that rhetorical accomplishments transcend the glory that comes with public office. Elsewhere in the *Dialogus* (4.2, cf. 39.1–4), Maternus expresses his own impatience with the "narrow confines" of such courts, and explains how they prevent one from giving free reign to his eloquence.

Aper's acknowledgment of the assertiveness of judges fits even less comfortably with the image of the orator presented at the opening of Cicero's dialogue *de Oratore*, where Crassus opens the discussion by saying, "It seems to me that nothing is more honorable than to be able to hold the minds of men by speaking, to influence their will, and drive them toward or lead them away from wherever one desires" (*de Or.* 1.30: *neque vero mihi quicquam...praestabilius videtur, quam posse dicendo tenere hominum [coetus] mentis, adlicere voluntates, impellere quo velit, unde autem velit deducere*). The poet Vergil likewise saw the orator as a commanding figure, whose ability to calm the spirits of a rebellious mob with his words offers the fitting simile for Neptune's mastery over the sea.[99] In contrast, Aper's pliant deference to the demands of the judges inverts this paradigm and calls into question his vision of oratory as a virile form of eloquence that provided its users with an independent source of power in the present.

The distinction between an orator who commands the respect of his listeners and an advocate who panders to the whims of judges seems to matter more to Messala, whose criticisms of contemporary rhetoric reflect the conservative cast of his thinking. When Messala's opportunity to speak finally arrives, he quickly reasserts the canonical status of Cicero, Calvus, and their contemporaries, and goes on to say that even the unsophisticated style of earlier orators such as Crassus and Gaius

---

[98] Plin. *Ep.* 6.2.5–9. Ironically, this lament about the water clocks is occasioned by the death of Regulus, whom Pliny praises for requesting *libera tempora* whenever they debated one another (6.2.3). See, in general, Parks (1945: 42–52), Crook (1995), also Fantham (1997).

[99] Ver. *Aen.* 1.148–56.

Gracchus would be preferable to the "curling irons of Maecenas or the jingles of Gallio" (*Dial.* 26.1: *calamistros Maecenatis aut tinnitus Gallionis*). The difference, he says, is like that between a rough-hewn toga and the prostitute's. Contemporary oratory is marked by "shameful vocabulary, lightweight sentiments, and license of arrangement" more appropriate to actors than to orators, or even real men (26.2: *ut lascivia verborum et levitate sententiarum et licentia compositionis histrionales modos exprimant*). By competing to provide audiences with what they want to hear, these so-called orators have become no better than entertainers whose professions incur the dishonor of *infamia*. This objection derives from the same essential concern for declining social status that underpinned Messala's previous distinction between contemporary *rhetores* and the Roman orators of old.

As the only interlocutor in the dialogue who represents the old Roman nobility, Messala is preoccupied with the moral issues that a new man such as Aper leaves out of his analysis.[100] When pressed by Maternus to focus on the causes of decline, he resorts to a familiar explanation:

> *quis enim ignorat et eloquentiam et ceteras artes descivisse ab illa vetere gloria non inopia hominum sed desidia iuventutis et neglegentia parentum et inscientia praecipientium et oblivione moris antiqui?*

> For who does not know that both eloquence and the other arts have declined from that ancient glory not through scarcity of men but through the sloth of the young, the negligence of their parents, the ignorance of their instructors, and forgetfulness of ancient habits? (*Dial.* 28.2)

In Messala's account, the decline of oratory is represented as part of a general decline of Roman moral traditions. In due course, he will even repeat the stock lament about dissolute youth who distract themselves with their love of the theater, gladiators, and horseracing (29.3). The broader contexts for this "forgetfulness of ancient habits" (*oblivio moris antiqui*) are not examined, however. Messala does not seek any more remote cause for this decline than the personal weaknesses of individual students, parents, and teachers. The only remedy (not that Messala offers one) would be a revival of old-fashioned morals, perhaps of the sort discussed in the previous chapter.

It has often been noted that Messala's analysis of the decline of Roman oratory is very close to that of Quintilian, the prominent rhetor whose teaching career under the Flavians had been devoted to combating the

---

[100] Messala gives a hint of his social differentiation from the others at *Dial.* 28.3. See Brink (1989: 488).

"style of speaking that is corrupt and broken up by all vices" (*Inst.* 10.1.125: *corruptum et omnibus vitiis fractum dicendi genus*), made popular through the influence of Seneca in the Neronian age.[101] What has not received sufficient attention, however, is how little Messala's conception of the orator's role in Roman society differs from the views expressed by his opponent. In his opening debate with Maternus, Aper had described forensic eloquence as "a defense as well as a weapon," equating advocacy with combat and rhetorical success with martial valor (*Dial.* 5.6). Messala adopts a similar position when he contends that "there can be no orator and never was one who did not go out into the forum armed with all these arts, just as if he were equipped with every weapon for the battle-line" (32.2: *quem non posse aliter existere nec extitisse umquam . . . nisi eum qui, tamquam in aciem omnibus armis instructus, sic in forum omnibus artibus armatus exierit*). Like Aper, Messala assumes that it ennobles the advocate to compare him to a combatant and to associate his education with military training. He also laments the fact that parents deposit their children in "the schools of those who are called rhetors" (35.1: *in scholas istorum qui rhetores vocantur*). Again, Messala stresses the Greekness of the term to draw a contrast with the Roman *oratores* of the past, betraying the same nativist outlook that lies behind Aper's objection to the plays Maternus has written about *Graeculi*.

Where Aper assails the uselessness of poetry and seeks to recall Maternus "from the auditoria and theaters to the Forum and to cases and to true battle" (10.5) Messala attacks declamation for its artificiality and praises the ancestral method of instruction, in which a young man was apprenticed to an orator who was engaged in public business, and thus "learned to fight in battle" (34.2: *pugnare in proelio disceret*).[102] This shared belief that advocacy is akin to combat even leads Messala to concede that Cassius Severus, the Augustan-era advocate whom Aper had credited with the realization that styles of oratory must change with the times, "could be called an orator if he were compared to those who came later" (26.4: *si iis comparetur qui postea fuerunt, posse oratorem vocari*).[103] In Messala's judgment, however, Cassius' style also exhibits many of the defects of the present day. He is described as "erratic in the use of his weapons and often

---

[101] Kennedy (1962: 134). See Barwick (1954: 5–14), Brink (1989), also Güngerich (1951), Barnes (1986: 235–6). Like Quintilian, Messala's views are shaped by the canonical authority of Cicero: Barwick (1954: 12–13), cf. Gowing (2005: 117–20).

[102] Eyben (1972).

[103] Cf. *Dial.* 19.1, Quint. *Inst.* 12.10.11. *PIR*² C 522, Rutledge (1999: 560). See Heldmann (1982: 163–98), Winterbottom (1964: 91–2).

stumbling in his eagerness to land a blow, such that he does not fight but rather mixes it up" (26.4: *ipsis etiam quibus utitur armis incompositus et studio feriendi plerumque deiectus, non pugnat sed rixatur*). This description, with its evocation of the arena, may be influenced by the fact that Cassius was said to have been taunted for his resemblance to the gladiator Armentarius.[104] More essentially, however, it underscores the view that an orator must be judged on how he performs in the rhetorical combat of forensic debate.

The intrusion of Cassius Severus into the dialogue, and Messala's concession that he might conditionally be regarded as an orator, has a further layer of significance for this debate about the proper role of oratory in defining one's social position. The elder Seneca reports that Cassius was less successful in declamation than in court cases, and that he consequently shared Messala's low opinion of these exercises. He presents what he says was Cassius' own explanation of this deficiency, which follows many of the lines of Messala's critique in the *Dialogus*. In Seneca's retelling, Cassius concluded his attack on declamation with a boastful account of how he once humiliated the rhetor Cestius for daring to compose a reply to Cicero's *pro Milone* by dragging him before the praetors to demonstrate the impotence of declamatory eloquence in the face of real dangers.[105] This tactic is remarkable, but the thrill of prosecution was evidently well known to Cassius, who Seneca says never defended anyone except himself (*Contr.* 3.*pr*.5). Like the powerful *delatores* Aper regards as the most successful advocates of the present day, Cassius was remembered by Tacitus as a person of obscure origins and questionable morals who made his way in the world by using his eloquence to attack others. His relationship with fellow senators was marked by extreme hostility, and ultimately he was exiled to Crete for publishing defamatory remarks about "illustrious men and women" (*Ann.* 1.72.3: *viros feminasque inlustres*).[106] Messala does not mention this aspect of Cassius' biography but simply notes that there was "more bile than blood" in the majority of his works.[107] There is, it

---

[104] Plin. *NH* 7.55. Cf. Quint. 2.12.2. Mayer (2001: 173).

[105] Sen. *Contr.* 3.praef.17, cf. Quint. *Inst.* 10.5.20. It may be worth mentioning that Cestius Pius was from Smyrna: *PIR*² C 694.

[106] Cf. Dio 56.27.1, D'Hautcourt (1995). There is some uncertainty about Tacitus' claim that this was the first punishment of its kind: Hennig (1973). See also Tac. *Ann.* 4.21.3, Rutledge (1999: 560).

[107] *Dial.* 26.4: *in magna parte librorum suorum plus bilis habeat quam sanguinis.* This is the accepted emendation of the manuscript reading, *plus vis habeat.*

seems, a more-or-less tacit acceptance of this use of rhetoric as a vehicle with which to attack one's peers.

In reading Messala's moralizing complaints about the decline of Roman oratory, it is important not to overlook the fact that his half-brother, whom Aper praises for eloquence but does not name (15.1), was Pliny's nemesis, M. Aquilius Regulus. Although he and Aper argue about whether the changing style of rhetoric reflects a decline in standards, the similarity in their thinking about the role of orators in Roman public life suggests a more fundamental agreement between the two men. Messala may have different views on what constitutes rhetorical skill, but he shares Aper's perspectives on the importance of such talent, which he regards as a manifestation of the speaker's martial *virtus*. Each in his own way reflects the common belief that the practice of oratory in the present represented a continuation of ancient, Republican traditions. Neither speaker gives any serious consideration to the political changes that have taken place since the era of Cicero. Nor do they seem bothered by the fact that under the Principate, the verbal combat that they valorize had a tendency to result in the exile or death of figures like Thrasea and the Helvidii. This unstated potential nevertheless lurks in the background as the merits of famous *delatores* such as Crispus, Marcellus, and Cassius Severus are discussed. Aper and Messala agree that the proper role for a Roman aristocrat continued to lie in an active engagement with the rough-and-tumble world of public life. Their failure to account for the significance of recent political prosecutions does not necessarily invalidate their arguments, but it does indicate a potential limitation in their historical perspective.

LUCROSAE HUIUS ET SANGUINANTIS ELOQUENTIAE USUS RECENS

The conclusion of Messala's discussion has been lost to a *lacuna* in the manuscripts.[108] When the text picks up again, the speaker is Curiatius Maternus, whose literary exploits and desire to abandon forensic advocacy provide the original impetus for this conversation about rhetoric's decline. As the author of a *Cato*, Maternus has a different historical perspective, and it has fallen to him to address the questions that have been omitted from the other speakers' analysis of the relationship between past and present.

---

[108] It is generally agreed that the gap is too short for Secundus to have had a speech of any length: See Häussler (1969), Murgia (1979), Steinmetz (1988), also Köves-Zulauf (1992), Bo (1993: 165–88).

In the first complete sentence following the break, Maternus introduces an arresting simile:

> *magna eloquentia, sicut flamma, materia alitur et motibus excitatur et urendo clarescit. eadem ratio in nostra quoque civitate antiquorum eloquentiam provexit.*

> Great eloquence, like a flame, is nourished by material, roused through disturbances, and shines by burning. The same principle applies to eloquence in our state just as it did to that of the *antiqui*. (*Dial.* 36.1)

At last, one of the speakers raises the importance of the political circumstances in which oratory is produced. As fire needs fuel, the quality of rhetoric depends on the nature of its subject matter. But fire, as Romans who had lived through the "long year" that brought the Flavians to power knew, is a destructive force. By defining the era of great eloquence as one of political turmoil, Maternus calls into question the value of these pursuits.

Maternus wholeheartedly accepts what both Aper and Messala contend, that the orator is like a soldier who goes out to do battle in the Forum and the courts. He brings to this metaphor a different historical perspective, however, one that takes into account the destructive violence of the recent civil wars. "Who does not know that it is more beneficial and better to be nourished by peace than to be vexed by war? Yet wars create more good fighters than peace," he observes (37.7: *quis ignorat utilius ac melius esse frui pace quam bello vexari? plures tamen bonos proeliatores bella quam pax ferunt*). To recover the great oratory of the past, it would be necessary to return to a state of crisis, which obviously is not desirable. Instead, Maternus prefers to enjoy the peace that comes with the current political order. In fact, the only sign of moral decline that he acknowledges in the present has to do with the warlike activities of the most powerful contemporary advocates. Following Aper's praise of Crispus and Marcellus in his opening speech, Maternus replies, "the practice of this lucrative and bloodstained eloquence is a recent thing, born of bad morals, and, as you were saying, Aper, created to take the place of a weapon" (12.2: *nam lucrosae huius et sanguinantis eloquentiae usus recens et ex malis moribus natus atque, ut tu dicebas, Aper, in locum teli repertus*).[109] Having brought ruin to their fellow senators to profit themselves, these *delatores* embody the corruption and violence that make Maternus long to abandon oratory for the "safe and quiet retreat of Vergil" (13.1: *securum et quietum Vergili secessum*).

---

[109] Winterbottom (2001: 143–4).

As established in the dramatic frame of the dialogue, Maternus prefers his poetry to the burdens of oratory and hopes to leave behind "the narrow confines of forensic cases" so that he can pursue the "more sacred and august eloquence" of the bards (4.2: *ut omissis forensium causarum . . . sanctiorem illam et augustiorem eloquentiam colam*). Unlike the committed traditionalists Aper and Messala, he does not assume that what advocates or orators do is worthwhile in itself. Speaking of the great crises in which Republican oratory flourished, Maternus concludes that the political conditions in which orators emerge are not desirable, and thus, perhaps, neither are orators. He feels that the "orators of our day" have achieved as much as they can in a "composed, peaceful, and happy *respublica*," while in the past they appear to have pursued "disorder and license (*licentia*)" more successfully.[110] In this analysis, Seneca's assertion that the moral character of an age is reflected in its oratory is turned on its head. The decline of Roman eloquence is not, as Messala interprets it, a sign of moral decay, but is rather the result of the peace and stability that the Principate has brought to the Roman world.

Rather than use his historical perspective to question the utility of the rhetorical style of the *antiqui* in the changed circumstances of the present, Maternus sets out to redefine the moral status of the Republican past altogether.[111] He explains that the age of great orators was also an age of great strife, in which factional hatreds were aired in public and led ultimately to armed conflict (36.3–37.8). This track leads, inevitably, to a reconsideration of the freedom associated with the Republic. Maternus exploits the ambiguity inherent in the Roman understanding of this term:

> *non de otiosa et quieta re loquimur et quae probitate et modestia gaudeat, sed est magna illa et notabilis eloquentia alumna licentiae, quam stulti libertatem vocant, comes seditionum, effrenati populi incitamentum, sine obsequio, sine severitate, contumax temeraria adrogans, quae in bene constitutis civitatibus non oritur.*

We are not talking about a leisured and peaceful pursuit that delights in integrity and decorum. Rather, this great and notable eloquence is a nursling of license (*licentia*), which fools call liberty (*libertas*), the companion of subversion, a prod for the unbridled populace that is without compliance

---

[110] *Dial.* 36.2: *nam etsi horum quoque temporum oratores ea consecuti sunt quae composita et quieta et beata re publica tribui fas erat, tamen illa perturbatione ac licentia plura sibi adsequi videbantur.* The hendiadys of *orator . . . consecuti sunt . . . adsequi videbantur* attracts the term *orator* into the present.

[111] Heldmann (1982: 275–9), Fantham (2004: 323–6), Gowing (2005: 115–16).

or strictness. It is a disagreeable, rash, and arrogant thing, which in well-established states does not occur. (*Dial.* 40.2)

It has been noted that these words directly contradict a claim made by Cicero, that eloquence was "the companion of peace, the ally of leisure, and to some extent the nursling of an already well-established state" (*Brut.* 45: *pacis est comes otique socia et iam bene constitutae civitatis quasi alumna quaedam eloquentia*).[112] Although Cicero had not mentioned the connection between eloquence and freedom, his own posthumous identification with the theme of Republican *libertas* is apparently enough to attract this concept into Maternus' refutation of his views. By introducing the topic of liberty, and by further delimiting its meaning within a framework that distinguishes it from license, Maternus is able to confront this as-yet-unmentioned, but nevertheless inescapably relevant aspect of Cicero's historical context, while also calling into question the authority of Cicero's views about the relationship between oratory and the "well-established state."[113]

This contradiction is not meant to suggest that Cicero's eloquence was itself the product of *licentia* – that would be inconsistent with his status as an orator. Maternus simply points out that Cicero could not have achieved greatness if it were not for the evils of the era in which he lived (37.6). He goes on to remark, "Neither was the eloquence of the Gracchi so valuable for the *respublica* that it should have suffered their laws, nor did Cicero properly balance his reputation for eloquence against such a demise" (40.4: *sed nec tanti rei publicae Gracchorum eloquentia fuit ut pateretur et leges, nec bene famam eloquentiae Cicero tali exitu pensavit*). The great orator's death was not just the end point for the era of Rome's greatest eloquence, it was also dramatic proof of the turbulence that had made this eloquence possible. If political turmoil is necessary for the flame of eloquence to thrive, then Maternus welcomes the decline of oratory as a fair price to pay for the peace and stability of the Principate.

QUID MATERNUS SIBI DEBUERIT

The inadequacy of "freedom" as a justification for the violence that accompanied the oratory of the late Republic also influences Maternus' view of contemporary advocacy. In response to Aper's celebration of two well-known *delatores* as "the most powerful men in the state and, as far as is

---

[112] Güngerich (1980: 176), see also Mayer (2001: 211–12), Gallia (2009: 186–8).
[113] On *libertas* and *licentia*, cf. Sen. *Clem.* 1.1.8.

permissible, the *principes* of the Forum," Maternus disparages their place in society:

> *nam Crispus iste et Marcellus, ad quorum exempla me vocas, quid habent in hac sua fortuna concupiscendum: quod timent, an quod timentur? quod, cum cotidie aliquid rogentur, ii quibus praestant indignantur? quod alligati cum adulatione nec imperantibus umquam satis servi videntur nec nobis satis liberi? quae haec summa eorum potentia est? tantum posse liberti solent.*

In the case of that Crispus and Marcellus, to whose examples you direct me, what do they have in this fortune of theirs that one should wish for: that they fear, or that they are feared? Is it that, even as they face constant requests, those whom they help resent it? Is it that, being bound through flattery, they seem neither servile enough to those in charge nor free enough to us? Are these things the height of their power? It is common for freedmen to have such power. (*Dial.* 13.4)

In Maternus' judgment, *delatores* are no different from the Imperial freedmen who oversaw many aspects of the emperor's administration.[114] They are nominally free but, due to the realities of power under the Principate, theirs is a circumscribed freedom, without meaningful independence. Their status, such as it is, is the result of fear and flattery – immoral qualities that will prove to be unstable sources of power. As the recriminations that followed the deaths of Nero and Domitian demonstrated, accusing one's fellow senators was not only a morally repugnant task, it was also a dangerous one as well. In fact, before the end of Vespasian's reign, Eprius Marcellus wound up taking his own life after being condemned for treason in the senate.[115] Assuming that Maternus' observation about Marcellus' fear can be taken as foreshadowing this event, the reader should be inclined to question Aper's previous claim that the prominence of *delatores* in the present reflects their possession of "something that they did not and cannot acquire from a *princeps*" (8.3: *quod non a principe acceperint nec accipi possit*).

For Maternus, true eloquence should be morally elevating, unsullied by the vicious imperatives of harming one's enemies and protecting one's friends from harm. Poetry, which is characterized by a pastoral existence secluded from the bustle and cares of the modern world, is closer to this pure form of eloquence.[116] Maternus claims that there were no orators in

---

[114] Gallia (2009: 182–3), cf. Boesche (1987: 198–9).

[115] Dio (Xiph.) 66.16.4. See Rogers (1980) *contra* Crook (1951), also Syme (1958: 101). Note the similarity in the formulation used by Pliny when he celebrates the banishment of *delatores* under Trajan, *Pan.* 35.3: *timeantque quantum timebantur.*

[116] *Dial.* 12.3–4. Heldmann (1982: 263–6), Manuwald (2001: 6–7), Häussler (1965: 193).

the golden age, because there were no crimes to prosecute, and expands on this point in his final speech (*Dial.* 12.3, cf. 41.3). Perhaps naively, he seeks to return to those utopian circumstances by rejecting oratory and embracing poetry as the only form of eloquence worth pursuing. Continuing along these lines, he observes:

> *quid enim opus est longis in senatu sententiis cum optimi cito consentiant? quid multis apud populum contionibus cum de re publica non imperiti et multi deliberent sed sapientissimus et unus? quid voluntariis accusationibus cum tam raro et tam parce peccetur? quid invidiosis et excedentibus modum defensionibus cum clementia cognoscentis obviam periclitantibus eat?*

> What need is there for long dissertations in the senate, when the best men agree quickly? Or for numerous meetings of the people, when it is not the inexperienced multitude but the one wisest man who determines the course of government? Or for voluntary prosecutions, when transgressions are so rare and so trivial? Or for hateful and excessive defenses, when the clemency of the judge reaches out to those in danger? (*Dial.* 41.4)

What Maternus offers here is nothing less than a new model for the Principate, in which the pretense of maintaining Republican tradition has been discarded in favor of a new set of moral and political obligations. Deliberative oratory, a topic largely ignored in the *Dialogus*, is pronounced dead, replaced by the judgment of an ideal, wise ruler and the rapidly obtained consent of his court advisors. Along with other forms of oratory, forensic advocacy also retreats from view as the show trials in which *delatores* visit ruin on their enemies become obsolete. Importantly for the tensions discussed in Chapter 3, self-restraint takes priority over punishment in this more perfect form of monarchy, and the ruler's *clementia* ensures that no one suffers unjustly.

Such an arrangement need not be inconsistent with *libertas*, which Maternus explicitly distinguishes from the *licentia* that prevailed under the Republic. In a previous exchange with Messala, Maternus encouraged the younger man to "employ that ancient *libertas*, from which we have degenerated more than from eloquence" (27.3: *utere antiqua libertate, <a> qua vel magis degeneravimus quam ab eloquentia*). The freedom to which he refers is the ability to speak openly, without fear of consequences.[117] Messala had just assured him that he was not offended by Aper's abuse of his "ancestors" and said that he expects the same indulgence from his listeners, "since you know that it is the law for this kind of discussion, that one should be disposed to offer his heartfelt opinion

---

[117] Sailor (2008: 127–9).

without penalty" (27.2: *cum sciatis hanc esse eius modi sermonum legem, iudicium animi citra damnum adfectus proferre*). This context suggests that Maternus' statement about the decline of *libertas* under the Principate is linked to the fear of malicious prosecutions that had grown with the rising influence of the *delatores*. The freedom that Maternus fears losing in the present is the same freedom he had exercised in delivering, and refusing to amend, his offensive *Cato*.

To the unsuspecting reader, it may seem incongruous that a poet who has written a provocative play entitled *Cato* should speak so enthusiastically about abandoning one of the few political and ethical obligations that had survived from the Republic. In fact, some modern commentators have suggested that the praise of monarchy in Maternus' final speech was meant to be read as self-contradictory "doublespeak," which exposes the impossibility of free speech under the Principate through its own insincerity.[118] This hasty dismissal of the character's stated opinions in favor of an imputed Catonian "Republicanism" cannot be accepted, however, because it ignores the complexity of the tradition surrounding Cato under the Principate. As has already been explained, Cato's famous suicide was more likely to be remembered by his admirers as a model of Stoic determination. It was, in fact, the opponents of these men who regarded Cato as a symbol of political opposition. The political views attributed to Maternus in the *Dialogus* – especially his ideal of a state guided by "the one wisest man" (*sapientissimus et unus*) – are wholly consistent with the dominant currents of Stoic thought in Tacitus' day.[119] The offenses of his *Cato* are probably better seen as part of a philosophical, rather than a political, manifesto.

In any case, the notion that we can reconstruct Maternus' "genuine" political views from the title of a lost play is extremely dubious.[120] It is true that Aper notes that Maternus "seem[s] to have deliberately chosen a famous character and one who would speak with authority" (10.6: *meditatus videris [aut] elegisse personam notabilem et cum auctoritate dicturam*), but the same witness also complains about the breadth of Maternus' subject matter as well (3.4). The follow-up to the offensive *Cato* will not be a *Brutus*, but rather a *Thyestes*. It is clear that Maternus was not limited to Roman, let alone Republican, themes. Despite Aper's complaints about the appropriateness of writing about *Graeculi*, the history of the Republic

---

[118] See esp. Bartsch (1994: 98–125), also Köhnken (1973), Murgia (1980: 123).
[119] Wistrand (1979: 94), cf. Brunt (1975: 17–21). Cf. Dio Chrys. 36.32, Schofield (1991: 86–90). See also Gowing (2005: 117).
[120] Gallia (2009: 192–200).

and the senate's conflict with Caesar do not occupy a privileged position as poetical subjects. These themes are instead particular aspects of a broader, cosmopolitan heritage of commonplaces that a poet could use to explore topics of contemporary interest.

The *Cato* nevertheless remains as important to the meaning of the *Dialogus* as Cicero's *Brutus* or *de Oratore*. As Aper sees it, the offense Maternus has given in his play represents a pointless risk:

> *nec pro amico aliquo sed, quod periculosius est, pro Catone offendis.*...
> *tolle igitur quietis et securitatis excusationem, cum tibi sumas adversarium*
> *superiorem. nobis satis sit privatas et nostri saeculi controversias tueri, in*
> *quibus [expressis] si quando necesse sit pro periclitante amico potentiorum*
> *aures offendere et probata sit fides et libertas excusata.*

> You offend not for some friend, but, what is more dangerous, for Cato.... Therefore abandon the excuse of peace and security, since you take a greater adversary for yourself. For me, it is enough to tend to private disputes and those of our era, in which, if it at some time it should be necessary to offend the ears of those more powerful on behalf of an endangered friend, your loyalty would be commended and your *libertas* would be excused. (*Dial.* 10.6–8)

Liberty, which in the *Dialogus* is equated with the ability to offend, is regarded by Aper as a quality best demonstrated in the courtroom. Aper admires this aspect of Maternus' character but wishes that he would utilize his courage on behalf of clients in the courts, rather than seeking fame by advocating on behalf of the long-dead Cato. Maternus' response, that the forensic use of liberty is really a form of license, has already been discussed.

In denying Maternus "the excuse of peace and security" for his poetic endeavors, however, Aper exposes his own arguments to another contradiction. The notoriety of Maternus' play undercuts Aper's previous contention that the fame attained by advocates outstrips anything that poets can achieve. He as much as admits to this fact when he acknowledges that "these things are especially praised in those auditoria and soon are passed on in the discussion of everyone" (10.7: ... *haec in ipsis auditoriis praecipue laudari et mox omnium sermonibus ferri*). A similar point is made by Maternus in an important passage, the interpretation of which has long been in dispute:

> *ego autem sicut in causis agendis efficere aliquid et eniti fortasse possum,*
> *ita recitatione tragoediarum et ingredi famam auspicatus sum, cum qui-*
> *dem †in Nerone† inprobam et studiorum quoque sacra profanantem Vatini*

potentiam fregi; hodie si quid in nobis notitiae ac nominis est, magis arbitror carminum quam orationum gloria partum.

Just as I perhaps was able to accomplish something and distinguished myself in pleading cases, I have done similarly through the recitation of my tragedies, and it augured well for me to earn my reputation when †in my Nero† I broke the shameful power of Vatinius, which was even profaning the holy traditions of the arts. Today if I have any fame and reputation, I judge that it derives more from the glory of my poems than from that of my speeches. (*Dial.* 11.2)

Some scholars accept the reading offered here, that Maternus broke Vatinius' power through a play entitled *Nero*, whereas others emend the text to suggest that he did so in his role as an advocate, during Nero's reign.[121] Ultimate certainty is impossible and, perhaps, unnecessary, because the meaning of the second sentence is clear enough. At the time of the *Dialogus*, Maternus was more famous as a poet than as an orator.

It is nevertheless significant that Maternus chooses to identify the origins of his reputation with an action he took against the insidious power of Vatinius. As described by Tacitus in the *Annals*, Vatinius was another despicable *delator*, who emerged from obscure origins in the Neronian age through what Tacitus describes as his "destructive strength" (*Ann.* 15.34.2: *vi nocendi*).[122] Whether the downfall of Vatinius was accomplished with a play or in a speech such as Pliny's *de ultione Helvidii*, Maternus' avowed hostility toward a figure who owed his wealth and status to destructive prosecutions, moreover one who was using his powers to profane "the holy traditions of the arts," accords well with the arguments attributed to him in the *Dialogus* about the moral superiority of poetry to oratory.

Moreover, it seems that this attack on a highly placed member of the Imperial court has important implications for the circumstances in which the dialogue is set. Tacitus says only that "it was going around that he had offended the sensibilities of the powerful" with this most recent play (2.1: *cum offendisse potentium animos diceretur*). If we admit the possibility that the views ascribed to Maternus in the discussion that follows this

---

[121] The idea that Vatinius' downfall was accomplished in a speech has been argued by Stroux (1931: 344–8), followed by Güngerich (1980: 44–6), Barnes (1986: 238–9), Mayer (2001: 122), Manuwald (2001: 8–9), and Zwierlein (2003). In favor of a play (probably entitled *Nero*) are Barwick (1954: 40–2), Heldmann (1982: 261–2), Kragelund (1987: 197–200), Bartsch (1994: 201–2), Levene (2004: 169–70), and Gallia (2009: 190–1).

[122] *PIR*[1] V 208, Rutledge (2001: 276–7), cf. Gallia (2009: 201–2).

statement have something to do with this notorious offense, it becomes likely that the unnamed powerful figures whom he targeted in his *Cato* were not Vespasian and Titus, but rather *delatores* such as Marcellus and Crispus.[123] In that case, the fame Maternus earned from this play would not be dissimilar from that which he claims to have acquired in his earlier confrontation with Vatinius. More importantly, by using the "innocent eloquence" of poetry to voice his criticism of these figures, Maternus avoided becoming a *delator* himself and participating in the cycle of licentious violence of prosecutions that he had come to despise.[124]

CONCLUSION

As a work of historical and literary inquiry, the *Dialogus* calls attention to the political and cultural uncertainties that three generations of life under a "restoration of the Republic" could not mask. When the character of Aper describes Eprius Marcellus and Vibius Crispus as being in a position to "handle and deal with everything," he does little to demonstrate the continued effectiveness of oratory as a wellspring of political authority. Instead, he exposes what Tacitus seems to have regarded as a particularly regrettable byproduct of monarchy – the ability of unscrupulous courtiers to acquire power through their influence with the ruler. The power that such men enjoyed was not derived from their tenure in traditional Republican magistracies, but from their prominence within the emperor's circle of friends. The influence of these detestable figures reminds us of Sallust's and Cassius Dio's concerns about kings' preference for bad men over good, and provides further evidence of the break with the moral traditions of *libertas* that had taken place under the Principate.[125]

Unwilling to take part in a system he finds corrupt, Maternus turns instead to the "good fortune and happy camaraderie of the bards" (*Dial.* 13.1: *fortunam quidem vatum et illud felix contubernium*). Herein lies the answer to Fabius' question. Because of the perceived destructiveness of public speaking in the present day, the good man chooses to exercise his eloquence in the pursuit of poetry instead. As described by Maternus, the glory of poetry has little to do with the blood-stained lucre that taints the oratorical success of the *delatores*, which Aper holds as an ideal. Instead, the poet's life offers a more satisfying social existence, in which success

---

[123] Gallia (2009), Heldmann (1982: 268–70).
[124] *Dial.* 11.4, Gallia (2009: 192), Williams (1978: 51).
[125] Cf. Paterson (2007) on the "subversive effect" of Imperial court culture. Livy (2.3.2) also identifies this unwelcome feature of monarchical systems.

depends purely on one's eloquence, not his willingness to attack fellow senators. This retreat from public life is not so much a step out of history as part of an effort to move it forward. Although he writes a play about Cato, Maternus does not look back to the Republic as a model for living in the present. What he desires instead is a new model of the Principate, which finally acknowledges the reality of the current political situation in order to produce a more accountable and morally acceptable form of autocracy.[126]

We do not know what came of the controversy provoked by Maternus' play, and the evidence for the poet's life beyond what is recorded in the *Dialogus* is ambiguous at best. It has been suggested, on the hypothesis of an analogy with figures such as Crassus in Cicero's *de Oratore* or Socrates in Plato's *Phaedo*, that Maternus died not long after the dramatic date of the dialogue, perhaps as a result of the dangerous offense of his *Cato*.[127] This interpretation has been broadly accepted, but prosopography offers several alternative possibilities. In a passage relating to the clampdown of 91, the epitomators of Dio record that a sophist named Maternus was put to death for declaiming against tyrants.[128] Alternatively, one of Martial's epigrams mentions the peaceful death of a certain Curiatius, who was stricken by an unexpected heat wave while summering at Tibur in 89.[129] Either of these figures could be the poet of the *Dialogus*. It has even been proposed that the author of the *Cato* should be identified with the M. Cornelius Nigrinus Curiatius Maternus recorded in inscriptions from Liria in Spain, who served as governor of Syria in the latter years of Domitian's reign and may have been among the candidates talked about as a potential successor to the Principate in the uncertain early months of Nerva's reign.[130] The range of possibilities is broad, and it is impossible to know whether Maternus faced exile and death, like the elder Helvidius

---

[126] Cf. von Fritz (1957: 565).

[127] Cameron (1967), followed by Alföldy and Halfmann (1973: 345–6), Luce (1993: 24), Bartsch (1994: 105–6), Rutledge (2000: 346–9), cf. Bo (1993: 228–34). *Contra*, Devreker (1986: 104–5), Gowing (2005: 113).

[128] Dio (Xiph.) 67.12.5, cf. (Zon.) 67.12.19. Identification of Tacitus' Maternus with this figure, assumed by the likes of Wissowa (*RE* 4.2 1834, citing the first edition of Norden's *Antike Kunstprosa*), was refuted by Gudeman (1914: 67), but then revived by Matthiessen (1970) and Barnes (1981).

[129] Mart. 4.60, with Friedländer (1886: 55–6) for the date. Perhaps the same Maternus mentioned elsewhere in the *Epigrams* (cf. 10.37, 1.96, 2.74). Identified with the poet of the *Dialogus* by Herrmann (1939), Devreker (1986: 106–8), also admitted as possible by Syme (1981: 138).

[130] *CIL* II² 14, 124. Barnes (1981) and Jones (1992: 187) would connect both this man and the sophist mentioned in Dio with our Maternus. He is more likely a nephew or adopted son: Alföldy and Halfmann (1973), Syme (1981: 136–7), Eck (1982: 324 n. 172).

did after his confrontation with Eprius Marcellus, or if his fate was more happy, like that of Pliny the Younger following his attack on Publicius Certus.

Because the main interlocutors in the *Dialogus* are so clearly drawn, each with his distinct point of view, it can be easy to forget that the opinions attributed to these characters are not necessarily those of actual historical persons, but rather the creations of an author writing about thirty years after the date of this supposed conversation.[131] Although the exigencies of Maternus' career (and those of Aper and Messala) provide a necessary framework for evaluating these ideas, it is Tacitus who is responsible for the particular formulation of the relationship between Cato, Cicero, and the present state of oratory that we find in the *Dialogus*. Although we should be cautious about oversimplifying the message of a complex and polyvocal text, a strong case can be made that what Maternus says about the undesirability of a return to the conditions of the Republic was not very far from Tacitus' own opinions.[132] When Tacitus seeks the root causes for the civil wars of 69 in the *Histories*, he traces the history of an "ancient and innate lust for power" (*Hist.* 2.38.1: *vetus ac iam pridem insita mortalibus potentiae cupido*) that lay behind the whole of Republican history, which led to the struggle of the orders, factionalism, and civil war. A similar view of the unsustainable violence of the Republican era is reflected at the beginning of the *Annals*, where Tacitus says that Augustus "accepted the whole state, which was worn out by civil strife, under his power with the name of *princeps*" (*Ann.* 1.1: *qui cuncta discordiis civilibus fessa nomine principis sub imperium accepit*). However grudgingly, the concentration of power into the hands of one man seems to be accepted as a necessary condition for peace.

Tacitus' views on these questions may be idiosyncratic. He likely gives a distorted picture of the predominance of *delatores* in Imperial oratory, just as he leaves out any discussion of deliberative and epideictic rhetoric and their place in contemporary training and practice.[133] Nevertheless, the analysis he presents in both the *Dialogus* and the *Histories* reflects a genuine concern about the way that notions of continuity with Republican traditions were used to justify the nature of public life under the Principate. As Regulus' comment about Pliny's emulation with Cicero suggests,

---

[131] Cf. Winterbottom (2001: 138).

[132] Syme (1958: 109–10), Williams (1978: 35), Winterbottom (2001: 153), cf. Sion-Jenkis (2000: 136–9). See also Keitel (1984) and (1992).

[133] Parks (1945: 30–1), also Fantham (1997).

the complexity of the relationship between Republican and Imperial oratory was something that every member of the Roman aristocracy had to negotiate on his own terms.

It seems fitting, therefore, to conclude this discussion by taking a brief look at one of Pliny's favorite poems, which commemorates his status as an emerging orator and patron of the arts. Composed by Martial late in Domitian's reign, the epigram describes Thalia's journey across the Subura and up the slope of the Esquiline to bring a book of poetry to Pliny's house. Referring to the poem in a letter prompted by the news of Martial's death, Pliny skips over the opening lines and a description of the statue group of Orpheus enchanting animals that stood near his house to quote the portrait of himself, which makes up the last ten lines of the poem:

> Sed ne tempore non tuo disertam
> pulses ebria ianuam videto:
> totos dat tetricae dies Minervae,
> dum centum studet auribus virorum
> hoc quod saecula posterique possint
> Arpinis quoque conparare chartis.
> Seras tutior ibis ad lucernas:
> haec hora est tua, cum furit Lyaeus,
> cum regnat rosa, cum madent capilli:
> tunc me vel rigidi legant Catones.

> But take care not to knock on that
> Cultured door drunk, at a time not yours.
> He devotes all day to stern Minerva,
> While he arranges for centumviral ears
> That which this and future eras may judge
> Equal even to the pages of Arpinum.
> Safer to arrive for the lamps that burn late:
> This hour is yours, when Lyaeus revels,
> When the rose holds sway, when hair is perfumed:
> Then I can be read even by stiff Catos.
>   (Mart. 10.20 (19).12–21, Plin. *Ep.* 3.21)

As in the *Dialogus*, the delectations of poetry are presented as an antidote to the demanding labors of public business, which Martial associates with the dual models of Cicero, the glory of Arpinum, and the *rigidi Catones* of the final verse.

Pliny might take pride in bridging these worlds, but Maternus evidently chose a different path. Knowledge of the fate that awaits Maternus would surely influence the final interpretation of the *Dialogus*, and of Maternus' stated wish that the portrait on his tomb be "not grave and menacing, but merry and crowned with laurel" (*Dial.* 13.6: *statuarque tumulo non maestus et atrox sed hilaris et coronatus*). It is possible that Maternus had reason for optimism. After all, Marcellus eventually fell from favor, and Tacitus does say that Vespasian was the first *princeps* ever to change for the better.[134] But Tacitus also knew the fate that awaited outspoken authors (and their books) in an age that sought to consign such expressions of *libertas* to oblivion.

[134] Tac. *Hist.* 1.50.4.

5

INSCRIPTION

Speculation about the form of Maternus' tomb brings us back to a facet of Roman cultural memory that we touched on briefly in Chapter 1, where one of the items adduced as evidence for the pervasive importance of *libertas* in the aftermath of the rebellion of Galba and Vindex was the epitaph of Verginius Rufus. It was noted that Nero's commander of the Rhine legions ultimately tried to settle the questions that had been raised about his loyalties during the battle of Vesontio by composing a brief epitaph in which his actions on that occasion were characterized as those of an *adsertor*, who acted not on his own behalf, but in the interests of his *patria* after Vindex's death. Whether these verses constitute special pleading or not, Verginius' act of self-justification serves to remind us that the contexts in which Imperial memories of the Republic were formulated were rarely oriented exclusively toward that distant past. As part of an ongoing ideological discourse in which the Roman elite continuously renegotiated their identity, this general's claim about asserting power "not for himself, but for the fatherland" was more about controlling the framework in which his own memory would be cast than about perpetuating a particular vision of the Republic. Contemplation of the past must have played some role in Verginius' sense of who he was and what he was doing at Vesontio, but the way in which this self-concept found expression was inextricably linked with a form of commemoration that looked to the future.

The Republic thus constitutes but one strand in a larger continuum of Roman memory, providing a backdrop against which contemporary concerns were mooted by men who sought to continue the old traditions while also contributing some new accomplishment for which they might be remembered themselves. Moreover, this was a continuum that constantly turned back on itself, seeing that the concern shown by figures such as Verginius for their own commemoration was itself a means of perpetuating cultural practices handed down from Republican forebears. By having one's achievements celebrated on a monumental tomb, the Imperial senator demonstrated his dedication to the principles of competition and glory seeking that can also be seen, for example, in the *elogia* preserved at the third-century BC tomb of the Scipios outside of Rome.[1]

In Verginius' case, however, the importance of the ideal was underscored by its nonfulfillment. When the younger Pliny visited the tomb nine years after Verginius' death, he found it unfinished, with no trace of the epitaph its occupant had crafted so carefully. This discovery prompted Pliny to bemoan the breakdown of trust (*fides*) that could consign so great a man to oblivion. The laziness of the heir to whom Verginius had entrusted the construction of his monument is presented as yet another sign of the moral collapse that threatened to overwhelm the Roman elite and cut them off from the traditions that formed such an important portion of their identity.[2] The problem was not with the tomb per se, but with an external process of commemoration that was supposed to be enacted through its construction. The fact of the matter is that, although monuments might be regarded as necessary for the propagation of memory, they were not in themselves sufficient to this task. Even a finished tomb could fall into disrepair if it was not maintained. The critical element, noted for its absence here, was the sense of obligation to the dead that joined past, present, and future together in an unbroken cycle of commemoration.[3] It is this ethical bond between generations (not the permanence of bronze or marble) that gave monuments much of their power as sites of cultural memory.

One consequence of the socially constituted nature of this kind of memory is that commemorative behaviors such as tending to funereal monuments also provided a way to define oneself as a participant in the ethical traditions that the honored dead were taken to represent. We have noted already the biographies that the Stoics wrote of Cato Uticensis and the declamations that would-be orators delivered concerning Cicero's final days. To these examples we can add that of Ti. Catius Asconius Silius Italicus, the epic poet whose reflections on the evocative power of public monuments in Rome has already been discussed.[4] According to Pliny, this wealthy consular enjoyed a prolonged retirement on the bay of Naples,

---

[1] *ILS* 1–10 (= *CIL* 1² 6–16), *LTUR* IV 280–5 s.v. "Sepulcrum (Corneliorum) Scipionum" [Zevi], Coarelli (1972), Wallace-Hadrill (2008: 218–23). On tombs as sites of memory, see Assmann (1999: 322-8).

[2] Plin. *Ep.* 6.10.2–6.

[3] Margalit (2002, esp. 91–4). Cf. Cic. *Tusc.* 5.64–6, with Jaeger (2002) on Archimedes' tomb, also Livy 38.56.2–3 on the tomb of Scipio Africanus.

[4] *PIR²* S 722. See Chapter 2.

where he dedicated himself to poetry and indulged a passion for buying villas and filling them with books, art, and portraits, which earned him a reputation as an "aesthete" (φιλόκαλος). Moreover,

> *quas non habebat modo, verum etiam venerabatur, Vergili ante omnes, cuius natalem religiosius quam suum celebrabat, Neapoli maxime, ubi monimentum eius adire ut templum solebat.*

> "He did not simply possess these things, but even venerated them, those of Vergil above all. He celebrated Vergil's birthday more religiously than his own, especially at Naples, where he tended to his tomb as one might a temple." (*Ep.* 3.7.8)

These commemorative gestures transformed the statues, portraits, and other objects that Silius collected from mere commodities into meaningful, quasi-sacred monuments, which served to bring their worshipful caretaker into closer association with the great figures of the past. It is clear that a devotion to Vergil's memory, which found particular expression at his tomb, was integral to Silius' construction of his own identity as a poet.

The interrelationship between monuments, memory, and the propagation of identity noted here could be extrapolated to the ways that Romans regarded the record of the past generally. It was in this regard that Livy described the purpose of his multivolume history of the Republic:

> *hoc illud est praecipue in cognitione rerum salubre ac frugiferum: omnis te exempli documenta in inlustri posita monumento intueri; inde tibi tuaeque rei publicae quod imitere capias, inde foedum inceptu, foedum exitu, quod uites.*

> In the study of events, this is a particularly wholesome and profitable aspect: that you look upon the lessons of every *exemplum* as if placed on a shining monument. Take from this for yourself and your state what to imitate, and what, foul in its undertaking and foul in its result, you should avoid. (Liv. 1.*praef.*10)

Before turning to the implications of the connection between monuments and literary texts made here, we should note that the terms of Livy's analogy conform to what has just been said. In stressing the eidetic quality of monuments (*inlustri... intueri*), the historian calls attention to the importance of the spectator's active response to what he sees. After first reconstructing the meaning of the *exempla* presented in his history/monument, the reader/viewer is then supposed to translate those lessons into action.[5]

---

[5] Jaeger (1997: 23–6), Miles (1995: 15–20), Moles (1993: 146), also Feldherr (1998: 4–12), Walter (2004: 422–5).

The monument can serve as a prompt to memory, but it is still up to the individual to supply the appropriate reaction.

If the attitude of Verginius and Silius to the commemorative function of monuments can be regarded as typical, it was not necessarily universal. As was discussed in the previous chapter, the question of how best to integrate ancestral traditions with the obligations of contemporary life did not always find a straightforward solution among the elite of the Flavian age. Not all forms of self-glorification, however hallowed by Republican precedent, were regarded as equally legitimate by everyone. Calvisius Ruso, one of Pliny's younger correspondents, was among those who found something to criticize in Verginius' epitaph. He offered as a counterweight the model of his uncle Sex. Julius Frontinus, whom we met briefly in Chapter 4 as the urban praetor who convened the senate meeting at which Helvidius Priscus renewed his offense with Eprius Marcellus.[6] Frontinus, his nephew suggests, acted better and more appropriately (*melius rectiusque*) by forbidding any monument to be constructed in his honor. This claim may reflect the influence of Stoic arguments about the indifferent nature of glory, but Pliny insists that Verginius' desire for immortality was appropriate and entirely praiseworthy. He points out that Frontinus was not actually unconcerned with his own memory, but merely skeptical about a tomb's efficacy in securing it:

> *vetuit exstrui monumentum, sed quibus verbis? "impensa monumenti supervacua est; memoria nostri durabit, si vita meruimus."*

> He refused to have a monument constructed, but in what terms? "The expense of a monument is wasteful. Our memory will last, if we earn it with our life." (*Ep.* 9.19.6)

The difference lies not in the desire to be remembered, but in the means by which this goal should be pursued. Frontinus argues that a tomb does little to enhance a reputation and that the best source of *memoria* is the life you lead.[7] Good deeds, rather than conspicuous monuments, are the only real prerequisite for posthumous fame. Although Pliny does not draw this connection, we may note that Frontinus' logic could be applied just as well to Verginius' circumstance, because Pliny had previously commented on the perversity of the fact that his ashes lay neglected while his memory traveled throughout the world (6.10.3: *neglectumque cinerem sine titulo sine nomine iacere, cuius memoria orbem terrarum gloria pervagetur*).

---

[6] Plin. *Ep.* 9.19. *PIR²* C 350. On the identity of the addressee, Syme (1958: 801–2), *contra* Sherwin-White (1966: 502). Frontinus: Tac. *Hist.* 4.39.1, *PIR²* I 322.

[7] Peachin (2004: 87–91), cf. Champlin (1991: 170).

Once again, it is not the tomb, but something else, that preserved this fame.

As pleased as Frontinus' heirs must have been about being spared the expense of building and maintaining a funerary monument for him, the nobility of this sentiment is complicated by the fact that the terms of its expression (*quibus verbis*) could be quoted from one of Frontinus' published works. Pliny points this out in his response to Ruso, arguing that it is less modest to discuss how one's memory will endure in a text available throughout the world (9.19.6: *per orbem terrarum legendum*) than to praise oneself in a brief inscription that can be read only in a single location (*uno in loco duobus versiculis*). As both Livy's preface and Horace's famous ode attest, a literary text was itself a kind of monument.[8] No doubt this is why Pliny was so careful to reproduce the verses originally intended for Verginius' tomb in his published correspondence. He had already noted with admiration that Verginius had lived to read his accomplishments celebrated in histories and song. Now the readers of Pliny's epistles are able to read the account that Verginius composed himself, for a monument that was never built. Thanks to the commemorative power of books, both Verginius' and Frontinus' memory were available to be transmitted globally.[9]

As the literary record takes on the characteristics of a physical monument, the same rules of commemorative ethics continue to apply. Just as Silius' reverence for Vergil's tomb established a link between himself and the great poet, Pliny's act of epistolary commemoration serves to secure a connection between himself and a celebrated statesman of the previous generation.[10] Moreover, by inserting himself in the place of the negligent heir as the true custodian of Verginius' memory, Pliny not only secures his mentor's place in history, but calls attention to his own literary renown at the same time. When approached with the appropriate commemorative disposition, a work of literature provided access not only to the memory of the people and events it chronicles (the function outlined in Livy's preface), but to that of the author as well (cf. Horace's *monumentum aere perennius*). This is what Pliny is getting at when he presents Frontinus' renunciation of a monument as disingenuous.

---

[8] *Carm.* 3.30.1, cf. Pind. *Pyth.* 6.5–14, Verg. *Georg.* 3.12–18, Suerbaum (1968: 165–7), Woodman (1974).

[9] Cf. *Ep.* 2.1.11: *vivit enim vivetque semper, atque etiam latius in memoria hominum et sermone versabitur, postquam ab oculis recessit.*

[10] This is all another example of Pliny's use of his correspondence for "self-fashioning": Beutel (2000: 135), Henderson (2002: 1–5).

In the context of this complicated nexus of monumentalism, literary endeavor, and self-praise, Imperial senators set out to establish a place for themselves (and, occasionally, the Republic) in the memory of their peers and progeny. Apart from the couplet that was to form his epitaph, Verginius never became famous as a producer of literary monuments. Frontinus and Silius, on the other hand, are remembered as both authors and prominent public figures, who left their mark not just in inscriptions and the writings of subsequent generations, but also through literary texts that they authored themselves. This chapter will look at some of the ways in which the memory of the Republic was transmitted in two works – Silius' *Punica*, a grandiose epic on the Hannibalic war, and Frontinus' *Strategemata*, a brief compendium of historical *exempla* relating to types of military cunning. Although frequently marginalized in the history of Latin letters, these texts merit close consideration (and, perhaps, comparison) as contemporary works by authors of identical social status, in which Republican history was remembered by and for an Imperial audience. Although their styles and approaches to literary fame were as different as their views on the commemorative function of monuments, Frontinus and Silius share a common interest in the military accomplishments of the Republic, which they set out to record in ways that reflect their distinctive understandings of that era's continued relevance for contemporary concerns.

DA, MUSA, MEMORARE

To place these works in their proper context, it is necessary to consider the authorial persona of each writer. The author of the *Punica* was not originally a poet. Like the advocates discussed in the previous chapter, Silius started out as a politician and pleader in the courts. Having reached the consulship in 68 by means of his eloquence, he saw his reputation suffer thereafter because of an involvement in the prosecutions that marred the end of Nero's reign. Although rewarded with further high office by Vespasian (who was no doubt grateful for his efforts to secure a smooth transfer of power from Vitellius to himself), Silius eventually abandoned Rome for Campania, where he reinvented himself as a devotee of Vergil.[11] According to Pliny, poetry offered a way to redeem himself: "he washed away the stain of his earlier efforts with admirable leisure" (*Ep.* 3.7.3: *maculam veteris industriae laudabili otio abluerat*). In the eyes of some,

---

[11] Plin. *Ep.* 3.7.5–8, Mart. 11.48, Pomeroy (1989: 120–1), D'Arms (1970: 207–8). Silius was proconsul of Asia in 77 but had eclipsed his fame as an orator with the *sacra* of Vergil by 92: Mart. 7.63.

at least, Silius accomplished the transformation from busy advocate to carefree poet that Maternus was said to have desired.

Unlike Maternus, however, Silius turned to Vergil's *sacra* in his old age, after a long and successful career of service to the state. This was not unusual. We may compare the activities of the congenial old commander T. Vestricius Spurinna, who spent his later years composing clever verses in Greek and Latin while perambulating on his country estate. Pliny speaks admiringly of Spurinna's daily routine and of his own desire to pursue a similar lifestyle when he should reach old age.[12] Republican examples – including that of Scipio Africanus – abound, but under the Principate senators had to be aware that retirement from public life was susceptible to dangerous interpretations. To abandon Rome so completely seemed remarkable to Pliny, and Silius appears to have raised some eyebrows when he failed to turn up among the ranks of those who came to welcome the recently inaugurated Trajan on his return to the capital in 99. Pliny notes, "there was great praise for the Caesar under whom this was allowed, as well as for the man who dared to make use of this freedom" (*Ep.* 3.7.7: *magna Caesaris laus sub quo hoc liberum fuit, magna illius qui hac libertate ausus est uti*).[13]

In leaving behind his public career so completely, Silius sought to craft a new identity for himself as an epic poet. Some indication of how he understood this role can be gleaned from his description of Ennius, who not only fought in the war against Hannibal, but also went on to describe it in his *Annales*, the first truly Roman epic. In the *Punica*, Silius gives Ennius a role in the fighting in Sardinia. He signals the character's place in literary history by invoking Calliope at the beginning of this *aristeia* and by having Apollo intervene in the battle to save the poet's life.[14] The god justifies this action with a prophecy:

> sacer hic ac magna sororum
> Aonidum cura est et dignus Apolline vates.
> hic canet inlustri primus bella Itala versu
> attolletque duces caelo.

> this one is holy, a great treasure
> for the Aonian sisters and a worthy bard for Apollo.

---

[12] Plin. *Ep.* 3.1.1, 7. *PIR*[1] V 308, Syme (1991: 541–50). Spentzou (2008: 133): "this belletristic approach to life suited a disempowered senator of the Domitianic era such as Silius."

[13] Scipio: Liv. 38.52.1, Scullard (1973: 151–2), D'Arms (1970: 1–2), cf. Cic. *Off.* 3.2, *Sen.* 19. Absenting himself from meetings of the senate was how Thrasea Paetus had fallen under suspicion: Tac. *Ann.* 16.21.1–22.5, Murray (1965: 54–6).

[14] Sil. *Pun.* 12.390–2. Manuwald (2007: 76–7, 80–2), Newman (1986: 226ff.), Suerbaum (2002: 119–42, esp. 133–9).

He will be the first to sing of the Italian war in radiant verse
and raise its commanders to the heavens. (*Pun.* 12.408–11)

This description echoes the *Punica*'s opening lines, in which Silius describes
his own aims as an epic poet:

Ordior arma, quibus caelo se gloria tollit
Aeneadum patiturque ferox Oenotria iura
Carthago. da, Musa, decus memorare laborum
antiquae Hesperiae . . .

I set out (to tell) the arms, with which the glory of the Aeneadae
raised itself to the sky and fierce Carthage submitted to
Oenotrian rule. Grant me, Muse, to remember the glorious achievements
of ancient Hesperia. (*Pun.* 1.1–4)

In the Ennius passage, however, Silius makes it clear that the glory of the
Romans had not simply "raised itself to the heavens" through feats of war.
A divinely inspired poet (*vates*) was also essential to the remembrance, and
thus the transmission, of this glory. This connection between the Muses,
poets, and memory went back to Homer, who also appears in the *Punica* in
an underworld *nekyia* scene, where he is described as a singer who "raised
our Troy to the stars" with his poetry (13.791: *ac vestram tulit usque
ad sidera Troiam*). Through the interplay of these metapoetic references,
Silius situates himself within a tradition of epic poets whose function is to
serve, with the help of the Muses, as agents of immortal memory.[15]

The transcendent power of epic may confer lasting fame on its subjects, but it redounds to the poet's immortality as well. Another place
"carried to the stars by Aonian song" in the *Punica* is Vergil's birthplace
of Mantua, itself described a home of the muses (*Pun.* 8.593–4: *Mantua, Musarum domus atque ad sidera cantu / evecta Aonio*). When Scipio
encounters Homer's shade in the underworld, the bard's appearance is
said to be like that of a god, an impression justified by the fact that he
used his divine talents to "encompass the land, the sea, the stars, and the
spirits of the departed in song" (13.788: *carmine complexus terram, mare,
sidera, manes*). All of these things are also represented in the verses of
the *Punica*, and thus this praise of Homer can also be read as aspirational,
suggesting that Silius is using poetry to pursue his own immortality as well.
The importance of this ambition, which gives added meaning to Martial's
praise for the "never dying volumes of endless Silius" (7.63.1: *perpetui
numquam moritura volumina Sili*), is underscored in Pliny's letter on the

---

[15] Manuwald (2007: 84–6). Cf. Hom. *Od.* 1.1–10, Vernant (1983: 76–80), Nagy (1974: 261),
(1999: 15–41), Detienne (1981: 9–27), Olson (1995: 14–16).

poet's death, which closes with a meditation of the brevity of human life and the usefulness of literary pursuits as a means to prolong one's existence (3.7.14: *certe studiis proferamus*).[16]

Noteworthy in the way Silius constructs his poetic heritage is how closely he aligns his Latin predecessors with earlier Greek tradition. Vergil's Mantua is not just a home to the muses, it is also a rival (*aemula*) to Homer's Smyrna (8.594). Ennius is praised as a bard who would "teach Helicon to sing in Latin meter and will not yield to the old Ascrean [i.e., Hesiod] in honor or reputation" (12.411–13: *resonare docebit / hic Latiis Helicona modis nec cedet honore / Ascraeo famave seni*). This sense of rivalry and interconnection can be traced back to Ennius, in fact, and his dream about the transmigration of Homer's soul into himself.[17] Although it is not new, Silius' emphasis on the Hellenic roots of epic has important implications for the self-consciously literary nature of his work. References to Smyrna, Aonia, and Ascrea, coupled with the use of Greek epithets such as Oenetria and Hesperia for places closer to home, suggest that Silius was writing to impress an audience of sophisticated *littérateurs* like himself, whose standards for evaluating his representation of the past were shaped by their broad reading and erudition in both languages.[18] Although his account of the Second Punic war derives most of its themes and narrative content from the works of historians such as Livy and Polybius, Silius also deliberately diverges from these sources in service of his own poetic aims.[19] It is as a divinely inspired bard, not a historian sifting through written accounts, that he claims to approach the Republican heritage.

Like other poets of the Flavian era, Silius was a self-conscious consumer and interpreter of the literary tradition in which he worked. It has been suggested that the genre of epic appealed to a writer such as Silius because it required the poet to execute a broad array of formally defined set pieces, within which he could test his powers of invention by interacting dynamically with the texts of multiple predecessors.[20] Taken as a whole, the *Punica* is an impressive monument to its author's broad reading and his almost compulsive drive to rework every possible generic commonplace in his own idiom. Silius' epic abounds with catalogs of forces (3.222–405, 8.352–621), *ekphraseis* of shields and armor (2.395–456, 5.132–48),

---

[16] Lefèvre (1989: 121–3).

[17] *Ann.* frs. ii–x Skutsch, Suerbaum (1968: 43), Brink (1972).

[18] Leigh (2000: 481–2). See, e.g., Tipping (2010a: 1–7) on the elaborate intertextuality of the *Punica*'s opening lines.

[19] See esp. Nesselrath (1986), also Steele (1922), Nicol (1936), Venini (1972), Lucarini (2004).

[20] Williams (1978: 197), cf. von Albrecht (1999: 295). See, in general, Hardie (1993), Hinds (1998).

and inspiring calls to battle (4.58–80, 5.149–85, 15.638–57). Rivers are forded, mountains transcended, and ships cut out across the sea (3.444–556, 6.521–8, 17.201–90). Battle scenes are punctuated by the *aristeiai* of individual heroes, unexpected deaths, and gruesome descriptions of bodies ripped apart by weapons (4.248–99, 5.268–332, 7.585–633). The underworld receives a visit (13.395–893) and funeral games are held (16.284–591, cf. 2.264–9), while bards come forward to enchant their listeners, prompting further metapoetic reflections on the power of song (11.288–97, 432–82, also 13.778–91). All the while, Silius embroiders his poem with vivid metaphors, etymologizing, and aetiological detail (3.420–41, 4.302–310, 5.9–23, 7.159–211).[21]

The significance of Silius' merging of the historical matter of Livy and Polybius with the epic mode of Vergil and Homer is perhaps most noticeable in his treatment of the gods. Unlike Lucan, who had excluded the gods from his epic treatment of historical events, Silius places divine forces at the center of his poetic program.[22] The proem of the *Punica* concludes with the following promise:

> *tantarum causas irarum odiumque perenni*
> *seruatum studio et mandata nepotibus arma*
> *fas aperire mihi superasque recludere mentes.*

> The causes of such anger, and a hatred that boundless
> energy preserved, and arms passed down through generations:
> I am granted to uncover these and to reveal the higher purpose.
> (*Pun.* 1.17–19)

In keeping with his special reverence for Vergil and implicit rivalry with Homer, Silius extends beyond the usual scope of human history to encompass supernatural events within his epic. Drawing on themes already established in the *Aeneid*, he locates the causes of the war in Juno's fondness for Carthage and her hatred of the race of Aeneas, making Hannibal an agent of the goddess's wrath (1.21–55, cf. Verg. *Aen.* 1.12–23).[23] Human motivations are sometimes attributed to the invisible influence of divine forces, while at other times, gods appear in dreams or disguise themselves in human form to manipulate the mortal heroes with their words.[24]

---

[21] Pomeroy (1989), Wilson (1993).

[22] Feeney (1991: 311), Wilson (1993: 221–2), von Albrecht (1999: 293).

[23] Ganiban (2010: 74–83), von Albrecht (1964: 47–8), Feeney (1991: 130–2, 303–4), Hardie (1993: 64).

[24] Fides, who enters men's hearts at Saguntum, is a notable source of inspiration: 2.513–25, cf. 6.609–18, 7.511–12, Vessey (1974a). Dreams: 3.168–213, 4.722–38, Vessey (1982: 329–30). Impersonation: 2.553–79, 10.45–71, 83–91.

Continuing in this epic mode, the gods also participate directly in the fighting, as when Apollo intervenes to save Ennius or when the youthful Scipio battles the river god of the Trebia and must be rescued from drowning by Vulcan (4.573–703, a scene that recalls the struggle between Achilles and the Scamander in *Iliad* 21.211–382).[25]

The prominence of the gods in a work that recounts historical events (rather than the wanderings of a mythical hero) may seem surprising, but it should be noted that the gods had a prominent role in Ennius' *Annales* as well.[26] Even prose historical accounts of Hannibal's invasion placed considerable emphasis on the war's religious dimension. Although he differs about the details, Silius follows Livy's lead in recounting the series of portents that preceded the disasters inflicted on Roman forces at Trebia, Trasimene, and Cannae.[27] The material clearly lent itself to reflections on the nature of the *pax deum* – a topic of particular interest to an author who had witnessed the events of 69. Nevertheless, the way in which Silius relies on a divine machinery to propel his narrative forward says far more about his adherence to the conventions of epic than it does about his use of what was recorded in the historical tradition. For the divinely inspired bard, the past is regarded as an object of poetic devotion, in which human events have importance not just in themselves but as manifestations of a larger cosmic order.

LONGUM EST . . . PER IMMENSUM CORPUS HISTORIARUM PERSEQUI

Although perhaps extraordinary in its intensity, Silius' turn to poetry was not, as Aper's criticism of Maternus in the *Dialogus* might suggest, an altogether unconventional or un-Roman gesture. From Cato the Elder to Cicero to Pliny the Younger, it had long been customary for Roman gentlemen to attempt to supplement their fame as orators with other literary

---

[25] Feeney (1991: 308–10), Santini (1991: 82–6). Mars had already intervened to save Scipio's life during this battle: 4.417–79. Cf. 1.535–55 (Jupiter wounds Hannibal with a spear at Saguntum, removed by Juno), 287–302, 449–523 (gods at Cannae). The culmination of this phenomenon occurs at 12.691–727, where Hannibal refuses to relent in his attack on Rome until Juno comes down and removes the clouds from his eyes to reveal all the gods who are fighting against him from their various locations in the city.

[26] For the gods in Ennius, see esp. frags. 1.xxxii, 7.xiii, 8.xv (Skutsch), Feeney (1991: 122–8). The influence of Ennius' now fragmentary text on the *Punica* is difficult to gauge: See Matier (1991).

[27] Sil. *Pun.* 4.103–35, 5.59–100, 610–26, 8.624–55, cf. Liv. 21.46.2, 22.3.11–12, 5.8, 36.6–9; Nicol (1936: 32). See also Levene (1993: 38–77).

pursuits.[28] Even Frontinus, who was as different from Silius in his commitment to public life as one could be, was commemorated by Martial for the time they spent together with the muses in the coastal resort of Tarracina. The thrust of Martial's poem, however, is his regret that the burdens of life in the capital have intruded on their literary friendship:

> *nunc nos maxima Roma terit.*
> *hic mihi quando dies meus est? iactamur in alto*
> *urbis, et in sterili uita labore perit*
>
> Now gigantic Rome wears upon us.
> When is a day here my own? We are overwhelmed by the city's waves
> and life slips by in fruitless endeavors.   (10.58.6–8)

Martial blames his own preoccupation with managing his estate on the Quirinal for his failure to pay his friend a visit, but the comical insincerity of this mock apology is apparent. Of the two men, Frontinus is the one who would have had the more significant burdens on his time.[29]

Frontinus' political prominence is evident from his first appearance in the historical record, where he shows up as praetor *urbanus* in January of 70, presiding over the inaugural meeting of the senate in the absence of the new emperor.[30] The high profile of this office, which he quickly ceded to the young Domitian, makes close ties to the Flavians likely, and subsequent activity indicates a genuine gift for military administration. Following a rapid advancement to the consulship, Frontinus went on to governorships in Britain, where he oversaw the subjugation of southern Wales, and later Asia, the crowning aspiration of only the most successful senatorial careers.[31] Unlike Silius, however, he did not subsequently retreat into a life of literary leisure. Pliny describes Frontinus as one of the "most prominent men in our state" during the latter years of Domitian's reign (*Ep.* 5.1.5: *quos tunc civitas nostra spectatissimos habuit*). Following Nerva's accession, he remained close to the seat of power, receiving a second consulship and important administrative posts, followed by the special honor of a third consulship, with Trajan as his colleague, in 100.

---

[28] Even in the midst of a busy career as an advocate and administrator, Pliny would take advantage of occasional moments of *otium* to compose hendecasyllables in the manner of Catullus: Plin. *Ep.* 6.14, 4.27.4, 5.3, cf. 5.8.6–7, 3.18.1, 1.6. See Hershkowitz (1995).

[29] *PIR*[2] I 322. Birley (2005: 68): "one of the most important figures of the Flavio-Trajanic era."

[30] Tac. *Hist.* 4.39.1. On Frontinus' origins, see Syme (1958: 790), Eck (1982: 48).

[31] Tac. *Agr.* 17.2, Birley (2005: 69–70), Eck (1970: 77–93), cf. Magie 1950: 579, 1442 n. 34. See also Birley (2000b), *contra* Campbell (1975).

His career can only be described as that of a man who remained deeply involved in affairs of state throughout his life.[32]

Although the acquaintance with Martial and his choice of Q. Sosius Senecio as son-in-law suggest a connection with the sophisticated literary circles of his day, Frontinus sensed that his talents lay elsewhere.[33] The literary activity for which he became famous – if it can properly be described as such – had little to do with the quiet relaxation enjoyed by poets. Instead, Frontinus promoted himself as a writer of instructional handbooks on topics such as land surveying, military tactics, and the water supply, which have been said to possess "somewhat limited pretensions to be literature."[34] Unadorned and straightforward in style, these manuals advertise their direct connection with the day-to-day responsibilities of the author's public career. Their only stated purpose is to provide practical instruction for others who might take up these duties in the future.

A vivid illustration of the close interweaving of Frontinus' official and literary careers can be found in the preface to his de Aquaeductu urbis Romae, a work on the administration of the urban water supply written soon after his appointment to the position of curator aquarum under Nerva.[35] Frontinus explains the difference between this composition and his earlier output as follows:

> in aliis autem libris, quos post experimenta et usum composui, succedentium res acta est; huius commentarii pertinebit fortassis et ad successorem utilitas, sed cum inter initia administrationis meae scriptus sit, in primis ad meam institutionem regulamque proficiet.

> In those other books, which I wrote after long experience and familiarity with the topic, it was the needs of my successors that were served. Perhaps the usefulness of this handbook will apply to my successor, but since it was written at the beginning of my administration, it will serve primarily for my own instruction and guidance. (Aqu. 1.2)

Although recent scholarship has raised doubts about the stated aims of the de Aqueductu and how useful it really might have been as a guide to

---

[32] Frontin. Aqu. 2.103, Plin. Pan. 61.6, 60.5. Far from avoiding Trajan's coronation, Frontinus is thought to have had a role in his selection as Nerva's heir: Eck (1982: 58–9).

[33] ILS 1105, 8820, PIR² S 560. "A man of taste and talent," according to Syme (1958: 122 n. 3), cf. Jones (1970a: 103).

[34] Goodyear in CHCL (1982: 672). Campbell (1996: 76), citing the low status of agrimensores, casts doubt on the attribution of works on land surveying to Frontinus, cf. Horster (2003: 191–2). On the de Aquis, see (Bruun 1991), Peachin (2004). Apart from dated controversies about the authenticity of portions of the text, the Strategemata has been relatively bereft of scholarly attention, but see Turner (2007).

[35] Frontin. Aqu. 1–2. The date of the appointment is provided at Aqu. 103.17.

the administration of the water supply, the utilitarian ethos that underpins Frontinus' authorial persona still needs to be taken seriously.[36] The claim that one's writings might be useful to others was not in itself remarkable. As we have seen, Livy also made reference to what was "wholesome and profitable" (*salubre ac frugiferum*) in his histories. But unlike the historian or philosopher who justified a retreat into leisure as potentially more beneficial to the common good than his continued participation in public office, Frontinus refuses to acknowledge that his literary efforts have any relationship to *otium* at all.[37] They are instead presented as a direct extension of services already rendered, or currently being undertaken, in public office.

The *Stratagems* clearly stands among the earlier efforts, in which Frontinus claims to have sought to assist others in performing some task he had already mastered through long experience. Conceived as a supplement to an already published treatise on military tactics, this work purports to "sum up the skillful deeds of generals, which are grouped by the Greeks under the single name of *strategemata*, in accessible handbooks" (*Str.* 1.*praef.*1: *ut sollertia ducum facta, quae a Graecis una στρατηγημάτων appellatione conprehensa sunt, expeditis amplectar commentariis*).[38] The benefit of such a compilation, Frontinus claims, is that it will allow commanders to consult the *exempla* of previous stratagems more easily than if they had to search through other histories and find them. "To my mind, busy men need to be instructed rapidly," he says, "for it is tedious to hunt down these things when they are scattered one by one over the vast body of histories" (*Str.* 1.*praef.*2: *sed ut opinor, occupatis velocitate consuli debet. longum est enim singula et sparsa per immensum corpus historiarum persequi*). For the commander who did not have the leisure, interest, or, indeed, the library to undertake historical research, the *Stratagems* offered a convenient (though perhaps not very effective) form of military instruction.[39]

---

[36] Peachin (2004: 84–6), Bruun (1991: 14–18), Blackman and Hodge (2001: 143–5), see also König (2007).

[37] Cf. Sall. *Iug.* 4.4, Cic. *Off.* 3.1.

[38] Now lost, the earlier work on *rei militaris scientia* is also referred to by Vegetius, *de Rebus Militaris* 1.8. It was perhaps comparable to the *Strategikos* of Onasander, written in the generation immediately preceding Frontinus', rather than a theoretical exposition of the art of war, as Bennett (1925: xviii–xix) suggests.

[39] Campbell (1987), cf. Goldsworthy (1996: 130–45). Precursors to the *Strategemata* include the Εἰσαγωγικός, a *commentarius* on senatorial procedure prepared by the antiquarian Varro for the politically inexperienced Pompey when he entered into his first consulship (Gell. *NA* 14.7), and of course, the περὶ τῶν στρατηγικῶν ὑπομνήματα of Aeneas Tacticus, which Polybius cites in the tenth book of his *Histories* (10.44.1).

In its basic conception, Frontinus' *Stratagems* is very similar to the collection of *Memorable Deeds and Sayings* compiled by the Tiberian writer Valerius Maximus.[40] Valerius offers a similar explanation of the nature of his work:

> *urbis Romae exterarumque gentium facta simul ac dicta memoratu digna, quae apud alios latius diffusa sunt quam ut breviter cognosci possint, ab illustribus electa auctoribus digerere constitui, ut documenta sumere volentibus longae inquisitionis labor absit.*

> The deeds and sayings that are worth remembering of the city of Rome and of external peoples are too widely scattered in other sources to be discovered quickly. I have decided to select these from noted authors and to arrange them so that the work of long discovery will be removed from those who wish to adopt them as precedents. (Val. Max. 1.*praef.*)

Like Frontinus, Valerius emphasizes the aim of brevity and expects his audience to reject the hard work that is required by the study of the past as it was conventionally presented in history books. He presents himself as providing a service for such readers, who lack the time or inclination to uncover the valuable information hidden away within the voluminous works of other writers.[41] By Frontinus' standards, however, Valerius was only partly successful in attaining this goal. It seems as though he has the nine books of the *Memorable Deeds and Sayings* in mind when he complains that "those who have picked out noteworthy passages have overwhelmed the reader by the very mass of material" (*Str.* 1.*praef*.2: *et hi, qui notabilia excerpserunt, ipso velut aceruo rerum confuderunt legentem*).[42] The indiscriminate scope of earlier collections has saddled them with the same disadvantages as the unwieldy histories they were meant to encapsulate. Frontinus embraces Valerius' functional aims, but he sets out to improve on their execution by providing a more narrowly tailored collection of *exempla*.

---

[40] Like the two-volume breviary of Roman history by his contemporary Velleius Paterculus, Valerius' work suggests a post-Livian/early Imperial "moment for brevity": Woodman (1975: 285–7). Compilations of *exempla* were not new, however: See Skidmore (1996: 33–49).

[41] Bloomer (1992: 11–16), Skidmore (1996: 31–3). Cf. the way in which the anonymous author of the *ad Herennium* characterizes the task of gathering *exempla* to demonstrate the art of eloquence, 4.3: *postremo, hoc ipsum summum est artificium – res varias et dispares in tot poematis et orationibus sparsas et vage disiectas ita diligenter eligere ut unum quodque genus exemplorum sub singulos artis locos subicere possis. hoc si industria solum fieri posset, tamen essemus laudandi cum talem laborem non fugissemus.*

[42] Cf. Gell. *NA praef.* 11, on earlier (esp. Greek) writers of scholarly *commentarii*, who *sine cura discriminis solam copiam sectati converrebant.*

Just as Silius' self-positioning as an epic poet sets him apart from Livy and Polybius, Frontinus' emphasis on utility distinguishes his approach to the past from that of the historians whose works he claims to have consulted. Frontinus does not pretend to preserve a record of events that might otherwise slip from memory. Nor does he seek to improve on the style or accuracy of his predecessors, as a historian approaching familiar material might be expected to do.[43] Instead, he describes the product of his labors as *commentarii* ("handbooks"), a term that has attracted much attention with regard to Frontinus' work.[44] Like its Greek equivalent ὑπόμνημα, the Latin word *commentarius* had broad application. In the most general sense, *commentarii* were written supplements to memory, collections of notes for personal or official use rather than formally crafted works of literature.[45] We might compare the 160 opisthographic volumes of extracts (*electorum commentarii*) that Pliny the Elder compiled over a lifetime of reading.[46] Whereas *historiae* (from the Greek ἱστορέω) constituted the formal results of an investigation into the past that could claim to have value in itself, Frontinus' *commentarii* are presented as simple conduits for information that readers could employ in pursuing other, more practical goals.

According to Frontinus, the rationale for producing this collection of "the skillful deeds of generals" is not the glory it will bring him as an author, but the prospect that knowledge of these *exempla* might foster contemporary generals' "ability to plan and carry out like things" (*Str.* 1.*praef.*1: *excogitandi generandique similia facultas*). His pedagogic approach is thus very close to that of Livy, who also emphasized the contemplation of *exempla* in his history, inviting readers to derive from them "what to imitate, and what, foul in its undertaking and foul in its result, you should avoid."[47] The basic principle of modeling one's behavior according to past *exempla* is the same, but Frontinus' narrow focus on

---

43 Cf. Livy 1.*praef.*2: *dum novi semper scriptores aut in rebus certius aliquid allaturos se aut scribendi arte rudem vetustatem superaturos credunt*, Moles (1993: 143–4). Goodyear (1982: 672–3): "Frontinus... purveys a mass of hackneyed material, Greek and Roman, compiled from literary sources, some of them, like Livy, painfully familiar.... The numerous errors of fact in the *Strategemata*, when tested against other better sources, enjoin a rather sceptical view of his abilities as a writer generally."

44 *Strat.* 1.*praef.*1. Cf. *Aqu.* 1.2, Bruun (1991: 17–19), Evans (1994: 53), DeLaine (1996: 117–19), Peachin (2004: 12–25).

45 Riggsby (2006: 134–50), Mourgues (1998: 123–32), Bömer (1953), *RE* 4 (1900): 726–59 s.v. "Commentarii" [von Premerstein], also Adcock (1956: 6–18).

46 Plin. *Ep.* 3.5.17: further proof of the inordinate scope that Frontinus set out to correct? The habit seems to have passed on to his nephew, who was busy copying out extracts from Livy when Vesuvius erupted in 79: *Ep.* 6.20.5.

47 Liv. 1.*praef.*10, Chaplin (2000: 6–29), Skidmore (1996: 7–27). Similar justifications for historiography can be found in Thuc. 1.22, Isoc. *Evag.* 75–80.

practical results ultimately sets him apart from Livy's emphasis on ethics, and from the moralizing tone of Roman exemplary discourse generally.[48]

As with Silius, Frontinus' treatment of the gods provides a convenient demonstration of the way his approach to the past is shaped by his choice of authorial persona and particular literary aims. Because of the narrow emphasis on the skillful deeds of generals, divine forces are almost entirely excluded from his text. His chapter on stimulating an army's will to fight does contain a subsection on omens (1.11.8–16), but the discussion centers on how signs can be interpreted profitably, not on the gods who sent them. This section begins with the story of the appearance of the Dioscuri at the battle of Lake Regillus, a miracle that stood as one of the central touchstones in the religious history of the Republic.[49] Frontinus presents the *exemplum* as follows:

> *Aulus Postumius proelio quo cum Latinis conflixit, oblata specie duorum in equis iuvenum animos suorum erexit, Pollucem et Castorem adesse dicens; ac sic proelium restituit.*

> Aulus Postumius: in the battle he fought with the Latins, when an image of two youths on horseback presented itself, he roused the spirits of his troops, saying that Pollux and Castor were present, and thus restored the battle. (*Str.* 1.11.8)

Although the author does not explicitly deny that the mounted youths were Castor and Pollux, the attribution of this claim (placed in indirect discourse dependent on the participle *dicens*) to Postumius suggest that the reality of the divine intervention was less important than the effect that the general's utterance had on the morale of his troops. This perspective is very different from that of Valerius Maximus, who states without equivocation in a comparable entry in his *Memorable Deeds and Sayings* that the Dioscuri did in fact come to the Romans' aid at Lake Regillus.[50] Rather than present the omen as evidence for the gods' involvement in human affairs or use it to stress the importance of the *pax deum* in Rome's military success, Frontinus focuses on the general's presence of mind in exploiting a chance occurrence to boost the morale of his troops. Postumius is remembered not as a pious leader whose vow to build a temple for the Dioscuri secured

---

[48] Bell (2008: 1–19), Roller (2004), Walter (2004: 51–70), also Litchfield (1914), Haight (1940: 3–9), Eyben (1972). See also Suleiman (1993: 25–61).

[49] Beard, North, and Price (1998: 31), Wissowa (1912: 216–17), Walter (2004: 146-8). Cf. Dion. Hal. *AR* 6.13, Cic. *ND* 2.6.

[50] Val. Max. 1.8.1a, Mueller (2002: 41). Silius also involves the Dioscuri in his account of the battle of Cannae, although as a careful mythographer he notes that they fought "in turns," because only one of them can rise from the underworld at a time: *Pun.* 9.295, cf. 13.804–5.

divine favor for the Romans, but as a crafty strategist who manipulated his soldiers' religious naïveté to gain a tactical advantage.

By omitting the moral and religious themes that preoccupy writers such as Livy and Valerius Maximus from consideration, Frontinus makes good on his promise to provide a ready collection of *exempla* for generals interested in what the Greeks called *strategemata*. But the value of Frontinus' *commentarii* goes beyond this exclusion of irrelevant material. As a further aid to the recovery of relevant information, handbooks of this type usually adhered to an explicit system of logical organization. Employing terms borrowed from Greek dialectic, Frontinus sketches a brief "table of contents" for his work:

> *quo magis autem discreta ad rerum varietatem apte conlocarentur, in tres libros ea diduximus. in primo erunt exempla quae competant proelio nondum commisso; in secundo quae ad proelium et confectam pacationem pertineant; tertius inferendae solvendaeque obsidioni habebit στρατηγήματα, quibus deinceps generibus suas species adtribui.*

> In order that these things, once divided up, might be placed together according to the variety of the material, I have organized them into three books. In the first are *exempla* that are suitable for cases in which the battle has not yet begun, in the second are those that relate to the battle and reestablishing the peace, the third contains stratagems for the imposition and the raising of sieges. I have assigned the corresponding *species* to each of these *genera* in order. (*Str.* 1.pr.2)

The subsequent addition of a fourth book, which some scholars regard as spurious because it is not mentioned here, complicates the picture somewhat, but what is clear is that Frontinus felt it was important to provide a systematic overview of the basic *genera* and *species* of the stratagems that make up his collection. Once again, the significance of this schema is more practical than theoretical. Frontinus is not attempting to outline a set of first principles from which he will derive a scientific system of strategic thinking. Rather, his goal is to provide a heuristic guide with which readers can navigate the material contained in his work.[51]

---

[51] "Tables of contents" were commonly provided as organizational aids in texts of this sort: Small (1997: 16–19), see, e.g., Plin. *NH praef.*33 ff., Gell. *praef.* 25 ff. See, in general, Fuhrmann (1960: 120), cf. Rawson (1978), Rüpke (1992: 213). Although Riggsby (2006: 137–9) is correct to stress that the division of Gaul into three parts at the beginning of Caesar's *commentarii de Bello Gallico* does not provide a framework for the work as a whole, he places far too much weight on Vitruv. 4.*praef.*1 in claiming that *commentarii* were, by definition, *non ordinita sed incepta*. On the problems surrounding the date and authenticity of Book 4 of the *Stratagems*, see Bendz (1938).

Frontinus' appeal to this system of classification underscores one of the basic principles of exemplary discourse, which is that the underlying lesson or rule that gives a story its force as an exemplary narrative should be repeatable in multiple different contexts.[52] Grouping *exempla* by type thus comes naturally to the genre, but it is also important to note that such an organizational scheme reflects the influence of habits of thought instilled in ancient rhetorical training. Frontinus' deliberate arrangement of material into these groupings is analogous to the system of ordered "places" and "images" employed in the art of memory, or mnemotechnics, developed by ancient orators to help them remember the elements of a speech or complex argument.[53] It has been demonstrated that training in the principles of classical mnemotechnics had a profound impact on the composition, organization, and even physical layout of medieval manuscripts. Although the nature of our evidence for the classical period precludes drawing firm conclusions, it seems plausible that similar mnemonic concerns were involved in the production of ancient texts as well.[54] It is unlikely that Frontinus expected his readers to commit the contents of his *commentarii* to memory, but the point remains that the principles of division and systemization he employs reflect his utilitarian approach to remembering. By rearranging his collection of *exempla* in a mnemonically convenient way, he made it easier to access the information that he had extracted from the cumbersome literary artifice of others' histories.

Once again, Frontinus invites comparison with Valerius Maximus, who also used a system of classification to organize his *Memorable Deeds and Sayings*. The broader compass of Valerius' work results in a different structure, which proceeds from the general principles of religion and social custom (books 1 and 2) to specific discussions of individual virtues (books 3–8) and concludes with a final book (9) on vices. Because of Valerius' emphasis on morals and their social underpinnings, one organizational principle that runs throughout his work is a strict division within each chapter between *exempla* that involve Romans and those drawn from foreign cultures. In fact, the very inclusion of "external" *exempla* in a work intended for a Roman audience is treated as something that requires justification. Valerius prefaces one such section with the disclaimer "I now take up external cases, which, though they have less authority when introduced

---

[52] Stierle (1972: 183–6), Demoen (1997: 136–7).

[53] Cf. Arist. *Rh.* 1358a, Cic. *Top.* 1.7. Yates (1966: 17–62) and Caplan (1970) provide standard accounts of the art.

[54] Carruthers (1990). A case for the influence of mnemonic principles in the composition of ancient texts is argued, primarily in terms of the practicalities of production, by Small (1995), (1997: 141–223).

in Latin literature, still may offer some pleasant variety" (1.6.*ext.praef.*: *attingam igitur externa, quae Latinis litteris inserta ut auctoritatis minus habent, ita aliquid gratae varietatis adferre possunt*). To perpetuate the customs that made Rome great, Romans were expected to model their behavior on that of their ancestors. Foreign *exempla* had less value in this formulation.[55]

Frontinus, on the other hand, makes no effort to distinguish between Roman and foreign generals. He moves freely between Macedonian, Roman, Carthaginian, and Greek *exempla* in the course of a single chapter (1.3). Indeed, the very title of Frontinus' work indicates his broader cultural horizons: Once an author has described the topic of his work as one "defined by the Greeks under the single name of *strategemata*," there is little reason to distinguish between individual *exempla* on the basis of their *Romanitas*. Valerius also calls attention to the lack of an adequate Latin equivalent for the Greek term *strategema* (7.4.*praef.*: *quia appellatione <Latina>vix apte exprimi possunt, Graeca pronuntiatione strategemata dicantur*), but he remains circumspect about the use of external *exempla* in his brief chapter on the subject. Although Valerius was able to accept the cunning of a Roman general such as Metellus, he could not bring himself to regard Hannibal as anything but a negative *exemplum*. His account of the Carthaginian leader's tactical superiority at Cannae concludes with the rebuke: "this was Punic courage, arrayed with trickery and traps and deceit, which now is the most secure apology for our undermined valor, since we were deceived rather than conquered" (7.4.ext.2: *haec fuit Punica fortitudo, dolis et insidiis et fallacia instructa, quae nunc certissima circumventae virtutis nostrae excusatio est, quoniam decepti magis quam victi sumus*). Comparison with the far more dispassionate account of the same stratagem in Frontinus' work (*Str.* 2.5.27) suggests the extent to which that author's emphasis on practical rather than moral concerns is reflected in the ecumenical scope of his collection.[56]

Filtered through the lens of these practical *commentarii*, Frontinus' approach to memory is clearly very different from that of a more "literary" author such as Silius Italicus. The famous accomplishments of past generations are not treated as though they demand celebration in their own right. Nor is the author's role in promulgating the memory of such things

---

[55] Bloomer (1992: 5), Skidmore (1996: 89–92), Demoen (1997: 140–1), cf. Margalit (2002: 37–44).

[56] Although 70 percent of the exempla in the *Stratagems* are drawn from Roman historical sources, the clever stratagems of Roman generals make up only 56 percent of the total.

worthy of much recognition. On the contrary, Frontinus emphasizes the tedium of poring through the "vast body of histories" in which the *exempla* he discusses had been so inefficiently preserved. Far from claiming glory for himself as an author whose text will bring his fame to the far corners of the world, Frontinus readily acknowledges the derivative nature of his work. Moreover, he makes little apology for its shortcomings. The preface closes with a remarkable admission:

> *at multa et transire mihi ipse permisi. quod me non sine causa fecisse scient, qui aliorum libros eadem promittentium legerint. verum facile erit <sua> sub quaque specie suggerere. nam cum hoc opus, sicut cetera, usus potius aliorum quam meae commendationis causa adgressus sim, adiuvari me ab his qui aliquid illi adstruent, non argui credam.*

> But I have allowed myself to pass over much, and anyone who has read the books of others presenting the same material will understand that I am not without reason in doing so. Because I have approached this work, like my others, with more concern for its usefulness to other than for my own praise, I will assume that I am being helped, not censured, by those who make additions to it. (*Str.* 1.*praef.*3)

Although this explicit invitation for readers to make additions to his work might give modern editors seeking to establish the authoritative text of the *Stratagems* headaches, it is also emblematic of Frontinus' unique position as an author who emphasizes utility over style or originality as the primary virtue of his work.[57] As Pliny's remarks about this author's refusal of a tomb suggest, this may be more of a posture than a genuine desire for self-negation. Even so, these are important claims, which suggests an alternate perspective on the openly self-aggrandizing approach of more literary contemporaries such as Silius.

EXCOGITANDI GENERANDIQUE SIMILIA FACULTAS

To appreciate more concretely how these two authors adapt the Livian tradition of Roman history to suit their own authorial aims, it will be useful to compare their versions of the same event. The ruse that Hannibal employed to escape from a blockade by the dictator Fabius, an event described by Livy, Polybius, and several other sources, provides a convenient

---

[57] See Ireland (1990: xxvi) on the difficulty of accessing the authenticity of individual portions of the work.

case in point.[58] Frontinus strips the story down to its most essential elements so that he can focus on the details of the stratagem itself:

> *Hannibal, ut iniquitatem locorum et inopiam instante Fabio Maximo effugeret, noctu boves, quibus ad cornua fasciculos alligaverat sarmentorum, subiecto igne dimisit; cumque ipso motu adulescente flamma turbaretur pecus, magna discursatione montes in quos actum erat conlustravit. Romani, qui ad speculandum concurrerant, primo prodigium opinati sunt: dein cum certa Fabio renuntiassent, ille insidiarum metu suos castris continuit. barbari obsistente nullo profecti sunt.*

> Hannibal: in order to escape an unfavorable position and scarce resources while Fabius Maximus was close at hand, he took cattle, to whose horns he had attached bundles of twigs, set them on fire, and released them at night. As the herd became agitated by the flames that increased with their motion, it lit up the mountains into which it had been driven by scattering widely. The Romans, who gathered to watch this, at first thought it was a prodigy. Then, when the truth was reported to Fabius, he kept his men in camp from fear of an ambush. The barbarians departed with no opposition. (*Str.* 1.5.28)

Although it might seem like a worthwhile point to make to commanders who might be called on to campaign in unfamiliar territory, Frontinus does not mention the linguistic mix-up that brought Hannibal to the rugged terrain outside Casilinum instead of the more favorable pass at Casinum (cf. Livy 22.13.6). In fact, he appears to generalize the topographical situation as much as possible. Specific references to the "Formian rocks and Liternum's sands and swamps" in Livy's account (22.16.4: *Formiana saxa ac Literni harenas stagnaque*) become the more generic "unfavorable position and scarce resources" in the *Stratagems*. Frontinus also leaves out any chronological marker that might indicate the stage of the war at which this episode occurred, and gives no indication of the repercussions that Hannibal's escape would have for the public perception of the effectiveness of Fabian tactics (cf. Livy 22.25.7). Although he is specific in attributing this stratagem to Hannibal, Frontinus manipulates his presentation of the event to produce a generalized *exemplum* that could be reproduced (theoretically, at least) by anyone in similar circumstances.[59]

---

[58] Livy 22.16.4–18.1, Plb. 3.92.10–94.6, cf. Nep. *Hann.* 5.1–2, Plut. *Fab.* 6.1–7.1, App. *Hann.* 14–15, Zon. 8.26.

[59] For those who are quick to question the practicality of Frontinus' work, it is interesting to note that de Sanctis (1917: 50 n. 79) cites a report of the use of a similar tactic along the Isonzo front in World War I.

Under the new organizational rubrics imposed by Frontinus' *commentarii*, events unrelated in time or place become juxtaposed in unexpected ways. It is interesting to notice, for example, that, although this is the only stratagem in the chapter *De evadendo ex locis difficillimis* to combine these elements, it is not the only circumstance in which fire (cf. Iphicrates, 1.5.24) or animals (cf. Darius, 1.5.25) were used to distract an enemy. Extracted from its unique historical context, the story of these immolated cattle is redefined as one of several ways in which a general could extricate himself from a difficult position. Hannibal's talent for escape is defined not by its significance to the progress or outcome of the war, but by its similarity to ruses employed by Sulla (1.5.17–18) and Spartacus (1.5.20–22).

Judged as the sum of its individual parts, the *Strategemata* does little to contradict Maslakov's assessment that learning history from rhetorical *exempla* "promoted a careless and fragmented image of the past."[60] Taken as a whole, however, the collection represents a vision of history that is more cohesive than what was possible in a narrative work of historiography. In this regard, the effect of Frontinus' approach might be compared to that of the gallery of "top men" (*summi viri*) on display in the Forum Augustum. Each statue, together with the biographical inscription that accompanied it, invited the viewer to contemplate the accomplishments of a single individual in isolation from the wider historical circumstances in which he lived. Collectively, the full series of statues offered a reassuring vision of a unified Republican past, in which messy issues of personal animus, political rivalry, and even civil war have been submerged.[61] Frontinus' collection of brief, decontextualized narratives accomplishes much the same effect. The *Stratagems* casts a much wider historical net, however, to bring together not just Marius and Sulla, but also Fabius and Hannibal (as well as Pericles and Brasidas) as more-or-less interchangeable icons in the history of successful generalship.[62]

In many ways, Silius' account of Hannibal's escape at Casilinum is more closely tied to the annalistic sources than Frontinus'. In the *Punica*, this stratagem remains contextualized as part of the larger narrative of Fabius' dictatorship, wherein he surpasses the noble deeds of his ancestors through delaying tactics and temporarily saves Rome from further disasters.[63] Livy's description of the terrain that Hannibal must confront

---

[60] Maslakov (1984: 445), cf. Ferrill (1978), Stierle (1972).
[61] See esp. *CIL* VI 40957 (= *ILS* 59), Geiger (2008: 155).
[62] Cf. Bloomer (1992: 155–63).
[63] Sil. *Pun.* 6.638–9: *pulcherrima quorum / cunctando Fabius superavit facta*, cf. Enn. *Ann.* 363 (Skutsch), Verg. *Aen.* 6.846. Tipping (2010a: 107–8).

in the Falernian region is also retained, although it is given a more poetic coloring:

hinc Laestrygoniae saxoso monte premebant
a tergo rupes, undosis squalida terris
hinc Literna palus

here he was oppressed by the rocky mountains of Laestrygonia,
with cliffs behind him, while the foul Liternan swamp stood opposite
with its wave-soaked plains.   (Pun. 7.276–8)

The details of the stratagem itself are similarly rendered into verse by Silius, who gives a more palpable impression of the Romans' initial terror at flames that seemed to require a supernatural explanation (7.351–76). Whereas Frontinus simplifies his narrative elements and rearranges them according to his own predetermined typology of strategic *exempla*, Silius keeps much of the structure and content of Livy's historical narrative.

To better situate this stratagem within the context of epic, however, Silius also seeks to expand on his source by interweaving material borrowed from Homer. Whereas Livy simply states that Hannibal "devised a trick for the eyes, frightening in appearance, to deceive the enemy" (22.16.6: *ludibrium oculorum specie terribile ad frustrandum hostem commentus*), Silius brings the reader into the Carthaginian camp to witness Hannibal's deliberations firsthand. The story begins at night:

cuncta per et terras et lati stagna profundi
condiderat somnus, positoque labore dierum
pacem nocte datam mortalibus orbis agebat.
at non Sidonium curis flagrantia corda
ductorem uigilesque metus haurire sinebant
dona soporiferae noctis. nam membra cubili
erigit et fulvi circumdat pelle leonis,
qua super instratos proiectus gramine campi
presserat ante toros. tunc ad tentoria fratris
fert gressus uicina citos.

All over both land and the calm of the wide deep sea
sleep has settled in, and with the days' toil cast aside,
the world enjoys the peace that night grants to mortals.
But a heart inflamed by cares and anxious vigilance
do not allow the Sidonian commander to take in
the gifts of soporific night. He roused himself
from his bedchamber and put on a tawny lion pelt,
which had been placed over the bolster that he spread out
on the grassy plain. Then he brought his rapid course
to the nearby tent of his brother.   (*Pun.* 7.282–91)

To readers who have even a passing familiarity with Homer's *Iliad*, this passage clearly evokes the opening scene of the Doloneia (*Il.* 10.1–24), in which the Achaean camp is submerged in soft slumber, but their commander is overwhelmed by a storm of anxiety.[64] Like Hannibal, Agamemnon rouses himself and "puts on the pelt of a tawny lion" (23: δαφοινὸν ἕεσσατο δέρμα λέοντος) before picking up his spear and heading out to consult with Nestor about a plan to save his hard-pressed army. The narratives are not perfectly parallel (there is no war council in Silius' version to match *Il.* 10.198–271), but the overall tone and the use of markers such as the lion pelt demonstrate that Silius is consciously following a Homeric model for introducing a nighttime stratagem. These similarities may suggest a connection between Fabius' blockade of Hannibal and the threat posed by Hector as the Trojans camped outside the Achaean palisade.[65] Of course, Silius' readers were also aware that the outcome of Rome's war with Carthage was different from that of the *Iliad*. In the latter contest, the descendants of the Trojans will prevail despite their opponent's trickery.

By introducing this intertextual relationship between his own epic and the *Iliad*, Silius expands the historical frame of reference in ways similar to what Frontinus accomplishes in the *Stratagems*. Although Roman history is not sorted and resystematized in the same way, the epic technique of the *Punica* nevertheless also invites the reader to consider multiple overlapping time frames simultaneously. Chronology becomes fluid, as the primary sequence of the Punic war narrative is constantly interrupted with scenes that either reflect on earlier moments of heroic valor or look forward in prophecies of later events.[66] But if Frontinus' collection of stratagems might be compared to the arrangement of statues in Augustus' gallery of *summi viri*, the *Punica* is perhaps closer to Vespasian's Temple of Peace, where masterpieces of Greek art were put on display for the public to enjoy.[67] Rather than derive practical lessons from Republican history, Silius wants his audience to appreciate the artistry with which these interconnections are developed. The poet's aims in reworking epic set pieces are perhaps more aesthetic than pedagogical, but the underlying implication, that the past is made up of a series of repeatable *exempla*, is similar.

---

[64] Juhnke (1972: 204–7).

[65] Cf. *Pun.* 7.305–9, *Il.* 10.43–52.

[66] Wilson (1993: 230–1), McGuire (1997: 136–44), Dominik (2003: 471), cf. Santini (1991: 7–8).

[67] Plin. *NH* 34.84, 35.102, 109, 36.27. Anderson (1984: 101–18), *LTUR* IV 67–70 s.v. "Pax, templum" [Coarelli], La Rocca (2001: 196–9), Millar (2005: 110–12). On the past as a "museum piece" in Silius, see Santini (1991: 9, 61–2), cf. von Albrecht (1999: 295).

UT BELLA SOLEBANT

At first glance, the logic of exemplarity that we find in both of these authors might seem to suggest an essentially ahistorical view of the relationship between past and present. Important cultural differences, such as those between Romans and Greeks (or even Romans and Carthaginians), and political changes, such as those that separated the Republic from the Principate, do not seem to have any impact on the relatability of individuals or events. Hannibal and Sulla are interchangeable, just as Hannibal and Agamemnon are. For Frontinus, this kind of reasoning is essential to the stated purpose of his collection, which is to instruct contemporary generals by encouraging them to replicate past *exempla*. Indeed, for these *exempla* to have the utility he claims for them, Frontinus must implicitly accept the officially postulated continuity between the era of the Roman Republic and the present circumstance of life under the Principate. Not only does he discount any changes in equipment or military organization that might affect the repeatability of certain *exempla*, he also ignores the altered political conditions in which generals of different eras operate.[68]

The first chapter of the first book of the *Stratagems*, which contains episodes from the Regal period, the Republic, and the reign of Domitian, as well as Sicilian and Athenian history, seems to confirm the claim that the past and the present can mingle indiscriminately. In Book 2, a stratagem employed by Claudius Nero in the Second Punic war (throwing the head of the defeated Hasdrubal into Hannibal's camp, 2.9.2) is repeated three times: first by Sulla in the siege of Praeneste (2.9.3), then by the German chieftain Arminius (2.9.4), and finally by Domitius Corbulo, during the siege of Tigranocerta in his Armenian campaign (2.9.5). Set in this context, it is difficult to imagine why Corbulo had ever lamented the changing fortunes of Roman generals who could no longer do as they saw fit under the constraints of the new Imperial system.[69] Frontinus' readers might remember that Corbulo was eventually recalled from his Armenian command and forced to kill himself by Nero, but it is also true that Hannibal's life ended in suicide, and even Scipio Africanus fell out of political favor at Rome and died in self-imposed exile at Liternum (cf. Sil. *Pun.* 13.885–93, 514–15). The inclusion of such details in the *Stratagems* might change how the accomplishments of any of these generals were perceived, but it would also undermine the stated purpose of these *commentarii*. Frontinus was not interested in reflecting on the vanity of human wishes any more

---

[68] Campbell (1987: 14), cf. Bloomer (1992: 204–7).
[69] Tac. *Ann.* 11.20.1. See Chapter 1.

than he appears to be interested in commenting on the political differences between the Republic and the Principate.[70] The omission of inconvenient facts such as the circumstances of Corbulo's death from his text suggests an author who was ready to forget them.

Corbulo is an exceptional case, however, and there is good reason to be suspicious of the proposition that his presence among Frontinus' *exempla* supports the claim that contemporary generals were no different from their Republican or Hellenic precursors, however. Because this commander's daughter, Domitia Longina, was also Domitian's wife, any praise of Corbulo's accomplishments could be regarded as flattery for the empress and by extension her husband.[71] Corbulo turns out to be the only recent general to be credited with successful stratagems in Frontinus' collection from outside the Imperial house, and his claim to inclusion in that category is tenuous at best. The German Arminius' deeds were also recent, but his annihilation of three Roman legions bespeaks the slowing of Imperial expansion that followed under Tiberius, or at least the incompetence of a general such as Varus (whose name appears twice in Frontinus' work in an adjectival formulation, describing the "Varian disaster," *Variana clades*: 3.15.4, 4.7.8).[72] The *Stratagems* thus offers very little in the way of tangible proof of the continued vitality of the art of Roman generalship under the emperors.

It is not that recent history lacked material for possible *exempla*, because warfare and Imperial expansion had continued during the Principate. But Frontinus' work contains no mention of men such as Aulus Plautius, who celebrated an *ovatio* for his role in Claudius' conquest of Britain, or his adoptive cousin (?) Aelianus, whose successful handling of a crisis along the Danube under Nero earned him a belated award of triumphal *insignia* from Vespasian.[73] More remarkable still, Frontinus provides almost no discussion of his own abilities as a military tactician. Although his accomplishments as a commander in Britain are vouchsafed by Tacitus, the author of the *Stratagems* is curiously silent about them.[74] There is, however, one instance of autobiography in the work, which some scholars dismiss as spurious because it appears in Book 4, a later appendage to the original plan.

---

[70] Cf. Juv. 10.147–87.

[71] *PIR*[2] D 181, Levick (2002).

[72] *PIR*[2] Q 30, cf. Sen. *Ep.* 47.10, Ov. *Trist.* 3.12.45–8, Vell. 2.117–20.

[73] Tac. *Ann.* 13.32.2, *PIR*[2] P 457; *CIL* 14.3608 (= *ILS* 986), *PIR*[2] P 480, Canole and Milns (1983), see also Campbell (1984: 320–5, 359–62). From Gordon's list of recipients of the *ornamenta triumphalia* (1952: 312–30), Vespasian and Corbulo are the only ones mentioned by Frontinus (*Str.* 2.1.17, 4.6.4, 2.9.5, 4.1.21, 28, 4.2.3, 4.7.2).

[74] Tac. *Agr.* 17.2, Syme (1958: 68), Eck (1982: 53), Birley (2005: 68–70).

If we accept the passage's authenticity (as I think we should), its wording merits close attention:

> auspiciis Imperatoris Caesaris Domitiani Augusti Germanici, eo bello quod Iulius Civilis in Gallia moverat, Lingonum opulentissima civitas, quae ad Civilem desciverat, cum adveniente exercitu Caesaris populationem timeret, quod contra exspectationem inviolata nihil ex rebus suis amiserat, ad obsequium redacta septuaginta milia armatorum tradidit mihi.

In the war fought under the auspices of Imperator Caesar Domitianus Augustus Germanicus, which Julius Civilis stirred up in Gaul, the wealthiest city of the Lingones, which had gone over to Civilis, feared devastation from the approaching army of Caesar. Because it was unharmed, against all expectations, and lost nothing of its property, it was brought back to obedience and surrendered 70,000 armed men to me. (*Str.* 4.3.14)[75]

Unlike the vast majority of *exempla* in Frontinus' collection, this one does not begin with the name of the general responsible for the successful stratagem in the nominative. Instead, it opens with the name of the Caesar under whose auspices the campaign was being fought, presented in a form that it attained only thirteen years later, when Domitian earned the title Germanicus (also with Frontinus' assistance) at the beginning of his reign.[76] The author is demonstrably deferential to the young prince (and current emperor), framing the story in such a way as to leave open the question of who was responsible for the restraint (*continentia*) that brought about the peaceful surrender of 70,000 Lingones. These shifts in grammar, although subtle, say a great deal about what it meant to be a Roman commander during the Principate.

Silius is more explicit about the nature of this change. The interconnections that link his Republican Romans to the paradigmatic heroes of other epics do not, as a rule, extend into the present. A justification for this boundary can be found in the poet's comment on the senate's noble response to the disaster at Cannae: "such was Rome then, whose habits would alter after you were gone, Carthage. If this was fated to occur, it would be better if you still stood" (10.657–8: *haec tum Roma fuit; post te cui vertere mores / si stabat fatis, potius, Carthago, maneres*).[77] The course of history, not to mention the history of civil war that formed the subject of Lucan's Roman epic, would seem to indicate a bleak future beyond the

---

[75] Bendz (1938: 27–30), Ward Perkins (1937: 102–3).
[76] Jones (1992: 128–31), cf. Eck and Pangerl (2003).
[77] Cf. 9.346–53. Marks (2005: 252–65), Tipping (2007: 224–31).

scope of the *Punica*.[78] We should be careful about oversimplifying or essen-
tializing Silius' pessimism, however. Concepts of decline are intrinsic to an
epic worldview, in which the deeds of past generations are idealized –
compare the boastful reminiscences of Nestor in the *Iliad* (1.259–74,
11.762) – so that the present, which is known to be imperfect, is put
at a disadvantage.[79] Silius gives this pattern a distinctively Roman moral
imprint, but he does not simply idealize the past as a way to denigrate
the present. Signs of decay are already in evidence in the early books
of the *Punica*, where we learn that the goddess Fides has already abandoned the world, driven into exile by mankind's wickedness and love of
luxury (2.496–506). Indeed, Jupiter asserts that the Romans had declined
from the glory of their ancestors and justifies the suffering that Hannibal
will inflict as a necessary test to restore their valor and make them worthy
of the empire they will receive as a result of the Punic wars (3.573–87).

This empire (*regnum*), as Jupiter further explains, is one which "not
even their descendants, with their luxury and thoroughly distorted minds
will be able to overthrow" (3.589–90: *quod luxu et multum mutata mente
nepotes / non tamen evertisse queant*). The irony in this statement represents an important wrinkle in Silius' historical thinking, which goes
beyond a perfunctory application of moralizing rhetoric. It is not just
that the acquisition of a vast empire and all the benefits that derive therefrom will bring about Rome's moral collapse, although the lament for
Carthage's destruction does indicate that Silius subscribes to the basic outlines of the *metus hostium* theme.[80] More importantly, Jupiter's prophecy
is an acknowledgment that Roman military dominance was able to exist
independently of the prevailing health of Roman *mores*. This happened
not, as the framing of Frontinus' *Stratagems* suggests, because morality
had nothing to do with martial success, but because the emperor's control
over provincial and military affairs ensured that these aspects of Roman
power could continue to be administered honestly. This new reality, which
has already been examined in Chapter 2, is reflected in Jupiter's prophecy
of Rome's future greatness, which moves swiftly from a description of
Scipio's successful conclusion of the war (3.590–92) to an encomium of
the "heavenly virtue" (*virtus caelestis*) of the Flavians that makes specific
reference to Domitian's rebuilding of the Capitoline temple (3.594–629,

---

[78] Tipping (2010b: 196–8), Ahl, Davis, and Pomeroy (1986: 2501–4), McGuire (1997: 57, 78–
85).

[79] Spaltenstein (1986: 247). Cf. Zerubavel (2003: 16–18).

[80] Ahl, Davis, and Pomeroy (1986: 2536), Tipping (2010a: 32), cf. Plb. 9.10, Marks (2005:
245–69).

esp. 622–4). Triumph, and the virtue that underpinned it, was now uniquely identified with the imperial house.[81]

The significance of this overlap between the changed political realities of the Principate and the principle of inevitable moral decline comes across most clearly in the conclusion to Book 14 of the *Punica*, where Silius begins by praising the restraint shown by Marcellus in the capture of Syracuse:

> sic parcere victis
> pro praeda fuit, et sese contenta nec ullo
> sanguine pollutis plausit Victoria pennis.

> thus, sparing the defeated
> replaced plunder and Victory, satisfied in herself,
> flapped her wings unpolluted by any bloodshed.
>
> (*Pun.* 14.673–5)

Although problematic when viewed alongside historical accounts of the fall of Syracuse, Silius' attempt to idealize Roman behavior receives confirmation from Cicero, who says the forum of Syracuse had been spared and was "untainted by slaughter" (*Ver.* 2.4.116: *purum a caede servatum est*) on Marcellus' entry into the city.[82] Like Cicero, Silius goes on to compare this wartime moderation with the rapacity of governors in peaceful provinces:

> felices populi, si, quondam ut bella solebant,
> nunc quoque inexhaustas pax nostra relinqueret urbes!
> at, ni cura viri qui nunc dedit otia mundo
> effrenum arceret populandi cuncta furorem,
> nudassent avidae terrasque fretumque rapinae

> Happy would people be, if, as wars once did,
> our peace left even emptied cities alone today!
> Still, if the care of the man who now gives rest to the world
> were not keeping our unbridled frenzy for global pillage in check,
> this insatiable rapine would have stripped bare land and sea.
>
> (14.684–8)

The poem's moral pessimism is tempered in this instance by a reference to the positive influence of Domitian over the administration of the empire.[83] If moral decline is inevitable, Imperial authority (and a policy of *correctio*

---

[81] Wilson (1993: 234).

[82] Pomeroy (1989: 134), Ripoll (1998: 453, 460–2), McDermott and Orentzel (1977: 30–1), cf. Ahl, Davis, and Pomeroy (1986: 2537–9). Cf. Liv. 25.31.8–9, 27.16.8, App. *Sic.* 4, Plut. *Marc.* 19.

[83] Marks (2005: 245–53), *contra* McGuire (1997: 82).

morum) offers a desirable counterweight. It is not necessary to insist on the sincerity of this claim to appreciate how useful it might be in bridging the gulf that separated the historical subject matter of Silius' epic from the contemporary reality of his audience's experience.

By acknowledging the importance of the emperor's ultimate control over military affairs, Silius redefines the nature of what divided the Republican past from the present. It is not simply that Roman morals have declined from their heroic apex, because political realities have shifted as well. As with Frontinus' *exempla*, parallels can still be drawn, but only where the emperor or his family are concerned. In this regard, the character of Scipio takes on particular significance for interpretations of Silius' work. What begins as a story of many men with no clear hero (1.5: *quot . . . viros*, cf. Verg. *Aen.* 1.1) ultimately becomes a more focused epic, centered on the accomplishments of a single triumphant general, who is secure in his power to command (17.625–54). The emergence of Scipio as the poem's central figure suggests a parallel with the monarchical position of Domitian, whose deeds received epic treatment in their own right in works such as Statius' *de Bello Germanico*.[84]

The lynchpin for this connection is provided by Hercules, who serves as a model of heroic behavior throughout the *Punica*.[85] Like Hercules, Scipio is the son of Jupiter (13.628–47, 17.653–4), and apotheosis awaits him as a reward for his pursuit of *virtus* (15.77–83, a theme already outlined by Ennius and Cicero).[86] This kinship with the gods would seem to distance Scipio further from any plausible connection with the present, but for the unique religious status that attached to emperors. Both Domitian's divine parentage and his anticipated (although not too eagerly) apotheosis are discussed in Jupiter's prophecy of Rome's happiness under the Flavians (3.601–2, 626–9). Whereas this status represented an obstacle for this emperor's attempt to exploit Republican precedents in the circumstances discussed above in Chapter 3, in Silius' epic the emperor's incipient divinity becomes a quality that further links him to the heroes of the past. The trinity of Domitian-Scipio-Hercules makes particular sense if, as seems likely, the overall prominence of Hercules in Flavian epic can be linked to an emerging interest in this hero as a model for interpreting the emperor's role as a protector of humanity.[87]

---

[84] Marks (2005: 113–243), Tipping (2010a: 164–5), (2010b), Courtney (1980: 195–9).

[85] Bassett (1966), Billerbeck (1986: 346–8), Ripoll (1998: 112–32), Tipping (2010a: 16–18).

[86] Enn. var. 24, *ap.* Cic. *Rep.* 6.26, Heck (1970: 168–73), Marks (2005: 155), Ripoll (1998: 79–83), Kennedy Klaassen (2010: 123–6).

[87] Ripoll (1998: 86–163). For Domitian in the guise of Hercules, Mart. 9.64, 65, Gsell (1894: 119).

In the opening scene of Book 15, the young Scipio, who has already undertaken a version of Odysseus' encounter with the shades of the underworld, reenacts the story of Hercules' decision at the crossroads, a myth attributed to the sophist Prodicus (*Pun.* 15.18–128, cf. Xen. *Mem.* 2.1.21–34).[88] Having taken a seat in the recognizably philosophical setting of a laurel tree's shade, the young hero is approached by the personified female figures of Virtus (Virtue) and Voluptas (Pleasure), who vie with one another to convince him to pursue their rewards. Scipio opts for Virtus, of course, but Silius also adds a new coda to the story, in which the spurned Voluptas flies off in a rage, promising, "My time will come – it will come someday when a pliant Rome strives to heed my commands and honor is paid to me alone" (15.125–7: "*venient, venient mea tempora quondam / cum docilis nostris magno certamine Roma / serviet imperiis, et honos mihi habebitur uni*"). Although the link between Hercules, Scipio, and Domitian is still operative in this parable, the addition of this prophecy imparts a further historical dimension that gives the story greater purchase as a commentary on contemporary concerns. In particular, the suggestion that *virtus* has been overwhelmed by the pursuit of hedonistic pleasure takes on considerable interest if viewed in the context of the debate about Maternus' poetic career discussed in the previous chapter or, for that matter, the younger Pliny's description of Silius' own habits in Campania.

Once the triumph that the Scipio celebrates at the close of the poem (where he is celebrated as a bona fide demigod: 17.647–54) is recognized as a source of glory available to Domitian alone, it becomes necessary to examine the nature of the epic heroism that the poet celebrates and to reassess the relevance of this theme for contemporary life. Unlike Frontinus, Silius is unwilling to accept the moral compromises that were sometimes required of generals. This leads him not only to condemn the stratagems employed by Hannibal, but also to whitewash the activities of his Roman commanders, as when he describes the recapture of Tarentum. Silius acknowledges that Fabius induced the commander of the garrison to betray his post by playing on his love for a woman, but he argues that this was justified because "the walls were captured without bloodshed" (15.324 *captis sine sanguine muris*). He even claims that "peaceful virtue approved this silent trick" (326–7: *tacitusque quietae / exin virtuti placuit dolus*). Livy, by contrast, says that after the Romans were let into the city

---

[88] Diels-Kranz 84, Heck (1970), von Albrecht (1964: 82–6), Spaltenstein (1990: 334–5), Marks (2005: 148–61). The story had been translated by Cicero (*Off.* 1.118), referenced in the preface of a historical work by Lucceius (*Fam.* 5.12.3), and even parodied by Ovid (Ov. *Am.* 3.1). See also D'Agostino (1954), Panofsky (1930).

walls, the capture of the citadel still required fierce fighting, and he suggests that the slaughter of the Bruttian contingent, whose commander had admitted the Romans, may have been done to cover up the fact of Fabius' reliance on treachery.[89] Not only does Silius distort the historical record, he does so in a way that celebrates the avoidance of violence, the putative focus of epic glory. Like Marcellus in his capture of Syracuse, Fabius is commemorated for sparing life, not for taking it.

Also in Book 15, Silius confronts the stratagem used by Claudius Nero to break Hannibal's will to fight (15.813–23). His description of the abuse that Hasdrubal's head receives, which is set at daybreak, involves its exhibition on spear point, and centers on Hannibal's reaction to the sight of his brother's face, suggests that the poet is imitating a scene from Vergil, in which Turnus displays the heads of Nisus and Euryalus to a distraught Trojan army (*Aen.* 9.459–72). This poetic context, particularly in its focalization, transforms what Frontinus regarded as a successful act of psychological warfare into a prideful display of cruelty.[90] As in the works of other Imperial poets, Silius' emphasis on the moral ambiguity of war complicates the process by which glory is conferred. Military accomplishments – the *arma* of the epic's opening line – are not always praiseworthy in and of themselves.[91]

More to the point, success in battle is not necessarily the central focus of Silius' commemorative project. It is important to note that one of the central themes of the *Punica* is trust (*fides*), which is a virtue more effectively displayed in defeat than in victory. The lengthy account of the fate of Saguntum, whose citizens chose suicide and destruction rather than betray their loyalty to Rome, shows not only the centrality of this theme to Silius' conception of the war with Hannibal, but also its connection with the immortality he seeks to perpetuate.[92] Similarly in Book 6, the poet introduces a long digression on M. Atilius Regulus, a general from the First Punic war who valued Fides above all other virtues (6.131–2). It is during his embassy to Rome as a Carthaginian prisoner of war that Regulus demonstrated not only the importance of this value, but its complexity as well (6.346–589, esp. 546–50). Silius appears to expand on the available

---

[89] Liv. 27.15.19–16.6, cf. Plut. *Fab.* 22.2–4.
[90] Ahl, Davis, and Pomeroy (1986: 2540–1), cf. McGuire (1997: 143), Tipping (2010a: 43–4) *contra* Marks (2005: 264–5), also (2008: 78–9).
[91] Tipping (2010b: 199).
[92] See esp. *Pun.* 2.510–13, 696–707, also von Albrecht (1964: 55–68), Liebeschuetz (1979: 175–9), Vessey (1974a), Fröhlich (2000: 413), McGuire (1997: 207–19), Ripoll (1998: 405–11), Dominik (2003: 477).

tradition by giving special prominence to the character of Regulus' wife Marcia, who begs with him to break his oath to return to Carthage and remain with his family in Rome.[93]

Like Dido, whose story is retold elsewhere in the *Punica* (8.81–156, cf. Verg. *Aen.* 4.584–629, Ov. *Fast.* 3.545–64), Marcia is modeled on the familiarly Roman poetic figure of the abandoned heroine. For all her passion and despair, however, she also registers points that are relevant to Silius' theme of *fides*, particularly when she castigates her husband for preferring his obligations to Carthage over family ties:

> *en, qui se iactat Libyae populisque nefandis*
> *atque hosti servare fidem. data foedera nobis*
> *ac promissa fides thalamis ubi, perfide, nunc est?*

> See who boasts of the faith he keeps with an enemy
> and the unholy peoples of Africa. Where now are
> the sworn vows and promised trust of our wedding, traitor?
>
> (*Pun.* 6.516–8)

An audience listening to these lines in the reign of Domitian might have been prompted to reflect on the competing claims that *fides* made on dissident senators under the Principate, who were sometimes forced to choose between their oath of loyalty to the *princeps* and other ethical obligations. It is clear that the fate of people such as the members of Helvidius' circle gave *fides* particular currency as a value shared by the Roman elite. Referring to the prosecutions that accompanied the latter portion of Domitian's reign, Tacitus speaks admiringly of "the fierce loyalty of slaves even under torture" (*Hist.* 1.3.1: *contumax etiam adversus tormenta servorum fides*), and Pliny the Younger boasts of the *fides* he displayed in looking after the interests of Arulenus Rusticus' family after his death (*Ep.* 2.18.4). Silius' portrayal of Regulus thus confirms what many already know, that a decision to keep faith could result in drastic and emotionally wrenching consequences for family and loved ones.[94]

The extent to which Silius' attitudes were shaped by his familiarity with Stoic philosophers such as Cornutus and Epictetus remains uncertain, but elements in his portrayal of Regulus suggest empathy if not

---

[93] Augoustakis (2006: 144–5), Mix (1970: 32–44). See esp. *Pun.* 6.436–52, 497–520, cf. Luc. 8.579–92.

[94] On the importance of these ethical conflicts within the Roman Stoa, Reydams-Schils (2005, esp. 171–6), Roller (2001: 64–87).

outright sympathy for the plight of certain members of this group.[95] Despite her complaints about Regulus' stubborn adherence to public *fides*, Marcia's ultimate willingness to share her husband's fate (6.511: *adest comes ultima fati*) recalls the exemplary bravery of Arria, the mother-in-law of Thrasea Paetus who fortified her condemned husband's resolve to commit suicide under Claudius by taking the dagger and stabbing herself first.[96] As others have pointed out, Regulus' response to these emotional appeals is a model of Stoic restraint (6.413–14, 519), but it is also interesting to note that Regulus' son, to whom this story is being told, remembers his father's appearance in terms that evoke the visage of an Imperial-era philosopher:[97]

humana maior species erat. horrida cano
vertice descendens ingentia colla tegebat
caesaries, frontique coma squalente sedebat
terribilis decor atque animi venerabile pondus.

His appearance was more than human. A great shaggy mass
hung down from his white head and covered his neck
with flowing hair, while on a brow covered with filthy hair sat
the awesome grace and venerable gravity of his soul.

(*Pun.* 6.426–9)

In Silius' account, Regulus is transformed from a heroic general who fought bravely (but recklessly) in Africa into something more familiar to his audience: an icon of Stoic endurance, who faces exile and even death because of his exacting sense of duty. This shift in emphasis reflects the way in which certain categories of virtue, such as personal *fides*, grew in importance as others, such as martial *virtus*, became increasingly difficult for anyone outside of the Imperial house to cultivate or display.

CONCLUSION

Like the forensic and declamatory activities discussed in the previous chapter, the command of legions continued to represent a vital arena in

---

[95] D'Arms (1970: 207–8), von Albrecht (1999: 292). See Charisius *GL* 159 Barwick, *PIR*² A 609, Pomeroy (1989: 121–2), Epictet. *Disc.* 3.8.7, Millar (1965), also Philostr. *Vit. Apol.* 7.10.2–15.3. Cf. Plin. *Ep.* 3.11.3, Dio (Xiph.) 67.13. Close friendship with Eprius Marcellus has also been proposed: Dessau (1911).

[96] Plin. *Ep.* 3.16, *PIR*² A 1113, C 103, Rudich (1993: 31).

[97] Billerbeck (1986: 351–2), Ripoll (1998). Fröhlich (2000). Cf. Sen. *Ep.* 5.2, Dio Chrys. 12.15, 72.2, also Plin. *Ep.* 1.10.6, Zanker (1995: 256–66).

which the Roman elite could contribute to public life under the Principate. Provinces needed governors, the frontiers needed protection, and opportunities for further conquest were sometimes still available. Ongoing conflicts in Britain and along the Rhine and Danube frontiers offered ample opportunity for the display of military acumen. The performance of these duties continued to confer prestige on officeholders, but it was the emperor alone who acquired titles such as Germanicus from the names of conquered territories (a tradition, Silius says, inaugurated by Scipio Africanus: *Pun.* 17.626). The differences from the Republic were clear: Soldiers all swore an oath of allegiance to the emperor, and the generals themselves were officially subordinated staff officers under his command. The responsibilities of these *legati*, as the scope of Frontinus' work suggests, were mostly tactical rather than strategic.[98]

These undeniable changes in the way that Romans campaigned had made civil wars less common, but they also meant that it was impossible for anyone who was not an emperor or his designated heir to rival fully the *exemplum* of a commander such as Scipio. As we have seen, Silius Italicus and Frontinus offer radically different visions of what Republican warfare was and how it related both to the present and to other eras. Although these authors tacitly or explicitly acknowledge the unique historical realities of the Principate, neither is prepared to suggest that the political organization of the Republic had anything to do with the success of Rome's Imperial expansion in that period. Frontinus simply ignores the issue, presumably because it might undermine the paradigmatic coherence of his collection. Silius, on the other hand, does acknowledge the political conditions in which the war with Hannibal was conducted. He presents these in a largely negative light, however, showing how the incompetence of popular leaders such as Flaminius, Minucius, and Varro led the Romans into one disaster after another. For Silius, the "blind vote" (*suffragia caeca*, 7.540, 8.255) of the common people represents yet another danger that Rome was forced to endure, as the wisdom of heroic nobles like Fabius Maximus went unheeded.[99] In either case, there was little interest in seeking a return to such a system.

Even as the Republic's political relevance for the present became increasingly attenuated, it did not fade from view. As the works of Frontinus and Silius attest, many Romans were still interested in remembering the history

---

[98] Campbell (1984:17–69, 317–62), Jones (1992: 126–59), cf. Lendon (1997: 176–236).
[99] McGuire (1997: 129–33).

of this period. As a matter of fact, the distance of these events made them easier to discuss in some ways. As Tacitus remarks in the *Annals*:

> *tum quod antiquis scriptoribus rarus obtrectator, neque refert cuiusquam Punicas Romanasve acies laetius extuleris: at multorum, qui Tiberio regente poenam vel infamias subiere, posteri manent.*

> Writers of ancient history have few detractors, because it does not matter to anyone whether you portray Carthaginian or Roman forces more favorably. But there are still descendants of those who suffered punishment or humiliation in Tiberius' reign. (*Ann.* 4.33.4)[100]

Discussions of recent events, such as the war to overthrow Nero or the prosecutions that took place under Domitian, invited controversy, but the passage of time (and the sheer generational distance this produced) made it possible to say what one wanted about the Republic without giving offence. Moreover, Tacitus' indifference to the relative praise of Carthage and Rome suggests the shifting cultural frame in which this period was remembered. As the historical distance that separated the Republic from the Principate grew, the field of vision expanded. Silius relates the great men of the Republic (and Hannibal) to the heroes of Greek myth, just as Frontinus cites *exempla* of good generalship without regard for cultural distinctions. As noted in the discussion of the *Dialogus* in the previous chapter, Maternus' juxtaposition of Cato and Thyestes as themes with which to comment on contemporary politics represented another instance of this phenomenon. With the passage of time, Republican accomplishments came to be situated in a broader context of human history, where they could be viewed with less obligatory chauvinism.

The significance of these expansive cultural horizons is epitomized in a revealing way by the poems that Martial and Statius wrote about a statuette owned by their friend Novius Vindex.[101] Although a political nonentity, Vindex was, like Silius Italicus, an epic poet who enjoyed collecting the works of famous Greek artists. Among these was an image of Hercules by Lysippus, which was manifestly a product of Greek culture (Martial says he had to use his Greek to read the sculptor's name inscribed on its base: 9.44.4–6), but also one with a remarkable provenance.[102] Before coming into Vindex's possession, it had been owned by Alexander the Great, Hannibal, and Sulla. Like the Capitoline monuments discussed in

---

[100] This comment precedes Tacitus' discussion of the prosecution of Cremutius Cordus' for having praised Cassius and Brutus (*Ann.* 4.34–35), on which, Sage (1991: 3387), McHugh (2004).

[101] Mart. 9.43, 44, Stat. Silv. 4.6. *PIR²* N 194. On the statuette itself, Bartman (1992: 147–86), de Visscher (1962).

[102] Kershaw (1997).

Chapter 2, this object provided a tangible link to the famous men of the past. The parallels between the hero and these three great generals would provide an obvious theme, but neither poet is very interested in pursuing it. Statius does describe how Hercules hated Hannibal for the destruction he unleashed on Italy and Saguntum (*Silv.* 4.6.75–84), but the only comment he can muster about Sulla has to do with his patrician heritage (4.6.85–8, cf. 107). Martial is more biting in his comment on Sulla, saying that Hercules commanded him to give up his savage power (9.43.10: *iusserat hic Sullam ponere regna trucem*), but the tendency of both poets is to discount the historical prelude to the statuette's present circumstance as an ornament in the house of Vindex, a role to which they find it better suited.[103]

It is fitting that Vindex's house is explicitly contrasted with the halls of power (*aulae*: Mart. 9.43.11, Stat. *Silv.* 4.6.90) Hercules had known previously, because this Lysippan statuette is different, both in stature and in form, from the counterpoised image of the god that stood in the grand hall of Domitian's palatine residence.[104] Unlike the heroic figure who provided a model for great commanders from Alexander the Great to the current emperor, Vindex's statuette is a more Callimachean Hercules, who reclines with a wine cup in his hand, just as he did when he took a break from his labors to enjoy the hospitality of the Nemean farmer Molorchus (Mart. 9.43.13, Stat. *Silv.* 4.6.51, cf. *SH* 257–65).[105] Rather than recount his own deeds to his host, as the figure in the *Aitia* does, this Hercules is able to sit back and listen as Vindex brings out a lyre and sings to him of those same accomplishments (Stat. *Silv.* 4.6.96–103). This poetic talent, which none of the statue's previous owners had possessed, makes Vindex a fitting curator of his Hercules.

In the private, literary context of Vindex's dining room, the pleasure of recounting heroic deeds has taken the place of the glory that comes from performing them. The accomplishments of the statue's previous owners, like those of Hercules, may prompt comment or criticism, but they do not instill a spirit of rivalry in the viewer. History functions like the statue itself, as an object of connoisseurship and aesthetic appreciation. Statius and Martial were both poets, of course, so their reinterpretation of Hercules as a figure of *otium* cannot be taken as proof of a monolithic shift in the attitudes of the Roman elite. In the same book of epigrams, Martial also writes in praise of a much larger statue of Domitian in the guise of

---

[103] Newlands (2002: 73–87), Coleman (1988: 192), Connors (2000: 515).
[104] Kleiner (1992: 183, fig. 152), cf. Winterling (1999).
[105] McNelis (2008: 262–6), Newlands (2002: 78–9).

Hercules, which stood along the via Latina (9.64–5).[106] Nevertheless, these observations about the Hercules Epitrapezios help to crystallize the simple point that, from any perspective, one of the surest ways to lay claim to the memory of the past was to write about it. The same holds true for Silius the poet as it does for Frontinus the man of action. Both were able to find in the Republic something worth keeping in memory. Like Vindex's Hercules, the objects of their interest might not be exclusively Republican or even Roman, but that did not necessarily diminish their importance for the cultural immortality that each author sought to establish for himself.

[106] Lorenz (2003).

6

RESTORATION

Rome's second dynasty came to an end on September 18, 96, when Domitian fell victim to a plot among his household staff.[1] Vespasian and his sons had held the position of supreme power in the state for over a quarter-century, but at the time of his death Domitian left no heir to take his place. Before a rush to arms could begin in the provinces, the senate acted quickly to assert its authority, naming M. Cocceius Nerva as its new *princeps*.[2] Even if this choice were unanimous, the new emperor faced a potential crisis of legitimacy. It was necessary to explain why he, and not somebody else, had been chosen to succeed Domitian. Nerva had fared well under the Flavians, but there was no intimate personal connection that could justify inheriting the familial *auctoritas* that formed the basis for most Imperial successions.[3] Nor had he saved the Roman world from the horrors of civil war, as Augustus and Vespasian could claim to have done in establishing their dynasties.

The strategy that would prove most successful for the new emperor was to cast himself as another *adsertor libertatis*, who would restore Rome to freedom following the *dominatio* of a cruel tyrant. As Domitian was cast into the role of Nero, Nerva took his cues from the rebels of 68.[4] In the coinage of his short reign, he reused a number of the types associated with that period, and especially with Galba. Both emperors represent the deity *Pax Augusta* on their coins, marking the stability that they sought to restore to the Roman world through their reigns. The associated theme of *Roma Renasc(ens)* is also repeated. Similarly, Galba's promise of

---

[1] Suet. *Dom.* 17.3, Dio (Xiph.) 67.17, Jones (1992: 193–6), Bengtson (1979: 243–6).
[2] See Syme (1958: 1–9), *PIR*² C 1227.
[3] Syme (1958: 627–8). Nerva did his best to placate the praetorians, disavowing any complicity in the assassination of Domitian and handing over those responsible to be executed.
[4] Shotter (1983: 217), cf. Ramage (1983).

stability throughout the empire, *Concordia Provinciarum* ("Harmony of the provinces"), is joined by Nerva with an icon of *Fides* (two hands clasped in agreement) to promote a hoped-for *Concordia Exercituum* ("Harmony of the troops"). But perhaps the fundamental ideological link between these two coinages is that of *Libertas Publica*, from which all other benefits were derived.[5] As was noted in Chapter 4, Nerva also bolstered his claim as a restorer of *libertas* by selecting Verginius Rufus as his colleague in the first ordinary consulship of his reign. Verginius' unexpected death in office seems to have been turned to Nerva's advantage with a funeral *laudatio* delivered by Tacitus celebrating the virtues of the new era.[6]

But still, the troops were restless. The commander Calpurnius Crassus threatened to revolt, and there was an uprising among the praetorian guards in Rome. In such a potentially unstable environment, Nerva went up to the Capitolium to announce his adoption of the vibrant young commander M. Ulpius Traianus.[7] This choice seems to have placated the troops, and in some ways could be said to justify the faith that Frontinus had shown in the continuity of Roman military valor into the present. Indeed, Frontinus may have played a role in the selection of Trajan as Nerva's heir.[8] In Trajan, military competence was not an anachronism, it was a means to political advancement of the most exalted kind.

RESTORATION IN CONTEXT

Nerva's reign as the self-proclaimed restorer of Roman *libertas* after the removal of Domitian's tyranny did not last very long, but it did serve to establish much of the ideological framework in which his heir would continue to operate. Following Nerva's death in 98, Trajan made sure that his adoptive father was consecrated as a *divus* and took pride in

---

[5] *Libertas Publica*: *RIC* I² 241 nos. 158–9, II 223–5 nos. 7, 19, 31(= *BMCRE* I 339 no. 176, 329 no. 121, III 3–8, nos. 16–18, 46–7, 60–1). The type appears in every issue of Nerva's reign: Shotter (1983: 221). *Pax Aug(usta)*: *RIC* I² 246 nos. 277–85, II 227–30 nos. 66, 88, 107 (= *BMCRE* I 329–31 nos. 123–33, III 15–25 nos. 92, 113, 137); *Roma Renasc(ens)*: *RIC* I² 233–43 nos. 24–9, 40–3, 57–8, 160–2, 197–204, 229–30, II 227–9 nos. 67, 91(= *BMCRE* I 339–40 nos. 178–84, III 15 *, 21 no. 118, 25 †); *Concordia Provinciarum/Exercituum*: *RIC* I² 223–8 nos. 35, 49, 104–8, 125–6, II 227–9 nos. 53–5, 69–70, 79–81, 95–7 (= *BMCRE* I 309–52 nos. 1–2, 216–25, 239–40, III 1–8 nos. 4–9, 27–30, 53–5), cf. *RIC* I² 213 no. 126 (= *BMCRE* I 306 no. 64).

[6] Dio (Xiph) 68.2.4, Plin. *Ep.* 2.1.6. See above, also Bennett (1997: 40).

[7] Dio (*Xiph.*) 68.3.2–4.2, Plin. *Pan.* 6, 8, 10. *PIR*² C 259. See Grainger (2003).

[8] Syme (1958: 16–17, 35), Eck (1982: 59–60).

the name of Imp. Caesar divi Nerva filius Nerva Traianus Augustus.[9] He also closely aligned himself with the policies of Nerva, particularly the proclamations relating to *libertas restituta*. According to Pliny the Younger, the enthusiasm shown for Trajan on his return to Rome from his review of Roman forces along the Danube was matched only by his modesty, and the absence of Silius Italicus on this occasion was proof of the freedom that men of senatorial status now enjoyed.[10]

The theme of restored liberty is implicated most interestingly in a small and very rare series of silver *denarii* issued by Trajan at some time following the end of his first Dacian war (in 102).[11] What makes these coins remarkable is that they present careful reproductions of fifty-one different Republican coins, reminted in an explicitly commemorative context. Unlike other official Imperial "reissues" of Republican coin types, which always present the portrait of the emperor on the obverse, these coins faithfully reproduce both the obverse and the reverse of original Republican exemplars. In fact, they would be practically indistinguishable from their models if not for the legend IMP CAES TRAIAN AVG GER DAC PP REST placed around the border of the reverse. The legend provides the only clear indication of the *princeps'* role in restoring these coin types.[12]

In addition to these Republican restorations in silver, Trajan also produced a smaller series of 22 gold *aurei* with the same reverse legend, which claim to reproduce coins of earlier emperors.[13] These were probably minted at the same time as the silver coins, which would seem to discredit any interpretation that the Republic was thought to be either more or less worthy of commemoration than the Principate. However, the gold coins have not been made with quite the same attention to detail as their silver counterparts. Some of the *aurei* are in fact "restorations" of coins that never existed, mixing obverse and reverse types that did not go together

[9] Plin. *Pan.* 11.1–4, *ILS* 283–304, cf. *Pan.* 23.4.

[10] Plin. *Pan.* 22, *Ep.* 3.7.6–7.

[11] Appendix B. See Seelentag (2004: 410–84) and Komnick (2001: 110–38). The discussion of Mattingly (1926, partly reproduced and updated in *BMCRE* III 138–41) remains fundamental. Unfortunately Strack (1931) ignores the series altogether. Fell (1992) and Bennett (1997), although useful on other points, provide only the barest summaries of these coins. Note also Duncan (1930), essentially rephrasing Mattingly's conclusions.

[12] The emperor's portrait was usually the most important marker of his authority over the coinage: Luke 20:24, Crawford (1983: 55), Wallace-Hadrill (1986). The point is not so much that the emperor actually selected coin types, but that he was thought to take an interest in their selection. See also Levick (1982a), (1999b), Ando (2000: 215–28).

[13] Komnick (2001: 125–32), Mattingly (1926: 256–64). *RIC* II 311–13 nos. 815–36.

in the original issues. The silver coins, in contrast, reflect a high degree of both accuracy and specificity. This suggests that Republican *denarii* were regarded as objects of particular interest under the reign of Trajan, at least to those few who paid attention to the images that appeared on coins.[14]

Any discussion of these coins must begin with the question of their date, and a single tantalizing piece of evidence. From the epitome of Cassius Dio, we know that Trajan melted down all the worn-out coinage in 107.[15] This date coincides with the chronological window provided by the emperors' titulature on the restorations, which indicates that they were minted after 102, when Trajan took the title *Dacicus*, but before 114, when he began to be called *Optimus* ("Best").[16] It has been suggested that the melting down of old coins in 107 was an obvious occasion to issue a series of restored coins as a commemoration of what was being taken out of circulation.[17] Such an act would be analogous to Vespasian's efforts to recover and restore the bronze inscriptions that were destroyed in the fire on the Capitol in 69.

Interpreting the series as a commemorative project of this type has appeal, but important objections can be made to this explanation.[18] The most likely reason for melting down old coins would have been to establish greater standardization in the value of the currency. Throughout the Republic and the early part of the Principate, Roman money had enjoyed remarkable stability in the weight and fineness of its precious metal content. Change came under Nero, who was notorious as the first emperor to debase the metal content of the coinage.[19] This modification of the real value of Roman coins caused people to look more closely at the money that was in circulation and to regard coins of recent date differently from older specie. Beyond the frontiers of the empire, Germans were said to be distrustful of newer Roman money, preferring to trade in coins with serrated edges, that is, silver coins from the Republican period, the value of which was well established.[20] Similar concerns seem to have influenced Romans as well. Ignoring practical motives of economic self-interest, moralists saw this break with the monetary standards of the past as further evidence of the ruin that Nero had brought to the Roman world, interpreting the

---

[14] See the discussion in Chapter 1.

[15] Dio (Xiph.) 68.15.3[1]: τὸ τε νόμισμα πᾶν τὸ ἐξίτηλον ἐξεχώνευσε. See Harl (1996: 92–6).

[16] Kienast (1996: 122).

[17] Mattingly (1926: 266–8), cf. Duncan (1930: 50–1).

[18] Strack (1931: 42), Komnick (2001: 158–63), Seelentag (2004: 413–18).

[19] Plin. *NH* 6.84, 33.3, Tac. *Ann.* 15.45. Harl (1996: 90–1).

[20] Tac. *Germ.* 5.5.

economic unpopularity of coins with his image on them as a popular expression of moral outrage against that emperor.[21]

One potential response to these objections would be for the emperor to attempt to restore the traditional standards of value to the coinage. In fact, such a move appears to have been attempted briefly by the rebels of 68. Drawing on the mineral resources of the Iberian Peninsula, Galba produced a series of *denarii* whose silver content was just below the standard established by Augustus (96.5 percent fine).[22] This may have been a response to Nero's perceived mismanagement of the Imperial finances. By minting coins with a silver content that was higher than Nero's, the rebels announced their desire for a return to good government with more honest financial standards and, thus, presumably, to the higher moral standards of past as well. Although he ultimately would return to the Neronian standard for silver content, Galba would continue to develop the rhetoric of monetary stability (*aequitas*) during his reign as emperor. The personification of Aequitas appears frequently in his coinage, and this Galban virtue was also advertised by Nerva, as part of the pattern discussed above.[23]

Trajan, on the other hand, made no attempt to reverse the process of devaluation. The image of Aequitas is absent from his coinage. Trajan's mint continued to produce coins on the Neronian standard, and the silver content of the coinage would be further devalued in time.[24] What Trajan's mint seems to have been doing in 107, therefore, was removing coins with higher silver content from circulation to produce a greater number of *denarii* from the same amount of precious metal. Given the negative public reaction to a similar move by Nero, it is difficult to reconcile the release of a series of restored coins commemorating Republican virtues with this policy of debasement. Even if the mint's actions were presented as an effort to increase economic stability by renorming the silver content across the money supply, to mark the occasion with so much fanfare would only have called attention to the fact that the Republican originals were being destroyed and replaced by new coins of lesser value.[25]

---

[21] Epictet. 3.3.3, Mart. 12.57.7–8. On Nero's extravagance, see, e.g., Suet. *Ner.* 30–1, Tac. *Ann.* 16.1.

[22] Harl (1996: 91–2), Walker (1977: 83–7). See also Sutherland (1987: 111–14, 126–8).

[23] *RIC* I² 238 nos. 121–2, 255 nos. 491–5 (= *BMCRE* I 351 no. 237); *RIC* II 223–6 nos. 1, 13, 25, 37, 51 (= *BMCRE* III 7 no. 52, 23 no. 127). Wallace-Hadrill (1981a: 20–39).

[24] Harl (1996: 92–4).

[25] I follow Jones (1956: 26) in being skeptical about the sophistication of ancient understanding of monetary policy.

THE EXEMPLARS

Even if we accept the notion that the melting down of old specie was the immediate impetus for issuing these coins, there is certainly no reason to assume so close a connection between the removal of coins from circulation and the minting of restorations that we must treat the series as a comprehensive record of every coin that was taken out of circulation in 107.[26] The chronological span of the originals is rather broad, going back even to the pre-*denarius* coinage. If Trajan's series was meant to reproduce all of the Republican-era coins that were melted down, it should contain a more extensive variety of types than it seems to have done. Although it is possible that lacunae exist in our evidence, the absence of many of the most common Republican coins from the series as we have it is notable.[27] This omission becomes more significant when we consider that some of the surviving coins in the series restore originals that were "decidedly rare" in their original issue. Two of them (nos. 18 and 20) refer back to coins that are estimated to have been minted from fewer than ten separate obverse dies.[28] Furthermore, the presence in the surviving series of clusters of related coins, such as the three coins of L. Rubrius Dossenus (11a–c) and both of the coins minted by L. Lucretius Trio (17a and 17b), points to the inescapable conclusion that there was a deliberate process of selection that accounts for the inclusion (and perhaps exclusion) of particular Republican coins in the series.

The most remarkable feature of these restored coins is how faithfully they reproduce their originals. Apart from some inevitable differences in the style of their execution, the restorations appear to have been produced by engravers who followed their models very carefully. In most cases, everything found on the Republican coin has been reproduced. It seems clear that the engravers were using actual coins as models when they carved the new dies. In fact, six of these coins reproduce features that were used as control marks in the initial issues (nos. 7, 8a, 12, 13, 14, 16). The faithful reproduction of particular control marks suggests that the mint workers had a single exemplar from which to work for each coin in the series and so were not surveying the entire corpus of Roman Republican coinage. The coins used by the engravers are likely to have been part of a collection, but

---

[26] Komnick (2001: 164–5), *pace* Gnecchi (*Riv. It. Num.* 1897), cited by Duncan (1930: 52).

[27] For example, there is no reflection of the vast issues by L. Piso Frugi (*RRC* 340/1: approximately 864 obverse dies) or C. Vibius Pansa (*RRC* 342/3–5: approximately 980 obverse dies). Crawford (*RRC* II 694) estimates that 30,000 coins were typically struck from a single obverse die.

[28] Mattingly (1926: 269). Die estimates in Crawford, *RRC*.

the nature of that collection is not clear.[29] It may have been housed in the mint of Rome, but this is far from certain. That a few of the coins differ from their originals in respect to small details could suggest that some of the model coins were worn, which would account for the alteration or the loss of certain features.[30] If the model coins were worn, however, this would mean that the collection of prototypes was not an official archive in the mint of Rome, where coins could be set aside before they had a chance to circulate. On the other hand, it may be that these minor deviations are better attributed to the die makers' carelessness.

A more significant obstacle to linking the restoration series with an official collection in the mint of Rome is the inclusion of coins that were not minted at Rome originally.[31] The most noticeable case is the reproduction of a coin minted by Sextus Pompey in Sicily after he had been declared an outlaw by Octavian (no. 41). This coin responds to Augustus' claims of filial *pietas* through Aeneas by invoking Sicilian Catanean brothers as a counterpoint. It is difficult to imagine a scenario in which this coin would be brought into an official collection of the Roman mint, so we may need to consider the possibility that the exemplars came from a private coin collection of some sort. Augustus was known to have given rare and old coins as gifts at the Saturnalia, so it is not unreasonable to retroject the modern antiquarian habit of coin collecting into the Roman context.[32] The uncommonness of a number of the coins in this series also points to the selective habits of a connoisseur. It would be too much to suppose that Trajan himself, emulating Augustus' numismatic interests, provided the originals of the coins restored in this series. But it is entirely possible some sort of semiprivate cabinet of historical coins was associated with the Imperial palace.

A clearer understanding of the nature of the collection that served as a source of these coins would be useful for assessing how numismatic images functioned within the context of Roman cultural memory, but its precise identification is ultimately incidental to the present investigation. We should not assume that the contents of Trajan's series are a direct reproduction of an individual coin collection any more than that they reflect an attempt to commemorate coins that were being removed from

---

[29] Duncan (1930: 63) makes some preliminary suggestions about the influence of the practice of coin collecting on restoration series.

[30] On no. 5, prows replace the two birds seen on the original; no. 27 lacks any of the three the control marks (hammer, anvil, or tongs) of the original; no. 32 is missing the praenomen letter T in its inscription.

[31] The importance of this point was suggested to me by William Metcalf.

[32] Suet. *Aug.* 75.

circulation. Even if a particular collection provided the exemplars from which the die engravers worked, the choice of coins to be reminted probably involved a further process of selection. The motivations that lay behind this decision-making process, insofar as they can be discovered, reveal a great deal about how Republican coins were viewed under the Principate and what they contributed to an understanding of the Republic's significance within the wider context of Roman visual communication. In examining the decision to restore particular Republican coins, we should wonder what Trajan stood to gain by their restoration. The question is far from simple, because Roman numismatic communication was polyvalent, both by nature and by design. Coins present both images and words, each of which might convey a broad variety of meanings. When presented together on a coin, these two registers of signification can be understood separately or in combination. To understand the process of selection that lay behind the Trajanic restorations, we will need to examine both.

NAMES AND INDIVIDUALS

Apart from the minor variations in iconography mentioned above, two coins in this series differ from their originals in a significant way (nos. 2, 3). The prototypes for these coins are recognizable as members of the anonymous series of early *denarii*, which showed a portrait of Roma on the obverse and the twin Dioscuri galloping on the reverse. With regard to their imagery, these restorations obey the established pattern of faithfully reproducing the details of their models. The reverses of both exhibit tiny identifying symbols – a female head on one, a shield and trumpet on the other – that are consistent with actual Republican coins.[33] The obverses, however, have been given legends that were not and could not have been present on the originals. In addition to the (authentic) denomination marker X, one also says COCLES (Fig. 6.1), the other DECIVS MVS. We now know that the first Roman *denarii* date to the Second Punic war.[34] It is therefore obvious that neither Horatius Cocles, legendary hero in the war against Porsenna, nor Decius Mus, legendary hero of the Samnite and Latin wars, could have minted *denarii* with their names on them. Nor did they have descendants who minted such coins during the Second Punic war.[35]

---

[33] Mattingly 1926: 234 notes the existence of variants of no. 2 without the female head, as in Belloni (1973: 20, 181), but cites Bahrfeldt in dismissing them as forgeries. See Komnick (2001: 112).

[34] Crawford, RRC 28–35, cf. Buttrey (1965).

[35] Crawford, RRC 207–8.

Figure 6.1. Restored *Denarius* of Trajan (modern forgery). Obverse: head of Roma with denomination mark X behind, legend COCLES added in front. Reverse: Dioscuri galloping, legend ROMA beneath (female head missing), explanatory legend IMP CAES TRAIAN AUG GER DAC PP REST around edge. (American Numismatic Society inv. 1980.109.444, *RIC* II 305 no. 767)

The assumptions that seem to lie behind the falsification of these coin legends are suggestive of the Romans' general ignorance about numismatic history. Pliny the Elder apparently had accurate information about when silver coins were first minted at Rome, but he mistakenly associates this event with the establishment of the *denarius*.[36] Yet Varro thought that silver coinage went back to the reign of Servius Tullius.[37] It is difficult to believe that officials working in the Roman mint would have been better informed than these noted antiquarians, especially because it is clear from the names that have been falsified on the two Trajanic coins that no one had an accurate concept of who was responsible for the anonymous coinage of the Middle Republic.[38] Perhaps the symbols on the reverses gave the engravers reason to attribute these anonymous coins as they did, but in that case it becomes more evident that the assignment of these names was arbitrary. The apparent absence of clear and reliable information about the history of coinage, even among the moneyers themselves, has important implications for the use of coins as a vehicle for the transmission of historical memory in the Roman world. Although modern numismatists may be able to attribute Republican coins with bona fide name legends to their original moneyers with greater confidence, there is little reason to assume

36 Plin. *NH* 33.44. See Crawford, *RRC* 35–7.
37 Varr. *Ann.* 1.
38 Mattingly (1926: 274–5). Komnick (2001: 113), citing Babelon and Beauvais, mentions their views on the potential importance of no. 6 for the position of members of the *gens Didia* under Trajan.

that Imperial Romans had access to similar information about the chronology and circumstances of the original issue of the *denarii* reproduced in Trajan's series.

Furthermore, we should consider why the names of famous individuals were added to these reissues at all. Apart from the early anonymous issues, most Republican silver coinage contains a legend giving the name of the moneyer. It is therefore not surprising that almost all the silver coins in Trajan's restoration series bear name legends of this sort. Even the two *denarii* with an obverse image of Augustus (nos. 43a and b) can be thought of as "Republican" in this sense, because they bear the name of Cossus Cornelius Cn. f. Lentulus and so at least give the appearance of continuing this formal freedom of self-promotion and self-expression by the lowly *monetales*. Nor should we underestimate how remarkable these legends would seem after more than a century of numismatic production in which the coinage from the mint of Rome presented not only the portraits but also the names of the members of the Imperial family exclusively. The falsification of name legends on what were originally anonymous coins suggests that these legends were seen as an important mark of authenticity in the restoration of coins from the Republican past.

In a very important sense, therefore, the names were a large part of what was being restored with these coins. This is significant, because it is frequently assumed that the legends on Roman Imperial coins were of little value as a means of communicating ideas.[39] In this case, however, it clearly was assumed that there was a literate audience who would care to read the words they found on their coins. The selection of which coins to include in the restoration therefore depended to a certain extent on the names that each coin bore. Once this principle has been established, one possible line of inquiry is to suppose that "the 'restoration' of a coin of a Republican family must have been felt as a great compliment to its posterity."[40] Insofar as the old Republican *gentes* still had descendants in Trajan's day, the restoration of coins emblazoned with their family name might have been taken as a mark of favor from the emperor. However appealing this notion may be as a possible explanation for the selection of types, it cannot be substantiated by the coins in this series.[41]

One case in particular argues against the interpretation of the restored coins as a means to flatter the descendants of Republican families. Among

---

[39] Jones (1956: 14–15), conceded by Sutherland (1959: 53).
[40] Mattingly (1926: 273).
[41] The gradual elimination of the Republican aristocracy under the Julio-Claudians is chronicled by Syme (1986).

the restored *denarii* is a coin with the reverse legend C MARI · C F S C (no.
16), which draws from a coin minted by the otherwise obscure personage
C. Marius Capito, apparently during Sulla's dictatorship. It is difficult to
interpret the restoration of this coin as a compliment to contemporary
descendants of the *gens Maria*, because the most prominent bearer of this
nomen in Trajan's day, Marius Priscus, is unlikely to have warranted such
a tribute. This was the infamous proconsul of Africa who was successfully
prosecuted by Pliny the Younger and Tacitus for *saevitia* in 99–100. His
trial in the senate was presided over by Trajan himself, and it is unlikely
that the *princeps* would have wished to contradict the senate's will or his
own supposed impartiality in the matter by deliberately rehabilitating the
prestige of the banished Marius.[42] What is far more likely is that the coin
was restored because the legend C MARI was seen as a reference to C.
Marius, victor over the Cimbri and Teutones. This despite the fact that the
inclusion of the moneyer's cognomen CAPIT on the obverse was meant
specifically to stress the absence of a relationship to the more famous Gaius
Marius or his eponymous son, whose defeat in the recent civil war had
unleashed the terror of Sulla's proscriptions.[43] It has been noted already
that the officials who restored these coins could be ignorant of the original
circumstances in which a particular Republican coin was struck.

In fact, various coin legends may have been misinterpreted by their
restorer as referring to more famous individuals who in fact had had
nothing to do with the original moneyer.[44] The early coin of a certain M
TVLLI (no. 4) was probably mistakenly associated with the more famous
orator and statesman M. Tullius Cicero. Another coin by M CATO (no. 9)
could have been interpreted as belonging to the well-known censor M.
Porcius Cato, or perhaps more likely the famous quaestor M. Porcius
Cato Uticensis. Although this is probably more of a stretch, a coin by
L LIVINEIVS REGVLVS (no. 39) may even have been thought to have
had some connection with M. Atilius Regulus, hero of the First Punic war
idealized for his *fides* by Silius. As we have seen, all three were important
cultural touchstones under the Principate. It is interesting to note that,
like Horatius Cocles and Decius Mus, each of these three figures was
particularly famous for the manner of his death.[45]

---

[42] Plin. *Ep.* 2.11, cf. *Pan.* 76. *PIR*[2] M 315, Morford (1992: 591–2), Talbert (1984: 476).

[43] Mattingly (1926: 243), cf. Vell. 2.27.4–28.3, App. *Civ.* 1.94, Crawford, *RRC* 392.

[44] Mattingly (1926) suggests many of these.

[45] Cf. Sen. *Suas.* 6.17 (Cicero), Luc. 2.302–3 (Cato), Sil. *Pun.* 6.62–551 (Regulus). Further possible misascriptions of the coins are noted in Appendix B.

Other coins in the series make reference to famous historical figures without requiring a mistaken interpretation of the meaning of their originals. The coins of Metelli tended to feature an elephant, a deliberate reference to L. Caecilius Metellus, the first Roman *imperator* to display these animals in his triumph. This image was picked up in the restorations of two coins from this famous family (nos. 15, 18). Similarly, a coin by FAVSTVS Cornelius Sulla showing the statue set up on the Capitol by the Numidian king Bocchus to commemorate the capture of Jugurtha by his father L. Cornelius Sulla FELIX is among the restorations (no. 23a).[46] The victory by L. Aemilius Paullus over king Perseus is depicted on the restoration of a coin originally minted by L. Aemilius Lepidus Paullus (no. 27). That man's brother, the triumvir M. Aemilius Lepidus, also minted a coin showing another ancestral relative, the famously chaste Vestal AEMILIA, which turns up among the restorations as well (no. 20, Fig. 6.11). As with the *denarius* of Faustus Sulla, which depicts not his father but a statue of his father, Lepidus' coin also commemorates another famous ancestor on the reverse with the image of a monument associated with him – in this case the basilica built by the censor M. Aemilius Lepidus in 179 BC.[47]

As we enter into the multiple possible frames of personal reference implicit in these coins, it becomes clear that the apparent focus on name legends in the choice of the *denarii* that were restored was useful not so much as a way to honor particular *gentes* still thriving under the Principate, but rather as a way to revive (or at least to perpetuate) the memories of famous individuals from Republican history, even some whose family traditions had already faded from the scene. This series of restored coins thus served as a kind of numismatic counterpart to the marble gallery of *summi viri* in the Forum Augustum, which provided a similar prospectus of Republican heroes.[48] Of the twenty-six fragmentary *elogia* that have been identified, seven correspond to figures named or represented in the coins

---

[46] On the Bocchus statue, see Flower (2006: 89–90), *LTUR* IV 360 s.v. "Statuae: C. Cornelius Sulla, Bocchus, Iugurtha" [Sehlmeyer].

[47] *LTUR* I, 183–7, s.v. "Basilica Paul(l)i," [Bauer]. The basilica had been adorned by shields by Lepidus' father: Plin. *NH* 35.13. For the cultural affinities between coins and other kinds of monuments, see Meadows and Williams (2001), also Burnett (1999: 154–5). On Aemilia, see Chapter 3.

[48] Gowing (2005: 138–45). The gallery of heroes in the Forum Augustum continued to receive additions in the Imperial period, and this process of augmentation was eventually transferred to the Forum of Trajan: Geiger (2008: 163–78, 191–2), Packer (2001: 4–5), Anderson (1984: 160–1).

restored by Trajan.[49] This overlap is striking, especially when we consider that the Forum Augustum may have had as many as 108 niches for statues, and there is little doubt that still more of the individuals referenced in the coins selected for restoration were also represented in the porticoes of the Augustan monument.[50] It seems likely that Augustus' Republican memory gallery may have exerted a great deal of influence on the selection of coin legends to restore, although we cannot say with certainty that other catalogs of Republican heroes did not exert influence as well.[51]

LIBERTAS AGAIN

Given the explicit connection between these coins and the heroes of the Republican period, it is perhaps not surprising to note the inclusion of coins that advertise the special Republican virtue of *libertas* as opposition to tyranny. Here again we find M. Brutus' pre-assassination obverse portrait of *Libertas*, paired with its original reverse scene depicting the founder of the free *respublica*, L. Junius Brutus as a consul, attended by two lictors and an accensor (no. 22, Fig. 6.2).[52] In addition, the coin labeled C SERVEIL C F could be taken as a reference to C. Servilius Ahala, another tyrannicide of the early Republican period, who put an end to the monarchical ambitions of Sp. Maelius in 439 BC (no. 21).[53] To these mythic champions of liberty must be added references to figures who became famous as enemies of Julius Caesar and Octavian. As noted above, Sextus Pompey has a coin (no. 41), representing the portrait of his father on the obverse and the

---

[49] no. 31: Aeneas = D(egrassi, *Inscr. It.* 13.3) 1, no. 35, Marcellus = D. 8, no. 8a, Scipio Asiagenus = D. 15; no. 33, Metellus Numidicus = D. 16; no. 29, Marius = D. 17, 83; no. 23, Sulla = D. 18; no. 27, Aemilius Paullus = D. 81. Excluding the side devoted to the *domus Julia*, twenty-five Republican heroes can be assigned to the gallery "with various degrees of certainty": Geiger (2008: 138–56).

[50] Degrassi, *Inscr. It.* 13.3 (1937: 2). Geiger (2008: 117–20) might place the number somewhat higher. Other probable candidates include Decius Mus (no. 3), Flamininus (no. 7), and Scaurus (no. 25). L. Brutus (no. 22) and Horatius Cocles (no. 2) are likely as well, although they already had famous statues on the Capitoline: Plin. *NH* 33.9, Gell *NA* 4.5.4, Platner and Ashby (1926: 498), *LTUR* IV 316 s.v. "Statua M. Horatii Coclitis" [Coarelli], 368 s.v. "Statuae Regum Romanorum" [Coarelli].

[51] Mattingly (1926: 275) alludes to the "pageant of Roman history" found in passages of the *Aeneid* (the *nekyia*, 6.756–885 and the shield *ecphrasis*, 8.626–728) and suggests a possible relationship between these coins and the poem. I have found some points of overlap, but not enough to suggest the poem functioned as a guide in choosing which coins would be restored.

[52] The obverse had reappeared in AD 68: See Chapter 1.

[53] Harlan (1995: 157) offers the entirely plausible explanation of the reverse type, showing two figures with shields and drawn swords, as a reference to M. Servilius Pulex Geminus, victor in twenty-three single combats.

Figure 6.2. Restored *Denarius* of Trajan. Obverse: head of Libertas with legend LIB-
ERTAS behind (cf. Fig. 1.1). Reverse: L. Junius Brutus (third from left), flanked by
attendants of consular office, name legend BRVTVS underneath. (© Trustees of the
British Museum, *BMCRE* III 135 no. 684)

Catanaean brothers – an all-too appropriate icon for Sextus' own familial
pietas – on the reverse.[54]

If we expand on the principle of the fluid interpretation of name legends,
other tyrannicides can also be found to accompany the coin of Brutus
just mentioned. There are two coins with the name of Q CASSIVS on
them (nos. 24a and b). The moneyer was obviously not the same as the
C. Cassius Longinus who rose to prominence as an assassin of Julius
Caesar, but, as the poet C. Helvius Cinna discovered, Romans were quite
capable of confusion in regard to the names of Caesar's assassins.[55] One
of these coins also has the head of *Libertas* on the obverse (no. 24b), so
the conjunction with M. Brutus' own *Libertas* types may have helped to
foster the misidentification of the author of these coins with Cassius the
tyrannicide. In addition to Brutus and Cassius, some of the names already
mentioned, such as M CATO (no. 9) and M TVLLI (no. 4), also could
have been confused with those of men whose deaths marked them out as
icons of the Republican *libertas* that was lost under the Caesars.

The inclusion of coins such as these in the Trajanic series of restorations
shows once again how easily the ideological theme of *libertas* could be
taken over into the official discourse of the Roman Principate. Nor was it

---

[54] Mattingly (1926: 270), "The enemies of the founders of the Empire – Cn. Pompey, Brutus,
Mark Antony – are deliberately included." I have been unable to identify an overt reference to
Antony in the series.

[55] Val. Max. 9.9.1, Suet. *Iul.* 85. On Cassius' fame, see Rawson (1986). Cinna: Wiseman (1974:
44–58).

necessary to forswear the memory of Caesar to appropriate the rhetoric of the Pompeian opposition, as it had been for Augustus.[56] Coins of both Julius Caesar and Augustus appear in the series (nos. 30, 31, 42, 43a and b). Even Caesar's extraordinary perpetual dictatorship is mentioned (no. 42).[57] In the case of Augustus, however, there seems to have been a particular effort to emphasize his continued sharing of honors with other *principes*. On the two coins that name AVGVSTVS on the obverse, the portrait of M. Agrippa is also depicted on the opposite side, along with the name of the moneyer, Cossus Cornelius Lentulus (nos. 43a and b). Here again Augustus provides the paradigm of a partnership between the ruler and the senate, in which men of talent can earn honors through good deeds. The model of Agrippa perhaps was stressed particularly under Nerva and Trajan, when men such as Verginius Rufus and Frontinus were also awarded for their service to the state with third consulships, a rare mark of distinction under the Principate, but one readily associated with M. Agrippa.[58]

Although it seems unlikely in the aggregate that the selection of coins for restoration was motivated by a desire to call attention to the Republican heritage of specific Imperial persons, it is difficult to resist seeing the coin of P GALBA (no. 19) in light of its connection to the emperor with that cognomen. Although the Sulpicii Galbae of the Republic had sufficient accomplishments to justify their continuing fame under the Principate, Ser. Galba's liberation of the Roman world from Nero's tyranny might be said to have imparted additional luster on the achievements of his ancestors. His association with *libertas* continued to make him a model for later emperors, and it was in light of this connection in particular that he was included in Trajan's parallel series of restored Imperial *aurei*.[59] Thus, a further link to the theme of freedom (beyond the intrinsic connection of this ideal with all things of Republican vintage) would have been provided in this case by the Imperial, rather than the Republican, associations of the name legend.

Another coin with intriguing implications for the continuity of *libertas* under the Principate is one that bears the name C NORBANVS (no. 13). That name attained prominence during the Republic with a new man who held the consulship in 83 and then committed suicide on Rhodes

---

[56] Syme (1939: 317).

[57] Caesar's prominence in the series is stressed (with distorting effect) by Harvey (2002).

[58] *CIL* VI 896 (= *ILS* 129, on the Pantheon).

[59] *RIC* I² 312 no. 824 (= *BMCRE* III 143 no. 701) has a standing figure of *Libertas* on the reverse. Mattingly (1926: 274).

in the following year after forces under his command were routed twice by Sullan armies. As a casualty of civil war, Norbanus might have been remembered as providing a prologue for the fashion of suicide-as-liberation made famous by the younger Cato.[60] There was also a more recent connection. According to Cassius Dio, a praetorian prefect named Norbanus was aware of the plan to assassinate Domitian in 96.[61] Whether the guard was involved in the plot or not is uncertain, but it is entirely possible that Norbanus, who had distinguished himself by his unstinting loyalty to Domitian during the suppression of Saturninus' rebellion, might have wanted to distance himself from the hated tyrant after his death, and thus promoted the story of his complicity.[62] In any case, there can be little doubt that the praetorian prefect was instrumental in securing the smooth transition to Nerva after Domitian was dead. Might the selection of this coin have been a way of commemorating Rome's most recent tyrannicide? That might be seen as establishing a dangerous precedent, but the connection would have been difficult to ignore once it was recognized.

Even in the case of Galba, the implication of Trajan's honoring the memory of an *adsertor libertatis* was that rebellion and tyrannicide were still viable methods for achieving political change under the Principate. Trajan had not taken part in the overthrow of his predecessor, so he did not need to invoke the theme of *libertas* to legitimate his position (as Galba or Vespasian had done) or to bridge a rupture in the charismatic authority of the office of *princeps* (as in Nerva's case). Instead, *libertas* would have been invoked more usefully as an element of Trajan's good government, consonant with the stability of his rule and its continuity with the moral traditions of the past. But such a neatly domesticated version of *libertas* is difficult to square with the restoration of coins connected with Brutus and Cassius. With these names, the association of this theme with a historical break from the past takes center stage, whereas the associations of Galba (and perhaps Norbanus) would relocate the disruptive sense of the term even closer to the present. We are thus left to conclude that Trajan's confidence in reviving these numismatic reminders of previous liberators was meant to reinforce the notion that only bad emperors should fear to mention *libertas*. The good emperor had nothing to fear from men who love freedom, because he was not an obstacle to it.[63]

---

[60] App. *Civ.* 1.91, cf. Livy *Per.* 89. Münzer (1932), MRR II: 70.

[61] Dio (Zon.) 67.15.26. PIR² N 162. See Syme (1983: 137–8), Jones (1992: 194), *contra* Gsell (1894: 327–8).

[62] Mart. 9.84.1–2, Friedländer (1886: 61).

[63] Cf. Seelentag (2004: 468–75).

CONTINUITY

By considering the fame of the individuals whose names appear on these coins, it is possible to offer explanations for the selection of many of the coins that were restored and to begin an analysis of their wider cultural significance. Other coins, however, remain shrouded in mystery, because the names they bear are those of men who were insignificant or are otherwise unknown to us. It is not possible to prove that every coin in the series was restored because of the name it bore, but the disappearance of the likes of CARISIVS (32) or NVMONIVS VAALA (38) from our general knowledge of Republican history should not lead us to conclude that these names were necessarily without resonance for a Trajanic audience.[64] Nevertheless, we may begin to see that a more important question remains unanswered in this analysis: *cui bono?* The simple answer might be that piety toward the past had its own rewards and that Trajan wanted to be seen as participating in the perpetuation of honors for Republican heroes. But this does not entirely explain the selection of the particular coins that appear in this series. Even if a clear correlation could be established between the individuals named on these coins and an "official list" of Republican heroes, we still should wonder what Trajan stood to gain by the detailed reproduction of the full visual and verbal content of these coins.

To begin to answer this question, it will be useful to turn to the iconographic features of the coins. From this vantage point, the interest of the Imperial mint officials in a coin such as that of T. Carisius becomes easier to explain. Carisius was a prolific moneyer, producing coins with images of everything from the goddess Roma to panthers and a sphinx. And yet the coin selected for restoration in the Trajanic series is one that offers a celebration of the work of the mint itself: It shows the die, anvil, hammer, and tongs used to produce coins on the reverse and Moneta, the tutelary goddess of this work, on the obverse (Fig 6.3). The continuity with the Republic being asserted here is thus one that has particular relevance to the medium in which it was presented.

Not all of the issues were of such narrow interest, however. The theme of Vaala's coin, which shows a soldier charging a well-defended rampart, seems to be the celebration of military valor. This martial quality, as we have seen in the works of Silius and Frontinus, was one of the enduring features of the memory of the Republic for many Romans living under the Principate. And yet it was not exclusively a Republican virtue. Trajan, with

---

[64] Carisius seems to have been a figure of some importance in the Triumviral period: App. *Civ.* 5.111, 5.25.8, *PIR*² C 422.

Figure 6.3. Restored *Denarius* of Trajan. Obverse: bust of Moneta, with legend MON-ETA behind. Reverse: tools of the minter's trade, with name of CARISIVS above, encircled by laurel wreath. (© Trustees of the British Museum, *BMCRE* III 136 no. 688)

his military background and success with expansionist wars into Dacia and later Parthia, was keen to promote the idea of a revival of Rome's martial spirit.[65] In this regard, it is important to realize that the coins of the restoration series were issued alongside the rest of Trajan's official coinage, into a world dominated by the imagery of his Imperial monuments.[66] As these coins mingled in circulation with the rest of the Imperial coinage, they would have served to highlight particular features of Republican visual language, out of which much of Roman Imperial numismatic imagery (and particularly Trajan's) grew, and to which it continued to refer both implicitly and explicitly. At this point in the discussion, therefore, we should begin to look for connections between the images contained in the restored series and other images communicated by Trajan. Shifting to the analysis of the thematic and iconographic content of the coins will not undermine what has already been said about the significance of the name legends in the selection of coins. On the contrary, what I hope to suggest is that these images worked with the legends to suggest a deeper connection between the *princeps* and the heroic figures of the Republic whose names they preserve.

In addition to Vaala's scene of matched warriors, several coins selected for restoration depict images of combat (nos. 6, 8, 21, 38). The battle scenes on the column of Trajan (dedicated in 113 and perhaps already envisioned when the restoration coins were minted) provide an important point of contact for these Republican images. We can safely imagine that

[65] See Plin. *Pan.* 13.4–5, cf. Bennett (1997: 66, 87).
[66] To set these coins aside from the "mainstream" coinage of Trajan's reign as an entirely self-contained series is, in my view, short-sighted, *pace* Strack (1931: 42).

Figure 6.4. Trajanic *Aureus*. Reverse: Trajan, mounted with javelin, military cloak flowing behind, trampling fallen Dacian, legend SPQR OPTIMO PRINCIPI above. (© Trustees of the British Museum, *BMCRE* III 66 no. 246)

some of these scenes were already presented in some fashion as part of the triumph that Trajan celebrated at the conclusion of his first Dacian war in 102. Furthermore, an important literary parallel for these scenes would have been provided in the *commentarii* that Trajan, following the model of Caesar, published about his campaigns.[67] In fact, Trajan's restoration of coins of Julius Caesar in both gold and silver has been described as a nod "from one great conqueror to another."[68] In this context we might also cite the portraits of Ancus (no. 28), Marcellus (no. 35), Sulla (no. 23b), Pompey (no. 41), and Agrippa (no. 43b), not to mention Hercules (no. 7).

These connections become more significant when we notice how closely the composition of certain restored coin types resembles that of other Trajanic issues. A noticeable parallel to the image of the galloping Dioscuri on the anonymous early coins that were restored with spurious name legends (Fig. 6.1) can be found on the reverse of a Trajanic *aureus*, which shows the emperor on horseback riding to the right, holding a javelin in his right hand (Fig. 6.4).[69] Instead of two riders there is one, and more action is seen in the way that Trajan brandishes his spear, but it is not difficult to

---

[67] *LTUR* II 356–9 s.v. "Forum Traiani: Columna" [Maffei], Lepper and Frere (1988), also Richmond (1935). For battle scenes in triumph, cf. Joseph. *BJ* 7.139, Beard (2007: 179–85). On the *Dacica* (of which only one line survives), see, e.g., Henderson (1927: 252). Celebration of the heroic deeds of the rank-and-file was a standard feature of such works. Perhaps Trajan described the scene of Maximus' attempt to capture Decebalus, in the same way that Cato had recorded the heroic exploits of the military tribune Caedicius. Caninius Rufus also undertook to write an epic poem about the wars: Plin. *Ep.* 8.4.1.

[68] Grant (1950: 100).

[69] *RIC* II 258 no. 208 (= *BMCRE* III 66 no. 246).

Figure 6.5. Great Trajanic Frieze. Battle scene showing Trajan on horseback, cloak flowing behind, trampling fallen Dacian. (Rome, Arch of Constantine, DAIR negative 1937.0329)

recognize the basic similarity between the two scenes, particularly in the horses' postures and the way the riders' cloaks trail behind them.[70] In terms of composition, the fallen Dacian being trampled under Trajan's horse does alter the impression of the scene somewhat, but here it is interesting to note that the models chosen both for the authentic version of the COCLES (no. 2) coin and for its counterpart, with the invented legend DECIVS (no. 3), include signature symbols (a female head, a crossed shield and carynx) that occupy the same position under the rampant horse's hooves as Trajan's vanquished Dacian.

In its basic elements, this image of a mounted figure rising up over a fallen foe was a deeply entrenched element of Trajanic iconography. Outside of the coinage, it can be seen most notably in the battle scene of the enormous frieze that originally graced porticoes in Trajan's Forum complex (Fig. 6.5). There probably was also a prominent equestrian statue

[70] Buttrey (1972: 95) suggests that a Vespasianic coin image showing Titus and Domitian riding right "may derive from a Republican Dioscurid type."

of the emperor in a similar pose whose form may be reflected in the imagery of both the coin and the monumental relief.[71] Trajan was not the only Roman to be depicted in this fashion. A similar scene appears toward the top of the frieze that encircles the column of Trajan, where the attempt by the cavalry soldier Ti. Claudius Maximus to capture the fallen king Decebalus before he killed himself is depicted. A version of this scene was engraved on the funeral stele set up for Maximus in his native Macedonia as well.[72]

Although this motif seems to have become particularly prominent in the imagery associated with Trajan's final victory in the Dacian wars, riders, of course, represented a common feature in ancient battle scenography going back to much earlier Greek and Hellenistic traditions.[73] There should be little surprise at the similarities among these images, because Roman visual culture operated through a common language of recognizable forms such as these.[74] Nevertheless, the restoration of Republican coins with Dioscuri types, along with others that display equestrian imagery (nos. 7, 28, 43a), serves to shape memory in a manner that reaffirms the notion that this kind of military heroism was uniquely embedded in a particular era of the Roman past. In their reference to specific exemplars, these coins cut across the broad cohesiveness of ancient rider imagery to draw attention to the connection between contemporary Trajanic imagery and its Republican precedents.

As discrete artifacts, the restored coins take the vague sense of cultural recognition associated with these representations and redefine them as specifically historicized memories of a Republican style of communication. Seen in the light of these numismatic traces, representations of the emperor on horseback can be identified as a reaffirmation of Republican precedents, rather than as a continuation of a style of self-representation that was also favored by Domitian, whose equestrian statue had dominated the Roman Forum before the condemnation of his memory.[75] In fact, *sestertii* commemorating Domitian's German triumph bear a much closer resemblance to the Trajanic rider scenes (Fig. 6.6), but these parallels are obscured (or at least cast in different light) by the restored Republican *denarii*.[76]

---

[71] Amm. Marc. 16.10.15–16, Hammond (1953). cf. Leander Touati (1987: 17–18, pl. 7.1), Packer (2001: 60, 72).

[72] Lepper and Frere (1988, Scene XCLV), Speidel (1970).

[73] Mackintosh (1995), Schleiermacher (1984), cf. Speidel (2004: 151–64).

[74] Hölscher (2004).

[75] Stat. *Silv.* 1.1, *LTUR* II 228–9 s.v. "Equus: Domitianus" [Giuliani], cf. Muscettola (2000: 29–45).

[76] *RIC* II² 280–301 nos. 205, 280, 358, 529–30 (= *BMCRE* III 364 *, 371 nos. 339, 380, 381).

Figure 6.6. *Sestertius* of Domitian. Reverse: Domitian, mounted with javelin, military cloak flowing behind, trampling fallen German, S C below. (© Trustees of the British Museum, *BMCRE* II 381 no. 380)

Republican precedents could also provide the cover of traditional authority in areas in which Trajan sought to expand on innovations that might have been associated with his discredited predecessor. As we saw in the previous chapter, the appeal of Hercules as a model of Imperial authority began to take shape under Domitian.[77] But this hero does not appear on that emperor's coinage, which is thoroughly dominated by the figure of Minerva. In contrast, Trajan's third consulship was marked by Hercules' reappearance on Roman coins, where he is shown nude in a frontal standing pose, with his trademark club and lion skin.[78] This was the same year in which Pliny the Younger compared Trajan's service to the empire under Domitian with the labors that Hercules performed for Eurystheus.[79] One of the restored *denarii* has a reverse image of a frontal standing figure of Hercules that is remarkably similar (no. 33), and two others present portraits with the hero's attributes on the obverse (nos. 7, 23b). The viewer who handles these coins is invited to locate the roots for Pliny's metaphor, which simultaneously marks an embrace of a much wider mythological framework, in the particular contexts of the Republic.

Also prominent in the restoration series are coins that evoke the pageantry of triumph, a key theme during Trajan's reign. Of particular interest is the presence of the three coins of L. Rubrius Dossenus, a moneyer who would be entirely unfamiliar today but for the fact that he minted

---

[77] See above.

[78] *RIC* II 247 nos. 37, 45, 49 (= *BMCRE* III 38–42 nos. 56–9, 81–93), Strack (1931: 95–104). Hercules Adsertor had appeared on the coins of the Gallic rebels in 68: *RIC* I² 207 no. 49 (*BMCRE* I 294 *).

[79] Plin. *Pan.* 14.5.

Figure 6.7. Restored *Denarius* of Trajan. Obverse: head of Jupiter Optimus Maximus, with scepter and legend DOSSEN behind. Reverse: triumphal *quadriga*, with Victory standing on front of car, legend L RVBRI beneath. (© Trustees of the British Museum, *BMCRE* III 133 no. 676)

coins that express the religious dimension of the Roman triumph so nicely (nos. 11a–c).[80] The reverses of these coins are all the same, showing a triumphal *quadriga* driven by a winged Victory (Fig. 6.7). The obverses of the three restored coins show, respectively, Jupiter, Juno, and Minerva – the gods of the Capitoline triad, in whose honor the triumphal celebration was held. Dossenus also minted a fourth coin in the series, showing Neptune on the obverse, but this coin seems to have been left out of the Trajanic restoration, despite the fact that it was by far the most numerous in the original issue.[81] This omission would seem to strengthen the argument that the association of these coins with the Capitoline triad and so with triumph was a primary reason for their restoration. The Capitoline triad is also represented for the first time on an Imperial coin on the reverse of a Trajanic *sestertius* dated between his fifth and sixth consulships.[82] One need not look long in the coinage of almost any Roman emperor to find triumphal imagery, but it had a particular prominence in the reign of Trajan. Trajan appears standing in a triumphal *quadriga* on both gold and silver coinage dating from his first Dacian triumph (Fig. 6.8).[83] The similarities between this image and that of Victory on the restored coins of Dossenus are readily apparent and invite comparison with the other images of *quadrigae* in the

[80] Seelentag (2004: 442–6).
[81] Crawford, *RRC* 362–3.
[82] Strack (1931: 197) (not in *RIC*).
[83] *RIC* II 247–9 nos. 48, 72, 86–7, 90 (= *BMCRE* III 49 §, ¶), cf. also *RIC* II 253 no. 138 (= 78 no. 350) (in figure).

Figure 6.8. *Denarius* of Trajan. Reverse: Trajan in triumphal *quadriga*, holding scepter and laurel branch, legend COS V P P OPTIMO PRINC around. (© Trustees of the British Museum, *BMCRE* III 78 no. 350)

restoration series (nos. 1, 8a, 25). In short, Trajan's triumphal imagery works in the same Republican idiom as Dossenus' coins.

Continuing the theme of conquest, Trajan also restored a coin commemorating L. Aemilius Paullus' victory over Perseus in 168 BC (no. 27). The reverse shows Paullus crowning a trophy while king Perseus and his two sons look on as captives. The composition of this type is remarkably similar to the reverse of a Trajanic *aureus* from the first Dacian war, in which a nude male figure crowns a trophy that stands above a conquered Dacian.[84] The implication of the parallel is that the *princeps* Trajan has taken the place of Paullus as a conquering hero. In a more zoologically specific register, one of the restored coins commemorates the submission of the Nabatean king Aretas to Aemilius Scaurus in 62 BC with an image of the Arabian ruler kneeling beside his camel (no. 25). The dromedary would reappear on Roman coinage following Trajan's organization of the province of Arabia in AD 106.[85]

Also in this military vein is the restored coin of C. Valerius Flaccus, showing a legionary eagle between two auxiliary standards (no. 14, Fig. 6.9). Trajan would mint coins in his sixth consulship with a similar eagle-and-standards reverse (Fig. 6.10).[86] Whether these parallels appeared before or after the restoration series was assembled, it is evident that the

[84] *RIC* II 249 nos. 70–1 (= *BMCRE* III 48 nos. 135–6).
[85] *RIC* II 250–61 nos. 94–5, 142–3, 245 (= *BMCRE* III 72–185 nos. 294–300, 474–7, 877), Strack (1931: 194–7). See also Bowersock (1983: 32–5, 81–5), *MRR* II 175.
[86] *RIC* II 264 nos. 294–6 (= *BMCRE* III 94 nos. 456–64).

Figure 6.9. Restored *Denarius* of Trajan. Obverse: bust of Victory, caduceus in front. Reverse: legionary eagle between two military standards, name VAL FLA IMPERAT on sides, EX SC in between. (© Trustees of the British Museum, *BMCRE* III 133 no. 679)

inclusion of so many coins that stress military and triumphal imagery created a pattern whereby the Republican precedents for Trajan's expansionist foreign policy were being brought into clearer focus.

As a counterpoint to this martial refrain, other coins in the series suggest more peaceful pursuits. In the restoration of these coins, the emperor's civic virtues could also be traced back to their Republican roots. One such virtue was *Liberalitas*.[87] Pliny the Younger celebrates Trajan's great improvements to Rome's system of grain supply in his *Panegyricus*, and these achievements are commemorated in the coinage with various types depicting the figures of Annona or the goddess Ceres.[88] For example, Annona is represented on COS V coins standing in front of a ship's prow, holding two corn ears over a *modius* measure with one hand and a cornucopia in the other.[89] Although the personified virtue Annona was unknown to Republican die engravers, her attributes were not. They can be seen quite clearly on the restored coin of Livineius Regulus, which presents two ears of corn and a *modius* on the reverse (no. 39). Ceres is also shown on one of the restored coins seated, holding a torch and an ear of corn (no. 29). This representation of the goddess can be compared with a Trajanic *denarius* that depicts her standing, but with the same attributes.[90] Although the discourse surrounding such divine figures and the human virtues they represent could only really flourish as it did under the unique conditions of

---

[87] Stylow (1972).
[88] Plin. *Pan.* 29–32, Strack (1931: 164–7).
[89] *RIC* II 255 nos. 165–7 (= *BMCRE* III 56 nos. 169–73). See also Kloft (1970).
[90] *RIC* II 251 no. 109 (= *BMCRE* III 54 no. 156).

Figure 6.10. *Denarius* of Trajan. Reverse: legionary eagle between two military standards, legend SPQR OPTIMO PRINCIPI around. (© Trustees of the British Museum, *BMCRE* III 95 no. 460)

the Principate, the restoration of Republican coins with similar features suggests an underlying continuity with much older values and practices.[91]

Another restored coin that may suggest a harvest-related theme is that of C. Marius Capito, depicting a figure plowing behind two yoked oxen on the reverse (no. 16). This coin bears striking resemblance to a COS V *sestertius* showing Trajan as a priest, probably performing the rite of the *primigenius sulcus* for the foundation of a new colony.[92] Once again, if the Republican coin was attributed by Trajan and his mint workers to the C. Marius from Arpinum, the interpretation of its plowing scene in connection with the ritual foundation of new colonies would not be inappropriate. If, as seems likely, the similarities of these types are the result of something more than mere coincidence, the restoration of this coin would have served to highlight the continuities between the civic and religious functions commonly performed by the *princeps* and those previously undertaken by an exalted Republican predecessor.

Another important subcategory among these restored *denarii* consists of coins that depict important monuments in the city of Rome, particularly sites in the Forum Romanum, such as the temple of Vesta (nos. 24a and b) and the nearby Puteal Scribonianum (no. 26).[93] The earliest in terms of its original issue is a coin of the *gens Aemilia* depicting the resplendent

---

[91] On Imperial virtues, see, e.g., Charlesworth (1937), Wallace-Hadrill (1981b), Fears (1981b), Noreña (2001).

[92] *RIC* II 284 nos. 567–8 (= *BMCRE* III 175 nos. 829–30), Strack (1931: 129–30), cf. Seelentag (2004: 436–8).

[93] *LTUR* V s.v. "Vesta, Aedes" [Scott], IV 171–3 s.v. "Puteal Libonis/Scribonianum" [Chioffi], Coarelli (1985: 166–76).

Figure 6.11. Republican *Denarius* of Type Restored by Trajan. Obverse: Vestal Aemilia, *simpulum* in front. Reverse: Basilica Aemilia, name M LEPIDVS beneath, AIMILIA REF S C around. (© Trustees of the British Museum, *BMCRR* I no. 3651)

basilica built in 179 BC during the censorship of M. Aemilius Lepidus (no. 20, Fig. 6.11). When examining the architectural representation on the reverse of this coin, it is difficult not to see certain basic similarities with the coins that Trajan would issue to celebrate the building of the Basilica Ulpia (Fig. 6.12), and to see in the restoration of this coin an anticipation of the plans for Trajan's enormous forum complex, as well as an attempt to underscore the traditional foundations of that architecturally ambitious project.[94] Similarly, the restoration of the coin of Marcius Philippus, which depicts the Aqua Marcia on the reverse (no. 28), might be connected with the Aqua Traiana – a project that would not be completed until AD 109, but for which work must have already been well under way in 107.[95] It is likely that the restoration of these coins gave an opportunity to reflect on the bustling program of public works that Trajan had begun, and to draw the implicit connection between this activity and some of the great public building projects of the Republican period.

Finally, it is possible to detect a different sort of contemporary relevance in the obverse image of the Aemilian coin (no. 20), which shows the portrait of a Vestal virgin, presumably the Aemilia who famously exonerated

[94] *RIC* II 261, 287 nos. 246–8, 616–18 (= *BMCRE* III 99, 207–8 nos. 492, 982–3). Seelentag (2004: 439–41), Packer (2001, esp. 182–3). The shield portraits of the Basilica Pauli/Aemilia (cf. Plin. *NH* 35.13), although clearly visible in the Republican coin, are not echoed in the numismatic representation of the Basilica Ulpia. *Imagines clipeatae* were, however, a prominent part of the architectonic decoration of the porticoes that ran down either side of the Forum of Trajan: Packer (2001: 61–4, figs. 54–5).

[95] *LTUR* I 70–2 s.v. "Aqua Traiana" [Virgili], Platner and Ashby (1926: 28). Seelentag (2004: 427–31). Cf. *RIC* II 278, 287 nos. 463, 607–9 (= *BMCRE* III 184–214 nos. 873–6, 975–6, 1008).

Figure 6.12. *Sestertius* of Trajan. Reverse: Basilica Ulpia, legend BASILICA VLPIA S C beneath, SPQR OPTIMO PRINCIPI around. (© Trustees of the British Museum, *BMCRE* III 207 no. 982)

her chastity when the sacred fire was extinguished.[96] This coin offers a pointed contrast to Domitian's essentially repressive approach to maintaining the sexual purity of that priesthood by calling attention to the story of a positive Vestal *exemplum*. There seems to be an effort to have it both ways in the series, however, because two other coins (nos. 24a–b) suggest a harder line regarding *incestum*. The common reverse image of both shows the temple of Vesta equipped with a curule chair and ballots for voting A(bsolvo) or C(ondemno) – the trappings of a trial. These features point to a connection between the obverse legend CASSIVS and L. Cassius Longinus Ravilla, the judge who acted as a *scopulus reorum* during the Vestal scandal of 113 BC, ensuring that the guilty were punished.[97] Once again, Domitian's detractors were able to reject his bad acts without abandoning the Republican value of *severitas* in principle.

More importantly, the portrait of Aemilia also provides a notable precedent for the prominence given to female members of the Imperial house. Trajan's later coins include the portraits of his wife Plotina, deified sister Marciana, and niece Matidia, marking a trend that would become more pronounced under his successors.[98] Of particular interest for our purposes is a coin that links Plotina's image with an altar of Chastity (*ara Pudicitiae*: Fig. 6.13), although other coins with her portrait show the goddess Vesta on the reverse.[99] As on the Aemilian coin, a female member of the

---

[96] See Chapter 3.
[97] Crawford *RRC* 452, see discussion in Chapter 3.
[98] *FOS* 631, 824, 681, Mattingly, *BMCRE* III lxxxii–iii, also Boatwright (1991, esp. 534–9).
[99] *RIC* II 298 no. 733, cf. 728–32 (= *BMCRE* III 107 no. 529, cf. nos. 524–8). If the altar in question was associated with the shrine of *Pudicitia patricia* in the Forum Boarium, it

Figure 6.13. *Denarius* of Trajan. Obverse: Empress Plotina. Reverse: Ara Pudicitiae, ARA PVDIC beneath, CAES AVG GERMA DAC COS VI PP around. (© Trustees of the British Museum, *BMCRE* III 107 no. 529)

household imparts honor to her male relatives through her association with an ideal of sexual purity. Similar praise for the emperor's wife can be found in Pliny's *Panegyricus*, where the speaker notably suggests that nothing was more holy, or more ancient, than Plotina was in her habits (*Pan.* 83.5: *quid enim illa sanctius, quid antiquius?*). The evocation of Aemilia's memory in Trajan's series of restored coins points to the same conflux of feminine virtue, religious distinction, and antiquity.

CONCLUSION

As the discussion presented in this chapter suggests, the Trajanic series of restored Republican *denarii* affords an excellent opportunity to examine how Romans of the Imperial period remembered their Republican past. Although this is a relatively small series of coins, its complexity makes it difficult to interpret within a single overarching framework. It is clear, however, that the restoration coins represent the revival of Republican sensibilities in a real and significant way. For the first time in over a hundred years, the accomplishments of people outside of the Imperial house were being commemorated on the coinage of Rome's mint. Previous restoration series had confined themselves to the coinage of earlier emperors. For Titus and Domitian, restored coins provided a means to advance a fictive sense of continuity between a select set of "good" Julio-Claudians and the

is interesting to note a topographical connection to the cult of Hercules, whose prominence under Trajan has already been mentioned: Livy 10. 23.3, *LTUR* IV 168 s.v. "Pudicitia Patricia, Sacellum, Ara, Templum" [Coarelli].

new Flavian dynasty.[100] In this special series of silver coins, however, the Imperial mint returned to an authentic Republican paradigm of diversity, invoking a broad range of persons from the pre-Imperial past, in whose coinage the essential models for all kind of contemporary iconography could be identified.

Unlike the projects of cultural or moral renewal discussed in previous chapters, in this last case Republican virtues were not presented as part of a communal Roman inheritance in which everyone was expected to participate. As the legend on each of these coins makes clear, the Republican glory commemorated in this series was being celebrated only by virtue of Trajan's special act of restoration. Whereas *exempla virtutis* were paraded under the Republic to promote the glory and familial *nobilitas* of a somewhat wider range of aristocratic *principes*, here they have been subordinated to the authority of a single, solely powerful *princeps*. The restoration of Republican military and triumphal imagery, along with representations of building programs and contributions to the food supply, all call attention to themes that were actively advanced by the current emperor. Insofar as these themes were primarily military and Imperial, we can assume that this co-opting of the past would not have met with much resistance. Long before the restoration of the Capitol and the triumph of Vespasian and Titus, the emperors' close connection with these themes had been well established. The ruler's unique authority in religious matters was also largely unchallenged, although Trajan's restoration of a coin with the image of the virtuous Vestal Aemilia on its obverse may have helped to smooth over some of the tensions exposed by Domitian during the events discussed in Chapter 3.

On the other hand, the coin with the legend M. TVLLI, insofar as it may have been used to suggest a connection between the emperor and Cicero, may have been more problematic in its implications. This is not because Cicero died as an opponent of tyranny, so much as the fact that his field of excellence, as discussed in Chapter 4, had not yet been ceded to the emperor in the same way. Although the opportunity for elite Romans to attain military glory had been curtailed under the Principate, rhetoric and other arenas of cultural production continued to provide an opportunity for men such as Pliny the Younger to continue Republican traditions and attempt to rival the achievements of the ancestors. In the reign of Domitian, however, the emperor was praised not only as a military commander, but also as a uniquely gifted orator and poet.[101] Scenes of the emperor in a

---

[100] Komnick (2001: 165–71), Mattingly (1920: 181–3).

[101] Stat. *Ach.* 1.14–19, Sil. *Pun.* 3.614–21, Mart. 5.5.6–7, Quint. *Inst.* 10.1.91, cf. Suet. *Dom.* 2.2, Tac. *Hist.* 4.86.2, Coleman (1986: 3088–95).

military cloak addressing his soldiers, which have no precedent in Republican iconography but begin to appear under Augustus, could be ascribed to the importance of these talents for military leadership.[102] Images such as the ones found on the Trajanic arch at Beneventum and the Roman *Anaglypha Traiani*, which show the emperor in civilian clothes addressing his fellow citizens, may suggest a closer connection between the *princeps* himself and the statesmen of the Republic, however.[103] The monumental commemoration of such addresses indicate not just the emperor's increased interest in public policy, but also his incursion into cultural territory that could still be cherished as a venue for elite self-promotion and cultural display.

Whether they increased the anxiety of senators or not, this series of restored *denarii* clearly redounded to the emperor's credit, as they framed a context of memory in which Trajan could be seen as the sole inheritor of the virtues of the Republican past. Unlike in previous chapters, where more emphasis was placed on the role of contingency and ambiguity in the production of memories of the Republic, the potential for contested meanings has been less in evidence here. In part this is because of the lack of a clear understanding of how any narratives, much less competing ones, were applied to the interpretation of these images. Equally important, however, is the fact that these coins were issued by the Imperial mint, and as such were the products of a more coherent ideological perspective than what we find, for example, in the multiple competing viewpoints of Tacitus' *Dialogus*.

Like other emperors, Trajan restored only those Republican precedents that he himself could claim to have surpassed. For the *optimus* ("best") *princeps*, however, the list of these *exempla* continued to expand, with the result that the ability of others to achieve a similar connection with the Republic was bound to fade from view. In a form of public communication dominated by the *princeps*, even the celebration of a recognizably Republican *libertas* could be put to the service of consolidating the stability of autocracy. The result was a paradox that Pliny openly celebrated in his *Panegyricus*, where he praised Trajan with the observation, "you command us to be free, and we shall" (*Pan.* 66.4: *iubes esse liberos, erimus*).

---

[102] *RIC* I² 59 no. 253 cf. II 253 no. 136 (= *BMCRE* I 100 no. 611, cf. III 77 no. 347). Campbell (1984: 69–87) cf. Goldsworthy (1996: 145–9).

[103] Kleiner (1992, figs. 190, 216), Torelli (1982: 106–8).

CONCLUSION

The last chapter closed with a return to the paradox examined at the outset of this book. This is as it should be, and not just because it fits an unruly mass of material into something resembling the pleasing order of ring composition. One of the things I have attempted to argue in this book is that efforts to find a normative definition of *libertas* in a post-Augustan context – one that was tidily reconciled with the realities of the Principate – could never achieve a wholly successful resolution. Even if Augustus was taken at his word when he co-opted the rhetoric of Caesar's assassins to justify his conduct in the civil wars, neither he nor his successors had the power to limit the meaning of political language in such a fundamental way. While Pliny defined the senate's freedom as originating with the emperor's power to command and Tacitus, in a roughly contemporary text, spoke of the unprecedented coexistence of *principatus ac libertas* under Nerva and Trajan, the fact remained that, on a basic level, freedom was conceptually incompatible with the fetters that an emperor's power imposed on contemporary political life. These senators may have been more willing to accept such contradictions than M. Brutus or Cato the Younger had been, but this does not mean that the problem of Caesar's relationship to liberty went away. In fact, Pliny and Tacitus remain keenly aware of the paradoxical nature of the reconciliation they are heralding, and may even be said to revel in that paradox.

By the same token, the choice of whether the Republic and the Empire represented distinct phases in the history of the Roman polity or whether they formed a continuous and interconnected whole also remained a difficult if not insoluble conundrum. For the sake of comparison, we might look at a passage from the fourth-century historian Ammianus Marcellinus, digressing to give some context for a riot that erupted over a wine short-age in Rome in 354:

> *eius populus ab incunabulis primis ad usque pueritiae tempus extremum, quod annis circumcluditur fere trecentis, circummurana pertulit bella, deinde aetatem ingressus adultam post multiplices bellorum aerumnas Alpes transcendit et fretum, in iuvenem erectus et virum ex omni plaga, quam orbis ambit inmensus, reportavit laureas et triumphos, iamque vergens in senium et nomine solo aliquotiens vincens ad tranquilliora vitae discessit. ideo urbs venerabilis post superbas efferatarum gentium cervices oppressas latasque leges fundamenta libertatis et retinacula sempiterna velut frugi parens et prudens et dives Caesaribus tamquam liberis suis regenda patrimonii iura permisit. et olim licet otiosae sint tribus pacataeque centuriae et nulla suf-fragiorum certamina, sed Pompiliani redierit securitas temporis, per omnes tamen quot orae sunt partesque terrarum, ut domna suscipitur et regina.*

From their first infancy to the end of childhood, which comprised about three hundred years, (Rome's) people waged wars around the walls. Then, passing into adolescence after the travails of several wars, they crossed the Alps and the sea. Having risen into youth and manhood, they brought back laurels and triumphs from every place in the wide world. And now, entering old age, with occasional conquest coming only because of their name, they have set out on a more tranquil life. After the proud necks of savage peoples were in harness and laws were passed to be the foundation and constant guards of freedom, the venerable city granted to the Caesars the right to administer its patrimony, just as a wise, wealthy, and temperate parent does to his children. Now that the tribal assemblies are left idle, the voting centuries have been pacified, and there are no more contests for votes, the stability of the time of (Numa) Pompilius has returned instead, and Rome has been embraced through all the countless regions of the world as mistress and queen. (Amm. 14.6.4–6)

In this passage, we can recognize the same themes of continuity, change, and decline that marked the memory of the Republic in the Flavio-Trajanic age. The perspective on these issues has continued to evolve, of course, as have the modalities within which they were discussed. The compari-son of the Caesars' power with an heir's administration of his patrimony reflects the development of ideas with roots in early discussions of Augus-tus' supreme title of authority, "father of the fatherland" (*pater patriae*).[1] Ammianus also employs a biological metaphor for Roman power first applied to the broad scope of Republican and Imperial history by the

---

[1] *RG* 35.1, cf. Strab. *Geog.* 6.4.2, Sen. *Clem.* 1.14.1-16.1, Roller (2001: 244).

Antonine historian Florus.[2] Although the chronological framework is left a bit uncertain, a connection is clearly implied between the quiescence of the voting assemblies of the Republic and Rome's transition from vigorous adulthood into secure old age. *Libertas* is still invoked, but here it is associated with the protections of a developed legal framework that, together with Rome's imperial dominion (*superbas... cervices oppressas*), were somehow handed over into the custody of the Caesars as *senium* set in.

Should continuity or rupture be stressed in this arrangement? The biological metaphor seems to privilege the integrity of the whole, and when Ammianus goes on to assail the vanity and snobbishness of the contemporary Roman elite, he cites such moral exemplars as Cato the Censor, Publicola, Regulus, and Scipio, suggesting their continued relevance, if only as a yardstick with which to measure present failures.[3] Elsewhere, and perhaps more often, incommensurability is suggested. Certainly the supposed protection of freedom under the law has been rendered a phantom by the description of the savagery of Gallus Caesar with which this book of Ammianus' *Res Gestae* begins.[4] Later in the text, we learn that even the emperor Julian was incapable of drawing the proper strategic lessons from Polybius' description of the capture of Carthage by Scipio Aemilianus.[5] Rome's status as a *lieu de mémoire* certainly seems to have been affected by the transfer of the Imperial seat to Constantinople.[6]

Ammianus' preoccupation with the memory of the Roman Republic is, of course, beyond the limited scope of the present study. It deserves brief mention nevertheless, if only to provide a necessary perspective from which to assess what has been accomplished here and determine what sort of larger claims are warranted. Although it may be true to say that the memory of the Republic underwent significant transformation during the period examined in this book, such a claim is meaningless without sufficient contextualization. Transformation, yes, but from what to what? It is not as though the Republic and the Principate were fundamentally incompatible ideas under Nero, but emerged into a happy reconciliation in the reign of Trajan. Nor is it legitimate to suggest that the myth of *respublica restituta*

---

[2] Florus, *praef.* 4–8. The application of the biological metaphor to constitutional history can be traced back at least as far as Polybius, 6.9.11–14, 6.51.4–8, etc. See also Barnes (1998: 173–5).

[3] Amm. Marc. 14.6.8–11, cf. 28.4.6–34, Matthews (2007: 414–16).

[4] Amm. Marc. 14.1.5: *nec vox nec vox accusatoris ulla licet subditicii in his malorum quaerebatur acervis ut saltem specie tenus crimina praescriptis legum committerentur, quod aliquotiens fecere principes saevi.* Cf. 30.4.3–22, Matthews (2007: 251–2).

[5] Amm. Marc. 24.2.16–17, Barnes (1990: 67–8).

[6] Amm. Marc. 16.10.13–17, Behrwald (2009: 78–86).

simply ceased to be important after some generational benchmark.[7] If the Republic had lost its meaning, why continue to remember it at all?

Although the preceding chapters are ordered chronologically, this book is not meant as a seamless account of the gradual progression of the Republican heritage from one location in Roman memory to another in the years between Nero's fall and Trajan's ascendancy. Instead, what I have tried to accomplish is to describe the involvement of the Republic, or rather the involvement of various concepts associated with the Republic, over as broad a range of the Roman cultural landscape as possible during the period in question. Republican tradition affected not just political and constitutional questions, but everything from literary aesthetics and architecture to issues of religious and moral authority. Tracing the multiple facets of Republican memory may strain the argument's cohesiveness at points, but even that is not entirely accidental. If there is a unifying thesis for the above discussion, it is that the multiplicity of contexts in which the Republican past could be remembered contributed to the basic incoherence of "the Republic" itself as an object of Roman memory. Remembering necessarily entails an effort to make sense of the past and its remains, but it need not apply the same reasoning in every instance.

As we have seen in various contexts, one man's Republicanism could become another's accommodation to the Principate. Whether one supported the current regime or not, it was possible to insist on the continuity of Republican moral standards, while accepting, or indeed embracing, the new political realities of the emperor's unrestrained authority. The *exempla* of the great heroes of Republican history were equally available to senators who sought to carry on the old traditions, those who retreated into lives of literary leisure, and unrepentant time servers alike. In some contexts the conceptual link between a particular relic of the Republican past and the political circumstances in which it was believed to have originated could be difficult to break, but the mnemonic framework one applied was always open to interpretation. Emperors could and often did appeal to Republican *exempla* as well, but they could not always be sure that the meaning they hoped to extract from the past would align with the memories their actions prompted in others. Domitian and Cornelia approached the same events (and the same religious heritage) from radically different points of view.

The complexity of the situation was amplified by the fact that the range of available material from which to construct a concept of Roman identity under the Principate was not limited to Republican memories alone.

---

[7] *CIL* 6.1033 (= *ILS* 425, Arch of Septimius Severus), cf. Gowing (2005: 151).

Emperors and their subjects had an ever-increasing stock of more recent examples to consider, such as those of Augustus and Agrippa, Claudius and his trusted advisor Vitellius, or even Nero and Thrasea Paetus. For the iconography of a commander in a triumphal chariot, Trajan did not have to go back to the coins of Dossenus to find a model. The image was also well established in Imperial art, as witnessed by material as diverse as the Arch of Titus and the Boscoreale cups.[8] By specifically invoking a Republican model in his series of restored coins, the emperor was able to make this connection clear, but the more recent contexts of Imperial image making remained available to any viewer who considered Trajanic iconography in its own right. Try as Trajan might to present himself as a continuator of the Republican ethos of military *virtus*, it would not be lost on certain members of his audience that his ability to triumph, like his claim to have restored *libertas* to the senate, was contingent on the power he exercised as emperor.

We may add to this growing store of Imperial memories the expanding cultural horizons of Roman Imperial culture, within which the Roman Republic came to be regarded as but one of many potential sources of authority. If anything threatened to undermine the continued vitality of the Republic as a touchstone of Roman identity during the period examined here, it was the willingness of the Roman elite to think of themselves in terms of Greek, rather than exclusively Roman, traditions. Or, to put it the other way around, perhaps the increasing acceptance of Greek cultural paradigms by members of the Roman elite can be attributed to their growing awareness of the distance that separated the Imperial present from its Republican past. The implied equivalence between Roman Republican and Greek *exempla* found in Silius' *Punica* and Frontinus' *Stratagems* constitutes an admission, albeit a tacit one, of how far the world of an Imperial senator stood apart from that of his Republican forebears.

Nevertheless, the Republic through its traces continued to assert itself as part of the cultural furniture of the world in which Imperial Romans lived. Every day, they read literature, examined monuments, and exchanged coins imbued with messages that originated in a Republican context. The advocate who donned a toga to go into the Forum and the Vestal virgin reciting prayers in her stola knew that they were participating in ancient cultural traditions, if only in the vaguest terms. They were surrounded by images and reports of figures from the past whose habits and dress were similar to their own. Every once in a while, when they were confronted with a portrait of Aemilia or the name of Tullius and stopped to consider some

---

[8] Kleiner (1992: 153–4, 187–8, figs. 129, 156), Pfanner (1983), Kuttner (1995).

particular *exemplum*, more specific narratives and historical frameworks began to impose themselves on the experience of social memory. As I have argued in the studies presented here, however, even as the memory of the Republic became an object of conscious contemplation, plenty of room could still be found to negotiate how to interpret the concepts and values embedded in these narratives. Whatever significance one chose to assign to these encounters with the past, it is clear that such moments of remembering the Republic remained an inescapable part of life under the Principate.

APPENDIX A: PLINY'S LETTER TO MINICIANUS (*EP.* 4.11)

C. Plinius Cornelio Miniciano suo[1]
s(alutavit)

(1) *Audistine Valerium Licinianum in Sicilia profiteri? nondum te puto audisse: est enim recens nuntius. praetorius hic modo inter eloquentissimos causarum actores habebatur; nunc eo decidit, ut exsul de senatore, rhetor de oratore fieret. (2) itaque ipse in praefatione dixit dolenter et graviter: "quos tibi, Fortuna, ludos facis? facis enim ex senatoribus professores, ex professoribus senatores." cui sententiae tantum bilis, tantum amaritudinis inest, ut mihi videatur ideo professus ut hoc diceret. (3) idem cum Graeco pallio amictus intrasset – carent enim togae iure, quibus aqua et igni interdictum est – postquam se composuit circumspexitque habitum suum, "Latine," inquit, "declamaturus sum."*

(4) dices tristia et miseranda, dignum tamen illum qui haec ipsa studia incesti scelere macularit. (5) confessus est quidem incestum, sed incertum utrum quia verum erat, an quia graviora metuebat si negasset. fremebat enim Domitianus aestuabatque in ingenti invidia destitutus. (6) nam cum Corneliam Vestalium maximam defodere vivam concupisset, ut qui illustrari saeculum suum eiusmodi exemplis arbitraretur, pontificis maximi

---

[1] *PIR*[2] C 1406, cf. Ep. 7.22.2: *ornamentum regionis meae.* The present letter touches on issues of rhetoric, law, and religion, which were all presumably shared interests of the author and his correspondent. Pliny was (or was soon to become) an augur: He joined the college in 104, following the death of Frontinus (*Ep.* 10.13, 4.8, Sherwin-White [1966: 79–80]. Minicianus held important priesthoods in the *municipia* of Cisalpina (*ILS* 2722), and Pliny also shares with him the details of the high-profile prosecution of Caecilius Classicus in letter 3.9.

iure,[2] *seu potius immanitate tyranni licentia domini, reliquos pontifices[3]
non in Regiam sed in Albanam villam convocavit. nec minore scelere quam
quod ulcisci videbatur, absentem inauditamque damnavit incesti, cum ipse
fratris filiam incesto non polluisset solum verum etiam occidisset; nam
vidua abortu periit.*

(7) *missi statim pontifices qui defodiendam necandamque curarent. illa
nunc ad Vestam, nunc ad ceteros deos manus tendens, multa sed hoc frequentissime clamitabat: "me Caesar incestam putat, qua sacra faciente
vicit triumphavit!"* (8) *blandiens haec an inridens, ex fiducia sui an ex
contemptu principis dixerit, dubium est. dixit donec ad supplicium, nescio
an innocens, certe tamquam innocens ducta est.* (9) *quin etiam cum in
illud subterraneum cubiculum demitteretur, haesissetque descendenti stola,
vertit se ac recollegit, cumque ei manum carnifex daret, aversata est et
resiluit foedumque contactum quasi plane a casto puroque corpore novissima sanctitate reiecit omnibusque numeris pudoris* πολλὴν πρόνοιαν ἔσχεν
εὐσχήμων πεσεῖν.[4] (10) *praeterea Celer[5] eques Romanus, cui Cornelia obi-
ciebatur, cum in comitio virgis caederetur, in hac voce perstiterat: "quid
feci? nihil feci."*

(11) *ardebat ergo Domitianus et crudelitatis et iniquitatis infamia.
arripit Licinianum, quod in agris suis occultasset Corneliae libertam. ille
ab iis quibus erat curae praemonetur, si comitium et virgas pati nollet, ad
confessionem confugeret quasi ad veniam. fecit.*

---

[2] Lovisi (1998: 716) suggests that the *pontifex maximus* decided *incestum* cases on his own and
was not bound by the majority decision of the pontifical college. Such may have been the reality
in Domitian's case (as Pliny implies, §6), but if this were the general rule, it seems strange that
the other *pontifices* were required to convene at all: cf. Cornell (1981: 30).

[3] For the possible influence of the other *pontifices* on Domitian's *clementia*, cf. the speculation
of Grelle (1980: 360–3) about the role of provincial *novi homines* such as Pegasus (*PIR²*
P 512) and Fabricius Veiento (*PIR²* F 91) in shaping Flavian moral policy. It is interesting
that Pegasus is the only member of Domitian's *consilium* to be praised by Juvenal, who
describes him as *interpres legum sanctissimus* (4.79). This influential jurist, who had risen to
prominence under Vespasian, probably died around 85: Champlin (1978: 278). Comparable
figures in the pontifical college at the start of Domitian's reign included C. Luccius Telesinus and
C. Rutilius Gallicus: *PIR²* L 366, R 248, Schumacher (1978: 667–8). Telesinus was reportedly
a friend of Apollonius who willingly went into exile when Domitian banished the philosophers
(Philostr. *VA* 4.40, 7.11.3–4). Gallicus, whom Statius (*Silv.* 1.4.4–6) celebrates as an invaluable
minister to the emperor, enjoyed the special honor of an iterated proconsulship of Asia: Eck
(1985: 480). He died in 92. Another *pontifex*, Cn. Julius Agricola (*PIR²* I 126), was away
campaigning in Britain during the first Vestal trial; Tacitus does not indicate whether he took
part in the second, which took place shortly before his death. On Domitian's *amici*, see also
Jones (1992: 50–7).

[4] Eur. *Hec.* 569. Quotations from Greek literature introduce a playful tone while advertising the
education and status of the writer and his addressee: Hoffer (1999: 219).

[5] Celer is a common name, and the identity of this equestrian is uncertain.

(12) *locutus est pro absente Herennius Senecio tale quiddam, quale est illud: "κεῖται Πάτροκλος."*[6] *ait enim: "ex advocato nuntius factus sum; Licinianus recessit."*[7] (13) *gratum hoc Domitiano adeo quidem ut gaudio proderetur, diceretque: "absolvit nos Licinianus." adiecit etiam non esse verecundiae eius instandum; ipsi vero permisit, si qua posset, ex rebus suis raperet, antequam bona publicarentur, exsiliumque molle velut praemium dedit.* (14) *ex quo tamen postea clementia divi Nervae translatus est in Siciliam, ubi nunc profitetur seque de fortuna praefationibus vindicat.*

(15) *vides quam obsequenter pareum tibi, qui non solum res urbanas verum etiam peregrinas tam sedulo scribo, ut altius repetam. et sane putabam te, quia tunc afuisti, nihil aliud de Liciniano audisse quam relegatum ob incestum. summam enim rerum nuntiat fama non ordinem.* (16) *mereor ut vicissim, quid in oppido tuo, quid in finitimis agatur – solent enim quaedam notabilia incidere – perscribas, denique quidquid voles dum modo non minus longa epistula nuntia. ego non paginas tantum sed versus etiam syllabasque numerabo.*

vale.

C. PLINIUS SENDS GREETINGS TO HIS FRIEND CORNELIUS MINICIANUS

(1) Have you heard that Valerius Licinianus is lecturing in Sicily? I don't imagine you have heard this yet, since the news is quite fresh. Only recently, this man was a praetorian senator, considered to be among the most eloquent pleaders of cases. Now his downfall is such that he has been transformed from a senator into an exile and from an orator into a rhetor. (2) He even said as much in the preface to his speech, declaring gravely and morosely: "What games you play, Fortune! You make senators out of professors, professors out of senators." There is so much bile and bitterness in this phrase that it seems to me that he only took up lecturing so that he could speak it. (3) Although he had entered wrapped in a Greek *pallium* (because those to whom fire and water is forbidden also are deprived of the right to wear the toga), after he had arranged himself and contemplated his costume, he announced, "I shall declaim *in Latin*."

(4) You will say that this is sad and pitiable, but nevertheless what that man deserves, who sullied these very pursuits with the crime of *incestum*. (5) In fact, he confessed to *incestum*, but it is not clear whether this was

---

[6] Hom. *Il.* 18.22 (Antilochus). Senecio himself was soon to be condemned for his association with Helvidius Priscus: Tac. *Agr.* 2.1, 45.1, *PIR*² H 128.

[7] Note the reappearance of the theme of transformation (cf. §1).

because it was true, or because he feared something more dire if he were to deny it, since Domitian was grumbling and was all worked up and left bereft by a tremendous ill-will. (6) For, since he longed to bury the chief Vestal Cornelia alive so that he might be thought to have enlightened his age with *exempla* of this sort, employing the right of a *pontifex maximus* – or rather the enormity of a tyrant or license of a master – he convened the other *pontifices*, not at the Regia, but at his Alban villa. With no less of a crime than the one he appeared to be punishing, he condemned her for *incestum* absent and unheard. Meanwhile he not only defiled his brother's daughter with *incestum*, but in fact even killed her, since while a widow she died from an abortion.

(7) The *pontifices* were sent straightway to attend to her burial and murder. She, stretching her hands now to Vesta, now to the other gods, cried out many things, but this most often: "Caesar thinks that I am unchaste, though he has conquered and triumphed when I perform the rites!" (8) Whether she said these things in flattery or derision, out of faith in herself or contempt for the *princeps*, is ambiguous. (9) She said them up until her death. I do not know whether she was innocent, but certainly she at least was regarded as innocent. Even as she was being sent down into that underground chamber, when her stola impeded her as she was climbing down and she turned to gather it up, although the executioner offered his hand, she turned away and with a final display of holiness repelled that shameful contact as though from an obviously pure and chaste body. And with all the enumerations of modesty, *"elle eut grand soin de tomber avec décence."*

(10) Furthermore, there was the Roman knight Celer, with whom Cornelia was linked. When he was being executed in the Comitium under the whips, he remained steadfast with this statement: "What have I done? I have done nothing."

(11) Consequently, Domitian was driven into a rage by the stigma of cruelty and injustice. He arrested Licinianus because he had harbored a freedwoman of Cornelia in his lands. That man was forewarned by those whom he held dear that if he did not want to suffer the Comitium and the whips he should take refuge in confession as though it were a pardon. This, he did.

(12) In his absence, Herennius Senecio spoke on his behalf in the fashion of that famous *"Patrocle est mort."* He simply stated, "From an advocate, I have been turned into a messenger. Licinianus has withdrawn." (13) This was so gratifying to Domitian that he was betrayed by his joy as he said, "Licinianus has exonerated us." He was sure to add that there was no need to impose upon the man's modesty, and he allowed him to plunder from

his own property as he was able before these goods were confiscated by the public treasury. A soft exile was granted as though it were a reward. (14) Subsequently, through the clemency of divine Nerva, he relocated to Sicily, where he currently is lecturing and avenging himself on fortune in his prefaces.

(15) You see how obediently I attend to you, since I write not only about city matters but even about overseas events with such diligence that I go into them rather deeply. And clearly I concluded that you, because you were away at the time, had heard nothing else about Licinianus than that he had been exiled for *incestum*. Rumor presents the outcomes rather than the full sequence of events.

(16) In response, I deserve to have you write out what is happening in your town and in the area (since notable things sometimes happen there) and then to tell me about whatever you wish, so long as the letter is just as long as this one. I will be counting not just the pages, but also the lines and even the syllables!

Farewell.

APPENDIX B: REPUBLICAN *DENARII* RESTORED BY TRAJAN

This appendix presents, in tabular form, the following information about Trajan's restored silver coinage:

Coin:	Numbering follows Mattingly (1926).
Obverse:	As described.
Reverse:	As described, with IMP CAES TRAIAN AVG GER DAC P P REST around on all.
Exemplar:	Unless otherwise indicated, exemplars are cited according to their number in Crawford, *RRC*.
Attribution:	Provides name of moneyer, followed, in square brackets, by those of other individuals with whom the coin might reasonably have been associated. *RE* numbers are given in parentheses.
Date:	Provides date of original issue. All dates are BC. In the event of a discrepancy, Crawford's date is listed first, followed by that of Mattingly in parentheses.
Size:	Estimated number of dies of original issue, after Crawford, *RRC*.

ANNOTATIONS:

† – Obverse legend not on original.
†† – Details altered from original.
*– Moneyer otherwise unknown.
§ – Original was serrated.
‡ – Reproduces control mark from original.

Coin	Obverse	Reverse	Exemplar	Attribution	Date	Size
1	Janiform head of Dioscuri.	Jupiter in quadriga driven by victory with thunderbolt and scepter, ROMA incuse on tablet below.	28/3, 31–34	anonymous	225–212 (c. 268)	huge
2	Helmeted head of Roma r., COCLES† in front, X behind.	Dioscuri on horseback charging r. over female head, ROMA below.	127/1	anonymous [Horatius (9) Cocles]	206–200 (c. 170)	[20]/ [25]
3	Helmeted head of Roma r., DECIVS in front, MVS† and X behind.	Dioscuri on horseback charging r. over crossed shield and trumpet (*carynx*), ROMA below.	128/1	anonymous [P. Decius (15) Mus]	206–200 (c. 170)	[<10]/ [<12]
4	Helmeted head of Roma r., ROMA behind.	Victory with palm branch in *quadriga* r., wreath above, X and M TVLLI below.	280/1	M. Tullius (11)* [M. Tullius (29) Cicero]	120 (133)	[163]/ [204]
5	Helmeted head of Roma r., X behind, ROMA below.	Roma seated r. on shields, with spear, helmet at feet, she-wolf and twins in front, two prows in field.††	287/1	anonymous	115/114 (c. 120)	[82]/ [102]
6	Helmeted head of Roma, r., ✳ below, Λ°A behind.	Two combatants, one with whip and shield, other with sword and shield, T DEIDI in ex.	294/1	T. Didius (5)	113/112 (c. 115)	[73]/ [91]

(continued)

(continued)

Coin	Obverse	Reverse	Exemplar	Attribution	Date	Size
7	Laureate bust of Hercules l., in lion skin with club on shoulder.	Two horses galloping l. with rider (*desultor*) on nearer, rat and TI Q below, D S S incuse on tablet in ex., ·S above.‡	297/1	Ti. Quinctius [Ti. Quinctius (45) Flamininus]	112 (110)	(87)/ 109
8	Helmeted head of Mars l.	Two combatants, one protecting fallen comrade with shield, other with horned helmet, Q THERM M F in ex.	319/1	Q. Thermus Minucius (66)	103	[253]/ [316]
8a	Laureate head of Jupiter l., Q in front.‡	Jupiter in *quadriga* galloping r. with scepter and thunderbolt, L SCIP ASIAG in ex.	311/1b	L. Cornelius (338) Scipio Asiagenus [L. Cornelius (337) Scipio Asiagenus]	106 (c. 102)	[143]/ [179]
9	Draped female bust (Libertas?) r., with hair in rolls and knotted at back, ROMA behind, M. CATO below.	Victory seated r. with *patera* and palm branch, VIC|RIX in ex.	343/1b	M. Porcius Cato (not in *RE*) [M. Porcius (9) Cato Censorius; M. Porcius (20) Cato Uticensis]	89 (c. 100)	[116]/ [129]
10	Male head (Mutinus Titinus?) r., with winged diadem and pointed beard.	Pegasus springing r. from tablet inscribed Q. TITI.	341/1	Q. Titius (33) Mutto*	90	[252]/ [280]

	Obverse	Reverse		Moneyer		
11(a)	Laureate head of Jupiter r., scepter and DOSSEN behind.	Victory in triumphal *quadriga* with wreath, thunderbolt, or eagle on side r., L RVBRI in ex.	348/1	L. Rubrius (17) Dossenus*	87 (89)	[187]/[208]
11(b)	Diademed, veiled head of Juno r., scepter and DOS behind.	Similar to 11(a).	348/2	"	"	[90]/[100]
11(c)	Helmeted bust of Minerva r., with *aegis*, DOS behind.	As on 11(a) but, above *quadriga*, Victory in *biga*, and bird on side of chariot.	348/3	"	"	[67]/[73]
12	Bust of Mercury r., with cloak and *petasus*, *caduceus* and letter E behind.‡	Ulysses walking r., welcomed by Argus on l., C MAMIL on l., LIMETĀN on r.	362/1§	C. Mamilius (8) Limetanus	82 (84)	[100]/[111]
13	Diademed bust of Venus r., C NORBANUS below, CCIII behind.‡	*Fasces* with ax, between ear of corn on l. and *caduceus* on r.	357/1b	C. Norbanus (6 and 9a)	83 (c. 84)	[156]/[173]
14	Winged, draped, bust of Victory r., *caduceus* in front.‡	Eagle between standards inscribed with H on l. and reversed P on r., C. \A_ FLA on l, IMPERAT on r., EX S C in field.	365/1c	C. Valerius (168) Flaccus [C. Valerius (170) Flaccus]	82 (83)	36/(39)

(continued)

(*continued*)

Coin	Obverse	Reverse	Exemplar	Attribution	Date	Size
15	Diademed bust of Pietas r., stork in front.	Elephant with bell hanging from neck walking l., Q C M P I in ex.	374/1	Q. Caecilius (98) Metellus Pius [L. Caecilius (72) Metellus]	81 (c. 79–7)	[88]/[98]
16	Draped bust of Ceres in corn wreath r., CAPIT LXXV behind, flower in front.‡	Farmer plowing l., C MARI · C F S C in ex.	378/1c§	C. Marius (33) Capito* [C. Marius (14)]	81 (c. 80)	100/100
17(a)	Radiate head of Sol r.	Crescent moon and seven stars, L LVCRETI below, TRIO above	390/1	L. Lucretius (33) Trio* [T. Lucretius (17) Carus?]	76	[32]/[36]
17(b)	Laureate head of Neptune r., trident behind shoulder.	Genius on dolphin r., L LVCRETI TRIO below.	390/2	"	76	[80]/[89]
18	Diademed head of Apollo with hair in ringlets r., ✶ under chin, ROMA behind.	Macedonian shield with elephant head at center, M METELLVS Q F around, laurel wreath encircling.	369/1	anonymous; M. Caecilius (77) Metellus [Q. Caecilius (94) Metellus Macedonicus; L. Caecilius (72) Metellus]	82–80 (82)	[<10]/[<11]
19	Draped and veiled bust of Vesta r., S C behind.	Sacrificial knife, *simpulum*, and axe, P GALB in ex., AE CVR l. and r. in field.	406/1	P. Sulpicius (55) Galba	69 (70)	[48]/[53]

20	Draped and veiled bust of Vestal Aemilia, *simpulum* beneath chin.	Facade of Basilica Aemilia adorned with shields, AEMILIA above, M. LEPIDVS below, REF on l., S C on r.	419/3b	M. Aemilius (73) Lepidus [Aemilia (150b); L. Aemilius (81) Paullus; M. Aemilius (68) Lepidus]	61 (65)	[<10]/ [<11]
21	Head of Flora r., in wreath of flowers, *lituus* behind, FLORA_ PRIMUS.	Two combatants with swords, C SERVEIL in ex., C F on r. in field.	423/1	C. Servilius (*RE* 16)* [C. Servilius (78) Pulex Geminus; C. Servilius (32) Ahala]	57 (c. 65)	[99]/ [110]
22	Diademed head of Libertas r., LIBERTAS behind.	L. Junius Brutus advancing l., between two lictors, preceded by herald, BRVTVS below.	433/1	M. Iunius (53) Brutus [L. Iunius (46a) Brutus]	54 (59)	[156]/ [173]
23(a)	Diademed bust of Diana r., with crescent on brow, *lituus* behind, FAVSTVS in front.	Bocchus, kneeling r., presenting branch to Sulla, seated l. on platform, Jugurtha kneeling l., with hands bound on r., FELIX on r. in field.	426/1	Faustus Cornelius (377) Sulla [L. Cornelius (392) Sulla Felix]	56 (60)	[<30]/ [<33]
23(b)	Diademed bust of Hercules (Sulla?) r., with lion skin on shoulders, FELIX above.	Diana holding *lituus* in *biga* galloping r., crescent above head, two stars above, star and FAVSTVS below.	426/2	"	"	[<30]/ [<33]

(continued)

(continued)

Coin	Obverse	Reverse	Exemplar	Attribution	Date	Size
24(a)	Draped, diademed bust of Vesta r., Q CASSIVS behind, VEST in front.	Temple of Vesta with *curule* chair inside, urn on l., tablet inscribed A C on r.	428/1	L. Cassius (65) Longinus [L. Cassius (72) Longinus Ravilla]	55 (58)	[36]/[40]
24(b)	Head of Liberty r., Q. CASSIVS in front, LIBERT behind.	similar to 24(a)	428/2	"	"	[60]/[67]
25	King Aretas kneeling r., offering branch and holding camel by reins, M · SCAVR · AED · CVR · above, EX S · C · l. and r. in field, REX ARETAS in ex.	Jupiter in *quadriga* l., scorpion below horses, P · HYPSAE · AED · CVR · above, C · HYPSAE · COS · PREIVE · CAPTV in ex.	422/1b	M. Aemilius (141) Scaurus; P. Plautius (18) Hypsaeus [M. Aemilius (140) Scaurus]	58	[336]/[373]
26	Diademed head of Bonus Eventus r., BON · EVENT · in front, LIBO behind.	Puteal Scribonianum, ornamented with lyres and laurel branch,†† PVTEAL above, SCRIBON below.	416/1	L. Scribonius (20) Libo [L. Scribonius (16) Libo]	62 (56)	[206]/[229]
27	Diademed, veiled head of Concordia r., CONCORDIA in front, PAVLLVS LEPIDVS behind.	L. Aemilius Paullus standing l., by trophy, by which on l. are Perseus and two children: TER above, PAVLLVS below.	415/1	L. Aemilius (81) Lepidus Paullus [L. Aemilius (114) Paullus]	62 (c. 56)	[240]/[267]

	Obverse	Crawford	Reverse	Moneyer	Date	Ref.
28	Diademed head of Ancus Marcius r., *lituus* behind, ANCVS below.	425	Equestrian statue r., on aqueduct with AQVA MAR · between arches, branch below horse, PHILIPPVS behind.	L. Marcius (74 and 77) Philippus [Ancus Marcius; Q. Marcius (90) Rex?]	56 (c. 54)	[447]/ [497]
29	Laureate, bearded head of Quirinus r., C MEMMI C F in front, QVIRINVS behind.	427/2	Ceres seated r., holding corn ear and torch, dragon at feet, MEMMIVS AED · CERIALIA PREIMVS FECIT around.	C. Memmius (9) [Memmius (1)]	56 (c. 58)	[39]/ [43]
30	*Apex, securis, aspergillum, simpulum.*	443/1	Elephant trampling dragon r., CAESAR beneath.	C. Iulius (131) Caesar	49–48 (bef. 49)	[750]/ [833]
31	Diademed head of Venus r.	458/1	Aeneas hurrying l., holding palladium, Anchises on shoulders, CAESAR in field on r.	"	47–46 (c. 48)	[390]/ [433]
32	Head of Moneta r., MONETA behind.	464/2	Anvil with punch die above, tongs on l., hammer on r., CARISIVS above,†† laurel wreath encircling.	T. Carissius (2)	46 (45)	[120]/ [133]
33	Head of Africa in elephant skin r., corn ear in front, plough below, Q METELL on r., SCIPIO IMP on l.	461/1	Hercules standing front, resting l. arm on club and lion skin, EPPIVS on r., LEG F C on l.	Q. Caecilius (99) Metellus Scipio; Eppius (2) [L. Caecilius (72) Metellus?]	47–46	[<30]/ [<33]

(continued)

(*continued*)

Coin	Obverse	Reverse	Exemplar	Attribution	Date	Size
34(a)	Radiate head of Sol r., *acisculus* and ACISCVLVS behind.	Diana with whip, in *biga* galloping r., L VALERIVS in ex.	474/5	L. Valerius (94) Acisculus	45	[<30]/ [<33]
34(b)	Apollo® with bound hair r., star above, *acisculus* and ACISCVLVS behind.	Europa on bull r., veil floating behind, L. VALERIVS in ex.	474/1a	"	"	[72]/ [80]
35	Bare head of consul M. Claudius Marcellus r., *triskelis* behind, MARCELLINVS in front.	Marcellus carrying trophy r., about to mount steps to temple of Jupiter Feretrius, MARCELLVS on r., COS. QVINQ. on l.	439/1	P. Cornelius (232) Lentulus Marcellinus [M. Claudius (220) Marcellus]	50 (44)	[30]/ [33]
36	Bearded head of Brutus? (Ser. Sulpicius Rufus?) r., L. SERVIVS RVFVS around.	Dioscuri standing front, holding spears and swords.	515/2	L. Servius (6) Rufus* [Ser. Sulpicius (95) Rufus; M. Iunius (53) Brutus]	41 (43)	[30]/ [33]
37	Laureate head of Apollo r., lyre behind.	Diana Lucifera standing front, head r., with long torch in each hand, P CLODIVS on r., M · F · on l.	494/23	P. Clodius (10)* [P. Clodius (48) Pulcher?]	42	[363]/ [403]

38	Bare head of man (Numonius Vaala?) r., C. NVMONIVS VAALA around.	Soldier attacking l., rampart defended by two enemies, VAALA in ex.	514/2	C. Numonius (1) Vaala	41 (43)	[<30/ <33]
39	Bare head of praetor L. Regulus r.	Modius between two corn ears, L. LIVINEIVS above, REGVLVS in ex.	494/29	L. Livineius (3) Regulus* [L. Livineius (see 2) Regulus M. Atilius (51) Regulus?]	42	[<30/ <33]
40	Head of Ceres/Tanit l., in wreath of corn ears.	Veiled, togate Q. Cornuficius with lituus, standing l., crowned by Juno Sospita standing l., in goat skin with sword and shield, raven on shoulder, Q CORNVFICI · AVGVR IMP around.	509/5	Q. Cornuficius (8)	42	[<30/ <33]
41	Bare head of Pompey the Great r., lituus in front, jug behind, MAG PIVS IMP ITER around.	The Catanaean brothers with parents on shoulders, Neptune, standing l. between them, with r. foot on prow, holding acrostolium, PRAEF above, CLAS · ET · ORAE MARIT · EX S · C in ex.	511/3a	Sex. Pompeius (33) Magnus [Cn. Pompeius (31) Magnus]	42–40	[51/ 57]

(continued)

(continued)

Coin	Obverse	Reverse	Exemplar	Attribution	Date	Size
42	Bare head of Octavian r., CAESAR III VIR R · P · C · around.	Laurel wreath set on curule chair, inscribed CAESAR DIC PER.	497/2b	C. Iulius (132) Caesar Augustus [C. Iulius (131) Caesar]	42 (43)	[<30]/ [<33]
43(a)	Bare head of Augustus r., AVGVSTVS in front.	Equestrian statue of Agrippa r., carrying trophy, on platform ornamented with two prows, COSSVS CN F LENTVLVS around.	RIC I² 73, 412	Cossus Cornelius (182) Lentulus [C. Iulius (132) Caesar Augustus; M. Vipsanius (2) Agrippa]	12	
43(b)	Laureate head of Augustus r., AVGVSTVS COS · XI around.	Head of Agrippa r., in rostral and mural crown, M. AGRIPPA COS · TER. COSSVS LENTVLVS around.	RIC I² 73, 414	"	"	

⊗ – Obverse listed by Mattingly "As on No. 34 (a)", but Robertson (1971: 73) identifies it as Apollo. See also Komnick (2001: 122–3).

BIBLIOGRAPHY

Abdy, R., and Harling, N. (2005) "Two Important New Roman Coins," *NC* 165: 175–8.

Adam, T. (1970) *Clementia Principis: der Einfluß hellenistischer Fürstenspiegel auf den Versuch einer rechlichen Fundierun des Principats durch Seneca.* Stuttgart.

Adcock, F. E. (1952) "A Note on *Res Gestae Divi Augusti* 34,3," *JRS* 42: 10–12.

Adcock, F. E. (1956) *Caesar as a Man of Letters.* Cambridge.

Ahl, F. (1976) *Lucan: An Introduction.* Ithaca.

Ahl, F. (1984) "The Art of Safe Criticism in Greece and Rome," *AJP* 105: 174–208.

Ahl, F., Davis, M. A., and Pomeroy, A. (1986) "Silius Italicus," *ANRW* II.32.4: 2492–561.

Albrecht, M. von (1964) *Silius Italicus: Freiheit und Gebundenheit römischer Epik.* Amsterdam.

Albrecht, M. von (1999) *Roman Epic: An Interpretative Introduction.* Leiden.

Alföldi, A. (1963) *Early Rome and the Latins.* Ann Arbor.

Alföldy, G. (1980) *Die Rolle des Einzelnen in der Gesellschaft des Römischen Kaiserreiches: Erwartungen und Wertmaßstäbe.* Heidelberg.

Alföldy, G. (1995) "Eine Bauinschrift aus dem Colosseum," *ZPE* 109: 195–226.

Alföldy, G., and Halfmann, H. (1973) "M. Cornelius Nigrinus Curiatius Maternus, General Domitians und Rivale Trajans," *Chiron* 3: 331–73.

Allen, W., Jr. (1944) "Cicero's House and *Libertas*," *TAPA* 75: 1–9.

Anderson, J. C., Jr. (1982) "Domitian, the Argiletum, and the Temple of Peace," *AJP* 86: 101–10.

Anderson, J. C., Jr (1984) *The Historical Topography of the Imperial Fora.* Coll. Latomus 182. Brussels.

Ando, C. (2000) *Imperial Ideology and Provincial Loyalty in the Roman Empire.* Berkeley.

Andrews, A. C. (1938) "Pliny the Younger, Conformist," *CJ* 34: 143–54.

Appel, G. (1909, repr. 1975) *De Romanorum precationibus.* New York.

Arena, V. (2007a) "*Libertas* and *Virtus* of the Citizen in Cicero's *De Republica*," *SCI* 26: 39–66.

Arena, V. (2007b) "Invocation to Liberty and Invective of *Dominatus* at the End of the Roman Republic," *BICS* 50: 49–73.

Arnim, H. von (1903–5) *Stoicorum veterum fragmenta*, 3 vols. Leipzig.

Ash, R. (1997) "Severed Heads: Individual Portraits and Irrational Forces in Plutarch's *Galba* and *Otho*," in *Plutarch and His Intellectual World*, ed. J. Mossman: 189–214. London.

Ashby, T. (1927) *The Roman Campagna in Classical Times*. London.

Assmann, A. (1999) *Erinnerungsraüme: Formen und Wandlungen des kulturellen Gedächtnisses*. Munich.

Assmann, J. (1988) "Kollektives Gedächtnis und kulturelle Identität," in *Kultur und Gedächtnis*, ed. J. Assmann and T. Hölscher: 9–19. Frankfurt am Main.

Assmann, J. (1992) *Das kulturelle Gedächtnis: Schrift, Erinnerung und politische Identität in frühen Hochkulturen*. Munich.

Assmann, J. (1997a) *Moses the Egyptian: The Memory of Egypt in Western Monotheism*. Cambridge, MA.

Assmann, J. (1997b) *Das kulturelle Gedächtnis: Schrift, Erinnerung und politische Identität in frühen Hochkulturen*, 2nd ed. Munich.

Assmann, J. (2000) *Religion und kulturelle Gedächnis. Zehn Studien*. Munich.

Assmann, J. (2006) *Religion and Cultural Memory: Ten Studies*, trans. R. Livingstone. Stanford.

Astin, A. E. (1963) "Augustus and 'Censoria Potestas'," *Latomus* 22: 226–35.

Astin, A. E. (1978) *Cato the Censor*. Oxford.

Astin, A. E. (1988) "Regimen morum," *JRS* 78: 14–34.

Augoustakis, A. (2006) "Coniunx in limine primo: Regulus and Marcia in Punica 6," *Ramus* 35: 144–68.

Augoustakis, A. (ed.) (2010) *Brill's Companion to Silius Italicus*. Leiden.

Austin, R. G. (1948) *Quintiliani Institutionis oratoriae liber XII*. Oxford.

Badian, E. (1968) Rev. of Degrassi, *ILLRP*. *JRS* 58: 240–9.

Baldwin, B. (1975) "Vespasian and Freedom," *RFIC* 103: 306–8.

Balsdon, J. P. V. D. (1951) "Sulla Felix," *JRS* 41: 1–10.

Baltrusch, E. (1989) *Regimen morum: die Reglementierung des Privatlebens der Senatoren und Ritter in der römischen Republik und frühen Kaiserzeit*. Vestigia 41. Munich.

Bardon, H. (1952) *La Littérature latine inconnue. Tome I: L'époque républicaine*. Paris.

Bardon, H. (1956) *La Littérature latine inconnue. Tome II: L'époque impériale*. Paris.

Barnes, T. D. (1981) "Curiatius Maternus," *Hermes* 109: 382–4.

Barnes, T. D. (1986) "The Significance of Tacitus' *Dialogus de Oratoribus*," *HSCP* 90: 225–44.

Barnes, T. D. (1990) "Literary Convention, Nostalgia and Reality in Ammianus Marcellinus," in *Reading the Past in Late Antiquity*, ed. G. Clarke: 59–92. Singapore.

Barnes, T. D. (1998) *Ammianus Marcellinus and the Representation of Historical Reality*. Ithaca.

Barrow, R. H. (1967) *Plutarch and His Times*. Bloomington.

Barry, W. D. (2008) "Exposure, Mutilation, and Riot: Violence at the Scalae Gemoniae in Early Imperial Rome," *G&R* n.s. 55: 222–46.

Bartlett, F. (1932) *Remembering*. Cambridge.

Bartman, E. (1992) *Ancient Sculptural Copies in Miniature*. Leiden.

Bartsch, S. (1994) *Actors in the Audience: Theatricality and Double Speak from Nero to Hadrian*. Cambridge, MA.

Barwick, C. (1964) *Charisii artis grammaticae libri V*. corr. ed. Leipzig.

Barwick, K. (1954) *Der Dialogus de Oratoribus des Tacitus. Motive und Zeit seiner Entstehung*. Berlin.

Barzanò, A. (1984) "La distruzione del Campidoglio nell'anno 69 d.C.," in Sordi (1984), 107–20.

Bassett, E. L. (1966) "Hercules and the Hero of the Punica," in *The Classical Tradition: Literary and Historical Studies in Honor of Harry Caplan*, ed. L. Wallach: 258–73. Ithaca.

Bauman, R. A. (1974) *Impietas in Principem: A Study of Treason against the Roman Emperor with Special Reference to the First Century A.D.* Munich.

Bauman, R. A. (1996) *Crime and Punishment in Ancient Rome*. London and New York.

Beard, M. (1980) "The Sexual Status of Vestal Virgins," *JRS* 70: 12–27.

Beard, M. (1995) "Re-Reading (Vestal) Virginity," in *Women in Antiquity: New Assessments*, ed. R. Hawley and B. Levick: 166–77. London.

Beard, M. (2003) "The Triumph of Flavius Josephus," in Boyle and Dominick (2003), 543–58.

Beard, M. (2007) *The Roman Triumph*. Cambridge, MA.

Beard, M., North, J., and Price, S. (1998) *Religions of Rome: Volume 1–A History*. Cambridge.

Beck, M. (2001) "Das dramatische Datum des *Dialogus de Oratoribus*." *RhM* 144: 159–71.

Behrwald, R. (2009) *Die Stadt als Museum? Die Wahrnehmung der Monumente Roms in der Spätantike*. Berlin.

Bell, A. A., Jr. (1989) "A Note on Revision and Authenticity in Pliny's Letters," *AJPh* 110: 440–66.

Bell, D. S. (2003) "Mythscapes: Memory, Mythology, and National Identity," *British Journal of Sociology* 54: 63–81.

Bell, S. (2008) "Role Models in the Roman World," in *Role Models in the Roman World: Identity and Assimilation*, ed. S. Bell and I. L. Hansen. MAAR Suppl. 7: 1–39. Ann Arbor.

Belloni, G. G. (1973) *Le monete di Traiano: Catalogo del Civico Gabinetto numismatico, Museo archeologico di Milano*. Milan.

Benario, H. W. (1979) "Agricola's Proconsulship," *RhM* 122: 169–72.

Bendz, G. (1938) *Die Echtheitsfrage des vierten Buches der frontinschen Stratege-mata*. (Diss. Lund).

Bengtson, H. (1979) *Die Flavier: Vespasian, Titus, Domitian. Geschichte eines römischen Kaiserhauses*. Munich.

Benjamin, W. (1969) "The Work of Art in the Age of Mechanical Reproduction," in *Illuminations*, 217–51. New York.

Bennett, C. E. (ed. and trans.) (1925) *Frontinus. The Stratagems. The Aqueducts of Rome*. LCL 174. Cambridge, MA.

Bennett, J. (1997) *Trajan, Optimus Princeps: A Life and Times*. Bloomington, IN.

Béranger, J. (1953) *Recherches sur l'aspect idéologique du principat*. Basel.

Béranger, J. (1973) *Principatus*. Geneva.

Berlin, I. (1969) *Four Essays on Liberty*. New York.

Bernardo, Y. (2000) *Severitas: A Study of a Roman Virtue in Cicero* (Diss. University of North Carolina).

Berriman, A., and Todd, M. (2001) "A Very Roman Coup: The Hidden War of Imperial Succession, AD 96–8," *Historia* 50: 312–31.

Beutel, F. (2000) *Vergangenheit als Politik: Neue Aspekte im Werk des jüngeren Plinius*. Frankfurt am Main.

Bianco, E. (1968) "Indirizzi programmatici e propagandistici nella monetazione di Vespasiano," *RIN⁵* 16: 145–224.

Billerbeck, M. (1986) "Aspects of Stoicism in Flavian Epic," *Papers of the Liver-pool Latin Seminar* 5: 341–56. Liverpool.

Birley, A. R. (2000a) "The Life and Death of Cornelius Tacitus," *Historia* 49: 230–47.

Birley, A. R. (2000b) "Senators as Generals," in *Kaiser, Heer und Gesellschaft in den römischen Kaiserzeit: Gedenkschrift für Eric Birley*, ed. G. Alföldy et al.: 97–119. Stuttgart.

Birley, A. R. (2005) *The Roman Government of Britain*. Oxford.

Blackman, D. R., and Hodge, A. T. (2001) *Frontinus' Legacy. Essays on Frontinus' De aquis urbis Romae*. Ann Arbor.

Blanckenhagen, P. H. von (1940) *Flavische Architektur und ihre Dekoration: Untersucht am Nervaforum*. Berlin.

Bleicken, J. (1972) *Staatliche Ordnung und Freiheit in der römischen Republik*. Kallmünz.

Bleicken, J. (1975, repr. 2004) s.v. "Freiheit II.2. Römische libertas," in *Geschichtliche Grundbegriffe: Historisches Lexicon zur politische-sozialen Sprache in Deutschland*, ed. O. Brunner et al. Vol. 2: 430–5. Stuttgart.

Bloomer, W. M. (1992) *Valerius Maximus and the Rhetoric of the New Nobility*. London.

Bloomer, W. M. (1997) "A Preface to the History of Declamation: Whose Speech? Whose History?" in Habinek and Schiesaro (1997), 199–215.

Blösel, W. (2000) "Die Geschichte des Begriffes *mos maiorum* von den Anfängen bis zu Cicero," in Linke and Stemmler (2000), 25–97.

Bo, D. (1993) *Le principali problematiche del Dialogus de oratoribus. Panoramica storico-critica dal 1426 al 1990.* Hildesheim.

Boatwright, M. T. (1984) "Tacitus on Claudius and the Pomerium: *Annals* 12.23.2–24," *CJ* 80: 36–44.

Boatwright, M. T. (1991) "The Imperial Women of the Early Second Century A.C.," *AJP* 112: 513–40.

Bobzien, S. (1998) *Determinism and Freedom in Stoic Philosophy.* Oxford.

Bodel, J. (1999) "Punishing Piso," *AJP* 120: 45–51.

Boesche, R. (1987) "The Politics of Pretence: Tacitus and the Political Theory of Despotism," *History of Political Thought* 8: 189–210.

Bömer, F. (1953) "Der Commentarius. Zur Vorgeschichte und literarischen Form der Schriften Caesars," *Hermes* 81: 210–50.

Bonneford, M. (1987) "Transferts de fonctions et mutation idéologique: le Capitole et le Forum d'Auguste," in *L'urbs: espace urbain et histoire (Ier siècle avant J.-C.–IIIe siècle apres J.-C.)* CEFR 98: 251–78. Rome.

Borgeaud, P. (1987) "Du mythe à l'idéologie: la tête du Capitole," *MusHelv* 44: 86–100.

Bowersock, G. W. (1969) *Greek Sophists in the Roman Empire.* Oxford.

Bowersock, G. W. (1983) *Roman Arabia.* Cambridge, MA.

Bowersock, G. W. (1990) "The Pontificate of Augustus," in Raaflaub and Toher (1990), 380–94.

Boyce A. A. (1938) "The Development of the Decemviri Sacris Faciundis" *TAPA* 69: 161–87.

Boyle, A. J., and Dominik, W. (eds.) (2003) *Flavian Rome.* Leiden.

Bradley, K. R. (1978) "The Career of Titus Clodius Eprius Marcellus, cos. II A.D. 74. Some Possibilities," *SymbOslo* 53: 171–81.

Bradley, K. R. (1984) *Slaves and Masters in the Roman Empire: A Study in Social Control.* Coll. Latomus 185. Brussels.

Bradley, K. R. (1994) *Slavery and Society at Rome.* Cambridge.

Briessmann, A. (1955) *Tacitus und das flavische Geschichtsbild.* Hermes Einzelschriften 10. Weisbaden.

Brilliant, R. (1999) "'Let the Trumpets Roar!' The Roman Triumph," in *The Art of Ancient Spectacle*, ed. B. Bergmann and C. Kondoleon. Studies in the History of Art 56: 221–9. Ithaca.

Brink, C. O. (1972) "Ennius and the Hellenistic Worship of Homer," *AJP* 93: 547–67.

Brink, C. O. (1989) "Quintilian's *de Causis Corruptae Eloquentiae* and Tacitus' *Dialogus de Oratoribus*," *CQ* 39: 472–503.

Brink, C. O. (1993) "History in the 'Dialogus de Oratoribus' and Tacitus the Historian: A New Approach to an Old Source," *Hermes* 121: 335–49.

Brink, C. O. (1994) "Can Tacitus' *Dialogus* Be Dated? Evidence and Historical Conclusions," *HSCP* 96: 251–80.

Brunt, P. A. (1959) "The Revolt of Vindex and the Fall of Nero," *Latomus* 18: 531–59.

Brunt, P. A. (1963) "Augustan Imperialism," *JRS* 53: 170–6.

Brunt, P. A. (1966) "The 'Fiscus' and Its Development," *JRS* 56: 75–97.

Brunt, P. A. (1975) "Stoicism and the Principate," *PBSR* 43: 7–35.

Brunt, P. A. (1977) "*Lex de imperio Vespasiani*," *JRS* 67: 95–116.

Brunt, P. A. (1980) "Free Labour and Public Works at Rome," *JRS* 70: 81–100.

Brunt, P. A. (1984) "The Role of the Senate in the Augustan Regime," *CQ* n.s. 34: 423–44.

Brunt, P. A. (1988) *The Fall of the Roman Republic and Related Essays*. Oxford.

Brunt, P. A. (1990) *Roman Imperial Themes*. Oxford.

Brunt, P. A., and Moore, J. M. (1967) *Res Gestae Divi Augusti: The Achievements of the Divine Augustus*. Oxford.

Bruun, C. (1991) *The Water Supply of Ancient Rome. A Study of Roman Imperial Administration*. Helsinki.

Buckland, W. W. (1963) *A Textbook of Roman Law*, 3rd ed., rev. P. Stein. Cambridge.

Burck, E. (1984) *Silius Italicus: Hannibal in Capua und die Rückeroberung der Stadt durch die Römer*. Wiesbaden.

Burgess, J. F. (1972) "Statius' Altar of Mercy," *CQ* 22: 339–49.

Burke, P. (1989) "History as Social Memory," in *Memory: History, Culture and the Mind*, ed. T. Butler: 97–113. Oxford.

Burnett, A. (1999) "Buildings and Monuments on Roman Coins," in *Roman Coins and Public Life under the Empire*, ed. G. M. Paul: 137–64. Ann Arbor.

Buttrey, T. V. (1965) "The Morgantina Excavations and the Date of the Roman Denarius," *Congresso Internazionale di Numismatica Roma 1961* vol. II: 261–7. Rome.

Buttrey, T. V. (1972) "Vespasian as Moneyer," *NC⁷* 12: 89–109.

Buttrey, T. V. (1975) "Domitian's Perpetual Censorship and the Numismatic Evidence," *CJ* 1975: 26–34.

Buttrey, T. V. (1976) "Vespasian's Consecratio and the Numismatic Evidence," *Historia* 25: 449–57.

Callataÿ, G. de (1996) *Annus Platonicus. A Study of World Cycles in Greek, Latin, and Arabic Sources*. Louvain.

Cameron, A. (1967) "Tacitus and the Date of Curiatius Maternus' Death," *CR* n.s. 17: 258–61.

Camp, J. (2001) *The Archaeology of Athens*. New Haven.

Campbell, B. (1975) "Who Were the 'Viri Militares'?" *JRS* 65: 11–31.

Campbell, B. (1984) *The Emperor and the Roman Army, 31 BC–AD 235*. Oxford.

Campbell, B. (1987) "Teach Yourself How to Be a General," *JRS* 77: 13–29.

Campbell, B. (1996) "Shaping the Rural Environment: Surveyors in Ancient Rome," *JRS* 86: 74–99.

Cancik-Lindemaier, H. (1990) "Kultische Privilegierung und gesellschaftliche Realität: ein Beitrag zur Socialgeschichte der virgines Vestae," *Saeculum* 41: 1–16.

Canole, P., and Milns, R. D. (1983) "Neronian Frontier Policy in the Balkans: The Career of Ti. Plautius Silvanus," *Historia* 32: 183–200.

Caplan, H. (1970) *Of Eloquence: Studies in Ancient and Mediaeval Rhetoric.* Ithaca.

Carlon, J. M. (2009) *Pliny's Women.* Cambridge.

Carney, T. F. (1962) "The Picture of Marius in Valerius Maximus," *RhM* 105: 289–337.

Carruthers, M. J. (1990) *The Book of Memory. A Study of Memory in Medieval Culture.* Cambridge.

Casey, E. (1987) *Remembering: A Phenomological Study.* Bloomington.

Casson, L. (1978) "Unemployment, the Building Trade and Suetonius, *Vesp.* 18," *BASP* 15: 43–51.

Castagnoli, F. (1981) "Politica urbanistica di Vespasiano in Roma," in *Atti del Congresso Internazionale di Studi Vespasianei*, 261–75. Rieti.

Castelli, E. A. (2004) *Martyrdom and Memory.* New York.

Castritius, H. (1982) *Der römische Prinzipat als Republik.* Husum.

Chalon, G. (1964) *L'edit de Tiberius Iulius Alexander.* Olten.

Champion, C. (1994) *"Dialogus* 5.3–10.8: A Reconsideration of the Character of Marcus Aper," *Phoenix* 48: 152–63.

Champlin, E. (1978) "Pegasus" *ZPE* 32: 269–78.

Champlin, E. (1991) *Final Judgments: Duty and Emotion in Roman Wills, 200 B.C.–A.D. 250.* Berkeley.

Champlin, E. (2003) *Nero.* Cambridge, MA.

Changeux, J.-P., and Ricoeur, P. (2000) *What Makes Us Think? A Neuroscientist and a Philosopher Argue about Ethics, Human Nature, and the Brain.* Princeton.

Chaplin, J. D. (2000) *Livy's Exemplary History.* Oxford.

Charlesworth, M. P. (1937) "The Virtues of a Roman Emperor: Propaganda and the Creation of Belief," *PBA* 23: 105–33.

Charlesworth, M. P. (1939) "The Refusal of Divine Honors, an Augustan Formula," *PBSR* 15: 1–10.

Chassignet, M. (1996–2004) *L'annalistique Romaine*, 3 vols. Paris.

Chilton, C. W. (1955) "The Roman Law of Treason under the Early Principate," *JRS* 45: 73–81.

Chilver, G. E. F. (1957) "The Army in Politics A.D. 68–70," *JRS* 47: 29–35.

Chilver, G. E. F., and Townend, G. B. (1985) *A Historical Commentary on Tacitus' Histories IV and V.* Oxford.

Chioffi, L. (1996) *Gli elogia Augustei del Foro Romano: aspetti epigrafici e topografici.* Opuscula Epigraphica 7. Rome.

Cizek, E. (1972) *L'époque de Néron et ses controverses idéologiques.* Leiden.

Cizek, E. (1982) *Néron.* Paris.

Clark, A. C. (1907) *Q. Asconii Pediani Orationum Ciceronis Quinque Enarratio.* Oxford.

Clarke, M. L. (1967) "Quintilian: A Biographical Sketch," *G&R* n.s. 14: 24–37.

Clarke, M. L. (1981) *The Noblest Roman. Marcus Brutus and His Reputation.* London.

Classen, C. J. (1988) "Virtutes Romanorum: römische Tradition und griechischer Einfluß," *Gymnasium* 95: 289–302.

Coarelli, F. (1969) "La *tyrannoctone* du Capitole et la mort de Tiberius Gracchus," *MEFRA* 81: 137–60.

Coarelli, F. (1972) "Il sepolcro degli Scipioni," *DArch* 6: 36–106.

Coarelli, F. (1983) *Il Foro Romano I: Periodo arcaico.* Rome.

Coarelli, F. (1985) *Il Foro Romano II: Periodo repubblicano e Augusteo.* Rome.

Coarelli, F. (1997) *Il Campo Marzio dalle origini alla fine della repubblica.* Rome.

Coleman, K. M. (1986) "The Emperor Domitian and Literature" *ANRW* II.32.5: 3087–115.

Coleman, K. M. (1988) *Statius, Silvae IV.* Oxford.

Colini, A. M. (1937) "Forum Pacis," *BullComm* 65: 7–40.

Confino, A. (1997) "Collective Memory and Cultural History: Problems of Method," *AHR* 102: 1386–403.

Connerton, P. (1989) *How Societies Remember.* Cambridge.

Connolly, J. (2007) *The State of Speech: Rhetoric and Political Thought in Ancient Rome.* Princeton.

Connors, C. (2000) "Imperial space and time: The literature of leisure," in Taplin (2000), 492–518.

Cooley, A. E. (2009) *Res Gestae Divi Augusti: Text, Translation, and Commentary.* Cambridge.

Cooper, D. E. (1986) *Metaphor.* New York.

Cornell, T. J. (1981) "Some Observations on the 'crimen incesti'," in *Le Délit religieux dans la cité antique.* CEFR 48: 27–37. Rome.

Cotta Ramosino, L. (1999) "L'opposizione a Nerone e le 'partes' di Galba," in *Fazioni e congiure nel mondo antico*, ed. M. Sordi. CISA 25: 218–36.

Courtney, E. (1980) *A Commentary on the Satires of Juvenal.* London.

Cramer, F. H. (1945) "Bookburning and Censorship in Ancient Rome: A Chapter from the History of Freedom of Speech," *JHI* 6: 157–96.

Cranston, M. (1953) *Freedom: A New Analysis.* London.

Crawford, M. H. (1983) "Roman Imperial Coin Types and the Formation of Public Opinion," in *Studies in Numismatic Method Presented to P. Grierson*, ed. C. N. L. Brooks et al.: 47–64. Cambridge.

Crescenzi, L. (1979) "La villa di Domiziano a Castel Gandolfo," in *Archeologia laziale* II: 99–106. Rome.

Crook, J. A. (1951) "Titus and Berenice," *AJP* 72: 162–75.

Crook, J. A. (1955) *Consilium Principis: Imperial Councils and Counselors from Augustus to Diocletian.* Cambridge.

Crook, J. A. (1995) *Legal Advocacy in the Roman World.* Ithaca.

Cugusi, P. (2003) "Qualche riflessione sulle idee retoriche di Plinio il Giovane: Epistolae 1,20 e 9,26," in *Plinius der Jüngere und seine Zeit*, ed. L. Castagna and E. Lefèvre: 95–122. Leipzig.

Culham, P. (1989) "Archives and Alternatives in Republican Rome," *CPh* 84: 100–15.

D'Agostino, V. (1954) "La favola del Bivio in Senofonte, in Luciano e in Silio Italico," *RSC* 3: 173–84.

Daly, L. J. (1975) "Verginius at Vesontio: The Incongruity of the *Bellum Neronis*," *Historia* 24: 75–100.

D'Ambra, E. (1991) "Pudicitia in the Frieze of the Forum Transitorium," *MDAI(R)* 98: 243–8.

D'Ambra, E. (1993) *Private Lives, Imperial Virtues: The Frieze of the Forum Transitorium*. Princeton.

Damon, C. (2003) *Tacitus. Histories Book I*. Cambridge.

Danti, A. (2001) "L'indagine archeologica nell'area del tempio di Giove Capitolino," *BullComm* 102: 323–46.

D'Arms, J. H. (1970) *Romans on the Bay of Naples: A Social and Cultural Study of the Villas and Their Owners from 150 B.C. to A.D. 400*. Cambridge, MA.

Darwall-Smith, R. H. (1996) *Emperors and Architecture: A Study of Flavian Rome*. Coll. Latomus 231. Brussels.

Dassow, E. von (2011) "Freedom in Ancient Near Eastern Societies," in *The Oxford Handbook of Cuneiform Culture*, ed. K. Radner and E. Robson. Oxford.

David, J.-M. (1984) "Du Comitium à la roche Tarpéienne. Sur certains rituels d'exécution capitale sous la République, les règnes d'Auguste et de Tibère" in *Du Châtiment dans la cité. Supplices corporels et peine de mort dans le monde antique*. CEFR 79: 131–76. Rome.

Degrassi, A. (1952) "Le dediche di popoli e re asiatici al Popolo Romano e a Giove Capitolino," *BullComm* 74: 19–47.

DeLaine, J. (1996) "'De aquis suis'? The 'commentarius' of Frontinus," in *Les Littératures techniques dans l'antiquité Romaine*, ed. C. Nicolet. Entretiens Hardt 42: 117–41. Geneva.

Demoen, K. (1997) "A Paradigm for the Analysis of Paradigms: The Rhetorical *Exemplum* in Ancient and Imperial Greek Theory," *Rhetorica* 15: 125–55.

Dessau, H. (1911) "Silius Italicus und Eprius Marcellus," *Hermes* 46: 621–6.

Detienne, M. (1981) *Les Maîtres de vérité dans la Grèce archaïque*. Paris.

Devine, E. (1970) "Stoicism and the Best Regime," *Journal of the History of Ideas* 31: 323–36.

Devreker, J. (1986) "Curiatius Maternus," in *Hommages à Jozef Veremans*, ed. F. Decreus and C. Deroux. Coll. Latomus 193: 101–8. Brussels.

D'Hautcourt, A. (1995) "L'exil de Cassius Severus: hypothèses nouvelle," *Latomus* 54: 315–18.

Diels, H. (1960) *Die Fragmente der Vorsokratiker*, 9th ed., ed. W. Kranz. Berlin.

Dixon, S. (2001) *Reading Roman Women: Sources, Genres and Real Life*. London.

Dominik, W. J. (1997) "The Style Is the Man: Seneca, Tacitus and Quintilian's Canon," in *Roman Eloquence: Rhetoric in Society and Literature*, ed. W. J. Dominik: 50–68. London.

Dominik, W. J. (2003) "Hannibal at the Gates: Programmatising Rome and *Romanitas* in Silius Italicus' *Punica* 1 and 2," in Boyle and Dominik (2003), 469–97.

Douglas, M. (1966) *Purity and Danger*. London.

Drexler, H. (1988) *Politische Grundbegriffe der Römer*. Darmstadt.

Duncan, T. S. (1930) "Roman Restoration Coins," in *Papers on Classical Subjects in Memory of John Max Wulfing*, ed. F. W. Shipley: 38–63. St. Louis.

Duncan-Jones, R. P. (1990) *Structure and Scale in the Roman Economy*. Cambridge.

Dunkle J. R. (1967) "The Greek Tyrant and Roman Political Invective of the Late Republic," *TAPA* 98: 151–71.

Durry, M. (1938) *Pline le Jeune. Panégyrique de Trajan*. Paris.

Dušanić, S. (1984) "Loci constitutionum fixarum," *Epigraphica* 46: 91–115.

Dyson S. L. (1975) "Native Revolt Patterns in the Roman Empire," *ANRW* II.3: 138–75.

Earl, D. (1967) *The Moral and Political Tradition of Rome*. Ithaca.

Ebbinghaus, H. (1913) *Memory. A Contribution to Experimental Psychology*. New York.

Eck, W. (1970) *Senatoren von Vespasian bis Hadrian: Prosopographische Untersuchungen mit Einschluss der Jahres- un Provinzialfasten der Statthalter*. Munich.

Eck, W. (1982) "Die Gestalt Frontins in ihrer politischen und sozialen Umwelt," in *Wasserversorgung im antiken Rom*, 47–62. Munich.

Eck, W. (1985) "Statius *Silvae* 1.4 und C. Rutilius Gallicus als Proconsul Asiae II," *AJP* 106: 475–84.

Eck, W. (1997) "Rome and the Outside World: Senatorial Families and the World They Lived In," in *The Roman Family in Italy: Status, Sentiment, Space*, ed. B. Rawson and P. Weaver: 73–99. Oxford.

Eck, W. (2003) *The Age of Augustus*, trans. D. L. Schneider. London.

Eck, W., Caballos, A., and Fernández, F. (1996) *Das senatus consultum de Cn. Pisone patre*. Munich.

Eck, W., and Pangerl, A. (2003) "Sex. Iulius Frontinus als Legat des niedergermanischen Heeres: zu neuen Militärdiplomen in den germanischen Provinzen," *ZPE* 143: 205–19.

Eder, W. (1990) "Augustus and the Power of Tradition: The Augustan Principate as Binding Link between Republic and Empire," in Raaflaub and Toher (1990), 71–122.

Eder, W. (2005) "Augustus and the Power of Tradition," in Galinsky (2005), 13–32.

Edmondson, J., Mason, S., and Rives J. (eds.) (2005) *Flavius Josephus and Flavian Rome*. Oxford.

Edwards, C. (1993) *The Politics of Immorality in Ancient Rome*. Cambridge.

Edwards, C. (1996) *Writing Rome: Textual approaches to the city*. Cambridge.

Equini, E. (1967) "Un frammento inedito dei fasti Ostiensi del 74," *Epigraphica* 29: 11–17.

Evans, H. B. (1994) *Water Distribution in Ancient Rome: The Evidence of Frontinus*. Ann Arbor.

Evans, J. D. (1990) "Statues of the Kings and Brutus on the Capitoline," *OpuscRom* 18: 99–105.

Evans, J. K. (1975) "The Dating of Domitian's War against the Chatti Again," *Historia* 24: 121–4.

Evans, J. K. (1976) "Tacitus, Domitian and the Proconsulship of Agricola," *RhM* 119: 29–84.

Evans, J. K. (1979) "The Trial of P. Egnatius Celer," *CQ* n.s. 29: 198–202.

Eyben, E. (1972) "The Concrete Ideal in the Life of the Young Roman," *AntCl* 41: 200–17.

Fantham, E. (1977) "Censorship, Roman Style," *EMC* 21: 41–53.

Fantham, E. (1978a) "Imitation and Evolution: The Discussion of Rhetorical Imitation in Cicero De Oratore 2. 87–97 and Some Related Problems of Ciceronian Theory," *CP* 73: 1–16.

Fantham, E. (1978b) "Imitation and Decline: Rhetorical Theory and Practice in the First Century after Christ," *CP* 73: 102–16.

Fantham, E. (1997) "The Contexts and Occasions of Roman Public Rhetoric," in *Roman Eloquence: Rhetoric in Society and Literature*, ed. W. J. Dominik: 111–28. London.

Fantham, E. (2003) "Three Wise Men and the End of the Roman Republic," *Papers of the Langord Latin Seminar* 11: 96–117.

Fantham, E. (2004) *The Roman World of Cicero's de Oratore*. Oxford.

Favro, D. (1996) *The Urban Image of Augustan Rome*. Cambridge.

Fears, J. R. (1980) "Rome. The Ideology of Imperial Power," *Thought* 55: 98–109.

Fears, J. R. (1981a) "The Cult of Jupiter and Roman Imperial Ideology," *ANRW* II.17.1: 3–141.

Fears, J. R. (1981b) "The Cult of Virtues and Roman Imperial Ideology," *ANRW* II.17.2: 827–948.

Fechner, D. (1986) *Untersuchungen zu Cassius Dios Sicht der römischen Republik*. Hildensheim.

Feeney, D. (1991) *The Gods in Epic: Poets and Critics of the Classical Tradition*. Oxford.

Feeney, D. (2007) *Caesar's Calendar: Ancient Time and the Beginnings of History*. Berkeley.

Feldherr, A. (1998) *Spectacle and Society in Livy's History*. Berkeley.

Fell, M. (1992) *Optimus Princeps? Anspruch und Wirklichkeit der imperialen Programmmatik Kaiser Traians*. Munich.

Fentress, J., and Wickham, C. (1992) *Social Memory*. Oxford.

Ferrary, J.-L. (1988) *Philhellénisme et impérialisme: aspects idéologiques de la conquête romaine du monde hellénistique, de la seconde guerre de Macédoine a la guerre contre Mithridate*. Rome.

Ferrill, A. (1978) "History in Roman Schools," *AncW* 1: 1–5.

Festinger, L., Riecken, H. W., and Schacter, S. (1956) *When Prophecy Fails.* Minneapolis.

Filippi, D. (1998) "L'*arx Capitolina* e la *primae Capitolinae arcis fores* di Tacito (*hist.*, III,71): una proposta di lettura," *BullComm* 99: 73–84.

Fishwick, D. (1987) *The Imperial Cult in the Latin West: Studies in the Ruler Cult of the Western Provinces of the Roman Empire* vol. I. Leiden.

Fishwick, D. (1991) *The Imperial Cult in the Latin West: Studies in the Ruler Cult of the Western Provinces of the Roman Empire* vol. II.1. Leiden.

Flaig, E. (1992) *Den Kaiser herausfordern. Die Usurpation im römischen Reich.* Frankfurt.

Flaig, E. (2003) *Ritualisierte Politik: Zeichen, Gesten und Herrschaft im Alten Rom.* Göttingen.

Flory, M. (1988) "*Abducta Neroni uxor*: The Historiographical Tradition on the Marriage of Octavian and Livia," *TAPA* 118: 343–59.

Flower, H. I. (1996) *Ancestor Masks and Aristocratic Power in Roman Culture.* Oxford.

Flower, H. I. (1998) "Rethinking '*Damnatio Memoriae*': The Case of Cn. Calpurnius Piso Pater in AD 20," *ClAnt* 17: 155–87.

Flower, H. I. (2000) "The Tradition of the *Spolia Opima*: M. Claudius Macellus and Augustus," *ClAnt* 19: 34–64.

Flower, H. I. (2006) *The Art of Forgetting: Disgrace and Oblivion in Roman Political Culture.* Chapel Hill.

Flower, H. I. (2010) *Roman Republics.* Princeton.

Fontana, B. (1993) "Tacitus on Empire and Republic," *History of Political Thought* 14: 27–40.

Fraschetti, A. (1981) "Le sepolture rituali del Foro Boario," in *Le Délit religieux dan la cité antique.* CEFR 48: 51–115. Rome.

Fraschetti, A. (1984) "La sepoltura delle Vestali e la Città," in *Du châtiment dans la cité: Supplices corporels et peine de mort dans le monde antique.* CEFR 79: 97–129. Rome.

Frede, D. (2003) "Stoic Determinism," in *The Cambridge Companion to the Stoics,* ed. B. Inwood: 179–205.

Fredrick, D. (2003) "Architecture and Surveillance in Flavian Rome," in Boyle and Dominik (2003), 199–227.

Friedländer, L. (1886) *M. Valerii Martialis Epigrammaton Libri.* Leipzig.

Friend, C. (1999) "Pirates, Seducers, Wronged Heirs, Poison Cups, Cruel Husbands, and Other Calamities: The Roman School Declamations and Critical Pedagogy," *Rhetoric Review* 17: 300–20.

Fritz, K. von (1957) "Tacitus, Agricola, Domitian and the Problem of the Principate," *CPh* 52: 73–97.

Fröhlich, U. (2000) *Regulus, Archetyp römischer Fides: das sechste Buch als Schlüssel zu den Punica des Silius Italicus.* Tübingen.

Frow, J. (1997) "Toute la mémoire du monde: Repetition and Forgetting," in *Time and Commodity Culture: Essays in Cultural Theory and Postmodernity*, 218–46. Oxford.

Fuhrmann, M. (1960) *Das systematische Lehrbuch. Ein Beitrag zur Geschichte der Wissenschaften in der Antike*. Göttingen.

Gagé, J. (1952) "Vespasian et la mémoire de Galba," *REA* 54: 290–315.

Galimberti, A. (2000) "L'opposizione sotto i Flavi: il caso di Elvidio Prisco," in *L'opposizione nel mondo antico*, ed. M. Sordi. CISA 26: 215–29. Milan.

Galinsky, K. (1996) *Augustan Culture: An Interpretive Introduction*. Princeton.

Galinsky, K. (ed.) (2005) *The Cambridge Companion to the Age of Augustus*. Cambridge.

Gallia, A. B. (2007) "Reassessing the 'Cumaean Chronicle': Greek Chronology and Roman History in Dionysius of Halicarnassus," *JRS* 97: 50–67.

Gallia, A. B. (2009) "*Potentes* and *potentia* in Tacitus' *Dialogus de Oratoribus*," *TAPA* 139: 169–206.

Gallivan, P. (1981) "The Fasti for A.D. 70–96," *CQ* 31: 186–220.

Ganiban, R. T. (2010) "Virgil's Dido and the Heroism of Hannibal," in Augoustakis (2010), 73–98.

Garthwaite, J. (1990) "Martial, Book 6, on Domitian's Moral Censorship," *Prudentia* 22: 13–22.

Gedi, N., and Elam, Y. (1996) "Collective Memory – What Is It?" *History and Memory* 8: 30–50.

Geiger, J. (1979) "Munatius Rufus and Thrasea Paetus on Cato the Younger," *Athenaeum* n.s. 57: 48–72.

Geiger, J. (2008) *The First Hall of Fame: A Study of the Statues in the Forum Augustum*. Leiden.

George, D. B. (1991) "Lucan's Cato and Stoic Attitudes to the Republic," *ClAnt* 10: 237–58.

Ghedini, F. (1986) "Riflessi della politica domizianea nei rilievi flavi di Palazzo della Cancelleria," *BullComm* 91: 292–309.

Gibbon, E. (1869) *The Autobiography and Correspondence of Edward Gibbon, the Historian*. London.

Giovannini, A. (1987) "Pline et les délateurs de Domitien," in *Opposition et résistance à l'empire d'Auguste a Trajan*. Entretiens Hardt 33: 219–48. Geneva.

Girard, J.-L. (1981) "Domitien et Minerve: une prédilection impériale," *ANRW* II.17.1: 233–45.

Girard, R. (1977) *Violence and the Sacred*, trans. P. Gregory. Baltimore.

Giuliani, L. (1986) *Bildnis und Botschaft: Hermeneutische Untersuchungen zur Bildniskunst der römischen Republik*. Frankfurt am Main.

Goar, R. J. (1987) *The Legend of Cato Uticensis from the First Century B.C. to the Fifth Century A.D.* Coll. Latomus 197. Brussels.

Goldberg, S. M. (1999) "Appreciating Aper: The Defence of Modernity in Tacitus' *Dialogus de Oratoribus*," *CQ* 49: 224–37.

Goldsworthy, A. K. (1996) *The Roman Army at War: 100 BC–AD 200*. Oxford.

Goodman, M. (1989) "Nerva, the *Fiscus Judaicus* and Jewish Identity," *JRS* 79: 40–4.

Goodman, M. (2005) "The Fiscus Iudaicus and Gentile Attitudes to Judaism in Flavian Rome," in *Flavius Josephus and Flavian Rome*, ed. J. Edmondson, S. Mason, and J. Rives: 167–77. Oxford.

Goodman, M. (2007) *Rome and Jerusalem: The Clash of Ancient Civilizations*. New York.

Goodyear, F. R. D. (1982) "Technical Writing," in *The Cambridge History of Classical Literature. Volume II. Latin Literature*, ed. E. J. Kenney and W. V. Clausen: 667–73. Cambridge.

Gordon, A. E. (1952) *Quintus Veranius Consul A.D. 49: A Study Based upon His Recently Identified Sepulchral Inscription*. Berkeley.

Gordon, R. (1990) "From Republic to Principate: Priesthood, Religion and Ideology," in *Pagan Priests: Religion and Power in the Ancient World*, ed. M. Beard and J. North: 179–98. New York.

Goud, T. E. (1996) "The Sources of Josephus *Antiquities* 19," *Historia* 45: 472–82.

Gowing, A. (2005) *Empire and Memory: The Representation of the Roman Republic in Imperial Culture*. Cambridge.

Gradel, I. (2002) *Emperor Worship and Roman Religion*. Oxford.

Grainger, J. D. (2003) *Nerva and the Roman Succession Crisis of AD 96–99*. London.

Granino Cecere, M. G. (1996) "Sacerdotes Cabenses e sacerdotes Albani: la documentazione epigrafca," in *Alba Longa: mito, storia, archeologia*, ed. A. Pasqualini: 275-316. Rome.

Grant, M. (1950) *Roman Anniversary Issues*. New York.

Grant, M. (1954) *Roman Imperial Money*. London.

Grelle, F. (1980) "La 'correctio morum' nella legislazione flavia," *ANRW* II.13: 340–65.

Griffin, M. T. (1968) "Seneca on Cato's Politics," *CQ* n.s. 18: 373–5.

Griffin, M. T. (1976) *Seneca: A Philosopher in Politics*. Oxford.

Griffin, M. T. (1984) *Nero: The End of a Dynasty*. New Haven.

Griffin, M. T. (1986) "Philosophy, Cato, and Roman Suicide" pts. I and II, *G&R* n.s. 33: 64–75, 192–202.

Griffin, M. T. (1989) "Philosophy, Politics, and Politicians at Rome," in *Philosophia Togata: Essays on Philosophy and Roman Society*, ed. M. Griffin and J. Barnes: 1–37. Oxford.

Griffin, M. T. (2003) "*Clementia* after Caesar: From Politics to Philosophy," in *Caesar against Liberty? Perspectives on His Autocracy*, ed. F. Cairns and E. Fantham: 157–82. Liverpool.

Grilli, A. (2002) *Vita contemplativa: il problema della vita contemplativa nel mondo greco-romano*. 2nd ed. Brescia.

Grimal, P. (1992) "Les Visages de la *Libertas* ches Sénèque et Lucain," in *La storia, la letteratura e l'arte a Roma da Tiberio a Domiziano*, 133–44. Mantua.

Groag, E. (1897) *Zur Kritik von Tacitus' Quellen in den Historien*. Leipzig.

Gros, P. (1976) *Aurea templa: recherches sur l'architecture religieuse de Rome à l'époque d'Auguste*. BEFAR 231. Rome.

Gruen, E. S. (1968a) *Roman Politics and the Criminal Courts, 149–78 B.C.* Cambridge, MA.

Gruen, E. S. (1968b) "M. Antonius and the Trials of the Vestal Virgins," *RhM* 111: 59–63.

Gruen, E. S. (1985) "Augustus and the Ideology of War and Peace," in *The Age of Augustus*, ed. R. Winkes: 51–72. Providence.

Gruen, E. S. (1992) *Culture and National Identity in Republican Rome*. Ithaca.

Gsell, S. (1894) *Essai sur le règne de l'empereur Domitien*. Paris.

Gudeman, A. (1894) *P. Cornelii Taciti Dialogus de Oratoribus*. Boston.

Gudeman, A. (1914) *P. Cornelii Taciti Dialogus de Oratoribus*. 2nd ed. Leipzig.

Guizzi, F. (1968) *Aspetti giuridici del sacerdozio romani: il sacerdozio di Vesta*. Naples.

Gundermann, G. (1888) *Iuli Frontini Strategematon libri IV*. Leipzig.

Gunderson, E. (2003) "The Flavian Amphitheatre: All the World as Stage," in Boyle and Dominik (2003), 637–58.

Güngerich, R. (1951) "Der *Dialogus* des Tacitus und Quintilians *Institutio Oratoria*," *CPh* 46: 159–64.

Güngerich, R. (1980) *Kommentar zum Dialogus des Tacitus*, ed. H. Heubner. Göttingen.

Haase, F. (1902) *L. Annaei Senecae opera quae supersunt. Supplementum*. Leipzig.

Habinek, T. and Schiesaro, A. (eds.) (1997) *The Roman Cultural Revolution*. Cambridge.

Haight, E. H. (1940) *The Roman Use of Anecdotes in Cicero, Livy, and the Satirists*. New York.

Hainsworth, J. B. (1962) "Verginius and Vindex," *Historia* 11: 86–7.

Halbwachs, M. (1925) *Les Cadres sociaux de la mémoire*. Paris.

Halbwachs, M. (1941) *La Topographie légendaire des évangiles en Terre Sainte*. Paris.

Halbwachs, M. (1950) *La Mémoire collective*. Paris.

Hammond, M. (1959) *The Antonine Monarchy*. PMAAR 19. Rome.

Hammond, M. (1963) "*Res olim dissociabiles: Principatus ac Libertas*. Liberty under the early Roman Empire," *HSCP* 67: 93–113.

Hammond, M. (1965) "The Sincerity of Augustus," *HSCP* 69: 139–62.

Hammond, M. (1968) *The Augustan Principate*. Enlarged ed. New York.

Hardie, P. (1993) *The Epic Successors of Virgil. A Study in the Dynamics of a Tradition*. Cambridge.

Harl, K. W. (1996) *Coinage in the Roman Economy, 300 B.C. to A.D. 700.* Baltimore.

Harlan, M. (1995) *Roman Republican Moneyers and Their Coins, 63BC–49BC.* London.

Harris, W. V. (2006) "A Revisionist View of Roman Money," *JRS* 96: 1–24.

Harvey, B. K. (2002) "Trajan's Restored Coinage and the Revival of the Memory of Caesar the Dictator," *AncW* 33: 93–100.

Haselberger, L. (2007) *Urbem Adornare: die Stadt Rom und ihre Gestaltumswandlung unter Augustus.* JRA Suppl. 64. Portsmouth, RI.

Häussler, R. (1965) *Tacitus und das historische Bewusstsein.* Heidelberg.

Häussler, R. (1969) "Zum Umfang und Aufbaus des *Dialogus de Oratoribus*," *Philologus* 113: 24–67.

Heck, E. (1970) "Scipio am Scheideweg: die *Punica* des Silius Italicus und Ciceros Schrift *De re publica*," *WS* 83: 156–80.

Hedrick, C. W. (1993) "The Meaning of Material Culture: Herodotus, Thucydides, and Their Sources," in *Nomodeiktes: Greek Studies in Honor of Martin Ostwald*, ed. R. R. Rosen and J. Farrell: 17–37. Ann Arbor.

Hedrick, C. W. (2000) *History and Silence: Purge and Rehabilitation of Memory in Late Antiquity.* Austin, TX.

Heinze, R. (1925) "Auctoritas," *Hermes* 60: 348–66.

Heldmann, K. (1982) *Antike Theorien über Entwicklung und Verfall der Redekunst.* Zetemata 77. Munich.

Hellegouarc'h, J. (1963) *Le Vocabulaire latin des relations et des partis politiques sous la république.* Paris.

Henderson, B. W. (1927) *Five Roman Emperors.* Cambridge.

Henderson, J. (2002) *Pliny's Statue: The Letters, Self-Portraiture, and Classical Arts.* Exeter.

Hennig, D. (1973) "T. Labienus und der erste Majestätprozess de famosis libellis," *Chiron* 3: 245–54.

Herrmann, L. (1939) "La morte de Curiatius Maternus," *Latomus* 3: 58–60.

Hershkowitz, D. (1995) "Pliny the Poet," *G&R* n.s. 43: 168–81.

Hesberg, H. von (2006) "Il potere dell'otium: la villa di Domiziano a Castel Gandolfo," *ArchClass* 57: 221–44.

Heubner, H. (1963) *P. Cornelius Tacitus, Die Historien. Kommentar Band I: Erstes Buch.* Heidelberg.

Heurgon, J. (1964) "L. Cincius et la loi du *clavus annalis*," *Athenaeum* n.s. 42:432–7.

Hickson, F. V. (1993) *Roman Prayer Language: Livy and the Aeneid of Vergil.* Stuttgart.

Hill, P. V. (1965) "Notes on the Ludi Saeculares of AD 88," in *Congresso Internazionale di Numismatica, Roma 11–16 Settembre 1961. Vol. II: Atti.* Rome.

Hinard, F. (1987) "Spectacle des exécutions et espace urbain," in *L'urbs: espace urbain et histoire (Ier siècle avant J.-C.–IIIe siècle apres J.-C.).* CEFR 98: 111–25. Rome.

Hinds, S. (1998) *Allusion and Intertext: Dynamics of Appropriation in Roman Poetry*. Cambridge.

Hirzel, R. (1895) *Der Dialog. Ein literarhistorischer Versuch*. Leipzig.

Hobsbawm, E. (1983) "Introduction: Inventing Traditions," in *The Invention of Tradition*, ed. E. Hobsbawm and T. Ranger: 1–14. Cambridge.

Hoffer, S. E. (1999) *The Anxieties of Pliny the Younger*. Atlanta.

Hölkeskamp, K.-J. (1996) "*Exempla* und *mos maiorum*: Überlegungen zum kollektiven Gedächtnis der Nobilität," in *Vergangenheit und Lebenswelt*, ed. H.-J. Gehrke and A. Möller: 301–38. Tübingen.

Hölkeskamp, K.-J. (2001) "Capitolium, Comitium und Forum. Öffentliche Räume, sakrale Topographie und Errinnerungslandschaften der römischen Republik," in *Studien zu antiken Identitäten*, ed. S. Faller: 97–128. Wurzberg.

Hölkeskamp, K.-J. (2010) *Reconstructing the Roman Republic: An Ancient Political Culture and Modern Research*. Princeton.

Hölscher, F. (2006) "Das Capitol – das Haupt der Welt," in Stein-Hölkeskamp and Hölkeskamp (2006), 75–99.

Hölscher, T. (2004) *The Language of Images in Roman Art*, trans. A. Snodgrass and A. Künzl-Snodgrass. Cambridge.

Hopkins, K. (1965) "Contraception in the Roman Empire," *CSSH* 8: 124–51.

Hopkins, K. (1978) *Conquerors and Slaves*. Cambridge.

Hopkins, K. (1980) "Taxes and Trade in the Roman Empire (200 B.C.–A.D. 400)," *JRS* 70: 101–25.

Hopkins, K. (1983) *Death and Renewal*. Cambridge.

Hopkins, K., and Burton, G. (1983) "Ambition and Withdrawal: The Senatorial Aristocracy under the Emperors," in Hopkins (1983), 120–200.

Horster, M. (2003) "Literarische Elite? Überlegungen zum sozialen Kontext lateinischer Fachschriftsteller in Republik und Kaiserzeit," in *Antike Fachschriftsteller: Literarischer Diskurs und socialer Kontext*, ed. M. Horster and C. Reitz: 176–97. Stuttgart.

Hosking, G. A. (1989) "Memory in a Totalitarian Society: The Case of the Soviet Union," in *Memory: History, Culture and the Mind*, ed. T. Butler: 115–30. Oxford.

Hurlet, F. (1993) "La *Lex de imperio Vespasiani* et la légitimité augustéenne," *Latomus* 52: 261–80.

Hutton, P. H. (1988) "Collective Memory and Collective Mentalities: The Halbwachs-Aries Connection," *Historical Reflections* 15: 311–22.

Huyssen, A. (2003) *Present Pasts: Urban Palimpsests and the Politics of Memory*. Stanford.

Huzar, E. (1984) "Claudius the Erudite Emperor," *ANRW* II.32.1: 611–50.

Imber, M. (2001) "Practiced Speech: Oral and Written Conventions in Roman Declamation," in *Speaking Volumes: Orality and Literacy in the Greek and Roman World*, ed. J. Watson, 199–216. Leiden.

Immerwahr, H. R. (1960) "*Ergon*: History as a Monument in Herodotus and Thucydides," *AJP* 81: 261–90.

Inwood, B. (2005) "Seneca on Freedom and Autonomy," in *Reading Seneca: Stoic Philosophy at Rome*, 302–21. Oxford.

Ireland, R. I. (1990) *Iuli Frontini Strategemata*. Leipzig.

Isaac, B. (2004) *The Invention of Racism in Classical Antiquity*. Princeton.

Jaeger, M. (1997) *Livy's Written Rome*. Ann Arbor.

Jaeger, M. (2002) "Cicero and Archimedes' Tomb," *JRS* 92: 49–61.

Jocelyn, H. D. (1969) *The Tragedies of Ennius: The Fragments*. Cambridge.

Johnstone, S. (1992) "On the Uses of Arson in Classical Rome," in *Studies in Latin Literature and Roman History VI*. Coll. Latomus 217: 41–69. Brussels.

Jones, A. H. M. (1939) "Civitates liberae et immunes in the East," in *Anatolian Studies Presented to William Hepburn Buckler*, ed. W. M. Calder and J. Keil: 103–17. Manchester.

Jones, A. H. M. (1950) "The Aerarium and the Fiscus," *JRS* 40: 22–9. (= *Studies in Roman Government and Law*, 99–114).

Jones, A. H. M. (1956) "Numismatics and History," in *Essays in Roman Coinage Presented to Harold Mattingly*, ed. R. A. G. Carson and C. H. V. Sutherland: 13–33. Oxford.

Jones, B. W. (1973a) "The Dating of Domitian's War against the Chatti," *Historia* 22: 79–90.

Jones, B. W. (1973b) "Some Thoughts on Domitian's Perpetual Censorship," *CJ* 68: 276.

Jones, B. W. (1979) *Domitian and the Senatorial Order: A Prosopographical Study of Domitian's Relationship with the Senate, A.D. 81–96*. Philadelphia.

Jones, B. W. (1992) *The Emperor Domitian*. London.

Jones, C. P. (1970a) "Sura and Senecio," *JRS* 60: 98–104.

Jones, C. P. (1970b) *Plutarch and Rome*. Oxford.

Judge, E. A. (1974) "'Res Publica Restituta': A Modern Illusion?" in *Polis and Imperium: Studies in Honour of Edward Togo Salmon*, ed. J. A. S. Evans: 279–311. Toronto.

Juhnke, H. (1972) *Homerisches in römischer Epik flavischer Zeit: Untersuchungen zu Szenennachbildungen und Strukturentsprechungen in Statius' Thebais und Achilleis und in Silius' Punica*. Munich.

Kammen, M. (1995) "Some Patterns and Meanings of Memory Distortion in American History," in Schacter and Tulving (1995), 329–45.

Kandel, E. R. (2006) *In Search of Memory: The Emergence of a New Science of the Mind*. New York.

Kapparis, K. (2002) *Abortion in the Ancient World*. London.

Kaster, R. A. (2002) "The Taxonomy of Patience, or When Is 'Patientia' Not a Virtue?" *CPh* 97: 133–44.

Keaveney, A. (1987) "Vespasian's Gesture," *GIF* 34: 213–16.

Keitel, E. (1984) "Principate and Civil War in the Annals of Tacitus," *AJP* 105: 306–25.

Keitel, E. (1992) "The Function of the Livian Reminiscences at Tacitus *Histories* 4.58.6 and 62," *CJ* 87: 327–37.

Kemp, A. (1991) *The Estrangement of the Past: A Study in the Origins of the Modern Historical Consciousness*. Oxford.

Kennedy, G. (1962) "An Estimate of Quintilian," *AJP* 83: 130–46.

Kennedy Klaassen, E. (2010) "Imitation and the Hero," in Augoustakis (2010) 99–126.

Kershaw, A. (1997) "Martial 9.44 and Statius," *CPh* 92: 269–72.

Kienast, D. (1984) "Der augusteische Prinzipat als Rechtsordnung," *ZRG* 101: 115–41.

Kienast, D. (1996) *Römische Kaisertabelle. Grundzüge einer römischen Kaiserchronologie*. Darmstadt.

Kierdorf, W. (1978) "Ciceros 'Cato': Überlegungen zu einer verlorenen Schrift Ciceros," *RhM* 121: 167–84.

Klein, K. L. (2000) "On the Emergence of Memory in Historical Discourse," *Representations* 69: 127–50.

Kleiner, D. E. E. (1992) *Roman Sculpture*. New Haven.

Kleiner, F. S. (1989) "Galba and the Sullan Capitolium," *AJN* 2nd Ser. 1: 71–7.

Kloft, H. (1970) *Liberalitas principis. Herkunft und Bedeutung. Studien zur Principatsideologie*. Cologne.

Koch, C. (1960) *Religio: Studien zu Kult und Glauben der Römer*. Nuremberg.

Köhnken, A. (1973) "Das Problem der Ironie bei Tacitus," *MH* 30: 32–50.

Komnick, H. (2001) *Die Restitutionsmünzen der frühen Kaiserzeit: Aspekte der Kaiserlegitimation*. Berlin.

König, A. (2007) "Knowledge and Power in Frontinus' *On Aqueducts*," in *Ordering Knowledge in the Roman Empire*, ed. J. König and T. Whitmarsh: 177–205. Cambridge.

Konstan, D. (2005) "Clemency as a Virtue," *CP* 100: 337–46.

Koortbojian, M. (2002) "A Painted *Exemplum* at Rome's Temple of Liberty," *JRS* 92: 33–48.

Kornhardt, H. (1936) *Exemplum: eine bedeutungsgeschichtliche Studie* (Diss. Götingen).

Koselleck, R. (2002) *The Practice of Conceptual History*, trans. T. S. Presner et al. Stanford.

Koselleck, R. (2004) *Futures Past: On the Semantics of Historical Time*, trans. K. Tribe. New York.

Köstermann, E. (1932) "Statio principis," *Philologus* 87: 358–68.

Köves-Zulauf, T. (1992) "Reden und Schweigen im taciteischen *Dialogus de Oratoribus*," *RhM* 135: 316–41.

Kraay, C. M. (1949) "The Coinage of Vindex and Galba, A.D. 68, and the Continuity of the Augustan Principate," *NC*[6] 9: 129–49.

Kragelund, P. (1987) "Vatinius, Nero and Curiatius Maternus," *CQ* 37: 197–202.

Kraus, C. S. (2000) "The path between truculence and servility: Prose literature from Augustus to Hadrian," in Taplin (2000), 438-67.

Kunkel, W., and Wittmann, R. (1995) *Staatsordnung und Staatspraxis der römischen Republik. Zweiter Abschnitt: die Magistatur*. Munich.

Künzl, E. (1988) *Der römische Triumph: Siegesfeiern im antiken Rom*. Munich.

Kuttner, A. (1995) *Dynasty and Empire in the Age of Augustus: The Case of the Boscoreale Cups*. Berkeley.

Kuttner, A. (1999) "Culture and History at Pompey's Museum," *TAPA* 129: 343–73.

Langlands, R. (2006) *Sexual Morality in Ancient Rome*. Cambridge.

La Rocca, E. (2001) "La nuova immagine dei fori Imperiale: Appunti in margine agli scavi," *MDAI(R)* 108: 171–213.

Latte, K. (1960) *Römische Religionsgeschichte*. Munich.

Leander Touati, A. M. (1987) *The Great Trajanic Frieze: The Study of a Monument and of the Mechanisms of Message Transmission in Roman Art*. Stockholm.

Lefèvre, E. (1989) "Plinius-Studien V, vom Römertum zum Ästetizismus: die Würdingungen des älteren Plinius (3,5), Silius Italicus (3,7) und Martial (3,21)," *Gymnasium* 96: 113–28.

Le Goff, J. (1992) *History and Memory*, trans. S. Rendall and E. Claman. New York.

Leigh, M. (1996) "Varius Rufus, Thyestes, and the Appetites of Antony," *PCPS* 42: 171–96.

Leigh, M. (2000) "Oblique politics: Epic of the imperial period," in Taplin (2000), 468–91.

Lendon, J. E. (1997) *Empire of Honour: The Art of Government in the Roman World*. Oxford.

Lepper, F. A., and Frere, S. S. (1988) *Trajan's Column: A New Edition of the Cichorius Plates*. Wolfboro, NH.

Letta, C. (1985) "La data fittizia del Dialogus de oratoribus," in *Xenia. Scritti in onore di Piero Treves*, ed. F. Broilo: 103–9. Rome.

Levene, D. S. (1993) *Religion in Livy*. Leiden.

Levene, D. S. (2004) "Tacitus' *Dialogus* as Literary History," *TAPA* 134: 157–200.

Levick, B. (1978) "Antiquarian or Revolutionary? Claudius Caesar's Conception of His Principate," *AJP* 99: 79–105.

Levick, B. (1982a) "Propaganda and the Imperial Coinage," *Antichthon* 16: 104–16.

Levick, B. (1982b) "Morals, Politics and the Fall of the Roman Republic," *G&R* n.s. 29: 53–62.

Levick, B. (1985) "L. Verginius Rufus and the Four Emperors," *RhM* 128: 318–47.

Levick, B. (1999a) *Vespasian*. London.

Levick, B. (1999b) "Messages on the Roman Coinage: Types and Inscriptions" in *Roman Coins and Public Life under the Empire*, ed. G. M. Paul: 41–60. Ann Arbor.

Levick, B. (2002) "Corbulo's Daughter," *G&R* n.s. 49: 199–211.

Liberman, G. (1998) "Les Documents sacerdotaux du collège 'sacris faciundis'," in *La Mémoire perdue: recherches sur l'administration romaine*. CEFR 243: 65–74. Rome.

Liebeschuetz, J. H. W. G. (1979) *Continuity and Change in Roman Religion*. Oxford.

Lind, L. R. (1979) "The Tradition of Roman Moral Conservatism" in *Studies in Latin Literature and Roman History I*. Coll. Latomus 164: 7–58. Brussels.

Lind, L. R. (1986) "The Idea of the Republic and the Foundations of Roman Political Liberty," in *Studies in Latin Literature and Roman History IV*. Coll. Latomus 196: 44–108. Brussels.

Linke, B., and Stemmler, M. (eds.) (2000) *Mos Maiorum. Untersuchungen zu den Formen der Identitätsstiftung und Stabilisierung in der römischen Republik*. Historia Einzelschrift 141. Stuttgart.

Lintott, A. W. (1972) "Imperial Expansion and Moral Decline in the Roman Republic," *Historia* 21: 626–38.

Lintott, A. W. (1978) "The Capitoline Dedications to Jupiter and the Roman People," *ZPE* 30: 137–44.

Lintott, A. W. (1999) *The Constitution of the Roman Republic*. Oxford.

Litchfield, H. W. (1914) "National *Exempla Virtutis* in Roman Literature," *HSCP* 25: 1–71.

Little, D. (1982) "Politics in Augustan Poetry," *ANRW* II.30.1: 254–370.

Lloyd-Jones, H., and Parsons, P. (eds.) (1983) *Supplementum hellenisticum*. Berlin.

Long, A. A. (1971) "Freedom and Determinism in the Stoic Theory of Human Action," in *Problems in Stoicism*, ed. A. A. Long: 173–99. London.

Long, A. A. (1986) *Hellenistic Philosophy: Stoics, Epicureans, Skeptics*. Berkeley.

Long, A. A. (1988) "Socrates in Hellenistic Philosophy," *CQ* 38: 150–71.

Lorenz, S. (2003) "Martial, Herkules und Domitian: Büsten, Statuetten und Statuen im Epigrammaton Liber Nonus," *Mnemosyne* 56: 566–84.

Lovisi, C. (1998) "Vestale, incestus et juridiction pontificale sous la République romaine," *MEFRA* 110: 699–735.

Lowenthal, D. (1985) *The Past Is a Foreign Country*. Cambridge.

Lucarini, C. M. (2004) "Le fonti storiche di Silio Italico," *Athenaeum* 92: 103–26.

Luce, T. J. (1986) "Tacitus' Conception of Historical Change: The Problem of Discovering the Historian's Opinions," in Moxon et al. (1986), 143–57.

Luce, T. J. (1990) "Livy, Augustus, and the Forum Augustum," in Raaflaub and Toher (1990), 123–38.

Luce, T. J. (1993) "Reading and Response in the *Dialogus*," in Luce and Woodman (1993), 11–38.

Luce, T. J., and Woodman, A. J. (eds.) (1993) *Tacitus and the Tacitean Tradition*. Princeton.

Ludolph, M. (1997) *Epistolographie und Selbstdarstellung. Untersuchungen zu den "Paradebriefen" Plinius des Jüngeren*. Tübingen.

MacBain, B. (1982) *Prodigy and Expiation: A Study in Religion and Politics in Republican Rome*. Coll. Latomus 177. Brussels.

MacCallum, G. C. Jr. (1967) "Negative and Positive Freedom," *Philosophical Review* 76: 312–34.

Mackie, N. K. (1986) "*Res Publica Restituta*: A Roman Myth," in *Studies in Latin Literature and Roman History IV*, Coll. Latomus 196: 302–40. Brussels.

Mackintosh, M. (1995) *The Divine Rider in the Art of the Western Roman Empire*. BAR 607. Oxford.

Macleod, C. (1983) "Thucydides and Tragedy," in *Collected Essays*, 140–58. Oxford.

MacMullen, R. (1966) *Enemies of the Roman Order: Treason, Unrest, and Alienation in the Empire*. Cambridge, MA.

MacMullen, R. (1986) "Judicial Savagery in the Roman Empire," *Chiron* 16: 147–66 (= *Changes in the Roman Empire*, 204–17).

Madvig, N. (1876, repr. 1963) *M. Tullii Ciceronis de finibus bonorum et malorum*. 3rd. ed. Hildesheim.

Magi, F. (1945) *I rilievi flavi del Palazzo della Cancelleria*. Rome.

Magie, D. (1950) *Roman Rule in Asia Minor*. Oxford.

Malcovati, H. (1955) *Oratorum romanorum fragmenta liberae rei publicae*. Turin.

Malitz, J. (1985) "Helvidius Priscus und Vespasian. Zur Geschichte der 'stoischen' Senatsopposition," *Hermes* 113: 231–46.

Manning, C. E. (1989) "Stoicism and Slavery in the Roman Empire," *ANRW* II.36.3: 1518–43.

Manuwald, G. (2001) "Der Dichter Curiatius Maternus in Tacitus' *Dialogus de oratoribus*," *GFA* 4: 1–20.

Manuwald, G. (2007) "Epic Poets as Characters: On Poetics and Multiple Intertextuality in Silius Italicus' *Punica*," *RFIC* 135: 71–90.

Manzoni, G. E. (1990) "Il retore Quintiliano di fronte ai filosofi," in *Aspetti della 'paideia' di Quintiliano*, ed. P. Cova et al.: 143–72. Milan.

Margalit, A. (2002) *The Ethics of Memory*. Cambridge, MA.

Marks, R. (2005) *From Republic to Empire: Scipio Africanus in the Punica of Silius Italicus*. Frankfurt am Main.

Marks, R. (2008) "Getting Ahead: Decapitation as Political Metaphor in Silius Italicus' *Punica*," *Mnemosyne* 61: 66–88.

Martin, P.-H. (1974) *Die anonymen Münzen des Jahres 68 nach Christus*. Mainz.

Martin, R. H. (1967) "The Speech of Curtius Montanus: Tacitus, *Histories* IV, 42," *JRS* 57: 109–14.

Marx, F. A. (1937) "Tacitus und die Literatur der exitus illustrium virorum," *Philologus* 92: 83–103.

Maslakov, G. (1984) "Valerius Maximus and Roman Historiography: A Study of the *Exempla* Tradition," *ANRW* II.32.1: 437–96.

Matier, K. O. (1991) "The Influence of Ennius on Silius Italicus," *Akroterion* 36: 153–8.

Matthews, J. (2007) *The Roman Empire of Ammianus*. Rev. ed. Ann Arbor.

Matthiessen, K. (1970) "Der Dialogus des Tacitus und Cassius Dio 67,12," *AC* 39: 168–77.

Mattingly, H. (1920) "The Restored Coins of Titus, Domitian and Nerva," *NC*[4] 20: 177–207.

Mattingly, H. (1926) "The Restored Coinage of Trajan," *NC⁵* 61: 232–78.

Maxfield, V. A. (1986) "Systems of Reward in Relation to Military Diplomas," in *Heer und Integrationspolitik: die römischen Militärdiplome als historische Quelle*, ed. W. Eck and H. Wolff: 10–25. Cologne.

Mayer, R. (1982) "What Caused Poppaea's Death?" *Historia* 31: 248–9.

Mayer, R. (2001) *Tacitus. Dialogus de Oratoribus*. Cambridge.

McDermott, W. C. (1969) "Pliniana," *AJP* 90: 329–32.

McDermott, W. C., and Orentzel, A. E. (1977) "Silius Italicus and Domitian," *AJP* 98: 24–34.

McDermott, W. C., and Orentzel, A. E. (1979) "Quintilian and Domitian," *Athenaeum* n.s. 57: 9–26.

McDonnell, M. (2006) *Roman Manliness: Virtus and the Roman Republic*. Cambridge.

McDougall, J. I. (1992) "Cassius Ravilla and the Trial of the Vestals," *AHB* 6: 10–17.

McGuire, D. T. (1989) "Textual Strategies and Political Suicide in Flavian Epic," *Ramus* 18: 21–45.

McGuire, D. T. (1995) "History Compressed: The Roman Names of Silius' Cannae Episode," *Latomus* 54: 110–18.

McGuire, D. T. (1997) *Acts of Silence: Civil War, Tyranny, and Suicide in the Flavian Epics*. Hildesheim.

McHugh, M. R. (2004) "Historiography and Freedom of Speech: The Case of Cremutius Cordus," in *Free Speech in Classical Antiquity*, ed. I. Sluiter and R. Rosen: 391–408. Leiden.

McKechnie, P. (1981) "Cassius Dio's Speech of Agrippa: A Realistic Alternative to Imperial Government?" *G&R* n.s. 28: 150–5.

McNelis, C. (2008) "*Ut Sculptura Poesis*: Statius, Martial, and the Hercules *Epitrapezios* of Novius Vindex," *AJPh* 129: 255–76.

Meadows, A., and Williams, J. (2001) "Moneta and the Monuments," *JRS* 91: 27–49.

Meier, C. (1990) "C. Caesar Divi filius and the Formation of the Alternative in Rome," in Raaflaub and Toher (1990), 54–70.

Meier, C. (1995, orig. pub. 1982) *Caesar*, trans. D. McLintock. New York.

Mellor, R. (1978) "The Dedications on the Capitoline Hill," *Chiron* 8: 320–30.

Melmoux, J. (1975) "C. Helvidius Priscus: disciple et héritier de Thrasea," *PP* 30: 23–40.

Merklin, H. (1991) "*Dialogus*-Probleme in der neueren Forschung," *ANRW* II.33.3: 2255–83.

Metcalf, W. E. (1989) "Rome and Lugdunum Again," *AJN* n.s. 1: 51–70.

Meyer, E. (2004) *Legitimacy and Law in the Roman World: Tabulae in Roman Belief and Practice*. Cambridge.

Miles, G. B. (1995) *Livy: Reconstructing Early Rome*. Ithaca.

Millar, F. (1963) "The Fiscus in the First Two Centuries," *JRS* 53: 29–42. (= *Rome, the Greek World and the East* II, 47–72).

Millar, F. (1964) *A Study of Cassius Dio*. Oxford.

Millar, F. (1965) "Epictetus and the Imperial Court," *JRS* 55: 141–8.

Millar, F. (1968) "Two Augustan Notes," *CR* n.s. 18: 263–6.

Millar, F. (1977) *The Emperor in the Roman World*. Oxford.

Millar, F. (1984) "State and Subject: The Impact of Monarchy," in Millar and Segal (1984), 37–60. (= *Rome, the Greek World and the East* I, 37–60).

Millar, F. (1988) "Imperial Ideology in the *Tabula Siarensis*," in *Estudios sobre la Tabula Siarensis*, ed. J. Gonzalez and J. Arce: 11–19. Madrid. (= *Rome, the Greek World and the East* I, 350–9).

Millar, F. (1995) "The Roman Libertus and Civic Freedom," *Arethusa* 28: 99–105.

Millar, F. (1998) *The Crowd in Rome in the Late Republic*. Ann Arbor.

Millar, F. (2002) *The Roman Republic in Political Thought*. Hanover, NH.

Millar, F. (2005) "Last Year in Jerusalem: Monuments of the Jewish War in Rome," in *Flavius Josephus and Flavian Rome*, ed. J. Edmondson, S. Mason, and J. Rives: 101–28. Oxford.

Millar, F., and Segal, C. (eds.) (1984) *Caesar Augustus: Seven Aspects*. Oxford.

Milnor, K. (2005) *Gender, Domesticity, and the Age of Augustus: Inventing Private Life*. Oxford.

Milnor, K. (2007) "Augustus, History, and the Landscape of the Law," *Arethusa* 40: 7–23.

Mix, E. R. (1970) *Marcus Atilius Regulus: exemplum historicum*. The Hague.

Moles, J. (1993) "Livy's Preface," *PCPS* n.s. 39: 141–68.

Momigliano, A. (1934) *Claudius: The Emperor and His Acheivement*, trans. W. D. Hogarth. Oxford.

Momigliano, A. (1969) "The Origins of the Roman Republic," in *Interpretation: Theory and Practice*, ed. C. S. Singleton: 1–34. Baltimore. (= *Quinto contributo*, 293–332).

Momigliano, A. (1996) *Pace e libertà nel mondo antico: lezioni a Cambridge gennaio-marzo 1940*, trans. R. Di Donato. Florence.

Mommsen, T. (1870) "Cornelius Tacitus und Cluvius Rufus," *Hermes* 4: 295–325. (= *Ges. Schr.* VII, 224–52).

Mommsen, T. (1878) "Der letzte Kampf der römischen Republik," *Hermes* 13: 90–105. (= *Ges. Schr.* IV, 333–47).

Mommsen, T. (1881) "*Adsertor libertatis*," *Hermes* 16: 147–52. (= *Ges. Schr.* IV, 347–52).

Mommsen, T. (1887, repr. 1952) *Römisches Staatsrecht. Erster Band: die Magistratur*, 3rd ed. Graz.

Mommsen, T. (1899) *Römisches Strafrecht*. Leipzig.

Mommsen, T. (1992) *A History of Rome under the Emperors*, ed. T. Wiedemann, trans. C. Krojzl. London.

Morford, M. P. O. (1992) "*Iubes Esse Liberos*: Pliny's *Panegyricus* and Liberty," *AJP* 113: 575–93.

Morford, M. P. O. (2002) *The Roman Philosophers from the Time of Cato the Censor to the Death of Marcus Aurelius*. London.

Morgan, G. (2006) *69 AD: The Year of Four Emperors*. Oxford.

Morr, J. (1926) "Poseidonios von Rhodos über Dichtung und Redekunst," *WS* 45: 47–63.

Mourgues, J.-L. (1998) "Forme diplomatique et pratique institutionnelle des *Comentarii Augustorum*," in *La Mémoire perdue: recherches sur l'administration romaine*. CEFR 243: 123–97. Rome.

Moxon, I. S., Smart, J. D., and Woodman, A. J. (eds.) (1986) *Past Perspectives. Studies in Greek and Roman Historical Writing*. Cambridge.

Mueller, H.-F. (2002) *Roman Religion in Valerius Maximus*. London.

Münzer, F. (1932) "Norbanus," *Hermes* 67: 220–36.

Münzer, F. (1937–8) "Die römischen Vestalinnen bis zur Kaiserzeit," *Philologus* 92: 47–67, 199–222.

Murgia, C. E. (1979) "The Length of the Lacuna in Tacitus' 'Dialogus'," *CSCA* 12: 221–40.

Murgia, C. E. (1980) "The Date of Tacitus' *Dialogus*," *HSCP* 84: 99–125.

Murison, C. L. (1999) *Rebellion and Reconstruction: Galba to Domitian. An Historical Commentary on Cassius Dio's Roman History*. Atlanta.

Murray, O. (1965) "The 'Quinquennium Neronis' and the Stoics," *Historia* 14: 41–61.

Muscettola, S. (2000) "The Sculptural Evidence," in *The Sacellum of the Augustales at Miseno*, ed. P. Miniero Forte: 29–45. Naples.

Mustakallio, K. (1992) "The 'crimen incesti' of the Vestal Virgins and the Prodigious Pestilence," in *Crudelitas: The Politics of Cruelty in the Ancient and Medieval World*, ed. T. Viljamaa, A. Timonen and C. Krötzl: 56–62. Krems.

Nagy, G. (1974) *Comparative Studies in Greek and Indic Meter*. Cambridge, MA.

Nagy, G. (1999) *The Best of the Achaeans: Concepts of the Hero in Archaic Greek Poetry*, rev. ed. Baltimore.

Nesselrath, H.-G. (1986) "Zu den Quellen des Silius Italicus," *Hermes* 114: 203–30.

Newbold, R. F. (1974) "Some Social and Economic Consequences of the A.D. 64 Fire at Rome," *Latomus* 33: 858–69.

Newlands, C. E. (2002) *Statius' Silvae and the Poetics of Empire*. Cambridge.

Newman, J. K. (1986) *The Classical Epic Tradition*. Madison, WI.

Nicol, J. (1936) *The Historical and Geographical Sources Used by Silius Italicus*. Oxford.

Nicolet, C. (1980) *The World of the Citizen in Republican Rome*, trans. P. S. Falla. Berkeley.

Nicolet, C. (1991) *Space, Geography, and Politics in the Early Roman Empire*. Ann Arbor.

Nodelman, S. (1975) "How to Read a Roman Portrait," *Art in America* 63: 27–33.

Nora, P. (1989) "Between Memory and History: *Les Lieux de Mémoire*," *Representations* 26: 7–25.

Noreña, C. (2001) "Communicating the Emperor's Virtues," *JRS* 91: 146–68.

Noreña, C. (2007) "Hadrian's Chastity," *Phoenix* 61: 296–317.

North, J. A. (1976) "Conservatism and Change in Roman Religion," *PBSR* 44: 1–12.

North, J. A. (1990) "Democratic Politics in Republican Rome," *P&P* 126: 3–21.

Oakley, S. P. (1985) "Single Combat in the Roman Republic," *CQ* 35: 392–410.

Ogilvie, R. M. (1965) *A Commentary on Livy Books 1–5*. Oxford.

Olick, J., and Robbins, J. (1998) "Social Memory Studies: From "Collective Memory" to the Historical Sociology of Mnemonic Practices," *Annual Review of Sociology* 24: 105–10.

Olson, S. D. (1995) *Blood and Iron: Stories and Storytelling in Homer's Odyssey*. Leiden.

Orlin, E. M. (1997) *Temples, Religion and Politics in the Roman Republic*. Leiden.

Orlin, E. M. (2007) "Augustan Religion and the Reshaping of Roman Memory," *Arethusa* 40: 73–92.

Orwell, G. (1949 repr. 1992) *Nineteen Eighty-Four*. New York.

Overman, J. A. (2002) "The First Revolt and Flavian Politics," in *The First Jewish Revolt: Archaeology, History and Ideology*, ed. A. M. Berlin and J. A. Overman: 213–20. London.

Packer, J. E. (2001) *The Forum of Trajan in Rome: A Study of the Monuments in Brief*. Berkeley.

Packer, J. E. (2003) "*Plurima et amplissima opera*: Parsing Flavian Rome," in Boyle and Dominik (2003), 167–98.

Paladini, M. L. (1985) "A proposito di 'pax Flavia'," in *La pace nel mondo antico*, ed. M. Sordi. CISA 11: 223–9. Milan.

Palmer, R. E. A. (1975) "The Neighborhood of Sullan Bellona at the Colline Gate," *MEFRA* 87: 653–65.

Palombi, D. (1997) "Cic. 2 Verr., V, 19, 48 e *Gloss. Ps. Plac.* f5 (= *GL*, IV p. 61) sulla costruzione del tempio di Giove capitolino," *BCAR* 98: 7–14.

Panofsky, E. (1930) *Hercules am Scheidewege und andere antike Bildstoffe in der neueren Kunst*. Studien der Bibliothek Warburg 18. Leipzig.

Panvini Rosati, F. (1996) "Ricerche sulla tipologia monetale Romana. Le personificazioni," *RIN* 97: 133–40.

Parke, H. W. (1988) *Sibyls and Sibylline Prophecy in Classical Antiquity*. London.

Parker, H. N. (2004) "Why Were the Vestals Virgins? Or the Chastity of Women and the Safety of the Roman State," *AJPh* 125: 563–601.

Parks, E. P. (1945) *The Roman Rhetorical Schools as a Preparation for the Courts under the Early Empire*. Johns Hopkins University Studies in Historical and Political Science 63.2. Baltimore.

Paterson, J. (2007) "Friends in High Places: The Creation of the Court of the Roman Emperor," in *The Court and Court Society in Ancient Monarchies*, ed. A. J. S. Spawforth: 121–56. Cambridge.

Patterson, O. (1991) *Freedom I: Freedom in the Making of Western Culture*. New York.

Peachin, M. (2004) *Frontinus and the curae of the curator aquarum*. HABES 39. Stuttgart.

Pecchiura, P. (1965) *La figura di Catone Uticense nella letteratura Latina.* Turin.

Peter, H. (1883) *Historicorum romanorum fragmenta.* Leipzig.

Pettit, P. (1997) *Republicanism: A Theory of Freedom and Government.* Oxford.

Pfanner, M. (1983) *Der Titusbogen.* Mainz am Rhein.

Phillips, E. J. (1978) "Nero's New City," *RFIC* 106: 300–7.

Pighi, J. B. (1965) *De ludis saecularibus populi romani Quiritium Libri Sex.* 2nd ed. Amsterdam.

Pigoń, J. (1992) "Helvidius Priscus, Eprius Marcellus, and *Iudicium Senatus*: Observations on Tacitus, *Histories* 4.7–8," *CQ* 42: 235–46.

Pigoń, J. (1999) "The Identity of the Chief Vestal Cornelia (*PIR2* C 1481): Some Suggestions," *Mnemosyne* 52: 206–13.

Platner, S. B., and Ashby, T. (1926) *A Topographical Dictionary of Ancient Rome.* Oxford.

Pleket, H. W. (1961) "Domitian, the Senate, and the Provinces," *Mnemosyne* 14: 296–315.

Pohlenz, M. (1966) *Freedom in Greek Life and Thought,* trans. C. Lofmark. Dordrecht.

Pomeroy, A. J. (1989) "Silius Italicus as 'Doctus Poeta'," *Ramus* 18: 119–39.

Price, S. R. F. (1979) "The Divine Right of Emperors," *CR* 29: 277–9.

Price, S. R. F. (1984) *Rituals and Power: The Roman Imperial Cult in Asia Minor.* Cambridge.

Proust, M. (1982) *Remembrance of Things Past, Vol. 1: Swann's Way, Within a Budding Grove,* trans. C. K. Scott-Moncrieff and T. Kilmartin. New York.

Pucci Ben Zeev, M. (1996) "Polybius, Josephus, and the Capitol in Rome," *JSJ* 27: 21–30.

Pulleyn, S. (1997) *Prayer in Greek Religion.* Oxford.

Purcell, N. (2003) "Becoming Historical: The Roman Case," in *Myth, History and Culture in Republican Rome. Studies in Honour of T. P. Wiseman,* ed. D. Braund and C. Gill: 12–40. Exeter.

Raaflaub, K. A. (1974) *Dignitatis contentio: Studien zur Motivation und politischen Taktik im Bürgerkrieg zwischen Caesar und Pompeius.* Munich.

Raaflaub, K. A. (2003) "Caesar the Liberator? Factional Politics, Civil War, and Ideology," in *Caesar against Liberty? Perspectives on His Autocracy,* ed. F. Cairns and E. Fantham. Papers of the Langford Latin Seminar 11: 35–67. Cambridge.

Raaflaub, K. A. (2004) *The Discovery of Freedom in Ancient Greece.* Chicago.

Raaflaub, K. A., and Samons, L. J., II (1990) "Opposition to Augustus," in Raaflaub and Toher (1990), 417–54.

Raaflaub, K. A., and Toher, M. (eds.) (1990) *Between Republic and Empire: Interpretations of Augustus and His Principate.* Berkeley.

Radice, B. (1968) "Pliny and the *Panegyricus*," *G&R* n.s. 15: 166–72.

Radke, G. (1972) "Acca Larentia und die fratres Arvales. Ein Stück römisch-sabinischer Frühgeschichte," *ANRW* I.2: 421–41.

Radke, G. (1987) *Zur Entwicklung der Gottesvorstellung und der Gottesvereh-rung in Rom.* Darmstadt.

Ramage, E. S. (1983) "Denigration of Predecessor under Claudius, Galba, and Vespasian," *Historia* 32: 201–14.

Raoss, M. (1960) "La rivolta di Vindice ed il successo di Galba," *Epigraphica* 22: 37–151.

Rawson, E. (1974) "Religion and Politics in the Late Second Century B.C. at Rome," *Phoenix* 28: 193–212. (= *Roman Culture and Society*, 149–68).

Rawson, E. (1978) "The Introduction of Logical Organization in Roman Prose Literature," *PBSR* 46: 12–34. (= *Roman Culture and Society*, 324–51).

Rawson, E. (1985) *Intellectual Life in the Late Roman Republic.* Baltimore.

Rawson, E. (1986) "Cassius and Brutus: The Memory of the Liberators," in Moxon et al. (1986), 101–19. (= *Roman Culture and Society*, 488–507).

Rawson, E. (1990) "The Antiquarian Tradition: Spoils and Representations of Foreign Armour," in *Staat und Staatlichkeit in der frühen römischen Republik,* ed. W. Eder: 158–73. Stuttgart. (= *Roman Culture and Society*, 582–98).

Rea, J. A. (2007) *Legendary Rome: Myth, Monuments and Memory on the Palatine and Capitoline.* London.

Rees, R. (2001) "To Be and Not To Be: Pliny's Paradoxical Trajan," *BICS* 45: 149–68.

Reggi, R. (1973) "La vindicatio in libertatem e l'adsertor libertatis," in *Studi in memoria di Guido Donatuti,* 1005–30. Milan.

Reydams-Schils, G. (2005) *The Roman Stoics: Self, Responsibility, and Affection.* Chicago.

Reynolds, J. M., and Ward Perkins, J. B. (1952) *The Inscriptions of Roman Tripoli-tania.* Rome.

Reynolds, L. (1991) *C. Sallusti Crispi: Catilina, Iugurtha, Historiarum fragmenta selecta, Appendix Sallustiana.* Oxford.

Rhodes, P. J. (2001) "Public Documents in the Greek States: Archives and Inscrip-tions," *G&R* 48: 33–44, 136–53.

Riccobono, S. (1950) *Il Gnomon dell'Idios Logos.* Palermo.

Rich, J. W., and Williams, J. H. C. (1999) "Leges et Ivra P. R. Restitvit: A New Aureus of Octavian and the Settlement of 28–27 BC," *NC* 159: 169–213.

Richardson, L., Jr. (1992) *A New Topographical Dictionary of Ancient Rome.* Baltimore.

Richmond, I. A. (1935) "Trajan's Army on Trajan's Column," *PBSR* 13: 1–40.

Richter, W. (1968) "Das Cicerobild der römischen Kaiserzeit," in *Cicero: ein Mensch seiner Zeit,* ed. G. Radke: 161–97. Berlin.

Riggsby, A. M. (1995) "Pliny on Cicero and Oratory: Self-Fashioning in the Public Eye," *AJP* 116: 123–35.

Riggsby, A. M. (1998) "Self and Community in the Younger Pliny," *Arethusa* 31: 75–97.

Riggsby, A. M. (2006) *Caesar in Gaul and Rome: War in Words.* Austin.

Ripoll, F. (1998) *La Morale héroïque dans les épopées latines d'époque flavienne: tradition et innovation.* Leuven.

Rives, J. (2005) "Flavian Religious Policy and the Destruction of the Jerusalem Temple," in Edmondson et al. (2005), 145–66.

Robertson, A. S. (1971) *Roman Imperial Coins in the Hunter Coin Cabinet, University of Glasgow II. Trajan to Commodus.* Oxford.

Rogers, R. S. (1949) "A Criminal Trial of A.D. 70," *TAPA* 80: 347–50.

Rogers, R. S. (1955) "Heirs and Rivals to Nero," *TAPA* 86: 190–212.

Rogers, R. S. (1960) "A Group of Domitianic Treason Trials," *CP* 55: 19–23.

Rogers, R. S. (1980) "Titus, Berenice and Mucianus," *Historia* 29: 86–95.

Roller, M. B. (1997) "Color Blindness: Cicero's Death, Declamation, and the Production of History," *CP* 92: 109–30.

Roller, M. B. (2001) *Constructing Autocracy: Aritsocrats and Emperors in Julio-Claudian Rome.* Princeton.

Roller, M. B. (2004) "Exemplarity in Roman Culture: The Cases of Horatius Cocles and Cloelia," *CP* 99: 1–56.

Rose, S. (1992) *The Making of Memory: From Molecules to the Mind.* New York.

Roxan, M., and Holder, P. (2003) *Roman Military Diplomas IV.* BICS Suppl. 82. London.

Rudich, V. (1993) *Political Dissidence under Nero. The Price of Dissimulation.* London.

Ruiz, U. E. (1982) *Debate Agrippa-Mecenas en Dion Cassio: Respuesta senatorial a la crisis del Imperio Romano en época severiana.* Madrid.

Rüpke, J. (1992) "Wer las Caesars *bella* als *commentarii*?" *Gymnasium* 99: 201–26.

Rutledge, S. (1998) "Trajan and Tacitus' Audience: Reader Reception of Annals 1–2," *Ramus* 27: 141–59.

Rutledge, S. (1999) "Delatores and the Tradition of Violence in Roman Oratory," *AJP* 120: 555–73.

Rutledge, S. (2000) "Plato, Tacitus, and the *Dialogus de oratoribus*," in *Studies in Latin Literature and Roman History*, ed. C. Deroux. Coll Latomus 254: 345–57. Brussels.

Rutledge, S. (2001) *Imperial Inquisitions. Prosecutors and Informants from Tiberius to Domitian.* London.

Ryan, F. X. (1993) "Some Observations on the Censorship of Claudius and Vitellius, A.D. 47–48" *AJPh* 114: 611–18.

Ryberg, I. S. (1942) "Tacitus' Art of Innuendo," *TAPA* 73: 383–404.

Ryberg, I. S. (1955) *Rites of the State Religion in Roman Art.* MAAR 22. Rome.

Sage, M. M. (1991) "The Treatment in Tacitus of Roman Republican History and Antiquarian Matters," *ANRW* II.33.5: 3385–419.

Sailor, D. (2008) *Writing and Empire in Tacitus.* Cambridge.

Saller, R. P. (1980) "Anecdotes as Historical Evidence for the Principate," *G&R* n.s. 27: 69–83.

Sancery, J. (1983) *Galba ou l'armée face au pouvoir.* Paris.

Sanctis, G. de (1917) *Storia dei Romani. Vol. 3: L'età delle guerre Puniche.* Part 2. Turin.

Santini, C. (1991) *Silius Italicus and His View of the Past.* Amsterdam. (trans. *La Cognizione del passato in Silio Italico,* 1983).

Saquete, J. C. (2000) *Las vírgenes vestales: un sacerdocio femenino en la religión pública romana.* Madrid.

Schacter, D. L. (2001) *The Seven Sins of Memory: How the Mind Forgets and Remembers.* Boston.

Schacter, D. L., and Tulving, E. (eds.) (1995) *Memory Distortion: How Minds, Brains, and Societies Reconstruct the Past.* Cambridge, MA.

Schanz, M. (1927) *Geschichte der römishcen Literatur II: die römishce Literatur in der Zeit der Monarchie bis auf Hadrian,* rev. C. Hosius. 4th ed. Munich.

Scheer, R. (1971) "Vindex Libertatis," *Gymnasium* 79: 182–8.

Scheid, J. (1981) "Le Délit religieux dans la Rome tardo-republicaine," in *Le Délit religieux dans la cité antique.* CEFR 48: 117–71. Rome.

Scheid, J. (1998) "Les Livres sibyllins et les archives des quindécimvirs," *CEFR* 243: 11–26.

Scheid, J. (2001) "Claudia the Vestal Virgin," in *Roman Women,* ed. A. Fraschetti: 23–33. Chicago. (trans. *Roma al femminile,* 1994).

Schiller, H. (1878) *Geschichte des römischen Kaiserreichs unter der Regierung des Nero.* Berlin.

Schleiermacher, M. (1984) *Römische Reitergrabsteine: die kaiserzeitlichen Reliefs des triumphierenden Reiters.* Bonn.

Schmitzer, U. (2000) *Velleius Paterculus und das Interesse an der Geschichte im Zeitalter des Tiberius.* Heidelberg.

Schofield, M. (1991) *The Stoic Idea of the City.* Cambridge.

Schöne, A. (1866, repr. 1967) *Eusebi Chronicorum Canonum Quae Supersunt.* 2nd. ed. Zurich.

Schowalter, D. N. (1993) *The Emperor and the Gods. Images from the Time of Trajan.* Minneapolis.

Schudson, M. (1995) "Dynamics of Distortion in Collective Memory," in Schacter and Tulving (1995), 346–64.

Schumacher, L. (1978) "Die vier hohen römischen Priesterkollegien unter den Flaviern, den Antoninen und den Severern (69–235 n. Chr.)" *ANRW* II.16.1: 655–819.

Schumacher, L. (2006) "AVGVSTVS PONT. MAX. – Wie wurde ein römischer Kaiser pontifex maximus?" *Klio* 88: 181–8.

Scott, J. C. (1990) *Domination and the Arts of Resistance: Hidden Transcripts.* New Haven.

Scott, K. (1936, repr. 1975) *The Imperial Cult under the Flavians.* New York.

Scott, R. T. (1968) *Religion and Philosophy in the Histories of Tacitus.* PMAAR 22. Rome.

Scullard, H. H. (1973) *Roman Politics 220–150 B.C.* 2nd ed. Oxford.

Sebesta, J. L. (1997) "Women's Costume and Feminine Civic Morality in Augustan Rome," *Gender & History* 9: 529–41.

Sedley, D. (1997) "The Ethics of Brutus and Cassius," *JRS* 87: 41–53.

Seelentag, G. (2004) *Taten und Tugenden Traians: Herrshaftsdarstellung im Principat.* Hermes Einzl. 91. Stuttgart.

Sehlmeyer, M. (1999) *Stadtrömische Ehrenstatuen der republikanischen Zeit: Historizität und Kontext von Symbolen nobilitären Standesbewusstseins.* Histora Einzl. 130. Stuttgart.

Shatzman, I. (1972) "The Roman General's Authority over Booty," *Historia* 21: 177–205.

Shaw, B. D. (1985) "The Divine Economy: Stoicism as Ideology," *Latomus* 44: 16–54.

Shaw, B. D. (2001) "Raising and Killing Children: Two Roman Myths," *Mnemosyne* 54: 31–77.

Shelton, J.-A. (1987) "Pliny's Letter 3.11: Rhetoric and Autobiography," *C&M* 38: 121–39.

Sherwin-White, A. N. (1966) *The Letters of Pliny. A Historical and Social Commentary.* Oxford.

Sherwin-White, A. N. (1969) "Pliny, the Man and His Letters," *G&R* n.s. 16: 76–99.

Sherwin-White, A. N. (1985) "Ancient Archives: The Edict of Alexander to Priene, a Reappraisal," *JHS* 105: 68–89.

Shotter, D. C. A. (1967) "Tacitus and Verginius Rufus," *CQ* n.s. 17: 370–81.

Shotter, D. C. A. (1975) "A Timetable for the *Bellum Neronis*," *Historia* 24: 59–74.

Shotter, D. C. A. (1978) "*Principatus ac libertas*," *AncSoc* 9: 235–55.

Shotter, D. C. A. (1983) "The Principate of Nerva: Some Observations on the Coin Evidence," *Historia* 32: 215–26.

Shotter, D. C. A. (2001) "A Considered Epitaph," *Historia* 50: 253–5.

Shotter, D. C. A. (2008) *Nero Caesar Augustus: Emperor of Rome.* Harlow.

Siber, H. (1951) "Zur Kollegialität der römischen Zensoren," in *Festschrift Fritz Schulz.* Vol. 1: 466–74. Weimar.

Simonelli, A. (1990) "La tradizione classica e l'origine del Capitolium," *A&R* n.s. 35: 71–7.

Sion-Jenkis, K. (2000) *Von der Republik zum Prinzipat: Ursachen für den Verfassungsweschel in Rom im historischen Denken der Antike.* Stuttgart.

Skidmore, C. (1996) *Practical Ethics for Roman Gentlemen: The Work of Valerius Maximus.* Exeter.

Skinner, Q. (1998) *Liberty before Liberalism.* Cambridge.

Small, J. P. (1995) "Artificial Memory and the Writing Habits of the Literate," *Helios* 22: 159–66.

Small, J. P. (1997) *Wax Tablets of the Mind: Cognitive Studies of Memory and Literacy in Classical Antiquity.* London.

Smith, A. D. (1999) *Myths and Memories of the Nation.* Oxford.

Snell, D. C. (2001) *Flight and Freedom in the Ancient Near East*. Leiden.

Sordi, M. (ed.) (1984) *I santuari e la guerra nel mondo classico*. CISA 10. Milan.

Sordi, M. (1985) "'Pax deorum' e libertà religiosa nella storia di Roma," in *La pace nel mondo antico*, ed. M. Sordi. CISA 11: 146–54. Milan.

Southern, P. (1997) *Domitian: Tragic Tyrant*. Bloomington.

Soverini, P. (1989) "Impero e imperatori nell'opera di Plinio il Giovane: aspetti e problemi del rapporto con Domiziano e Traiano," *ANRW* II.33.1: 515–54.

Spaltenstein, F. (1986–90) *Commentaire des Punica de Silius Italicus*, 2 vols. Geneva.

Spawforth, A. J. S. (ed.) (2007) *The Court and Court Society in Ancient Monarchies*. Cambridge.

Speidel, M. (1970) "The Captor of Decebalus: A New Inscription from Philippi," *JRS* 60: 142–53.

Speidel, M. (2004) *Ancient Germanic Warriors: Warrior Styles from Trajan's Column to Icelandic Sagas*. London.

Speidel, M., and Lieb, H. (eds.) (2007) *Militärdiplome*. Stuttgart.

Spentzou, E. (2008) "Eluding Romanitas: Heroes and Anti-heroes in Silius Italicus' Roman History," in *Role Models: Identity and Assimilation in the Roman World*, ed. S. Bell and I. L. Hansen. MAAR Suppl. 7: 133–46. Ann Arbor.

Stambaugh, J. E. (1978) "The Functions of Roman Temples," *ANRW* II.16.1: 554–608.

Stamper, J. W. (2005) *The Architecture of Roman Temples*. Cambridge.

Stanton, G. R. (1971) "*Cunctando Restituit Rem*: The Tradition about Fabius," *Antichthon* 5: 49–56.

Staples, A. (1998) *From Good Goddess to Vestal Virgins: Sex and Category in Roman Religion*. London.

Starr, C. (1952) "The Perfect Democracy of the Roman Empire," *AHR* 58: 1–16. (= *Essays on Ancient History*, 262–77).

Steele, R. B. (1922) "The Method of Silius Italicus," *CP* 17: 319–33.

Stein-Hölkeskamp, E., and Hölkeskamp, K.-J. (eds.) (2006) *Erinnerungsorte der Antike: die römische Welt*. Munich.

Steinmetz, P. (1988) "Secundus im Dialogus de oratoribus des Tacitus," *RhM* 131: 342–57.

Stepper, R. (1999) "Der Oberpontifikat von Caesar bis Nerva: Zwischen Tradition und Innovation," in *Zwischen Krise und Alltag. Antike Religionen im Mittelmeerraum*, ed. U. Egelhaaf-Gaiser and R. Stepper: 171–85. Stuttgart.

Stepper, R. (2003) "Der Kaiser als Priester: Schwerpunkte und Reichweite seines oberpontifikalen Handelns," in *Dei Praxis der Herrscherverehrung in Rom und seinen Provinzen*, ed. H. Cancik and K. Hitzel: 157–87. Tübingen.

Stewart, R. (1994) "Domitian and Roman Religion: Juvenal, Satires Two and Four," *TAPA* 124: 309–32.

Stierle, K. (1972) "L'Histoire comme exemple, l'exemple comme histoire: contribution à la pragmatique et à la poétique des textes narratifs," *Poetique* 10: 176–98.

Strack, P. L. (1931) *Untersuchungen zur römischen Reichsprägung des zweiten Jahrhunderts. Teil 1: die Reichsprägung zur Zeit des Traian.* Stuttgart.

Strong, D. (1994) "Roman Museums," in *Roman Museums: Selected Papers on Roman Art and Architecture*, 13–30. London.

Strothmann, M. (2000) *Augustus – Vater der res publica: Zur Funktion der drei Begriffe restitutio – saeculum – pater patriae im augusteischen Principat.* Stuttgart.

Stroux, J. (1931) "Vier Zeugnisse zur römischen Literaturgeschichte der Kaiserzeit," *Philologus* 86: 338–68.

Stuart, D. R. (1905) "Imperial Methods of Inscription on Restored Buildings: Augustus and Hadrian," *AJA* 9: 427–49.

Stylow, A. U. (1972) *Libertas und Liberalitas: Untersuchungen zur innenpolitischen Propaganda der Römer.* Munich.

Suerbaum, W. (1968) *Untersuchungen zur Selbstdarstellung älterer römischer Dichter.* Spudasmata 19. Hildesheim.

Suerbaum, W. (ed.) (2002) *Handbuch der Lateinischen Literatur der Antike. Erster Band: Die Archaische Literatur von den Anfängen bis Sullas Tod.* Munich.

Suleiman, S. R. (1993) *Authoritarian Fictions: The Ideological Novel as a Literary Genre.* Princeton.

Suolahti, J. (1963) *The Roman Censors: A Study on Social Structure.* Helsinki.

Sutherland, C. H. V. (1959) "The Intelligibility of Roman Imperial Coin Types," *JRS* 49: 46–55.

Sutherland, C. H. V. (1970) *The Cistophori of Augustus.* London.

Sutherland, C. H. V. (1984) "The Concepts *Adsertor* and *Salus* as Used by Vindex and Galba," *NC* 144: 29–32.

Sutherland, C. H. V. (1986) "Compliment or Complement? Dr Levick on Imperial Coin Types," *NC* 149: 85–93.

Sutherland, C. H. V. (1987) *Roman History and Coinage 44 BC–AD 69: Fifty Points of Relation from Julius Caesar to Vespasian.* Oxford.

Swan, M. (1970) "Josephus, *A.J.* XIX,251–252: Opposition to Gaius and Claudius," *AJPh* 91: 149–64.

Syme, R. (1930) "The Imperial Finance under Domitian, Nerva, and Trajan," *JRS* 20: 55–70. (= *Roman Papers* I 1–17).

Syme, R. (1939) *The Roman Revolution.* Oxford.

Syme, R. (1953) rev. Degrassi (1952), *JRS* 43: 148–61. (= *Roman Papers* I 231–59).

Syme, R. (1957a) "How Tacitus Came to History," *G&R* n.s. 4: 160–67. (= id. 1970a: 11–18).

Syme, R. (1957b) "The Friend of Tacitus," *JRS* 47: 131–7. (= id. 1970a: 110–18).

Syme, R. (1958) *Tacitus*, 2 vols. Oxford.

Syme, R. (1968) "The Ummidii," *Historia* 17: 72–105. (= *Roman Papers* II 659–93).

Syme, R. (1969) "Pliny the Procurator," *HSCP* 73: 201–36. (= *Roman Papers* II 742–73).

Syme, R. (1970a) *Ten Studies in Tacitus*. Oxford.

Syme, R. (1970b) "Domitius Corbulo," *JRS* 60: 27–39. (= *Roman Papers* II 805–24).

Syme, R. (1981) "Governors Dying in Syria," *ZPE* 41: 125–44. (= *Roman Papers* III 1376–92).

Syme, R. (1982a) "Partisans of Galba," *Historia* 31: 460–83. (= *Roman Papers* IV 115–39).

Syme, R. (1982b) "Tacitus: Some Sources of His Information," *JRS* 72: 68–82. (= *Roman Papers* IV 199–222).

Syme, R. (1983) "Domitan: The Last Years," *Chiron* 13: 121–46. (= *Roman Papers* IV 252–77).

Syme, R. (1986) *The Augustan Aristocracy*. Oxford.

Syme, R. (1991) *Roman Papers*. Vol. 7, ed. A. Birley. Oxford.

Takács, S. A. (2008) *Vestal Virgins, Sibyls, and Matrons: Women in Roman Religion*. Austin, TX.

Talbert, R. J. A. (1977) "Some Causes of Disorder in A.D. 68–69," *AJAH* 2: 69–85.

Talbert, R. J. A. (1984) *The Senate of Imperial Rome*. Princeton.

Taplin, O. (ed.) (2000) *Literature in the Greek and Roman Worlds: A new perspective*. Oxford.

Taylor, L. R. (1929) "Tiberius' Refusal of Divine Honors," *TAPA* 60: 87–101.

Taylor, L. R. (1931, repr. 1975) *The Divinity of the Roman Emperor*. New York.

Thein, A. (2002) *Sulla's Public Image and the Politics of Civic Renewal*. (Diss. University of Pennsylvania).

Thompson, L. A. (1982) "Domitian and the Jewish Tax," *Historia* 31: 329–42.

Thompson, L. A. (1984) "Domitianus Dominus: A Gloss on Statius *Silvae* 1.6.84," *AJP* 105: 469–75.

Tipping, B. (2007) "*Haec tum Roma fuit*: Past, Present and Closure in Silius Italicus' *Punica*," in *Classical Constructions: Papers in Memory of Don Fowler, Classicist and Epicurean*, ed. S. J. Heyworth: 221–41. Oxford.

Tipping, B. (2010a) *Exemplary Epic: Silius Italicus' Punica*. Oxford.

Tipping, B. (2010b) "Virtue and Narrative in Silius Italicus' *Punica*," in Augoustakis (2010): 193–218.

Torelli, M. (1982) *Typology and Structure of Roman Historical Reliefs*. Ann Arbor.

Tortorici, E. (1991) *Argiletum: commercio speculazione edilizia e lotta politica dall'analisi topografica di un quartiere di Roma di età repubblicana*. Rome.

Townend, G. B. (1961) "Some Flavian Connections," *JRS* 51: 54–62.

Townend, G. B. (1962) "The Consuls of A.D. 69/70," *AJP* 83: 113–29.

Townend, G. B. (1981) "The Reputation of Verginius Rufus," *Latomus* 20: 337–41.

Townend, G. B. (1987) "The Restoration of the Capitol in A. D. 70," *Historia* 36: 243–8.

Toynbee, J. M. C. (1944) "Dictators and Philosophers in the First Century A.D.," *G&R* 13: 43–58.

Toynbee, J. M. C. (1957) *The Flavian Reliefs from the Palazzo della Cancelleria in Rome.* London.

Tränkle, H. (1965) "Der Anfang des römischen Freistaats in der Darstellung des Livius," *Hermes* 93: 311–37.

Trapp, M. (2007) *Philosophy in the Roman Empire: Ethics, Politics and Society.* Burlington, VT.

Traub, H. W. (1955) "Pliny's Treatment of History in Epistolary Form" *TAPA* 86: 213–32.

Travlos, J. (1971) *A Pictorial Dictionary of Ancient Athens.* New York.

Treggiari, S. (1969) *Roman Freedmen during the Late Republic.* Oxford.

Trouillot, M.-R. (1995) *Silencing the Past: Power and the Production of History.* Boston.

Tung, A. M. (2001) *Preserving the World's Great Cities. The Destruction and Renewal of the Historic Metropolis.* New York.

Turner, A. (2007) "Frontinus and Domitian: *Laus Principis* in the *Strategemata*," *HSCP* 103: 423–49.

Urban, R. (1999) *Gallia rebellis. Erhebungen in Gallien im Spiegel antiker Zeugnisse.* Historia Einzelschrift 129. Stuttgart.

Vahlen, I. (1928) *Ennianae poesis reliquiae.* 2nd ed. Leipzig.

Várhelyi, Z. (2005) "A Sense of Change and the Historiography of the Turn from Republic to Empire," in *A Tall Order: Writing the Social History of the Ancient World. Essays in honor of William V. Harris*, ed. J.-J. Aubert and Z. Várhelyi: 357–75. Munich.

Varner, E. R. (2004) *Mutilation and Transformation: Damnatio Memoriae and Roman Imperial Portraiture.* Leiden.

Vasaly, A. (1993) *Representations: Images of the World in Ciceronian Oratory.* Berkeley.

Venini, P. (1972) "Cronologia e composizione nei Punica di Silio Italico," *RIL* 106: 518–31.

Verbrugghe, G. P. (1982) "L. Cincius Alimentus – His Place in Roman Historiography," *Philologus* 126: 316–23.

Vernant, J. P. (1983) *Myth and Thought among the Greeks.* London. (trans. *Mythe et pensee chez les Grecs* 1965).

Vessey, D. (1974a) "Silius Italicus on the Fall of Saguntum," *CPh* 69: 28–36.

Vessey, D. (1974b) "Pliny, Martial and Silius Italicus," *Hermes* 102: 109–16.

Vessey, D. (1982) "The Dupe of Destiny: Hannibal in Silius, *Punica* III," *CJ* 77: 320–35.

Veyne, P. (1990, orig. pub. 1976) *Bread and Circuses*, trans. B. Pearce. London.

Vinson, M. P. (1989) "Domitia Longina, Julia Titi, and the Literary Tradition" *Historia* 38: 431–50.

Visscher, F. de (1962) *Héraclès Epitrapezios.* Paris.

Vogel-Weidemann, U. (1979) "The Opposition under the Early Caesars: Some Remarks on Its Nature and Aims," *AClass* 22: 91–107.

Wachsmuth, C. (1860) "Ueber die Unächtheit des vierten Buchs der Frontinischen *Strategemata*," *RhM* 15: 574–83.

Wachsmuth, C. (1883–4) *Ioannis Stobaei Anthologii libri duo priores*, 2 vols. Berlin.

Walbank, F. W. (1957–79) *A Historical Commentary on Polybius*, 3 vols. Oxford.

Walbank, F. W. (1985) *Selected Papers. Studies in Greek and Roman History and Historiography*. Cambridge.

Walker, D. R. (1977) *The Metrology of Roman Silver Coinage*, 2 vols. BAR suppl. 22. Oxford.

Wallace-Hadrill, A. (1981a) "Galba's Aequitas," *NC* 141: 20–39.

Wallace-Hadrill, A. (1981b) "The Emperor and His Virtues," *Historia* 30: 298–323.

Wallace-Hadrill, A. (1982a) "*Civilis Princeps*: Between Citizen and King," *JRS* 72: 32–48.

Wallace-Hadrill, A. (1982b) "The Golden Age and Sin in Augustan Ideology," *P&P* 95: 19–36.

Wallace-Hadrill, A. (1986) "Image and Authority in the Coinage of Augustus," *JRS* 76: 66–87.

Wallace-Hadrill, A. (1997) "*Mutatio morum*: the idea of a cultural revolution," in Habinek and Schiesaro (1997), 3–22.

Wallace-Hadrill, A. (2008) *Rome's Cultural Revolution*. Cambridge.

Walser, G. (1955) "Der Kaiser als Vindex Libertatis," *Historia* 4: 353–67.

Walter, U. (2004) *Memoria und res publica. Zur Geschichtskultur im republikanishen Rom.* Frankfurt am Main.

Walzer, A. (2003) "Quintilian's *vir bonus* and the Stoic Wise Man," *Rhetoric Society Quarterly* 33.4: 24–41.

Wardle, D. (1996) "Vespasian, Helvidius Priscus and the Restoration of the Capitol," *Historia* 45: 208–22.

Wardman, A. (1982) *Religion and Statecraft among the Romans*. Baltimore.

Ward Perkins, J. B. (1937) "The Career of Sex. Julius Frontinus," *CQ* 31: 102–5.

Waters, K. H. (1964) "The Character of Domitian," *Phoenix* 18: 49–77.

Waters, K. H. (1969) "Traianus Domitiani Continuator," *AJPh* 90: 385–405.

Watkins, M. J. (1990) "Mediationism and the Obfuscation of Memory," *American Psychologist* 45: 328–35.

Watson, A. (1973) "Vespasian: *adsertor libertatis publicae*," *CR* n.s. 23: 127–8.

Weinstock, S. (1960) "Pax and the 'Ara Pacis,'" *JRS* 50: 44–58.

Weinstock, S. (1971) *Divus Iulius*. Oxford.

Wellesley, K. (1956) "Three Historical Puzzles in *Histories* 3," *CQ* n.s. 6: 207–14.

Wellesley, K. (1964, repr. 1995) *Tacitus: The Histories*. New York.

Wellesley, K. (1972) *Cornelius Tacitus: The Histories Book III*. Sydney.

Wellesley, K. (1975) *The Long Year A.D. 69*. London.

Wellesley, K. (1981) "What Happened on the Capitol in December, A.D. 69?" *AJAH* 6: 166–90.

Wheeler, E. L. (1988) *Stratagem and the Vocabulary of Military Trickery.* Mnemosyne Suppl. 108. Leiden.

White, H. (1978) "The Historical Text as Literary Artifact," in *Tropics of Discourse: Essays in Cultural Criticism*, 81–100. Baltimore.

Whittaker, C. R. (1994) *Frontiers of the Roman Empire: A Social and Economic Study.* Baltimore.

Wickert, L. (1949) "Der Prinzipat und die Freiheit," in *Symbola Coloniensia Iosepho Kroll Sexagenario A.D. VI Id. Nov. A. MCMIL Oblata.* 111–41. Cologne.

Wickert, L. (1954) "Princeps (civitatis)," *RE* XXII.2: 1998–2296.

Wiedemann, T. E. J. (1985) "The Regularity of Manumission at Rome," *CQ* 35: 162–75.

Wiedemann, T. E. J. (1996) "From Nero to Vespasian," in *CAH* X², 256–82.

Wildfang, R. L. (2001) "The Vestals and Annual Public Rites," *C&M* 52: 223–56.

Wildfang, R. L. (2006) *Rome's Vestal Virgins.* London.

Williams, C. A. (2004) *Martial Epigrams Book Two.* Oxford.

Williams, G. (1978) *Change and Decline: Roman Literature in the Early Empire.* Berkeley.

Williamson, C. (1987) "Monuments of Bronze: Roman Legal Documents on Bronze Tablets," *ClAnt* 6: 160–83.

Williamson, C. (1995) "The Display of Law and Archival Practice in Rome," in *Acta Colloquii Epigraphici Latini Helsingiae 3–6 Sept. 1991 Habiti*, ed. E. H. Solin et al.: 239–51. Helsinki.

Williamson, C. (2005) *The Laws of the Roman People: Public Law in the Expansion and Decline of the Roman Republic.* Ann Arbor.

Wilson, E. (2007) *The Death of Socrates.* London.

Wilson, M. (1993) "Flavian Variant: History. Silius' *Punica*," in *Roman Epic*, ed. A. J. Boyle: 218–36. London.

Winkler, H. (2002) "Discourses, Schemata, Technology, Monuments: Outline for a Theory of Cultural Continuity," *Configurations* 10: 91–109.

Winterbottom, M. (1964) "Quintilian and the *Vir Bonus*," *JRS* 54: 90–97.

Winterbottom, M. (1975) "Quintilian and Rhetoric," in *Empire and Aftermath: Silver Latin II*, ed. T. A. Dorey: 79–97. London.

Winterbottom, M. (1982) "Cicero and the Silver Age," in *Éloquence et rhétorique chez Cicéron.* Etretiens Hardt 28: 237–66. Geneva.

Winterbottom, M. (2001) "Returning to Tacitus' *Dialogus*," in *The Orator in Action and Theory in Greece and Rome*, ed. C. W. Wooten: 137–55. Leiden.

Winterbottom, M., and Ogilvie, R. M. (1975) *Cornelii Taciti opera minora.* Oxford.

Winterling, A. (1999) *Aula Caesaris: Studien zur Institutionalisierung des römischen Kaiserhofes in der Zeit von Augustus bis Commodus (31 v Chr.–192 n.Chr).* Munich.

Wirszubski, C. (1950) *Libertas as a Political Idea at Rome during the Late Republic and Early Principate*. Cambridge.

Wiseman, T. P. (1974) *Cinna the Poet and Other Roman Essays*. London.

Wiseman, T. P. (1978) "Flavians on the Capitol," *AJAH* 3: 163–78.

Wiseman, T. P. (1979) *Clio's Cosmetics: Three Studies in Greco-Roman Literature*. Leicester.

Wiseman, T. P. (1986) "Monuments and the Roman Annalsists," in Moxon et al. (1986), 87–100.

Wiseman, T. P. (1987) "*Conspicui postes tectaque digna deo*: The Public Image of Aristocratic and Imperial Houses in the Late Republic and Early Empire," in *L'urbs: espace urbain et histoire (Ier siècle avant J.-C.–IIIe siècle apres J.-C.)* CEFR 98: 393–413. Rome.

Wissowa, G. (1912) *Religion und Kultus der Römer*. 2nd ed. Munich.

Wistrand, E. (1976) *The So-Called Laudatio Turiae: Introduction, Text, Translation, Commentary*. Lund.

Wistrand, E. (1979) "The Stoic Opposition to the Principate," *StudClass* 18: 93–101.

Woodman, A. J. (1974) "*Exegi monumentum*: Horace, *Odes* 3.30," in *Quality and Pleasure in Latin Poetry*, ed. A. Woodman and D. West: 115–28. Cambridge.

Woodman, A. J. (1975) "Questions of Date, Genre, and Style in Velleius: Some Literary Answers," *CQ* n.s. 25: 272–306.

Woodman, A. J. (1988) *Rhetoric in Classical Historiography: Four Studies*. Portland.

Woodside, M. S. A. (1942) "Vespasian's Patronage of Education and the Arts," *TAPA* 73: 123–9.

Wright, A. (2001) "The Death of Cicero. Forming a Tradition: The Contamination of History," *Historia* 50: 436–52.

Yates, F. A. (1966) *The Art of Memory*. London.

Yavetz, Z. (1969a) *Plebs and Princeps*. Oxford.

Yavetz, Z. (1969b) "Vitellius and the Fickleness of the Mob," *Historia* 18: 557–69.

Yavetz, Z. (1975) "Forte an Dolo Principis (Tac., *Ann*. 15.38)," in *The Ancient Historian and His Materials: Essays in Honour of C. E. Stevens on His Seventieth Birthday*, ed. B. Levick: 181–97. Westmead.

Yavetz, Z. (1983) *Julius Caesar and His Public Image*. London.

Yerushalmi, Y. H. (1982) *Zakhor: Jewish History and Jewish Memory*. Seattle.

Zanker, P. (1988) *The Power of Images in the Age of Augustus*, trans. A. Shapiro. Ann Arbor.

Zanker, P. (1995) *The Mask of Socrates: The Image of the Intellectual in Antiquity*, trans. A. Shapiro. Berkeley.

Zecchini, G. (1980) "La morte di catone e l'opposizione intellettuale a Cesare e ad Augusto," *Athenaeum* n.s. 58: 39–56.

Zecchini, G. (1984) "La profezia dei druidi sull'incendio del Campidoglio nel 69 d.C.," in Sordi (1984), 121–31.

Zehnacker, H. (1987) "Tensions et contradictions dans l'empire au Ier siècle: les témoignages numismatiques," in *Opposition et résistance a l'empire d'Auguste a Trajan.* Entretiens Hardt 33: 321–57. Geneva.

Zerubavel, E. (2003) *Time Maps: Collective Memory and the Social Shape of the Past.* Chicago.

Zevi, F. (1995) "Demarato e i re 'corinzi' di Roma," in *L'incidenza dell'antico: Studi in memoria di Ettore Lepore I,* ed. A. Storchi Marino: 291–314. Naples.

Zimmermann, M. (1995) "Die 'restitutio honorum' Galbas," *Historia* 44: 56–82.

Zinserling, G. (1959/60) "Studien zu den Historiendarstellungen der römischen Republik," *Wissenschaftliche Zeitschrift der Friedrich-Schiller-Universität Jena, Gesellschafts- und Sprachwissenschaftliche Reihe* 9: 403–48.

Ziolkowski, A. (1992) *The Temples of Mid-Republican Rome and Their Historical and Topographical Context.* Rome.

Zwierlein, O. (2003) "Der Sturz des Vatinius durch den Redner Maternus," *GFA* 6: 111–16.

INDEX

imperium, 9, 35, 74, 77, 79, 85, 139, 206, 207. *See also* Capitoline Temple; conquest
incestum, 92, 93, 94, 95, 103, 104, 108, 110
inscriptions, 77, 79, 81, 183. *See also* Capitoline hill, inscriptions on

Javolenus Priscus, L., 131
Jerusalem, 82
  Second Temple, 86, 87
Judaea, 73, 84, 86, 87
Julia (Titus' daughter), 100, 103, 104
Julius Agricola, Cn., 132, 145, 250
Julius Caesar, C., 24, 29, 52, 68, 137, 138, 149, 156, 229, 231, 235
  assassination, 6, 27, 29, 37, 230
  dictatorship, 25, 36, 105
  portrait, 25
Julius Cornutus Tertullus, C., 131, 132
Julius Frontinus, Sex. *See* Frontinus
Julius Secundus, 148, 149, 153, 155, 156
Julius Vestinus, L., 73, 74, 83
Julius Vestinus, M., 18
Julius Vindex, C., 15, 21, 25, 28, 36, 178
  as *phileleutheros*, 22
  death of, 33
  rebellion of, 12, 14, 28, 35, 44, 47, 217
Junius Arulenus Rusticus, Q., 129, 130, 132, 134, 211
Junius Brutus, L., 23, 27, 28, 46, 65, 229
Junius Brutus, M., 27, 28, 29, 45, 46, 66, 136, 140, 156, 229, 232, 248
Junius Mauricus, 129, 130
Juno Moneta, 65
Jupiter, 33, 206, 208
Jupiter Liberator, 17, 21, 32
Jupiter Optimus Maximus, 75, 77, 84, 85, 125, 239. *See also* Capitoline Temple (Temple of Jupiter Optimus Maximus)
Juventius Celsus, 125

Kraay, Colin, 28

Lake Regillus, 194
Lars Porsenna, 51, 224
legions. *See* armies
lex de imperio Vespasiani, 79, 87
libertas, 9, 35, 37, 43, 54, 63, 65, 71, 81, 82, 102, 103, 109, 136, 137, 138, 142, 166, 171, 177, 184, 219. *See also* slavery; *adsertor libertatis*

and free speech, 34, 149, 169, 170
and law, 36, 250
and Principate, 17, 25, 27, 28, 29, 30, 31, 32, 35, 41, 44, 45, 70, 71, 84, 85, 89, 102, 132, 138, 141, 173, 230, 231, 232, 247, 248
and renewal, 22, 28, 218
and Republic, 9, 11, 14, 23–27, 29, 36, 41, 43, 45, 64, 136, 167
and the fall of Nero, 13, 15, 27, 44
and *virtus*, 39–40, 101, 138, 173, 232
and Virtus, 150
in imperial context, 17
opposite of slavery, 15, 19, 20, 27
opposite of tyranny, 23, 32, 46, 217, 229, 232, 248
polyvalence of, 13, 17, 21, 32, 45
Libertas (deity), 16, 17, 22, 27, 229
Licinius Crassus, M., 43, 160
lieu de mémoire, 4, 9, 56
literature, 129, 155, 182, 183, 186, 189, 190
Livy, 23, 42, 62, 180, 186, 188, 191, 193, 198, 199, 200, 201, 209
Lucan, 24, 54, 137, 187, 205
ludi Saeculares, 97
Lugdunum, 21
Lutatius Catulus, Q., 37, 63, 66, 68, 70, 72, 84

Maecenas, C., 39, 158, 161
Maelius, Sp., 65, 104, 229
Manlius Capitolinus, M., 65, 104
Marcia (wife of Atilius Regulus), 210–211
Marius, C., 52, 200, 227, 242
Marius Priscus, 227
Mars Ultor, 29
Martial, 101, 114, 125, 176, 185, 189, 190, 214, 215
Maternus. *See* Curiatius Maternus
memory, 68, 117, 136, 139, 147, 182, 185, 216, 225, 228, 237, 245
  and bodily practice, 119
  and ethics, 179, 182
  and history, 4, 58
  and identity, 5, 8, 21, 43, 130, 150, 178, 180
  and monuments, 58, 60, 114, 179, 180, 181, 237
  and politics, 6, 85, 91, 247
  and texts, 62, 64, 76, 182, 185, 193, 196, 197